THIS DIFFICULT INDIVIDUAL,
EZRA POUND

This Difficult Individual, Ezra Pound

By EUSTACE MULLINS

"... drop in some day at your convenience ... to discuss this difficult individual, Ezra Pound ..."

—Christian Herter, Under Secretary of State, in a letter to Dr. Winfred Overholser, Superintendent of St. Elizabeths Hospital, January 2, 1958.

FLEET PUBLISHING CORPORATION

230 PARK AVENUE • NEW YORK 17, N.Y.

ACKNOWLEDGEMENTS

The author wishes to acknowledge the following for permission to quote excerpts in this biography:

Abelard-Schuman Limited, for excerpts from *Intimations* by Oliver St. John Gogarty, copyright 1950; Richard Aldington, for excerpts from *Life for Life's Sake;* Margaret Anderson, for excerpts from *The Little Review* and *My Thirty Years' War;* Janice Ford Biala, for excerpts from *Thus to Revisit, No Enemy, Return to Yesterday,* and *New York Essays* by Ford Madox Ford; Cassell & Co., for excerpts from *The Crowning Privilege* by Robert Graves; Christy & Moore, Ltd., for excerpts from *J. B. Yeats: Letters to His Son W. B. Yeats; Commentary,* for excerpts from "Pure Poetry, Impure Politics, and Ezra Pound" by Peter Viereck (copyright American Jewish Committee); Constable and Company Limited, for excerpts from *South Lodge* by Douglas Goldring; Caresse Crosby, for excerpts from Ezra Pound's *Imaginary Letters* published by the Black Sun Press; *Esquire,* Inc., for excerpts from "Aftermath: The Question of Ezra Pound", February, 1958 issue; Farrar, Straus & Cudahy, Inc., for excerpts from *On Poetry and Poets* by T. S. Eliot, copyright 1943, 1945, 1951, 1954, 1956, 1957 by T. S. Eliot, and *The Apprenticeship of Ernest Hemingway* by Charles A. Fenton, copyright 1954 by Charles A. Fenton; Mrs. M. A. Goldring, for excerpts from *People and Places* by Douglas Goldring; Victor Gollancz, Ltd., for excerpts from *W. B. Yeats* by Joseph Hone; Harcourt, Brace & World, Inc., for excerpts from *The Letters of Ezra Pound, 1907–1941* edited by D. D. Paige, copyright, 1950; Gerald W.

Henderson, for excerpts from *I Have This To Say* by Violet Hunt;
Holt, Rinehart and Winston, Inc., for excerpts from *Life Is My Song* by
John Gould Fletcher; Houghton Mifflin Company, for excerpts from
Amy Lowell: A Chronicle by S. Foster Damon, and *A Critical Fable* by
Amy Lowell; Mrs. G. A. Wyndham Lewis, for excerpts from *Blasting
and Bombardiering* by Wyndham Lewis; J. B. Lippincott Company, for
excerpts from *It Was The Nightingale* by Ford Madox Ford; The Mac-
millan Company, for excerpts from *King of the Great Clock Tower* by
William Butler Yeats, *The Letters of W. B. Yeats* edited by Allen Wade,
and *Yeats: The Man and the Mask* by Richard Ellman; Frederick Mor-
gan, for excerpts from his essay on the *Pisan Cantos,* in *The Hudson
Review,* Spring 1951; *The Nation,* for excerpts from their editorial on
Ezra Pound, April 1958; New Directions, for excerpts from the works
of Ezra Pound; *The New Yorker,* for excerpts from "Talk of the
Town", August 14, 1943 issue; Oxford University Press, Inc., for ex-
cerpts from *The Identity of Yeats* by Richard Ellman, copyright 1954;
G. P. Putnam's Sons, for excerpts from *Let There Be Sculpture* by
Jacob Epstein, copyright 1940 by Jacob Epstein; Random House Inc.,
for excerpts from *The Autobiography of Alice B. Toklas* by Gertrude
Stein, copyright 1933 and renewed 1960 by Alice B. Toklas, and *Auto-
biography of William Carlos Williams;* Routledge & Kegan Paul Ltd.,
for excerpts from *W. B. Yeats, Man and Poet* by Norman Jeffares;
Saturday Review; The New Republic, for excerpts from "The Ezra
Pound Controversy" by Malcolm Cowley; The Viking Press, Inc., for
excerpts from *The Portable Nietzsche* translated by Walter Kaufman,
Exile's Return by Malcolm Cowley, *The Letters of D. H. Lawrence*
edited by Aldous Huxley, and *The Letters of James Joyce* edited by
Stuart Gilbert; and *The Yale Literary Magazine* for excerpts from
Babette Deutsch's article on Pound in the December, 1958 issue.

Special thanks go to Dorothy Pound, for permission to quote from
the Rome Broadcasts; to Omar Pound, for his reading and correction
of the manuscript, and to Ezra Pound, for his encouragement in the
planning of this book. In addition, the author would like to thank
E. E. Cummings, Frederick Morgan and Arnold Gingrich for their
comments on the galleys, and James Laughlin, for his kind cooperation.

for D. P.

THIS DIFFICULT INDIVIDUAL,
EZRA POUND

THE LOFTIEST rise of land in that territorial oddity known as the District of Columbia is occupied by an insane asylum. I have not been able to ascertain what humorist in the victorious Federal Government, immediately following the Civil War, selected this dominant ground for the site of St. Elizabeths Hospital, so that the employees of the various departments could look up, as they emerged from their offices at the close of the day, and see in the distance the solemn brick buildings of that Valhalla of the government clerk, the madhouse.

In 1949, I was introduced to the poet Ezra Pound, who was at that time an inmate of St. Elizabeths Hospital. There had been conflicting reports as to his mental condition; that is to say, the reports of the government psychiatrists, and the reports of everyone else who knew him. The hospital officials avoided the issue by describing him to prospective visitors quite honestly as a "political prisoner". In the interests of national security, Pound was being kept under guard by the Federal Bureau of Health, Education and Welfare. I also was a ward of the government. My status as a veteran of the Second World War had won me paid subsistence at the Institute of Contemporary Arts in Washington.

In those days, the Institute housed the sad remnants of the "avant-garde" in America. It was inevitable that the name of Ezra Pound, who for nearly half a century had personified all that was

13

new and daring in the fine arts, should be mentioned there, although its directors preferred the work of one of Pound's earliest discoveries, T. S. Eliot. In 1948, a reception had been held at the Institute in honor of Eliot, who had just been awarded the Nobel Prize (as have several of Pound's students, although he himself has been passed by repeatedly). At this reception, I had first seen Ezra Pound's wife, Dorothy Shakespear Pound, who appeared briefly, squired by Eliot in his most high Episcopal manner.

True to his calling, Pound had not allowed a treason indictment or a cell in a madhouse to interfere drastically with his work. He was translating the Confucian *Odes*. One of the students at the Institute was also a nurse at St. Elizabeths. Like many other members of the staff, she had peeked at Pound's confidential file, although this was nominally forbidden. My fellow student informed me that Ezra was a source of considerable annoyance to his "captors", as his doctors were sometimes called. Not only had he refused "treatment", as the doctors termed their excursions into barbarism, but he would not take part in the activities of the hospital.

In reality, persons under observation for mental illness are immediately deprived of all their civil rights, a dilemma that the writers of the Constitution unfortunately overlooked. It has been very simple for bureaucrats to designate their critics as being "mentally ill", and to shut them away from the eyes of the world in the various Bastilles that have been built for that purpose. No one dares to intervene on behalf of a person who is "mentally ill". It is much safer to be a Communist or a hoodlum. The sculptor John B. Flannagan, who was a patient at Bloomingdale Hospital in New York (reputedly one of the best in the country), wrote of his experiences, "There are actually more legal safeguards for a felon than checks on the psychiatrist to whom civil liberty is a joke."[1]

The superintendent of St. Elizabeths, Dr. Winfred Overholser, was a genial type who wished the patients to help him create the atmosphere of a YMCA summer camp, but the assorted rapists, dope addicts, and political prisoners refused to cooperate. The staff employed the latest methods of "therapy" (which were constantly changing), such as acting out one's repressions, without weapons of course. For those who wished to write—a category that includes everyone suspected of mental illness—a mimeographed journal, called *St. Elizabeths Sunshine,* was circulated among the patients. The doctors were peeved because Ezra would not contribute to this journal, and the nurse informed me that they had marked him down as "uncooperative". This is the most serious charge that can be lodged against an inmate of a mental institution.

Despite the fact that it is a federal institution, and much more amply budgeted than comparable state hospitals, St. Elizabeths is a heart-breaking and appalling Bedlam. Visiting doctors from other countries are seldom asked to tour it, for they would doubtless be horrified. The dank, dark buildings reek of the foul stench of a century's urine. I once dined in the employees' cafeteria, and was ill for two days. It seemed impossible for me to get the smell of the place out of my system.

The medical techniques used at St. Elizabeths are regarded as incredibly backward and inhumane by more advanced European physicians. Although the members of the staff no longer cure "mental illness" by removing the entire large intestine, this was a popular remedy there until the Second World War. The superstitious doctors of several decades ago believed that mental disorder was caused by bacteria in the gut, the bacteria that in reality are responsible for the osmotive digestive process. The operation had no visible effect on the patients' mental capacities, but more than eighty per cent of them died from its aftereffects.

The staff at St. Elizabeths is also quite excited about a cure that has been in vogue in the Congo for some twenty thousand years, according to such anthropologists as Frobenius. This is a method for relieving mental illness by splitting open the skull and removing part of the brain. The operation is known as "lobotomy". European physicians have denounced this process as excessively barbaric, as well as demonstrably worthless in the treatment of mental illness, but it is still employed by the federal psychiatrists and surgeons.

A more recent treatment, electric shock, was blithely described by Dr. Overholser in an interview published in *U.S. News and World Report,* November 18, 1955:

"An electric current is passed between the temples and causes a period of unconsciousness with very violent, convulsive movements."

"Isn't it just like getting electrocuted?" the interviewer asked. "There's a certain amount of risk," Dr. Overholser replied. "I think rather slight, but there is some risk to it."

"What does it do? How does it cure them?"

"We don't know. It's entirely empirical."

The electric shock treatment is very closely allied to the practice of electrocution as a capital punishment, with this difference: the murderers are only electrocuted once, but those accused of mental illness have to endure three or more shocks on consecutive days. Electrodes are strapped on to the patient's temples, and he is bombarded with currents not quite powerful enough to cause death. A patient who had been "cured" by this treatment assured me that it was one of the most terrifying experiences that anyone can undergo.

Dr. Overholser concluded the interview by pointing out that there was no longer any stigma attached to those who had been inmates of mental hospitals. He said proudly, "We have a great many of our patients who go back to work in government agencies."

The statistics on the number of government workers in Washington who have histories of mental illness have been suppressed. One of my fellow students at the Institute was a lady who had undergone a lobotomy. She constantly complained that she was going to sue the doctor, a resolve that we encouraged, but by the time she had reached the doctor's office, she always would forget why she had come. She was employed at the White House during the Truman administration, but I do not believe that she held a policy-making position.

Ezra was not forced to undergo either the lobotomy or the electric shock treatment while he was imprisoned at St. Elizabeths. His worldwide reputation as a poet perhaps protected him from such ordeals. The electric shock technique had received some unfavorable publicity at the Nuremberg Trials, when inmates of Nazi concentration camps testified that they had been forced to submit to this treatment. In her book, *Hitler's Ovens,* Olga Lengyel says that she employed the ruse of insanity to escape from Auschwitz and visit her husband at Buna. She was included in a convoy of mentally ill inmates who were being sent to Buna for this treatment, and she describes their reception there:

"The (mentally) sick were led into an experimental room. There, under the surveillance of a German doctor, they were injected with a new product intended to produce a shock in the nervous system. The reactions were noticed with much care. While these experiments were going on, our S.S. guards were eating and drinking in the German medical director's office. I was able to rejoin my husband."[2]

Psychiatrists comprise a fascinating group for future study in the field of mental disorder. Dr. Overholser's predecessor at St. Elizabeths had been shot dead by his wife while he was sitting in an automobile with his mistress in front of a fashionable dress shop on Washington's F Street. A few months later, a series of brutal muggings and rapes, committed by employees of St. Elizabeths, had moved a Washington editor to complain that the attendants should be locked up at night with the patients, and that they should not be allowed to come into the city.

When a creative personality falls into their clutches, the psychiatrists run about like chickens in the shadow of the hawk's wing. Pound's records were constantly being pawed by curious doctors and attendants, and when, in 1949, a souvenir-hunter on the staff absconded with a large part of his case history, the remainder of the tattered file was placed in a safe. Dr. Overholser parries all inquiries about it with the standard reply: "These are confidential government papers, and cannot be shown to anyone."

John Flannagan wrote of his Bloomingdale experience, to his friend Carl Zigrosser in December, 1934, "Psychiatric sophistry finds I've been too interested in my work—it should have a less dominant place in my life—and my life no longer seems my own."[3]

It is a favorite theme of the psychiatrists, this notion that the creative artist is a mentally-ill, compulsive manic-depressive with a non-controllable personality disorder. He must be "adjusted". Once he has been adjusted to society, he will no longer feel the urge to write fine poetry or to create splendid music. Instead, he will settle down to "normal" living; he will turn out knickknacks for the dime stores or write verses for the community newspaper, as Pound was asked to do at St. Elizabeths. The psychiatrist fears above all else the healthy, cleansing effect of the creative personality upon society.

During Pound's imprisonment, American editorial writers were carried away by an exhilarating sense of freedom whenever they mentioned him. He was a federal prisoner and in no position to sue for libel, so he was a tempting target. The jackals of the press usually described him by such epithets as "the crazy traitor", "the convicted traitor", or "the mad poet". Not only was it libelous to term him a traitor when he had not been convicted of treason, let alone tried, but the continued usage of such terms by the press over a period of years made it impossible to assure him a fair trial. Public opinion was carefully schooled to believe that he was guilty *without* having been tried. The background of his broadcasts, which will be revealed for the first time in this book, and which explains why he risked the death penalty in order to defend the Constitution of the United States, was never discussed by the American press.

In the preface to one of Robert Harborough Sherard's books, Lord Alfred Douglas writes, "I always had an instinctive feeling that once Oscar Wilde had been sent to prison, prison became the obvious goal for any self-respecting poet, and I never rested until I got there. It took me about twenty-five years to do it, but I succeeded in the end, and I did six months' imprisonment in the Second Division for libelling Mr. Winston Churchill about the battle of Jutland. The result is that I am one of the very few Englishmen of letters now living, or who has been living since 1895, who can go to bed every night without feeling more or less ashamed of being an Englishman."[4]

The imprisonment of Ezra Pound caused some uneasiness among America's men of letters, although they really had nothing to fear, for, no matter what sort of regime came to power, they would still be considered harmless.

Pound was flung into Howard Hall when he was brought from the death camp at Pisa in November, 1945. He was surrounded by rapists and killers who had been adjudged criminally insane, often as a result of clever maneuvering by highly-paid attorneys. In this milieu, it was not to be expected that he should survive very long. He lasted eighteen months there, shut away from the daylight, among men and women who screamed day and night, foamed at the mouth, or tried to choke one another. Those who wallowed in their own filth had their clothes removed.

After thirteen months in this dungeon, Pound was removed to the less turbulent atmosphere of the "Chestnut" ward, a section of the hospital containing mostly senile patients who were harmless. This was a belated response to the vigorous protests of some of Pound's visitors, such as T. S. Eliot, who had been horrified by the medieval surroundings in which the poet had been imprisoned.

Dorothy Pound had finally learned through the press that her husband was imprisoned in Washington. When she arrived there, her funds were nearly exhausted. Government officials promptly declared her an "enemy alien", although she had been married to an American citizen for forty-two years. As an enemy alien, she was not allowed to draw upon her savings in England. Cummings and Hemingway generously advanced money, which carried her through those difficult days. She was allowed to visit her husband for only fifteen minutes each afternoon, as she began a vigil that was to last for more than twelve years. A guard was present during these brief meetings. Dr. Overholser explained this extra precaution by saying that Pound was under indictment for the most serious offense in American jurisprudence.

On January 29, 1947, Ezra's attorney, Julian Cornell, appeared before Judge Bolitha Laws in Washington and asked for bail, as he had done several times before. He cited Dr. Overholser's statement that Pound would never "improve" while being kept at St. Elizabeths. Cornell argued that if Pound could be given bail, he could be removed from St. Elizabeths and placed in a private institution. The government attorney argued that this "merely would place him (Pound) in a happier and more comfortable position", thus indirectly admitting that almost any institution would be more comfortable than St. Elizabeths. This was reported in the New York *Times* of February 1, 1947.

This argument exposed the government's position in keeping Pound at St. Elizabeths as a punishment, rather than as a patient suffering from mental illness. Judge Laws denied the defense attorney's motion for bail, and the order was signed by Assistant Attorney General Theron Caudle, who was soon to win fame as the hero of the "mink coat" scandal.

The use of the term "mental illness" as a weapon to dispose of political opponents is by no means rare in American history. A recent book, *The Trial of Mary Todd Lincoln,* by James A. Rhodes and Dean Jauchius (Indianapolis, The Bobbs-Merrill Company,

1959), exposes the rigged insanity trial of President Lincoln's widow to invalidate the possible influence of her son, Robert Todd Lincoln, in the elections of 1876. As soon as they were over, and only two hours after the results were known, Mrs. Lincoln was given a new sanity hearing and released. As Rex Lampman said of the inmates of St. Elizabeths, "Most of these people are here because somebody wants them to be here."

While Ezra Pound labored under the disabilities of life in a madhouse, I continued my studies at the Institute. I learned that a very devoted and talented couple who taught there, Rudd and Polly Fleming, were regular visitors to Ezra Pound. They often went directly from our classrooms, driving past the Capitol building on their way to the madhouse. One afternoon, they suggested that I might like to meet Pound. Out of modesty, I demurred, but when the invitation was repeated the following week, I accepted. On a gray November afternoon in 1949, I rode with them to the grim walled fortress of St. Elizabeths.

Before we went into the admitting office, Polly Fleming cautioned me to say that I had already visited Pound. The procedure for obtaining permission to see him was rather complicated and time-consuming. A letter of clearance had to be obtained from Dr. Overholser, as well as a note from Pound, saying that he was willing to meet me. This red tape could be avoided by replying to the attendant on one's first visit, in answer to the query, "Have you visited Pound before?", a cheerful "Yes."

I managed this answer without difficulty, but I was rather nervous as we left the administration building. Although I had met a good many celebrities, I realized that Pound might prove to be disconcerting. He was a living legend who overshadowed every other figure in modern letters, and I hardly felt prepared to meet him.

My hesitancy was not a personal weakness, for in later years I often made appointments for well-known personalities to meet Pound, only to have them back out at the last moment. One cosmopolitan lady, a principal backer of the magazine *Poetry,* got cold feet three days in succession before I gave up the effort to introduce her to Pound. On another occasion, a famed literary critic fled Washington on the day that I had agreed to take him to St. Elizabeths.

A previous administrator had attempted, with little success, to enliven the dreary atmosphere of the hospital by naming the wards after various trees. The ward in which Ezra was lodged was known as the "Chestnut" ward, which we reached by crossing the court-yard. I followed the Flemings up a steep spiral of iron stairs. The walls were covered with dirty, flaking enamel, and obviously they had not been cleaned for many years. I was instinctively repelled by the unpleasant odor of the ward. One flight up, we came to a door that was closed and locked. Rudd pressed a tiny button in the wall, and we heard an electric bell echoing through the unseen interior.

After a wait of several minutes, the door was opened by a stocky gentleman with kindly eyes. A ring of enormous keys was strapped to his waist, reminding me of a drawing I had once seen of a medieval gaoler. I later learned that he was the brother of a Congressman, and I delighted Pound by observing that both of these admirable brothers had devoted their lives to the care of the mentally retarded.

We were led down a long, gloomy corridor, which was never lit by the light of the sun. A radio blaring from an alcove showed that the patients did not lack for recreation, although the volume indicated that some of them must be deaf. At the further end of the hall, partially shielded by a folding screen, which failed to conceal him or his guests from the glares of the livelier inmates, sat Ezra Pound.

As the Flemings introduced me, Pound sprang up from his chair and grasped my hand. His piercing eyes and pointed beard reminded me at once of the late King George V of England. Despite the aura of gloom that pervaded this place of shadows, he seemed cheerful and energetic. This was his way of withstanding the hell into which Fate, as the federal government is sometimes known, had deposited him. During the ensuing decade, I seldom saw one of his visitors who was as filled with vitality and optimism as himself.

Ezra sank back into his chair and leaned his head against a cushion. He informed me that he was unable to hold up his head for long because of some difficulty with the vertebrae in his neck. In the chair next to him sat his wife, Dorothy Shakespear Pound. Hers is a classic English profile; her eyes are as bright, courageous, and youthful as her husband's. We dragged up some more chairs, and formed a semi-circle in front of Pound.

At that time, he was receiving very few visitors, and no one else joined us that afternoon. Many people who would have liked to visit him were fearful of doing so because they had to apply by letter. Since Ezra had been accused of treason against the present office-holders, those who visited him incurred considerable risk. A visitor might be promptly investigated by government agents, and some of them lost their jobs.

Later on, journalists began to carp about the fact that some of Pound's visitors were anarchists or other types of extremists, the forerunners of the beatniks. But people who had something to lose could not afford to visit Pound and incur the inevitable penalties. Despite the fact that many literate persons who occupied subordinate positions in the government read and admired Pound's work, none of them dared to visit him. Even Huntingdon Cairns, who holds a fairly lofty post at the National Gallery, would only risk seeing Pound a few times during the twelve and a half years of his imprisonment in Washington.

Consequently, Pound's visitors could be divided into two groups, the youthful and reckless art students, or beatniks, and those admirers of his work who came from other countries and were therefore immune to reprisals by the federal government. This group included scholars and diplomats from almost every country in the world except Russia.

The Flemings were respectful but somewhat wary in their attitude toward Pound. They conducted themselves in the manner of Gray Ladies visiting a sickroom. They were proud to know him, but they were like a prim couple calling on a wealthy old uncle of whom they disapproved but whom they did not wish to alienate. They later complained to me that they had to endure harsh criticism from many of their liberal friends because they had been visiting Pound. It did not occur to them that their liberal friends should not dictate their choice in this matter. When John Kasper became a celebrated figure, the Flemings vanished from the scene and did not reappear for many months, although Pound neither sponsored nor approved of Kasper's political activities.

For his part, Pound was very fond of the Flemings. They had been his earliest and most faithful visitors during the gloomiest years in the madhouse. They had arrived on the scene while he was still confined in the "Hellhole", as he termed Howard Hall, the ward for the criminally insane.

The Flemings came to see him about three times a week during most of the years of his imprisonment. Rudd was doing some Greek translations, and Polly was translating Laforgue and other French poets whom Ezra had introduced in America some years before. Although they had many literary interests in common, their politics were at the other extreme from Pound's, and any discussion that ventured into this realm would soon become acrimonious, as Polly was, like most of her persuasion, rather loquacious. Nevertheless, Pound delighted in teasing them by making an unfavorable reference to some "liberal" hero, perhaps to spur the conversation along.

On this, my first visit, politics was not mentioned. Ezra and Rudd chatted about the Greeks, and Polly talked with Mrs. Pound. Occasionally, Ezra would screw his features into a terrible grimace and partly rise from his chair, as if he were trying to ward off some unseen threat. Neither his wife nor the Flemings would pay any attention to these actions, although they suggested that he might be suffering from an acute fit of madness. Thus did Macbeth envisage Banquo, and, looking behind me, I saw a lanky hillbilly, a rawboned fellow about twenty years old, with staring eyes and a face like an advertisement for a horror movie.

Seeing that I was disturbed, Ezra rose from his chair and pushed the fellow out of the way. His actions on this occasion reminded me of Trotsky's quote from Tolstoy in his *History of the Russian Revolution*. Tolstoy describes an old man who was sitting by the side of the road and making wild gestures and fierce grimaces. Tolstoy at first supposed him to be mad, but on drawing near, he saw that the old man was merely sharpening a knife upon a stone.

The hillbilly annoyed us again on subsequent visits, and Ezra sometimes got rid of him by giving him some small change. He was finally transferred to another ward, and we saw him no more. He was not at all like the other "Chestnuts", who were, if one may be excused this pleasantry, less violent nuts. The old men paced up and down the long corridor most of the day, or sat apathetically in chairs spaced along the walls. As Ezra said, "One can't be associated with gooks for long without being affected by it."

I remember one of the more pathetic "Chestnuts", an old man

named Bolger, who walked back and forth, wringing his hands and moaning again and again in a piteous voice, "Oh God, Oh God, don't let them retire me!" I learned that he had been a prominent executive who had stayed at his desk too long and become senile. Out of pity, his fellow officers had delayed retiring him despite the seriousness of his condition. He knew that they were thinking of unloading him, and this knowledge only made his condition worse. They kept him on, and he finally ruined the corporation and was retired penniless to the madhouse.

In this atmosphere, Ezra led a monastic existence. He spent most of the day studying and writing in an incredibly tiny room that had a single narrow window. He was able to close his door partially, but this did not keep out the blare of the radios, or the roar of the television, which came after 1952. Nor did the door protect him from the murmur of the old men's voices as they paused in the hall, muttering over and over the arguments that they had used, or had meant to use, in some long-forgotten crisis.

I had said very little on this first visit, and supposed that I was making no impression. As the hospital bell tolled four, the signal for visitors to leave, Ezra fixed those very piercing eyes on me and asked, "What day would you like?"

"Oh, Tuesday would be all right with me," I replied hesitantly, without knowing what was meant.

"Let's see, we don't have anyone coming on Tuesday, do we?" he asked his wife.

"Not at the present," she answered. "Dick[5] has gone off on some sort of expedition, and he won't be around for awhile."

"Good," he said to me. "I'll see you then."

He vigorously shook hands with each of us, as the gaoler came up with his bunch of keys and unlocked the door. Ezra kissed his wife goodbye, and we were let out into an atmosphere of freedom. Once we were on the lawn, I breathed deeply, trying to get that terrible musty odor out of my lungs. Dorothy Pound was observing me, and she smiled gently but said nothing. After all, she was going in and out of that hellish place every day.

The Flemings drove Dorothy Pound home to the tiny apartment that she occupied a few blocks from the hospital. Later, as they took me downtown, Polly triumphantly exclaimed, "I thought he would like you!"

"How do you know?" I asked. "He didn't seem to pay much attention to me."

"Oh yes," she said. "Why, he has given you your own day!" She explained that this was quite unusual. Only a few of Pound's friends were allowed a specific day of their own each week, and to their knowledge, Pound had never extended this privilege to anyone on his first visit.

I had first read Pound's *Pisan Cantos* because of the furor over the Bollingen Prize in 1948, and from there I had gone on to the earlier *Cantos*. Now that I felt the necessity of knowing more of Pound's work, I found that this was not so easily done. Although he had published some thirty volumes of verse and criticism during the past four decades, they had been issued by obscure publishers in small quantities and were not readily available. Fortunately, the Library of Congress was at hand, but I discovered that nearly all of his books were kept in the Rare Book Room. This was a rather ornate room protected by velvet ropes, and the reader had to sign his name in a ledger before being admitted. Once I began to order the slender volumes of Pound's early work, I realized the precision and the direction that had led so relentlessly to the form of the *Cantos*.

When I checked the listings of Pound in the guides to periodicals, both in the United States and in England, I found many letters and short articles that were not available in the collected volumes. A letter that appears in *The Nation* of April 18, 1928, was of particular interest. He characterized Henry Ford as the "epitome of the American hired man." This struck me as a very apt summation. Most of the great American fortunes had been founded by hired men and tinkerers rather than by robber barons, as the scholars who are so heavily subsidized by the Ford Foundation contend. It was inevitable that the hired men should become easy marks for professors and other confidence men, and that the hired men should turn over their fortunes to these types so that the professors could use this money to proclaim that the hired men were saps.

Pound's characterization of Ford as the American hired man was an important revelation to me. It was the first time that I realized the importance of *placing* people, an art that must be mastered by great hostesses and critics.

On the following Tuesday, I took the bus out to the hospital. As justification for my existence, I brought along the manuscript of a novel. The Pounds and I spent a pleasant afternoon. No other visitors turned up, and I had an opportunity to appreciate the man. This was an important day for me. I had not known the details of his case, except that he had been locked up on a charge of treason and had been the subject of much controversy. Now, as I watched him sitting there, enveloped in the enormous gloom of the madhouse, I was suddenly committed to him and to his ideals, and I knew that from that point on I would be involved in his struggle. He has written in *The Pisan Cantos,*

Neither Eos nor Hesperus has suffered wrong at my hands[6][.]

The tragedy of the First World War, which signified the downfall of an orderly Western civilization, spurred Pound to seek justice. It is impossible for the artist to complete himself, or do significant work, without committing himself to this struggle. Sooner or later, he will be asked to become a lackey to the existing order, regardless of that order's merits. His life then becomes a precarious existence, if he chooses to carry on without submitting, or an empty one, if he surrenders.

I now began a routine that I maintained for the next three years. At one o'clock each afternoon, I walked down to the F.B.I. building at Tenth Street and Pennsylvania Avenue to take the Congress Heights bus. I arrived at St. Elizabeths about a quarter to two, and usually remained a half hour after the bell until four-thirty, when Ezra had to go in for his evening meal.

I have often been asked what we could find to talk about for three hours each day over a period of years. Many of Pound's visitors came only for an hour's visit, or less. The Flemings usually arrived about three, and left promptly when the bell tolled four. But they were not being educated by Ezra. The *Cantos* explain the nature of these conversations:

And they want to know what we talked about?
    "de litteris et de armis, praestantibusque ingeniis,

Both of ancient times and our own; books, arms,
And of men of unusual genius,
Both of ancient times and our own, in short the usual subjects
Of conversation between intelligent men."[7]

As the press of visitors grew each year, I seldom knew whom I
might encounter there. Dorothy Pound was always present, with the
exception of two brief "vacations", when she visited relatives in
Philadelphia and Virginia. She was related to the St. George
Tuckers, and to Randolph of Roanoke as well, so we were cousins
many times removed. Ezra was quite pleased to learn that I was
one of "them Randolphs", and he included some fiery passages about
Randolph's battle against the Bank of the United States in his *Cantos*.

I often encountered Dorothy Pound in the administration building in the early afternoon, and we would go up to the "Chestnut"
ward together. During at least seven months of the year, we sat
with Ezra in that peculiar hell. It is difficult to convey in words the
sordid horror of the situation in which Pound spent a considerable
portion of his life—the rank, dead odor, the atmosphere of futility
as the blank-faced old men paced up and down the hall, the sense
of utter hopelessness.

Archibald MacLeish described the scene in a review that appeared in the New York *Times,* December 16, 1956:

". . . Not everyone has seen Pound in the long dim corridor
inhabited by the ghosts of men who cannot be still, or who can be
still too long. . . . When a conscious mind capable of the most
complete human awareness is incarcerated among minds which are
not conscious and cannot be aware, the enforced association produces a horror which is not relieved either by the intelligence of
doctors or by the tact of administrators or even by the patience and
kindliness of the man who suffers for it. You carry the horror away
with you like the smell of the ward in your clothes, and whenever
afterward you think of Pound or read his lines, a stale sorrow
afflicts you."

The winter months that confined Ezra to the gloomy hole were
most depressing for him. After greeting his daily visitors, he sometimes leaned back in dejection. Perhaps he was thinking, "When
will this end?" Usually he carried the conversation, but on some of

those gray afternoons, he lapsed into periods of silence. Since he was always the center of attention, this would put a damper on the talk.

One afternoon, I did not bother to report in at the office, thinking it a useless formality and not required of anyone who visited so frequently. I sat down on the lawn with the Pounds, and a few minutes later, an attendant came rushing up, demanding to know why I had not reported in at the desk. We were several hundred feet from the office, and this incident proved that Ezra was under constant surveillance. He cautioned me that I must always make sure to report; otherwise, it might result in the curtailment of his privilege of receiving visitors. I was surprised to learn that Dorothy Pound was required to report every afternoon as though she were visiting her husband for the first time.

On another occasion, I persuaded a fellow student at the Institute, Michael Reck, to come out with me. He was a crew-cut type, more an admirer of Cummings than of Pound. I believe that I finally lured him out to the hospital by saying that Cummings was to be there, or that he might turn up. Despite Ezra's fame, there were many young people who thought of him as some sort of evil genius who might corrupt them, and they seemed determined not to pursue the matter any further.

With a continued show of reluctance, Reck accompanied me. When we approached the admitting office, I cautioned him to tell the attendant that he had visited Ezra before. He fluffed the line, however, possibly through fear that he might get into serious difficulties with the "government", and finally stammered that this was his first visit. It was then that I realized he would never become a poet, for he obviously had no talent as a liar.

I tried to repair the damage by attempting to bulldoze him in. I stepped in front of him, but it was too late. The attendant was new at the job, and he went into a rear office, reappearing with a grave type in his mid-thirties, no doubt an on-the-job-training psychiatrist. He informed us that it would be impossible for Reck to see Pound without going through the requisite preliminaries, as Pound was "a political prisoner".

Ezra was delighted to learn that the officials were being so frank about his status, and it gave me new insight into the opposition of the state that held him in bondage. As I plunged deeper into the study of his work, I was forced to take into account the entire circumstances that had led him to make the broadcasts from Italy, resulting in his indictment on a charge of treason. I learned that he could have avoided the indictment by renouncing his American citizenship, but he had purposely refused to make this sacrifice, for behind his every act was his loyalty to his country.

It was this inescapable fact that had caused the government attorneys to place him in the madhouse, rather than to publicly try a man whose only crime was his unswerving and uncompromising patriotism. I reflected that I owed my education to three Americans who were indicted for high treason against duly constituted authority, although none of the three "traitors" was ever tried on this charge. I had previously studied at Washington and Lee University, which had been founded with a grant from George Washington, whom the British had promised to hang as a traitor, and brought to its present eminence by Robert E. Lee, who also had been promised a hangman's noose for the crime of treason.

Washington and Lee are now enshrined in the hearts of their fellow countrymen, and no one could think of them as traitors. With the passage of time, and a deeper understanding of the unseen forces at work that promoted the Second World War, his fellow citizens will erase for all time the charge of treason laid against Ezra Pound.

The government of the United States admitted that there was no case against him when the charges were dropped in 1958. For the first time, the case *for* Ezra Pound, which should have been presented at the trial that the government refused him, is being presented in this book. In order to do so, it is necessary to recount his literary career from its inception, for the same ideals and values that guided him from his student days led to the broadcasts and the indictment for treason as inevitably as they led to the *Cantos*. As everyone who has been privileged to know him can testify, he has found it impossible to maintain his strict standards of artistic integrity without also maintaining those standards in his dealings with that perennial foe of the artist, the State.

II

EZRA POUND was born on October 30, 1885, in Hailey, Idaho. He was the son of Homer Loomis Pound and Isabel Weston Pound. In later years, the sculptor Lekakis humourously referred to Ezra as "Homer's son", a *mot* that was repeated among the Greeks.

Hailey was a frontier town, such as those that can be seen today on any American television screen. Homer Pound was employed in the government land office. Ezra recalls seeing some burly gentlemen striding about with large six shooters strapped to their waists. In 1888, Homer Pound was appointed assayer to the United States Mint in Philadelphia. The family was caught in the famed "Blizzard of '88" during their return to the East. They settled in Wyncote, Pennsylvania, a prosperous suburb, with such neighbors as a certain Mr. Curtis, who published a well-known periodical of that era.

Ezra's interest in money as a phenomenon, in contrast to the usual attitude toward money as something to get, is a legitimate one. His paternal grandfather, Thaddeus Coleman Pound, had been a pioneer railroad-builder and lumberman in Wisconsin. He served several terms as a Congressman and became an ardent advocate of monetary reform. While he was in Washington, his lumber interests were wiped out by the rapid expansion of the Weyerhaeuser firm. He returned home to salvage what he could, and for a time, he paid his workers in scrip money. Ezra inherited a few bills of this unique currency, and used one of them as an illustration for his own monetary theories.

His father sometimes allowed Ezra to stroll through the Mint, and he has described to me one of his earliest memories, when he watched men stripped to the waist as they shovelled heaps of gold coins into large sacks. Perhaps this familiarity is responsible for Ezra's apparent contempt for money as a personal possession, since he has never made any effort to acquire it, or to become a slave to it. He has been annoyed because the lack of money prevented him from carrying out one of his many projects, or from subsidizing other writers, but his regard for money is, to say the least, an unconventional one.

One of Ezra's London friends, Phyllis Bottome, later described his parents, whom she came to know well: "They were a quiet old-fashioned and extremely pleasant type of American—common to our early childhood, but less easily discerned now."[1] Homer Pound was a civil servant when that profession was as highly regarded as an occupation for an intelligent man as the law or the ministry. Ezra grew up in a comfortable middle-class home of the 1890s, the sort of place that only a millionaire can afford today. In 1900, he leaped into the world of the arts by enrolling at the University of Pennsylvania. He obtained the status of "special student", by stating that he wished to avoid "irrelevant subjects".

Among Pound's closest friends during his student days were William Carlos Williams, who was studying medicine at the graduate school, and Hilda Doolittle, daughter of Professor Charles Doolittle, Flower Professor of Astronomy at the University. Hilda Doolittle, later known as the poetess H.D., was a student at Bryn Mawr. Among her classmates there was Marianne Moore.

Williams had been introduced to Pound by a student named Van Cleve. He relates that Pound often came to his dormitory room to read aloud his poems. Some of these works later appeared in Pound's first volume, *A Lume Spento* (1908). Pound was then writing a sonnet a day. He burned the lot of them at the end of the year. Williams also was engaged in writing poetry, an epic that he was too shy to read to anyone.[2]

"I was fascinated by the man," Williams writes of Pound. "He was the liveliest, most intelligent and unexplainable thing I'd ever seen and the most fun—except for his painful self-consciousness and his coughing laugh."[3]

A small group of students occasionally gathered at Pound's home for a Sunday afternoon sandwich and song fest. Williams says that Pound never learned to play the piano, and Mrs. Pound, whom he describes as "erect and rather beautiful in an indifferent, middle-aged way," usually played for them.[4]

With great gusto, Pound involved himself in extracurricular activities. He took up fencing under the tutelage of the University's master, Signor Terrone, but dropped it when Williams, who had had the benefit of a year's study at a Swiss school, informed him that the French style was much superior to the Italian style that was taught by Signor Terrone.

In 1903, Pound, irritated by the faculty at the University, decided to make a change. He enrolled at Hamilton College. In his *Autobiography*, Williams says that Pound may have left the University because of some difficulty with his parents,[5] but he may have forgotten that Pound enrolled as a special student, rather than as a candidate for a degree, indicating that he had not planned to spend more than a year or two there.

Pound continued to visit his parents and his friends in Philadelphia on weekends. One result of this was the first known character analysis of Pound, expressed in a letter written by Williams to his mother, dated March 30, 1904:

"He is really a brilliant talker and thinker but delights in making himself exactly what he is not: a laughing boor. His friends must be all patience in order to find him out and even then you must not let him know it, for he will immediately put on some artificial mood and be really unbearable. It is too bad, for he loves to be liked, yet there is some quality in him which makes him too proud to try to please people."[6]

Pound could hardly have known of this letter when he later described Williams as "bloody inarticulate", for it is one of the most expressive things that Williams has written.

At the age of eighteen, Pound was already exhibiting those traits that were to excite contumely for the rest of his life. It has often seemed that Pound did exactly what Williams describes in this passage, that is, to deliberately obscure his finer qualities, and put his worst foot forward. Malcolm Cowley has observed that Pound does this in order to remain free of the crowd, and of the admirers who are attracted by his daring.[7] For a half-century he has been the tightrope walker of modern letters, and for a half-century the audience has been waiting for him to lose his footing. If his manner seems unduly rude to some people, it has served two purposes. First, it tests the tensile strength of the subject's mind, and, second, it keeps civilian sightseers from lingering too long in the captain's tent.

This mode of self-defense may be described as armor, if one desires to tread the manure-strewn path of psychology; some of it is due to a self-toughening process; but much of it is sheer perversity. Whatever it is, it has operated to his benefit through the years. Think of the consequences had he settled down for any protracted period with Mr. Joyce, Mr. Antheil, or Peggy Guggenheim! Yet this would have been Pound's fate had he not occasionally bristled his spine, and the ensuing loss of work would have been incalculable.

Through the courtesy of *The New Yorker,* we have two descriptions of Pound at Hamilton College. His roommate, Claudius Alonzo Hand, now general counsel for a Wall Street bank, said that Pound would sometimes come in around midnight, wake him, and shove a glass of beer into his hand. Then he would read his poems aloud. When he had finished, he would ask Hand how much he had understood.

"Not a word," the still sleepy Hand would confess.

"Oh God!" Ezra would exclaim, seizing the glass of beer and downing it in desperation.

"It must have been pretty discouraging," said Mr. Hand, some four decades later, as he analyzed his role in Ezra's flight from the homeland.[8]

Another Hamilton boy, Mr. Conklin Mann, became a genealogist. He discovered, after some years of research, that Ezra had changed his name from Ezra Weston Pound to Ezra Loomis Pound. His mother, Isabel Weston Pound, had been a great-niece of Henry Longfellow, and perhaps Ezra felt that the tell-tale Weston in his own name might cause someone to remember the connection.

Mann says that Pound did not join a fraternity at Hamilton,

although he received a bid. During a rather undignified part of the initiation ceremony, he is said to have attacked one of the elders, and he was subsequently blacklisted as one who had no respect for constituted authority. The episode is illustrative of what Ortega terms "the sportive origin of the State."

This resulted in an uneasy truce between Pound and his fellow-students, which was broken on at least one occasion. Mann records that the students played a prank on Pound one afternoon when his parents were scheduled to visit the school. While Pound was at the train station waiting for them, the students removed all of the furniture from his room and placed it on the campus. The bed was neatly turned down, and a pair of pajamas lay on top of it when the Pounds arrived.[9]

Mann describes Pound as "a tall, long-striding dirty-collared boy with tawny, leonine hair, who talked about getting a position with the American Embassy in London."[10] Pound had gone abroad with his aunt in 1898, and he was already chafing at the bit, anxious to return to Europe. He was aware that there were few opportunities in poetry for him in the land of "The Blue Flower", and he had no desire to become imprisoned in its cultural strait jacket.

After obtaining a degree at Hamilton, Pound returned to the University of Pennsylvania to take a master's degree in 1906. He was given a fellowship as an instructor with professorial functions. Williams relates that Pound performed impressively in the chorus of Euripides' *Iphigenia in Aulis,* which the senior class staged at the Philadelphia Academy of Music.[11]

Another close friend of Pound's in Philadelphia, H.D., had had a nervous breakdown, and had withdrawn from Bryn Mawr. She was living quietly at home, devoting her time to working on her poems.

In June, 1906, Pound left for Europe. He had been awarded a traveling fellowship by the University for the purpose of gathering material on the work of Lope de Vega. He went to Spain, France and Italy, returning to the United States the following summer. The University board refused to renew the fellowship, and he decided to become a teacher. He accepted an offer of a position at Wabash College, in Crawfordsville, Indiana. In the autumn of 1907, he arrived there to take up his duties as Professor of Romance Literature.

His stay in these bucolic surroundings lasted but four months. In *The Nation* of April 18, 1928, he writes of this experience, "At twenty-two, stranded in Devil's Island, Indiana." One evening, he went out to post a letter. It was snowing heavily, and he encountered a girl in the storm who told a sad story. She had been stranded in the town with a burlesque show, when the manager took what cash was on hand and purchased a single ticket to more favorable climes. She had no money, and no place to go. The centennial history of the college recounts that Pound took her home with him. He gave her his bed, and slept on a pallet that he had prepared on the floor.

The next morning, he left early to give an eight o'clock class. His landladies, the maidens Hall, rushed upstairs, ostensibly to clean his room, but actually to see for themselves the creature who had sullied their home. Pound was too young to know that no female can enter a house inhabited by maiden ladies without their antennae registering the alien craft. The young lady was booted out by one Hall, while her sister was frantically buzzing the town's lone telephone operator. Having established the fact that an emergency did indeed exist, she had the lines cleared while she talked to the president of the college and two of the trustees. By noon of that day Pound's career in the Groves of Academe was over.

Although no wrongdoing was charged, the president informed Pound that he was too much the "Latin Quarter" type, a phrase that he had read somewhere, and that to him summed up all of the vice that pervaded the decadent world surrounding Crawfordsville, Indiana. Some critics have seized upon this episode as at least a partial explanation for Pound's years as an expatriate, while others, leaning heavily upon the syndrome theory, have imagined that it accounts for his continual biting criticism of life as it is lived in America.

Such observations ignore the fact that all of Pound's criticism of his homeland is soundly based upon educational and cultural grounds. On no occasion has he suggested that the reins of the prevailing sexual mores be lightened in the United States. Most of these suggestions have come from his critics.

H. Glenn Hughes, historian of the Imagist movement, questioned Pound about the Wabash College incident in 1930. He said that the episode was recalled without embarrassment or rancour. Instead, Pound responded "with considerable amusement, and insists that he was absolutely innocent of any misdemeanour."[12]

Pound returned to Wyncote for a brief visit. His father agreed that if he could get a favorable opinion from an expert about his poetry, he would finance another trip to Europe. A visit to Witter Bynner, then literary editor of *McClure's* Magazine, produced the necessary recommendation, but apparently not much money was forthcoming, for Pound says that he landed in Europe in January, 1908, with eighty dollars in his pocket. He had taken passage on a cattle boat, landing at Gibraltar. From there, he made his way on foot across the continent to Venice, an excursion that he still recalls with relish. The important thing, he says, is that he was able to make such a trip without a passport. He had no identification papers, these personal indignities being largely unknown until after the First World War.

When he arrived in Venice, he still had sufficient funds to finance the printing of one hundred copies of his first book of poems, *A Lume Spento*. As contrasted to the approximately one thousand dollars that a young poet has to advance in order to get out a slender volume of verse in the United States, Pound had this one produced for the equivalent of eight dollars! It was offered for sale at the modest price of one dollar per copy. Pound noted in the 1930s that copies were bringing as much as fifty dollars. James Laughlin, Pound's publisher, says that he paid one hundred and twenty-five dollars for his copy, and that the price has since gone higher.

From Venice he set out once more, again on foot (youth hostelers, please note). He now had his box of poems, in addition to his modest luggage. He had decided to assault the citadel of London, and stopped over for but one night in Paris. From London, he applied again for the renewal of his fellowship on the Lope de Vega study, but he was refused. He applied a third time the following year, with the same result.

The name of Pound at that time was a familiar one in London. A Sir John Pound had been Lord Mayor in 1904–5, and in 1908 he was the chairman of the London General Omnibus Company. If worst had come to the worst, Pound could probably have appealed to his namesake for a job as bus driver. But he was able to make his own way, and he never met Sir John.

He devoted his energies to crashing the literary world of London, where Sir John was no better known than Ezra. Despite his dwindling funds and his lack of acquaintances in this enormous, sprawling, smoky city, Ezra had the confidence of youth and his copies of *A Lume Spento*.

The little book was duly sent to the literary critics, who received it favorably. The *Evening Standard* reviewer wrote, ". . . wild and haunting stuff . . . coming after the trite and decorous stuff of most of our decorous poets, this poet seems like a minstrel of Provence at a suburban musical evening."

From the outset, Pound was viewed by Londoners as an American novelty, and he did not shirk the role. He grew a bushy beard, and this, combined with his thick, wavy hair and piercing eyes, and his Byronic costume, caused him to stand out jarringly in a milieu where, says Wyndham Lewis, a sophisticated post-1890s society was dreaming wistfully of the eighteenth century.

There was a strong Georgian movement among the younger London poets when Pound arrived. These writers were enchanted by visions of secluded country estates, where swallows darted about through the low-hanging branches of willow trees. Pound launched a number of furious attacks against the members of this group, using suffragette papers, the columns of the daily press, and his own adequate talent for stirring up conversation in the literary clubs. He went so far as to challenge the leader of the Georgians, Lascelles Abercrombie, to a duel, with indifferent results.

One of Pound's first successful campaigns in London resulted in his capture of the leading publisher of the old *Yellow Book* crowd, Elkin Mathews.[13] He soon learned that Mathews, far from being a daring publisher of avant-garde work, was one of the most cautious men in London. He had made his reputation during the 1890s, while he was a partner of John Lane, a clerk who had gone into publishing and had been very successful. Lane had severed the partnership, and he was then publishing under the Bodley Head imprint. He was financed by a wealthy partner with the appropriate name of Money-Coutts (later Lord Latymer), who also wrote a slender volume of verse.[14]

Percy Muir, who eventually incorporated the Mathews firm into Chatto and Windus, says that Lane had "in overflowing measure that buccaneer spirit, a modicum of which is indispensable to any publisher." Muir describes Mathews as "timid and almost entirely unadventurous."[15]

But Pound, as he entered Mathews' office at the end of Vigo Lane, which has been called the most narrow, inconvenient and curious street in London, knew of him only through the *Yellow Book* connection, and as publisher of such writers as Oscar Wilde, Arthur Symons, Aubrey Beardsley, and Lionel Johnson. Across the street was the firm with which Pound would later be associated, Lane's Bodley Head Company, which was at that time ensconced in the old *Saturday Review* offices.

Pound has described the encounter with Mathews as follows: Mathews suggested that, as an unknown poet, Pound should pay at least part of the printing costs.

POUND: "I have a shilling in my clothes, if that's of any use to you."

MATHEWS: "Well, I want to print them. Anyhow."[16]

In April, 1909, Mathews brought out *Personae*. It was a critical success. The *Evening Standard* critic said, ". . . a queer little book which will irritate many readers."

Edward Thomas wrote a three-and-one-half page praise of Pound in *The English Review,* saying, in part, ". . . He cannot be usefully compared with any living writers . . . full of personality, and with such power to express it that from the first to the last lines of most of his poems he holds us steadily in his own pure, grave, passionate world."

The *Oxford Magazine* critic said, "This is a most exciting book of verse."

"No new book of poems for years had contained such a freshness of inspiration, such a strongly individual note, or been more alive with indubitable promise," wrote the critic of *The Bookman*.

Encouraged by the success of *Personae,* Mathews brought out Pound's *Exultations* a few months later. His poems were now appearing in the *Evening Standard, St. James Gazette, The English Review,* and other important English newspapers and periodicals.

Inevitably, he came to the attention of *Punch,* and was treated to the following example of British humor:

"Mr. Welkin Mark (exactly opposite Long Jane's) begs to announce that he has secured for the English market the palpitating works of the new Montana (U.S.A.) poet, Mr. Ezekiel Ton, who is the most remarkable thing in poetry since Robert Browning. Mr. Ton, who has left America to reside for awhile in London and impress his personality on English editors, publishers and readers, is by far the newest poet going, whatever other advertisements may say. He has succeeded, where all others have failed, in evolving a blend of the imagery of the unfettered West, the vocabulary of Wardour Street, and the sinister abandon of Borgiac Italy."[17]

In October, 1909, on his twenty-fourth birthday, Pound achieved a sudden success with the publication of his poem "The Ballad of the Goodly Fere," in *The English Review.* An account of the last hours of Christ, the poem was quoted everywhere. It threatened to provide him with an easy method of composition that would hamper his development. He later remarked, "After the success of the 'Goodly Fere', all I had to do was to write a ballad about each of the disciples, and I would have been set for life."[18]

But Pound had no intention of taking such an easy path. "The Ballad" did bring him to the attention of his native land, and *The Literary Digest,* which was the *Time* Magazine of its era, reprinted the poem, with an introductory note about its author, "Mr. Eyra Pound," on October 30, 1909.

The following month, in the issue of November 27, 1909, the *Digest* ran a picture of a still-beardless Pound, probably a college photograph, and quoted *The Bookman,* " . . . he has written and burnt two novels and 300 sonnets." These were the works that undoubtedly would have won him fame and fortune among his fellow countrymen. He was correctly named as "Ezra Pound" in this issue, someone having called the editor's attention to the previous error. Twenty years later, *The Literary Digest* boasted of having been the first American publication to print Pound's work.

By coincidence, this same issue of *The Literary Digest* carried a note about Senator Nelson Aldrich's tour of the West to gain support for a new banking plan, the Aldrich Plan, which would give the nation a central bank. When this plan was enacted as the

Federal Reserve Act, Ezra Pound, Congressman Charles Lindbergh, and many other Americans criticized it as too great a concentration of credit.

One of Pound's London enthusiasts, Miss May Sinclair, had made the publication of "The Ballad of the Goodly Fere" possible by introducing its author to Ford Madox Hueffer, editor of *The English Review*. Soon Pound was spending much of his time in the offices of the *Review* with the genial Hueffer.

The magazine had been launched in December, 1908, shortly after Pound's arrival in London, by a group of writers incensed because Thomas Hardy had been unable to get one of his poems published in the established magazines. This melancholy work, "A Sunday Morning Tragedy", is not a very exciting poem, and, no doubt, Hueffer had been planning such a venture for months, without a sufficient excuse to rally his supporters. His helpmate, Violet Hunt, has described the fevered manner in which Hueffer planned the new periodical. He summoned his friends to all-night meetings, and the details of the venture were worked out as though they were plotting a political conspiracy.

Then, as now, the main problem of a would-be editor was to finance the publication. Hueffer's friend, Arthur Marwood, agreed to put up some of the money. For the remainder of the needed sum, says Violet Hunt, Hueffer approached the various branches of his family on the Continent, the German Hueffers, the Dutch Hueffers, and the French Hueffers. Hermann Hueffer, a prominent banker in Paris, who had secured the Duke de Tancourville as a suitable husband for his daughter, agreed to support the *Review*. The initial issue of December, 1908, boasted the names of Thomas Hardy, Joseph Conrad, Henry James, John Galsworthy, Count Tolstoi, and H. G. Wells as contributors. It is doubtful if any single copy of a literary periodical has ever contained so much new work by such an array of world-famous writers.

Hueffer was able to call upon them because he was their intimate friend. His father, Franz Hueffer, had come from Germany to edit the Tauchnitz edition of Dante Gabriel Rossetti's poems. He fell in love with, and married, the daughter of Ford Madox Brown, an artist whose home was the meeting-place for the pre-

Raphaelites. The young Hueffer grew up as a familiar of the best-known writers and artists of England.

At the age of sixteen, Hueffer published his first book, *The Brown Owl* (1892). A gregarious fellow, he spent much of his time in the company of other writers, chatting about his favorite subjects, wine and food.

Despite the splendor of these names, the new magazine failed to pay its way, possibly because of inadequate "promotion" on the part of its publisher and editor. The backers grew uneasy, for Hueffer had painted a glowing picture of the profits that would soon be forthcoming. In all sincerity, he had devised elaborate charts for the division of the enormous dividends that would be paid by the *Review*.

Not only were there no profits, but the backers were called upon to advance more money, for each new issue of the magazine increased its debts. The backers refused to put up any more money, leaving Hueffer with the choice of paying the deficits himself or giving up the enterprise. Despite the fact that he had no private fortune, and was dependent upon the income from his own writing as his only source of livelihood, he poured his savings into the breach. Within a few months after the first issue, he wrote to Arnold Bennett that the *Review* was costing him three hundred pounds per month out of his own pocket. Violet Hunt estimates that the net loss was about one hundred pounds per month, which was probably the sum that Hueffer was contributing, but since Hueffer was serving without salary, he may have included this sum in the larger figure.

Violet Hunt made frantic efforts to save the *Review,* approaching many of her acquaintances in London for contributions. She tried to find a purchaser who would merely subsidize it, and allow Hueffer to continue as editor. Willa Cather was then in London, and Miss Hunt suggested that Miss Cather's publisher, S. S. Mc-Clure, who was at that time the giant of the publishing world in America, might wish to buy the magazine as an English outlet. Mr. McClure was not interested.

At last, Miss Hunt snared one of the wealthiest men in England, Lord Alfred Mond, head of the mushrooming chemical trust, Imperial Chemical Industries. Lord Mond was at once interested in taking over the magazine, and he invited Hueffer and Miss Hunt to spend the weekend with him at his estate, Goring Hall, and work out the details of the transfer.

Hueffer had now put out thirteen issues of the *Review,* and his funds were exhausted. He was disappointed to find that Lord Mond was quite anxious to acquire the *Review,* but that he did not need the services of its founder. He saw the possibilities of the magazine as a political weapon, for, despite its losses, it had attracted an influential audience in England, and it was now an important organ of opinion.

Knowing that he could not purchase Hueffer's political support, Lord Mond proposed to purchase the magazine and let Hueffer go elsewhere. Nor was Hueffer to be repaid for his losses. Lord Mond proposed that he would continue to publish the magazine, and would be fully responsible for any further debts incurred, but he could not afford to pay anything for the audience that Hueffer had built up for him.

Hueffer quixotically agreed to this odd proposal, because he was anxious that the magazine should survive. Perhaps he thought he might be able to repurchase it at some future date. He was always extremely optimistic and careless about financial matters. In this instance, he was not able to recover the magazine. He went down to Goring Hall as the publisher and editor of one of the most influential reviews of the day, and he returned to London with nothing. Hueffer had met his first millionaire.

Pound memorialized the event in "Canto 104":

> Mond killed the English Review
>   and Ford went to Paris (an interval)[19][.]

During the months that he edited the review, Hueffer did not confine himself to publishing the works of the established reputations. He also introduced the work of several important writers. Ezra Pound and D. H. Lawrence were two of the poets who first appeared in its pages. Violet Hunt, who was acting as Hueffer's reader, had first read the poems that D. H. Lawrence, then a young schoolteacher, had sent in, and she passed them on to the editor with an enthusiastic note. Hueffer was greatly impressed by the poems, and sent off a wire that he had accepted them. He invited Lawrence up to London for a lunch to celebrate the first publication of a writer whose importance he had already recognized.

On the day that the November, 1909, issue of *The English Review* was sent out to its subscribers, Lawrence arrived for his lunch. Pound was also present at this affair. Roast beef and plum pudding were served with champagne (Violet Hunt had been entrusted with the responsibility for the arrangements; Hueffer has written somewhere that champagne is appropriate only for children's birthday parties and for Americans!). Hueffer jocularly asked Lawrence, a miner's son, how he liked having champagne for lunch, and assured him that that was the way successful authors lived. He did not mention the sad state of affairs at the *Review*, nor the fact that he was exhausting his own savings in the effort to keep it going.

The offices of the *Review* were at 84 Holland Park Avenue, a "maisonette over a poulterer's and fishmonger's combined,"[20] according to Violet Hunt. The rooms also served as the living quarters of the editor. He had engaged, without salary, a subeditor, Douglas Goldring, who worked by day as a writer for *Country Life,* the sedate periodical of the English squirearchy. His evenings were spent in laboring for the *Review,* for Hueffer had assured him of its great expectations. While Goldring was answering correspondence and wondering how to pay the printer's bills, Hueffer, surrounded by his many friends, was host to the continual party which went on in the office.

"Gobbets of blood," complains Goldring, "oozing from the suspended carcases of rabbits, made the threshold positively unsafe."[21] Henry James, who had been informed of the circumstances in which the *Review* was published, refused to come near the place. Whenever he was required to confer with the Master, Hueffer usually disappeared for a day or two, going down to James' place in Rye.

Violet Hunt says that the doors to the office were never locked, and that a strange assortment of characters came and went during the day. The Russian spy Azef, notorious as the murderer of Father Gapon, often stopped in to rifle the editor's desk while Hueffer was away. A lady who, in the style of those days, was

known simply as "Vera F.," and who had shot at Stolypin and
missed, also was a frequent visitor. The neighborhood drunkard,
Geordie McKnite, was often sprawled across the threshold oblivious to the dripping blood, but one merely stepped over him.[22]

Despite his gory hands, the landlord, Mr. Chandler, seems to
have been a perfect type of the English butler. In response to
the urging of his wife, he periodically gave Hueffer notice to move,
but he never enforced the order. The neighborhood was a dangerous one, and a man was sandbagged and robbed in broad daylight
outside the shop. Mr. Chandler lived in fear of being knifed in the
back when he made his daily trip to the bank, but Hueffer came
and went without noticing the risks that were peculiar to that area.
His only recorded complaint was made on the day that a finicky
burglar made off with his supply of spare tall hats. This was no
slight inconvenience, for he was a fixture at fashionable garden
parties, and these accoutrements formed an indispensable portion
of his wardrobe.

Among the regular evening visitors to the office was R. B.
Cunninghame-Graham, who in his youth had greatly resembled
Pound. He also had been a very controversial figure. He was a
former member of Parliament who had been jailed for participating
in a riot in Trafalgar Square. He had been hit over the head and
sentenced to six weeks in prison. Other habitués included W. H.
Hudson, Wyndham Lewis, Stephen Reynolds, Edward Garnett,
Percival Gibbons, Edgar Jepson, May Sinclair, and Ethel Colburt
Mayne. Pound was usually present for he had taken rooms just
down the street.

Hueffer has given us some interesting accounts of Pound's first
years in London. In reading these paragraphs, one can almost hear
the voice that H. G. Wells has described as Hueffer's "languid,
plangent tenor."

In his reminiscences, Hueffer, who later changed his name to
Ford Madox Ford to escape the charge of being a German spy
during the First World War, and who shall hereafter be known as
Ford in these pages, makes several amusing references to Pound.
In discussing a creature whom he terms the "Typical Academic
Critic", Ford says, ". . . in the drawing rooms of lady leaders of,
let us say the Fabian Society, he (the Typical Academic Critic)

will be observed to be looking at Mr. Pound knocking over small teatables and whatnots."[23]

Ford intensely admired Pound, for he describes him in this book as "the kindest-hearted man who ever cut a throat,"[24] comparing him in this regard favorably with Bertran de Born. As for Pound's impact upon London society, and the *Punch* caricature of him, Ford says, "Youth ought to go in sombreroes, trousers of green billiard cloth, golden whiskers, with huge cravats, and to be found in cafes if not in hedge alehouses or the cabarets of Montmartre. . . . Indeed, you might put it that a public which, unconsciously, remembers Villon, will believe in no other youth, and so the drawing-rooms are dead."[25]

Ford recalls his first meeting with Pound:

"When I first knew him, his Philadelphia accent was still comprehensible if disconcerting; his beard and flowing locks were auburn and luxuriant; he was astonishingly meagre and agile. He threw himself alarmingly into frail chairs, devoured enormous quantities of your pastry, fixed his pince nez firmly on his nose, drew a manuscript from his pocket, threw his head back, closed his eyes to the point of invisibility, and looking down his nose, would chuckle like Mephistopheles and read you a translation from Arnaut Daniel. The only part of that verse you would understand would be the refrain.

'Ah me, the darn, the darn, it comes toe sune!'

"We published his Ballad of the Goodly Fere," continues Ford, "which must have been his first appearance in a periodical except for contributions to the Butte Montana Herald. Ezra, though born in Butte in a caravan during the great blizzard of—but perhaps I ought not to reveal the year. At any rate, Ezra left Butte at the age of say two. The only one of his poems written and published there that I can remember had for refrain,

'Cheer up, Dad . . .'

"Born in the blizzard," says this fanciful historian, "his first meal consisted of kerosene. That was why he ate such enormous quantities of my tarts, the flavour of kerosene being very enduring. It accounted also for the glory of his hair."[26]

Ford's joshing contained some truth, for Pound, although not born in the great blizzard of '88, nearly lost his life because of it. He explained this to Kate Buss in a letter dated March 9, 1916: "We came East behind the first rotary snow plough, the inventor of which vortex saved me from death by croup by feeding me with lumps of sugar saturated with kerosene."[27]

In describing this efficient frontier remedy for the croup, Ezra calls attention to the grain of truth that runs throughout Ford's ornate prose. For instance, Ford says that Ezra's grandfather, Thaddeus Coleman Pound, was a "periodic millionaire", who usually went broke just as he was planning to make some munificent gift to his grandson. While he was in Washington as a Congressman from Wisconsin, from 1871 through 1882, his holdings were wiped out.

He must have been as out of step as his grandson, for the custom in those days was that an impecunious man could go into Congress for a few years and retire as a wealthy man, enriched through the granting of special dispensations to insurance companies and railroads (*viz.* the Ames case). Pound reversed this rags to riches theme. He came to Congress a rich man and went home broke. One can only conclude that he must have been honest. The senior Pound called down the fates upon his head when he became an advocate of monetary reform, just as his grandson was to do some decades afterwards.

Those critics who bemoan Ezra's "desertion of poetry for economics" know nothing of the family background that prompted these interests. Ezra took up where his grandfather had left off. His battle against bankers and monopolies, his passion for various forms and problems of monetary issue, and his native self-reliance in these matters, were qualities that he had legitimately inherited from his forebears, and from such pillars of the Republic as crusty old John Adams as well. It is of interest that Ezra liked to be addressed by his disciples as "Grampaw".

At any rate, the bankrupt grandfather was unable to contribute to the European "Grand Tour" which was to have been his graduation present to the limb of Satan. The result was Pound's cattle-boat excursion to Europe.

"Many poets have done that," writes Ford of this experience (although he does not cite any other instances of would-be poets arriving in Europe by cattle boat). "But I doubt that any other ever made a living by showing American tourists about Spain without previous knowledge of the country or language. It was, too, just after the Spanish-American war, when the cattle-boat dropped him in that country."[28]

"The living" to which Ford refers was occasioned by Pound's meeting an American family in Spain who were the proverbial Innocents Abroad. He agreed to show them around, without mentioning that this was also his first view of the sights, and received in return a modest honorarium. There is an advantage to having a guide who is also seeing the wonders for the first time, as enthusiasm may be communicated. The guidebooks carried him triumphantly through his first European venture.

Critics have always complained of Pound, whether he leads us into the Middle Ages, Greece, or China, that he does not know the country well enough to function as a guide. But guiding parties across wildernesses that one had not yet traversed was an old Western custom.

"It was with that aura of romance about him," says Ford, "that he appeared to me in my drawing-room. I guessed that he must be rather hard up, bought his poem at once, and paid him more than it was usual to pay for a ballad. It was not a large sum, but Ezra managed to live on it for a long time—six months, I think—in unknown London. Perhaps my pastry helped."[29]

Ford was continually amused by Pound's impact upon the society of lady novelists and plump gentlemen of letters who maintained a virtually impassable barrier against new talent. In *Thus to Revisit,* a book that he wrote to boost the young Imagist poets of London, Ford remarks, "I wish I had Mr. Pound's knack of cutting the heart out of a subject."[30]

"Mr. Pound's harsh aphorisms," he continues, "are like sharp splinters of granite struck off by a careless but violent chisel. But whatever Mr. Pound is or is not, of this the Reader may be certain: wherever two or three men of Letters—of Printed Matter—are found united in irritations, some splinters from one or other of Mr. Pound's chippings will be found at the bottom of their poor, dear abscesses."[31]

Ford was one of Pound's earliest and most steadfast supporters, but he was never able to remain in a position of strength, that is, in a place where he could assist deserving talents and expose the unworthy. Although his background fitted him for the editorship of any literary journal in England, he was much too well-qualified. After all, this is the century of the Third-Raters, and a First-Rater can only accept the penalties against him that are inescapable, because he is not of his time. The only editorships ever held by Ford were those on two journals that he himself had founded, *The English Review,* and the *transatlantic review.*

Although Pound's literary excursions provoked nervous admonitions from Oxford dons who had staked their claims many years earlier. Ford greeted his translations with enthusiasm. He welcomed Pound's *Cathay* as "one of the most beautiful volumes of poems in the world."[32] It was this book of translations from the Chinese that led T. S. Eliot to term Pound the inventor of Chinese poetry for our time.

His months of association with Pound on Holland Park Avenue are delightfully chronicled by Ford in his *New York Essays.* He refers to a time when he courted "a Beautiful Lady, so beautiful that Mr. Bernard Shaw broke up the City Socialist Club by drinking champagne out of her shoe."[33] It is typical of Ford's sly wit that he should depict the Socialists as sitting around and drinking champagne.

The Beautiful Lady was wont to carry a red string bag, through which the tips of onions protruded. She was joined on her morning walks by Ford and Pound. "Ezra had a forked red beard," says Ford, "luxuriant chestnut hair, an aggressive lank figure; one long blue single stone earring dangled on his jawbone. He wore a purple hat, a green shirt, a black velvet coat, vermilion socks, openwork, brilliantly tanned sandals, and trousers of green billiard cloth in addition to an immense flowing tie that had been hand-painted by a Japanese Futurist poet."

In his casual way, Ford gives an encompassing picture of the Beaux Arts society of pre-war London, where Japanese poets painted ties and ballet dancers created sculpture.

"So, with the Beautiful Lady on my left," continues Ford, "and Ezra on my right, Ezra scolding at the world and making at it fencers' passes with his cane, we would proceed up Holland Park

Avenue. The Beautiful Lady in the most sonorous of voices would utter platitudes from Fabian Tracts on my left, Ezra would mutter vorticist half-truths half-inaudibly in a singularly incomprehensible Philadelphia dialect into my right ear. And I had to carry the string bag."[34]

No doubt Ford lived in fear that one of his friends from the Peerage would see him carrying a bag of onions. Men have been ostracized from London society for less serious offenses. He later claimed to have been revenged for this indignity, for which he blamed Pound. He knew that an American, and one from the West to boot, could not possibly be disgraced by carrying a bag of onions. The occasion of his revenge, also described in *New York Essays,* was an award that Pound won in France:

"Mr. Pound is an admirable, if eccentric, performer of the game of tennis. To play against him is like playing against an inebriated kangaroo that has been rendered unduly vigorous by injection of some gland or other. Once he won the tennis championship of the south of France, and the world was presented with the spectacle of Mr. Pound in a one-horse cab beside the Maire of Perpignan or some such place. An immense silver shield was in front of their knees, the cab was preceded by the braying fanfare of the city, and followed by defeated tennis players, bull-fighters, banners and all the concomitants of triumph in the South. It was when upon the station platform, amid the plaudits of the multitudes, the Maire many times embraced Mr. Pound that I was avenged for the string bag and even the blue earring!"[35]

The amiable Ford was beset most of his life by serious marital and financial problems. At the age of twenty-four, as befitted a successful young writer who could be counted upon to become a pillar of the establishment, he had taken in marriage one Elsie Martindale, whose father was President of the Pharmaceutical Society of Great Britain. The issue consisted of two daughters, but the wife showed less concern for Ford's literary efforts when they became non-profitable, and *The English Review* proved to be the breaking-point. Ford left her in 1909, and went to the offices of the *Review* to live with Violet Hunt.[36] His wife, being Catholic, refused to grant him a divorce.

Ford had persuaded Violet Hunt to live with him by painting, as only he could do, a grim picture of his increasing depression and his determination to end his life. He had thought it through very carefully, he told her, and had decided to dose himself with poison. As this began to take effect, he would throw himself under one of the omnibuses that rolled past on Notting Hill. No one, he assured her, would think to perform an autopsy on a man who had been run over by a bus. The insurance company would provide for his family, as he intended to insure himself for a large sum just before undertaking this "accident", and his own problems would be over.

The Ford-Hunt affair seems to have been more literary than passionate—the protagonists had both been listed in the British *Who's Who* for their efforts—and Violet Hunt was not seriously inclined to assume charge of the depressed writer until she discovered, in a pocket of Ford's dressing gown, which he had left temptingly near, a large bottle that was dramatically labelled "POISON". She moved into the offices of the *Review*.

A marriage is said to have taken place at some point between the married Ford and the unmarried Violet Hunt, perhaps in Germany, where the couple resided for several years after the collapse of the *Review*. Ford claimed, in his customary vague manner, that he had gotten a divorce from his first wife in Germany, but apparently she had never been informed of it. At any rate, when the consort wrote a letter to the London press about some literary matter, she signed it impressively as "Violet Hunt Hueffer," indicating that she was now the legitimate spouse. The first, or original, Mrs. Hueffer was outraged by this act, which she considered to be unpardonable insolence, and she sued Violet Hunt for libel. At the same time, she had Ford jailed for nonpayment of alimony.[37]

Thus he joined the great company of twentieth century writers and artists who have served their time. The lack of a prison record today is a serious indictment of one's talent, and it excites suspicion among one's fellow artists as well. Having spent much of the last two decades in visiting various imprisoned intellectuals, I have become familiar with the sort of government housing that is provided for the creative personalities of the time. Ezra's first advice to me was "Keep out of jail. It is too great a restriction on your activities."

After leaving the Holland Park office to Mr. Chandler, the Ford-Hunt ménage was established at South Lodge. The open house for their friends continued, despite their lack of funds. There was a summer place, which Ford describes as "hidden away in a green corner of England." Roast suckling pig was one of the delicacies served here, and Pound was a regular visitor. He wrote to his mother, December 24, 1913,

"Am down here for a week with Hueffers in a dingy old cottage that belonged to Milton . . . Impossible to get any writing done here. Atmosphere too literary. Three 'Kreators' all in one ancient cottage is a bit thick."[38]

In his inimitable way, Ford tells us that "Mr. Pound appeared, aloft on the seat of my immensely high dogcart, like a bewildered Stuart pretender visiting a repellent portion of his realm. For Mr. Pound hated the country, though I will put it on record that he can carve a suckling pig as few others can."[39]

This rural ménage has been described by Pound in his farewell poem to London, "Hugh Selwyn Mauberley":

> Beneath the sagging roof
> The stylist has taken shelter,
> Unpaid, uncelebrated,
> At last from the world's welter.
>
> Nature receives him;
> With a placid and uneducated mistress
> He exercises his talents
> And the soil meets his distress.
>
> The haven from sophistications and contentions
> Leaks through its thatch;
> He offers succulent cooking;
> The door has a creaking latch.[40]

In 1910, J. M. Dent of London published Pound's first work of criticism, *The Spirit of Romance*. This book was the outcome of the University of Pennsylvania fellowship, which had not been renewed. The study had grown considerably from the initial examination of Lope de Vega, who was included almost as an afterthought. It was principally concerned with Pound's greater enthusiasm, Arnaut Daniel, the poet of Provence, whom Dante termed *"il miglior fabbro."*

The book attracted little attention and was the only work of Pound's to be published by Dent. Several decades were to elapse before Pound's passion for the Provençal was to find an audience.

In the "Prefatio" to *The Spirit of Romance,* Pound included a statement that was not calculated to improve his popularity with the poetasters of London, and that probably had been inspired by his observations of them: "the history of an art is the history of masterwork, not of failures, or of mediocrity."

In 1911, Elkin Mathews published Pound's *Canzoni,* which met with a more favorable reception. The book was dedicated to his future mother-in-law, at whose home he was a frequent dinner guest. Mathews also had success with *Provença* (1909), which also was reviewed favorably. *The Tablet* critic declared, "Mr. Pound is sometimes Celtic; he has the love of out-of-the-way legends, and his high authority in Provence literature and lore is made evident on nearly every page."

The Spectator said, "Mr. Pound is that rare thing among modern poets—a scholar. He is not only cultivated but learned."

The Nation chimed in with this chorus of praise by stating, "If Mr. Pound will go on with the development in method shown in this latest volume, he will add to English poetry something which is unusual riches."

This was heady praise for a poet still in his twenties, coming as it did from journals that were not given to snap judgments or radical tastes. And these criticisms were made in a city that was accustomed to handing on, twenty years after, its shopworn tastes to its culturally shabby cousin across the seas. It took two world wars to reduce English literary standards to those of America.

Eliot wrote in 1917 of Pound's early volumes, "Few poets have ever undertaken the siege of London with less backing; few books of verse have ever owed their success so purely to their own merits. Pound came to London a complete stranger, without either literary patronage or financial means."[41]

More important, Pound had established an important beachhead on the Continent for those American writers and artists who came over in a constant stream after his initial success in 1908. Although he had been preceded by other American expatriates, such as Henry James, these early arrivals were men of independent means, who had no interest in helping young writers.

The dominance of Pound in such movements as Imagism and Vorticism stemmed from his position in London. The headquarters of the American expeditionary forces were confined to his tiny rooms in Holland Park Chambers, almost a decade before the soldiers arrived. Newly-beached immigrants, refugees, or expellees, as they might have called themselves, went to Pound to get their introductions in London and to prepare for their own assault on the city.

With his next book of poems, Pound came to the inevitable parting of the ways with Mathews. The timid publisher refused to print two poems of the manuscript of *Lustra,* as being entirely too daring. Pound allowed him to bring out the mutilated volume, and he simultaneously brought out the complete *Lustra* elsewhere at his own expense. The appearance of these two "Lustras" did not cause any great confusion in the world of poetry, for they both appeared in small editions.

Although Mathews realized that Pound was now too independent for him, he continued to boost his poetry. When Harriet Monroe, a poetry-lover from Chicago, arrived in London on her round-the-world trip in 1912, Mathews told her about his star poet, and she purchased his books. She read them during a long train ride across Siberia and became a Pound enthusiast.

She was not to meet Pound until 1923, but when she returned to Chicago, she began to publish a new magazine, *Poetry.* She asked Pound to become the London correspondent, and he agreed. Unfortunately, Miss Monroe was committed to print a certain amount of work from financial supporters of the magazine, and she and Pound could never agree as to the quality of this work. She did introduce his poems in Chicago, and a group of Pound enthusiasts circulated his books.

Parodies of his style appeared in the "Line O'Type" column of the Chicago *Tribune,* a sure sign of immortality. Floyd Dell, editor of the Chicago *Evening Post Literary Review,* became a Pound convert. In an editorial dated April 4, 1913, he wrote, "Ezra Pound, we salute you! You are the most enchanting poet alive . . . There is no mistake about you, Ezra Pound. You are a creator of beauty in a world where only by a divinely creative process beauty exists."

It is fitting that this first biography of Pound should have been written in Chicago, even though he had a greater audience there in 1913 than he has today, for Chicago can take credit for having discovered Pound long before he was admired in New York. And if Pound refers to this city as "Hogville" in recent correspondence, it is with affection rather than disdain.

III

LTHOUGH POUND, who had arrived unknown in London, had within a few years achieved fame on two continents, he was profoundly discontented. The cause of his unrest was the breakdown in communications. The failure of *The English Review* was a great setback. For the next decade, he busied himself with a number of inadequate successors, in order to have an outlet for his work. He finally realized that it is easier to write an epic poem than to manage an intelligent periodical in the twentieth century, and he retired to Italy to work on his *Cantos*.

The magazines that he edited or contributed to during the remainder of his London period were supplemented by his activities in the literary clubs. The artistic life of prewar London was centered in these groups, which were informal in character, and usually built around a central personality. There were few salons worthy of note, but some of the writers and artists entertained at home once a week, an event known as an "evening".

T. E. Hulme's evenings in his rooms at 67 Frith Street attracted many of the wits of London, and indirectly, the Imagist and Vorticist movements, with which Pound was involved, were born of these associations. His interest in the writings of the East also stemmed from the *paideuma* that he accrued through attendance at these affairs. In the dedication to Amiya Chakravarty of his translation entitled *The Unwobbling Pivot and the Great Digest of Confucius* (1952), he writes, as follows:

"Dear Chak

"When you gave me the hope that these two books of Confucius might be issued in India, I sat down and translated the Analects. Is there anything more I can say that belongs with an edition of them?

"The memory of Rabindranath singing his poems in London nearly four decades ago belongs to our two biographies not as prefatory matter to a living classic, though it was at Sarojini Naidu's that I met Fenollosa's widow through whom came my first contact with the great poetry of Japan and China, and among Fenollosa's papers she gave me the first text of the 'Pivot' I had seen.

" 'All flows, and the pattern is intricate.' Gitanjali, or the first poems from it, went from London to America at that time, and if you succeed in printing the 'Pivot' in Bengal, it will have come via Italy.

Ezra Pound
Washington, D.C."

Pound mentions in a memorial to Harold Monro, which he included in his *Polite Essays,* that Monro had missed the fun of Hulme's dinner at the Tour Eiffel in 1909, and he does not remember him at Mrs. Kibblewhite's evenings at the old Venetian Embassy.[1] In effect, he is calling attention to the fact that Monro was not a member of the London Bohemia at that time. Later, through his Poetry Bookshop and his publications, Monro did assume a prominent role in the literary world of London. By that time, Pound had gone on to Paris.

The Irish poet, William Butler Yeats, was a familiar guest at many of these club meetings. He was an active member of the Ghosts' Club, which met monthly at Pagani's Restaurant on Great Portland Street. He attended the Thursday luncheons of his friend Edward Garnett, which were given at the Mont Blanc Restaurant on Gerrard Street. And he had founded one of the most exclusive writers' clubs in London, the Rhymers' Club, in the 1890s.

Private and little-publicized, its members met almost nightly in an upper room of the Cheshire Cheese, an ancient eating-place in the Strand. In this bare room with sanded floors, Yeats and his friends were wont to drink black coffee and smoke hashish until dawn. The group included Ernest Rhys, Lionel Johnson, Thomas Hardy, Ernest Dowson, Arthur Symons, Francis Thompson, and the Poet Laureate, Robert Bridges.

Yeats was the grandson and namesake of the Reverend William Butler Yeats, the late Rector of Tullylish, County Down. He was the eldest of four children of the painter, John Butler Yeats. The family was consecrated to the arts. Yeats was a poet, his brother Jack was a painter, his sister Lily taught the country girls fine handicrafts, such as embroidery, in the ancient Gaelic tradition, and his youngest sister, Elizabeth, affectionately known as "Lolly", enlisted the local maidens in the craft of book publishing.

They made their own paper from rags and pulp, set type, printed and bound beautiful little books, which were issued under the imprint of the Cuala Press. The editions, which were sold in series by private subscription, appeared in lots of from one hundred to five hundred copies. The Cuala Press brought out some of Yeats' best work, such as his enchanting essay, *A Packet for Ezra Pound* (1929). "Lolly" also published Pound's edition of the *Selected Letters of John Butler Yeats* (1917).

Yeats had recently come through a harrowing experience with the self-professed master of black magic, Alistair Crowley. The two men, both interested in psychic phenomena, had founded a Society for Psychical Research. They set up a "temple" in order to perform their works, but Yeats soon discovered that he, a practitioner of beneficial "white magic", had been lured into an association with a practitioner of evil, or "black magic".

To counteract Crowley's baneful activities, Yeats moved into "the Temple". A titanic struggle for the soul of one of the members ended in a draw between the master of white magic and the lord of black magic. Tiring of the contest, Crowley decided to move to the Continent. He insisted on selling all of the furnishings of "the Temple" before he left, with the proceeds to be divided between the two founders. Yeats refused to let him enter "the Temple", and Crowley, finding his black magic insufficient for the purpose, resorted to the courts. The lawsuit was grist for Crowley's mill, but Yeats found the court battle very upsetting.

Crowley left the field, and soon turned up in New York. As a joke, Austin Harrison, Ford's successor to the editorship of *The English Review,* had given Crowley a letter of recommendation, which stated that he was the most important lyric poet in England. On the strength of this letter, George Sylvester Viereck hired Crowley to write anti-British propaganda for Viereck's paper, *The Fatherland,* in 1915.

At this time, American sentiment was overwhelmingly pro-German. Crowley's bitter propaganda against his homeland was so absurd that it became embarrassing to be pro-German, and sentiment began to swing to the British. Crowley later claimed that he had done this deliberately, and wanted credit for having sent the United States into the British camp during the First World War. Others have also claimed credit for this feat, but a realistic study of the situation reveals that, like most important decisions in American foreign policy, it was largely accidental.

In 1894, Lionel Johnson introduced Yeats to his cousin, the novelist Olivia Shakespear. Yeats fell in love with her, an emotion that soon ripened into a lifelong friendship. About one-third of Yeats' published letters are addressed to Olivia Shakespear, but these do not include the ones written to her in his later years. The collected edition of Yeats' letters also is marred by another serious omission, the absence of his correspondence with Pound, which had been stored in Rapallo at the time the volume was compiled.

Dorothy, Mrs. Shakespear's daughter, who was four years old at the advent of Yeats, supposed that he was a clergyman, because of the black suit that he customarily wore "for beauty and for elegance."

Robert Graves' comments, in *The Crowning Privilege,* that his father was once informed by John Butler Yeats that "Willie has found a very profitable little by-path in poetry."[2] Although Yeats enjoyed a modest income from his work, it was hardly the most profitable bypath which an intelligent man could pursue in London. The elder Yeats himself was rather impractical, and he lived out his last years on a tiny income in New York City, boarding at the Petitpas.

For some years, Yeats had been madly in love with the actress Maud Gonne, heroine of the Irish Revolution. Together they had been entranced by the flame of rebellion that flickered in the un-dimmed and eagle eyes of the aged John O'Leary. They sat for hours at a time listening to the revolutionist as he told stories of his career. He had spent many years in prison, and twice he had heard a death sentence pronounced upon him.

Although Maud Gonne was willing to smoke hashish with Yeats, she was not willing to marry him. Each time that he was rebuffed, he went back to his verses with renewed determination. Perhaps poets should not consummate their love affairs.

When Ezra Pound came onto the scene, Yeats was nearly fifty years old. His *Collected Works* (1908), in eight volumes, had already been published by the Shakespeare Head Press, at Stratford-on-Avon. Not only was his reputation secure, but it seemed that his important work was now behind him.

Yeats had a brief influence upon the poetry of Ezra Pound, as indicated by Louis MacNeice, in *The Poetry of W. B. Yeats*. MacNeice cites the following lines from *Personae* as an example of Pound under the influence of Yeats:

> There are many rooms and all of gold,
> Of woven walls deep patterned, of email,
> Of beaten work; and through the claret stone,
> Set to some weaving, comes the aureate light.[3]

Pound soon abandoned this subdued glow in favor of hotter blazes, notably the sun of Provence. He was to have a much more profound and lasting influence upon Yeats than Yeats had had upon him.

The first mention of Pound in Yeats' writings appears in a letter to Lady Gregory of December 10, 1909:

". . . this queer creature Ezra Pound, who has become really a great authority on the troubadours, has I think got closer to the right sort of music for poetry than Mrs. Emery [the actress Florence Farr]—it is more definitely music with strongly marked time and yet it is effective speech. However, he cannot sing, as he has no voice. It is like something on a very bad phonograph."[4]

William Carlos Williams, in several of his letters, has recorded the impact of Pound upon Yeats. In the first of these, written to Babette Deutsch, and dated January 18, 1943, he says that Pound gave Yeats "a hell of a bawling out" for some of his archaisms, and that Yeats turned over his manuscripts to Pound for correction.[5]

The second letter was written to Richard Eberhart, October 23, 1953. When they first met in London, Yeats asked for Ezra's opinion of his poetry. "Ezra was forced to say that he admired them greatly, as was the truth, but that they were marred by a deforming inversion of the phrase which was deplorable. Yeats at once set about correcting the defect and worked diligently at it for several years."[6]

There may be some over-emphasis in Williams' phrase "bawling out", but there is little doubt that with one swoop, the hawk, Pound, brought Yeats down into the modern world.

John Butler Yeats wrote to his son on February 11, 1911,

"Quinn met him [Pound] and liked him very much. The Americans, young literary men whom I know, find him surly, supercilious and grumpy. I liked him myself very much, that is, I liked his look and air, and the few things he said, for tho' I was a good while in his company, he said very little."[7]

Yeats' desire to bring poetry back to the common people prompted him to take rooms at 18 Woburn Buildings, in a rather dangerous neighborhood in London. He no longer frequented the Rhymers' Club at the Cheshire Cheese, but met his friends at his "evenings". Not only did the "common people" show no interest in poetry, but Yeats' visitors objected to traveling through the slum area. As the months went by without incident, they mastered their fears, and Yeats enjoyed a goodly company.

John Masefield, who was a regular at Yeats' "Mondays", has described the quarters as they were in 1910, when Pound was in attendance. The rooms were decorated in a somber range of blues and browns. The walls were hung with engravings by William Blake, with two large portraits of Yeats by his father, and a painting of Sligo Harbor by his brother Jack, which bore the title "Memory". Against one wall stood a blue wooden lectern, which supported, between two giant candles, the Kelmscott Press Chaucer. A dark high wooden settle jutted out some five feet into the room, with shelves of books behind it. At the opposite wall was a red earthenware tobacco jar, with an embossed design of writhing black dragons, which contained Virginia cigarettes. He also provided a jug of claret and siphons of soda water for his visitors.[8]

It was the custom of Yeats to let in the first comer, although his landlady, Mrs. Old, sometimes performed this function. After that, the last arrival was expected to answer the bell. In this sedate atmosphere, Pound reigned for some months. Douglas Goldring somewhat irreverently describes the scene in *South Lodge:*

"I shall never forget my surprise, when Ezra took me for the first time to one of Yeats' 'Mondays,' at the way in which he dominated the room, distributed Yeats' cigarettes and Chianti, and laid down the law about poetry. Poor golden-haired Sturge Moore, who sat in a corner with a large musical instrument by his side (on which he was never given a chance of performing) endeavoured to join the discussion on prosody, a subject on which he believed himself not entirely ignorant, but Ezra promptly reduced him to a glum silence. My own emotions on this particular evening, since I did not possess Ezra's transatlantic *brio,* were an equal blend of reverence and a desire to giggle. I was sitting next to Yeats on a settle when a young Indian woman in a sari came and squatted at his feet, and asked him to sing 'Innisfree,' saying she was certain that he had composed it to an Irish air. Yeats was anxious to comply with the request, unfortunately, like so many poets, was completely unmusical, indeed almost tone-deaf. He compromised by a sort of dirge-like incantation calculated to send any unhappy giggler into hysterics. I bore it as long as I could, but at last the back of the settle began to shake, and I received the impact of one of the poet's nasty glances from behind his pince-nez. Miraculously, I recovered, but it was an awful experience."[9]

At this time, Yeats was undergoing an intensive graduate course with Ezra, which was modified by the presence of a poet of the old school, T. Sturge Moore. Although Yeats appreciated the benefits of the association, the strain sometimes was too much for him, as evidenced by a letter to Lady Gregory dated January 3, 1913:

"My digestion has got rather queer again—a result I think of sitting up late with Ezra and Sturge Moore and some light wine while the talk ran. However, the criticism I got from them has given me new life and I have made that Tara poem a new thing and am writing with new confidence having got Milton off my back. Ezra

is the best critic of the two. He is full of the middle ages and helps
me to get back to the definite and concrete away from modern abstractions. To talk over a poem with him is like getting you to put
a sentence into dialect. All becomes clear and natural. Yet in his
own work he is very uncertain, often very bad though very interesting sometimes. He spoils himself by too many experiments and has
more sound principles than taste."[10]

Norman Jeffares, in his biography of Yeats, describes the initial
impact of Pound upon Yeats' work, during 1913, the first of the
three winters that Pound spent as Yeats' secretary:

"A bitter note underlies the strangeness of some poems which
Yeats wrote at the time, notably 'The Three Beggars,' 'The Three
Hermits,' 'Running to Paradise,' and 'The Hour Before Dawn'—
These are written in a style which seems Yeats' imitation of Synge,
and perhaps too by the influence of Pound's vitality and mockery.
They are at once remote and humourous poems, a strange combination. 'The Three Hermits' was written at Stone Cottage, March 15,
1913, where he had settled for the autumn with Ezra Pound, who
had become an intimate friend, and spent the two following winters
with him there. Pound read aloud to him when his eyes were bad,
and taught him to fence. 'I sometimes fence for a half hour before
the day's end, and when I close my eyes upon the pillow I see a
foil before me, the button to my face,' Yeats wrote of this rather
trying period, in his 'Essays.'

"His health was bad," continues Jeffares, "and affected his
spirits; in fact he became aware that he was fifty . . . Pound's
effect upon his poetry was to make it harsher and more outspoken,
says Mrs. William Butler Yeats. For instance, 'The Scholars' was
originally written, under Pound's influence, in 1915 in a harsher
vein than the final version, toned down when Pound was not there
to protest."[11]

Jeffares also mentions another important element in the association of Yeats and Pound, "the 'Noh' drama of Japan, to which
Ezra Pound had introduced him. He found these plays an incentive
to return to an early ideal of recreating the Irish scenery he loved
by means of an art form."[12]

Richard Ellmann, in *Yeats: The Man and the Mask,* also has paid
lengthy tribute to Pound's influence:

"In putting his principles into practice, to use 'a speech so natural and dramatic that the hearer would feel the presence of a man thinking and feeling:' Yeats had signal assistance from Ezra Pound. Pound had breezed into London in 1908, confident and full of information about obscure literature, persuaded that Yeats was the best poet writing in English, but that his manner was out of date. The poet must be a modern man, he must be clear and precise, he must eliminate all abstractions and all words which sense did not justify as well as sound. Everything must be hard and concrete, a statement of Ezra Pound, not a musical composition by Debussy.

"Pound himself was a very mixed personality," says Ellmann. "His instincts, as he once remarked, were to write in the manner of the 1890's, but he curbed and scorned them. He was now very much the man of the new movement, the organizer, busy from the time of his arrival in separating both living and dead poets into the readable and the unreadable. His strong prejudices were directed partly against all that seemed to him stodgy, such as the poetry of Wordsworth, and on one occasion he is said to have challenged a reviewer on the *Times* to a duel for having too high an opinion of Milton. Pound and Yeats got along well from the first, with the younger man assuming towards the older a mixed attitude of admiration and patronage. 'Uncle William,' as he called him, was making good progress but still dragging some of the reeds of the 90's in his hair. Pound set himself the task of converting Yeats to the modern movement, and had many opportunities from 1912 to 1916 to apply pressure. In 1912 he impudently altered without permission some poems which Yeats had given him to send to *Poetry* Magazine; Yeats was infuriated but then forgave him. During the winters of 1913–14, 1914–15, and 1915–16, Pound acted as Yeats' secretary in a small cottage in Ashdam Forest in Sussex, reading to him, writing from his dictation, and discussing everything. It was Pound who, knowing that Yeats had spent six or seven years trying to write the Player Queen as a tragedy, suggested that it be made into a comedy, with such effect that Yeats completely transformed the play at once. At Ashdam Forest, Pound would have liked to read contemporary literature to Yeats, but Yeats insisted on *Sordello* and Morris' *Sagas*. Pound would frequently urge Yeats to make changes in words or lines so as to get further away from the 90's. The older poet asked him to go through his verse and point out to him which words were abstractions, and was surprised at the large number that were so marked. He made a renewed effort to purge his verse of its weaknesses in *At the Hawks Nest,* his first play in six years, which he dictated to Pound early in 1916. The improvement is noticeable at once, the new verse is more spare, the images are exactly delineated, every shadow is removed. The tone, too, is definitely that of Yeats and no one else,

> I call to the mind
> A well long choked up and dry
> And boughs stripped by the wind,
> And I call to the mind's eye
> Pallor of an ivory face
> Its lofty dissolute air,
> A man climbing up to a place
> The salt sea wind has left bare.[13]

"The first play," Ellmann continues, "shows the effect of the young American's stimulating influence in its dramatic form as well as its style. During the first year that Pound acted as his secretary, Yeats was working on an essay to prove the connection between the beliefs of peasants, spiritualists, Swedenborg, and Henry Moore; his thoughts were full of ghosts, witches and supernatural phenomena. Pound, on the other hand, had a project of his own. He was the literary executor of Ernest Fenollosa, a scholar who had spent many years in Japan studying the Noh drama. It was very exciting to Yeats, always on the lookout for new ways of using occult research, to hear that the Japanese plays were full of spirits and masks, and that the crises in the plays usually occurred when a character who had appeared to be an ordinary mortal was suddenly revealed to be a good spirit. He was delighted to learn from Pound that the Noh 'was one of the great arts of the world, and quite possibly one of the most recondite. The art of the illusion is at the root of the Noh. These plays, or eclogues, were made only for the few; for the nobles; for those trained to catch the illusion. In the Noh we find an art based upon the god-dance, or upon some local apparition, or, later, on gestes of war and feats of history; an art of splendid posture, of dancing and chanting, and of acting that is not mimetic. It is a symbolic stage, a drama of masks—at least they have made masks for spirits and gods and young women. It is a theatre of which both Mr. Yeats and Mr. Craig may approve.'

"A little school of devotees of the Noh plays grew up in London," says Ellman, "including Pound, Yeats, Arthur Waley, and Edmund Dulac. Pound began to publish his translations of the plays in magazines and then in a small volume, with a preface by Yeats, at the Cuala Press. The difficulty was that none of the devotees had ever seen a Noh play, but late in 1915 Pound discovered, living in poverty in a backstairs room, the Japanese dancer Ito, who had acted in the Noh in Japan."[14]

It seems uncanny that Pound should have been able to locate an actor of the Noh in post-Victorian London. Joseph Hone, in his biography of Yeats, says "one of his [Yeats'] collaborators was a Mr. Ito [a traditional dancer of Japan] who attracted considerable note at the London Zoo by prancing about outside the cages of the birds of prey, and behaving in such a weird way that people supposed he must be either mad or a follower of some unknown Eastern religion who worshipped birds. Presently Mr. Ito was set to evolve a dance based on the movements of the birds as they hopped about and stretched their wings, and Yeats was often beside him at the Zoo, all attention."[15]

Pound was aware of the effect he was having upon Yeats for he mentions it in a letter to his mother, written in November, 1913:

"My stay in Stone Cottage will not be in the least profitable. I detest the country. Yeats will amuse me part of the time and bore me to death with psychical research the rest. I regard the visit as a duty to posterity."[16]

As foreign editor of *Poetry,* Pound had secured for Harriet Monroe some of the finest talents. One of these poets was Yeats. Perhaps Pound was taking his duties as an editor too seriously when he revised the final line of a poem, "Fallen Majesty", which Yeats suggested that he send to Miss Monroe. The line, which originally read, "Once walked a thing, that seemed as it were, a burning cloud," was altered by Pound, without consulting the author, to "Once walked a thing that seemed a burning cloud".

Ellmann cites this incident, in *The Identity of Yeats,* as proof of his contention that Pound's editing of Yeats' poems "rendered them more compact and effective."[17]

Although Yeats at first was angered by this presumption, he agreed that the excised phrase had weakened the line, and the act was forgiven. The outcome of this impertinence, recklessness, and discourtesy of Pound's was that Yeats received a two hundred and fifty dollar award by *Poetry*. He was enjoying comfortable circumstances at the time, and he decided that the award should be given to a younger and needier poet. He wrote to Miss Monroe in December, 1913:

"Why not give the 40 pounds to Ezra Pound? [Yeats had agreed to keep 10 pounds and return 40 pounds to Miss Monroe for an award to someone who needed it.] I suggest him to you because, although I do not really like with my whole soul the metrical experiments he has made for you, I think those experiments show a vigorous creative mind. He is certainly a creative personality of some sort, though it is too soon yet to say of what sort. His experiments are perhaps errors, I am not certain; but I would always sooner give the laurel to vigorous errors than to any orthodoxy not inspired."[18]

Miss Monroe was a very tractable person in dealing with her geniuses, and she agreed to award the forty pounds to Ezra, who had already served two years as her foreign editor without pay. He was quite pleased to get the award, and he wrote to William Carlos Williams that he had purchased a new typewriter.

Two marriages resulted from the Yeats-Pound association, each of the bachelors marrying young ladies introduced through the other. Pound had met at Yeats' "Mondays" Mrs. Olivia Shakespear and her daughter Dorothy, whom he married in 1914. The Pounds had a very good friend, Miss Georgie Hyde-Lees, whom Yeats married in 1917. Each was best man at the other's wedding.

One account of Pound's marriage is to be found in the Philadelphia *Evening Bulletin* of February 20, 1928, in an interview with Homer Pound:

" 'He always had a lot of nerve,' said Mr. Pound, the affectionate, reminiscent smile appearing once more, 'even the way he met his wife was nervy. He found funds were getting low, as usual, so he went to the Polytechnic Institute in London (he was only about 21 years old) and presented his name. 'Do you want to register as a student?' he was asked. 'No,' said Ezra, 'I want to register as a teacher. I want to give a course on the Romance Literature of Southern Europe.' 'But we don't want a course on the Romance Literature of Southern Europe,' he was told; 'besides, who are you?' 'Let me give the course,' said Ezra, 'and you'll see.' Well, they let him give it, heaven knows why. And among the students who registered for the course was a Miss Dorothy Shakespear and her mother. Ezra promptly fell in love with his pupil and she with him, and they were married and lived happily ever after."

The elder Pound's recollection of his son's age at the time of meeting Dorothy Shakespear is faulty—Pound was twenty-five. And the courtship lasted for several years before they were married. But the statement that they lived happily ever after is quite true.

John Butler Yeats wrote to his daughter Lily on March 24, 1914; "He (Willie) mentioned that he was to hurry home for Ezra Pound's marriage. He is to marry Mrs. Shakespear's daughter. She is beautiful and well off and has the most charming manners . . . Both are clever, and I fancy Ezra is a nice fellow. As Willie remarks, when rich and fashionable people bring up a daughter to be intellectual, naturally she will turn away from the 'curled darlings' of her own class and fall in love with intellect which is mostly to wed in poverty as well. I hope it will turn out that Ezra is not an *uncomfortable* man of genius."[19]

Dorothy Shakespear Pound could hardly have foreseen that she would have to sit outside the walls of a madhouse for thirteen years, waiting for a hostile government to release her husband. I never heard her complain about it, nor do I suppose that anyone else heard any recriminations from her.

The bridal couple went off to France; a walking tour through Provence served as their honeymoon trip. Dorothy Pound later recalled that they used Toulouse as their base for this excursion. They carried rucksacks and slept outdoors much of the time. These happy days were interrupted by the outbreak of the First World War, and they returned to London.

Yeats wrote to his father, December 26, 1914, "The week after next I go to the Stone Cottage and Ezra Pound will be my secretary. He brings his wife with him this time. She is very pretty and had a few years ago seven generals in her family all living at once and all with the same name—Johnson, relations of Lionel Johnson."[20]

Pound could never be a silent partner, and throughout their association, he was pressing Yeats to sponsor persons and causes of which the Irishman was wary. One such instance was Pound's successful maneuver to get Yeats to recommend James Joyce for a grant from the Royal Literary Fund. Another was an event which bewildered everybody except the instigator, Pound.

There was living on a secluded country estate in Sussex a gentleman who had long been known as the "gadfly of the British Empire", Wilfrid Scawen Blunt. Retired from revolutionary activities at that time, Blunt composed sedate Victorian lyrics, hardly the type of poetry that would excite Pound's enthusiasm. But because of his background (Blunt had been jailed for speaking on behalf of Irish Home Rule, had been banned from Egypt because of his role in promoting Egyptian nationalism, and had agitated on behalf of Hindu revolutionaries), Pound decided to give him an award for his poetry.

He rounded up a committee, consisting of himself, Yeats, T. Sturge Moore, John Masefield, Victor Plarr, F. S. Flint, and Richard Aldington. The committee commissioned Gaudier-Brzeska to carve an alabaster box, in which the poets would place presentation copies of their poems in homage to Blunt.

Blunt was then invited to a dinner party in his honor, to be given in London. He declined, perhaps suspecting a police trap, and suggested instead that the committee journey down to his charming Jacobean estate, Newbuildings Place, and take dinner with him there. The offer was accepted, and the poets came to Blunt. Pound has described the occasion in *The Pisan Cantos:*

> But to have done instead of not doing
>   this is not vanity
> To have, with decency, knocked
> That a Blunt should open
>   To have gathered from the air a live tradition
> or from a fine old eye the unconquered flame
>   This is not vanity.
>   Here error is all in the not done,
> all in the diffidence that faltered,[21] [.]

These lines conclude Pound's great soliloquy (Yeats has re-marked that all that is great in modern literature is soliloquy) in which he examines his past career to see if he has committed the sin of vanity.

Yeats provided a roast peacock as his contribution to the Blunt festivities. Although Masefield was unable to be present, the others enjoyed themselves, and ate heartily. Most of them had two help-ings of the peacock, which had been brought before them in full plumage, and when that was gone, Blunt had a roast beef for them.

The press had been notified by the specialist in public relations, Pound, that the award was to be presented to Blunt, and the occa-sion caused widespread public indignation. Blunt was then as con-troversial a figure as Pound is today, and the poets were denounced when they returned to London. The *Times* quoted one critic as say-ing, "A man at the Foreign Office says he will never speak to any of those men again."[22]

Pound's association with Yeats produced a phrase that critics have been using ever since, the "later Yeats". Hart Crane, in a letter to Allen Tate, May 16, 1922, says that he has read and admired Yeats, "the later poems," he adds.[23] Douglas Goldring, who knew both Pound and Yeats well, has written, "The 'later Yeats', who is now so universally admired, was unmistakably in-fluenced by Pound."[24]

It was the "later Yeats" who received the Nobel Prize in 1923. There have been many critical judgments on the effect of Pound's onslaught against the complacency of the "Collected Yeats" of 1908. T. R. Henn says, "Pound's mind and talk offered many things; pity for the underdog; a studied violence of language; an attempt to combine classical pattern and form in the intensity of the last Romantics."[25]

Although Pound has never referred to any assistance that he may have been able to render Yeats, the contribution has not gone unnoticed. The distinguished poet Valentine Ironmonger has sug-gested, in a letter to *The Irish Times,* November 3, 1952, that no better use of a Yeats Memorial Fund could be made than to turn it over to Ezra Pound, so that he could live out his last years in any place of his choosing, and in the comfort he has earned.

IN RETROSPECT, the furor over the literary movement known as Imagism seems excessive only if we forget that it represented a courageous revival of *vers libre*. Free verse opened the gates to all sorts of outpourings, but it was a healthy reaction against the Victorian metronome.

Imagism, as did its Poundian successor, Vorticism, had its origins in the personality of Thomas Edward Hulme, a youthful London intellectual who once had walked across Canada for the exercise. Hulme started a Poetry Club in 1908 with a government clerk, F. S. Flint. They advanced some of the principles which would later be known as Imagist, but the other members of the club proved to be too stodgy, and they withdrew. Hulme and Flint started another club the following year, which met weekly, and in 1910, Hulme inaugurated his brilliant "Tuesdays" at 67 Frith Street.

Most of the "bright young men" of London were to be found there until 1914, when Hulme went off to the war. He stood up when everyone else was ducking, and a direct hit by a high explosive shell blew him to bits. Wyndham Lewis relates that they were unable to find any remains. Richard Aldington used this event as the basis for his first successful book, the novel *Death of a Hero* (1929).

Pound printed some of Hulme's poems as an appendix to his volume, *Ripostes* (1912), under the heading "The Complete Poetical Works of T. E. Hulme". A bust of Hulme by Epstein also survives.

Poems which could be described as Imagist began to appear in 1911, and they enjoyed a vogue under Pound's inspiration until 1916, when Amy Lowell appeared on the scene. She turned the movement into a chintzy parlor piece for her New England mansion, and the images that had seemed so important to the young poets disappeared in the clouds of cigar smoke in which Miss Lowell veiled her bulk.

A young American of independent means, John Gould Fletcher, from Little Rock, Arkansas, had arrived in London a few months after Pound. H.D., Pound's college friend, came to London in 1911, and an English solicitor's son, Richard Aldington, also joined the group. They were the core of the Imagist movement.

Fletcher, a shy, neurotic youth who was determined to become a poet, had taken rooms near George Bernard Shaw in Adelphi Terrace, but he could never muster the courage to call upon him. He led a solitary life during his first year in London. He had met a few would-be writers at Harold Monro's Poetry Bookshop, but they could not afford to dine with him at the expensive French restaurant where he usually took his meals. He ate alone, reading at table.

In 1910, Fletcher brought out five small volumes of his poetry, engaging four separate London publishers for the work. He paid the entire costs of publication himself, and hopefully sent the books to critics. There was no enthusiastic reception, such as had greeted Pound, for the poems, although well-written, offered nothing new. Most of the recipients did review them, and the unsold copies were kept in storage until the outbreak of the First World War, when Fletcher contributed them to the British war effort as paper pulp.

In addition to his duties as foreign editor of *Poetry,* Pound had also created for himself the post of literary editor of a suffragette newspaper, *The New Freewoman,* which had formerly been known as *The Freewoman.* Pound's position on suffragism is not clear; he once remarked in a letter to me that each new dilution of the suffrage weakened the entire system on which voting was based. His alliance with the staff of *The New Freewoman* may have been occasioned by the fact that the journal was militantly opposed to the excessive virility of the Pankhurst wing.

These suffragettes chained themselves to fences, in a poor imitation of the Andromeda myth, and also re-enacted other folktales which this writer does not care to discuss. In order to re-emphasize the intellectual facets of the suffragette movement, such as they were, a wealthy lady named Miss Harriet Weaver had financed this newspaper. It was written and edited by her friend Dora Marsden. Miss Weaver felt that the paper was not attracting a sufficiently wide audience, and when Ezra Pound chanced upon her at one of Hulme's evenings, he persuaded her that she could get more readership by incorporating a literary review with the suffragette editorials. He agreed to furnish this department without salary, and thus he obtained an English outlet for the promotion of his various disciples and enthusiasms.

Pound praised one of Fletcher's volumes in *The New Freewoman,* and soon afterwards, he called upon the Arkansas bard at his French restaurant in London. Fletcher has recorded the occasion in his autobiography:

"I must confess that I eyed Pound with considerable interest, having already heard about him while in London, and having read with attraction and repulsion about equally balanced, his own early volumes. What I saw was a man of about my own age and height, dressed in a brown velvet coat, a shirt open at the neck and no necktie, and pearly-gray trousers. His fine-chiseled, forward-jutting features were set off by a rounded mass of fiery, curly red hair and beard and mustache similarly red and curly, trimmed to a point. Gray-blue penetrating eyes, shielded by a pince-nez, peered at the world behind his projecting cheekbones; and a high-pitched, shrill, almost feminine voice provided strange contrast to the pugnacious virility of the poet's general aspect. He had, I soon saw, slender feminine hands, which, as he talked, he fluttered to and fro. His body was almost equally mobile, jumping and twitching in his chair, with a backward jerk of the head, as he emphasized each point."[1]

Ezra was quite the innovator in dress, for it took considerable courage to wear an open-necked sport shirt in London at that time. He has told me of an occasion in Rapallo, on a scorching afternoon, when a little Frenchman approached him in the town square. The Frenchman was choking in a high starched collar, as he passed by the comfortable Ezra, who was sauntering along in his customary sport shirt, open wide at the neck. The Frenchman's eyes protruded, first in hate, and then in envy. He reached up and with a single violent gesture ripped open his tie and shirt. It may be said that Ezra found the world writhing in stiff collars and left it in sport shirts.

"I discovered him to be as baffling a bundle of contradictions as any man I have ever known," says Fletcher, continuing his description of Pound. "Internationally Bohemian in aspect, he yet preserved marked farwestern ways of speech and a frank, open democracy of manners. Hating the academicians of England, he yet laid claim to be a great scholar in early Provençal, Italian and Latin. Keen follower of the dernier cri in arts and letters, his own poetry was often deliberately archaic to a degree that repelled me. In short, he was a walking paradox."[2]

Fletcher was unable to understand how a man could dislike academicians and yet devote himself to the study of the classics. Apparently he was unfamiliar with the type of scholar who had grown up in the universities of England like a particularly difficult type of clinging ivy, and is epitomized by T. S. Eliot's pronouncement on Professor Gilbert Murray's translations of the Greek: "He has erected a barrier between the student and the plays greater than that represented by the original Greek."[3]

At first, Pound and Fletcher got along, to such an extent that Fletcher contributed some money to *The New Freewoman.* Having pumped this masculine source, Pound proposed to Miss Weaver that the journal's title be altered to a noun of more neutral gender. He suggested *The Egoist,* and she agreed to it.

On January 1, 1914, the first issue of *The Egoist* appeared. Dora Marsden remained as editor, assisted by Richard Aldington as sub-editor. When he went to war, Aldington was replaced by Rebecca West, and still later by T. S. Eliot.

In *Make It New,* Pound says,

"In the spring of 1912, H.D., Richard Aldington and myself decided that we were agreed upon the three principles following:

"1. Direct treatment of the 'thing' whether subjective or objective.

"2. To use absolutely no word that does not contribute to the presentation.

"3. As regarding rhythm: to compose in the sequence of the musical phrase, not in sequence of a metronome."[4]

It was the third point that opened the doors to the camp-followers of *vers libre,* and created a certain amount of confusion. A lengthier version of these principles, "A few Don'ts by an Imagiste", was contributed by Pound to the March, 1913 issue of *Poetry.* It attracted, among others, Amy Lowell, who immediately wrote her first Imagist poem, "In a Garden". Pound later included this poem in *Des Imagistes,* an anthology, which was published in New York on April 20, 1914.

Of the early Imagists, only H.D. continued to write in this vein throughout her career. Richard Aldington considered her poem, "Hermes of the Ways," which appeared in *The Egoist,* February 2, 1914, one of the best works in this style. The following stanza illustrates the mode:

> The great sea foamed,
> gnashed its teeth about me;
> But you have waited,
> where sea-grass tangles with
> shore-grass.

H.D. and Richard Aldington, both having a passion for things Greek, had become infatuated with each other while making the rounds of the museums. They were married on October 28, 1913. Aldington says that when he returned from the war, he was rather nervous. He and H.D. were divorced. She went off to Europe with the bride of another intimate of the Poundian circle, the novelist Winifred Bryher. Bryher was the only daughter of Sir John Ellerman, the richest ship-owner in England.

Bryher had introduced Aldington to her father, who invited him to dinner. Learning that the young man was a struggling poet,

Ellerman offered him fifty pounds as a contribution to the arts. Aldington mentions in this connection that when Sir John died a few years later, he left forty million pounds. Aldington refused the gift, but said that he would like to get some sort of post in the writing field that paid a salary. Ellerman gave him letters of introduction to take to the editors of two newspapers, the *Times*, and the *Sphere*. Since Ellerman owned a large share of both newspapers, the editors were willing to hire Aldington. He wrote for these papers regularly for some years.

In 1912, when Pound, H.D., and Aldington were formulating the principles of Imagism, Aldington recorded the process. In his autobiography, *Life For Life's Sake*, he wrote,

"Like other American expatriates, Ezra and H.D. developed an almost insane relish for afternoon tea, a meal with which I can most willingly dispense. Moreover, they insisted on going to the most fashionable and expensive tea-shops (which I thought a sad waste of money) not only in London but in Paris. Thus it came about that most of our meetings took place in the rather prissy milieu of some infernal bun-shop full of English spinsters. However, an extremely good time was had by all, and we laughed until we ached—what at, I haven't the slightest recollection. No doubt we all got off some splendid cracks, but for the life of me I can't remember one of them. I suspect that the cream of the wit lay in the fact that we were young, entirely carefree, and having a glorious time just being alive. Naturally, then, the Imagist mouvemong [perhaps a slur on Ezra's French accent] was born in a tea-shop—in the Royal Borough of Kensington. For some time Ezra had been butting in on our studies and poetical productions, with alternate encouragement, and the reverse, according to his mood. H.D. produced some poems, which I thought excellent, and she either handed them or mailed them to Ezra. Presently each of us received a ukase to attend the Kensington bun-shop. Ezra was so worked up by these poems of H.D.'s that he removed his pince-nez and informed us that we were Imagists. Was that the first time I had heard that Pickwickian word? I don't remember. According to the record, Ezra swiped the word from the English philosopher T. E. Hulme: and anyone who can find a copy may read in Ezra's 'Ripostes' the five or six poems Hulme wrote to illustrate his theories. They are pretty good, especially the one about the moon like a red-faced farmer looking over a gate. Ezra's note on Hulme's poems contains the ominous threat: 'as to the future, that is in the hands of the Imagists.'

"But at that time who and where were the Imagists? My own belief is that the name took Ezra's fancy, and that he kept it in petto for the right occasion. If there were no Imagists, obviously they would have to be invented. Wherever Ezra has launched a new movement—and he had made such a hobby of it that I always expect to find one day that Pound and Mussolini are really one and the same person—he has never had any difficulty about finding members. He just calls on his friends."[5]

As Pound's Imagist movement took hold in London, T. E. Hulme and Wyndham Lewis made an effort to reassert themselves in it. They announced a series of lectures at the Kensington Town Hall to discuss this new development in poetry, but Ezra was not asked to speak. Michael Roberts, in his biography of T. E. Hulme, describes the first of these lectures:

"Hulme was not a good lecturer and Wyndham Lewis read a paper supporting Hulme and came off pretty badly himself, mumbling in a husky voice, with his head buried in his manuscript. The audience felt as if they could snatch the papers from the poets and read them for themselves—there was so obviously something very worthwhile buried in all their abstract mumbling. To end it all, Ezra Pound stood up, all self-possessed, complete with velvet coat, flowing tie, pointed beard, and a halo of fiery hair. Lolling against the stage, he became very witty and fluent, and with his yankee voice snarled out some of his poems. Somehow, such a voice rather clowned verse."[6]

Pound emerged as the victor that evening, still the leader of the Imagists. He now occupied a dominant position, due to his role as foreign editor of the leading American magazine of verse, *Poetry,* and to his free hand in editing the literary section of *The Egoist.* His department had mushroomed until it had all but pushed Miss Marsden and her suffragette propaganda out of the magazine. She still held forth on the front page and a few paragraphs inside, but Pound, who had started modestly on the back page, now filled most of the paper.

So strong had his position become that Pound sometimes devoted entire issues of *The Egoist* to his current enthusiasms. He presented the May 1, 1915 issue as an "Imagist Number". F. S. Flint contributed an account of the origins of the movement, and Pound's mother-in-law, Olivia Shakespear, wrote a study of the poetry of D. H. Lawrence, which Pound was boosting at that time.

Lawrence was nervous about becoming one of Pound's "protégés", and he got out from under as soon as possible. He had written to Edward Garnett, on June 21, 1913, "Ezra Pound asked me for some stories because 'he had got an American publisher under his wing.' The tenant of Pound's wing-cover turns out to be the editor of The American Review—a reincarnation of The Smart Set—and I think his name is Wright."[7]

He wrote again to Garnett from Italy on October 6, 1913, ". . . I have asked Ezra Pound to forward to the English Review two stories he had, which were returned from the Smart Set."[8]

And on December 30, 1913, Lawrence wrote the following request to Garnett: "I wish you would send to Ezra Pound, 10 Church Walk, Kensington W—three or four copies of my poems, and send me the bill for them. I owe him something like a sovereign, which The Smart Set sent him as commission, for getting them my two stories. The commission he sent on to me 'as being averse from returning anything to the memorandum of an editor and unable to take commission on my work!'—I didn't want Pound's pound of commission. So now he says he would like three or four copies of my poems, to get them into the hands of the members of the Polignac prize committee, or some such reason. The Hueffer-Pound faction seems inclined to lead me around a little as one of their show-dogs. They seem to have a certain ear in their possession. If they are inclined to speak my name into the ear, I don't care."[9]

On March 14, 1914, Lawrence again wrote to A. D. McLeod from Italy: "I think there will be some of my poems in a paper called *The Egoist*. I don't know anything about it. Ezra Pound took some verses and sent me three pounds three shillings. Try to get a copy, will you?—I believe it will be next month—it may be this, but I think not. But unless I can get hold of a copy, I absolutely don't know what they have printed."[10]

This is the last time that Pound's name is mentioned in Lawrence's published letters. To say that Lawrence disliked Pound is meaningless unless one is to believe that he disliked everybody. He was one of the unhappiest creative minds of our time, but in those moments when the sun broke through, as in some of the short pieces collected in *Phoenix,* he is superb. In his preoccupation with sex, he is actually concerned with survival. As Norman Douglas wrote, "D. H. Lawrence opened a little window for the bourgeoisie. That was his life-work."[11]

A kind of "Third Force" in London poetry circles at that time was led by Harold Monro, keeper of the Poetry Bookshop, which had become a meeting place. Monro was little more than a dilettante and wrote uninspired work. By remaining in one place, he became quite an authority, and long after Pound had left for Paris, and Amy Lowell had returned to America, Monro continued to hold forth in London. He traveled around England, giving lectures, and was introduced as the acknowledged leader of English poetic endeavors. He also wrote a book, *Some Contemporary Poets,* which is of interest. He refers to the leader of the Imagists,

"It is related that when a young countryman of Pound's, arriving in England, visited the master with a species of his work, Pound sat for long at the table, in deep consideration of a certain poem, and at length, glancing up, remarked, 'It took you ninety-seven words to do it; I find it could have been managed in fifty-six.' "[12]

Pound's dominance in London poetry circles was seriously challenged from the distaff side, a quarter that he might have reasonably felt he had no cause to fear. His outlets were publications owned by women: *Poetry,* in Chicago, owned and edited by Miss Harriet Monroe; *The Egoist,* the property of Miss Harriet Weaver; and later, *The Little Review* of Margaret Anderson. It may seem odd that the virile Pound was forced to deal almost exclusively with women, but masculine conservatism is nowhere more drearily expressed than in the field of publishing. Women are much more radical than men, and much more willing to venture into new modes of expression.

Although Pound maintained literary relationships with women

for protracted periods, the result was often non-literary, and the parting inevitable. What woman, after all, could watch this red-maned rooster strutting about and still think logically about his ideas? Consequently, his associations with lady writers and editors degenerated into Strindbergian battles between the sexes, with Pound achieving a series of Pyrrhic victories.

After having obtained possession of a suffragette publication, which in itself was an ironic event, he could hardly have supposed that he would be vulnerable to an attack from a female poetaster. Yet this was the threat which now loomed on the horizon. Miss Amy Lowell, wealthy, eccentric, cigar-smoking sister of the President of Harvard College (of whom Oliver St. John Gogarty wrote, "Dr. Lowell came to visit me wearing a frock coat and brown shoes, and the brown shoes distracted me so that I cannot remember what was said."[13]), was on the high seas. She had been a common, or garden variety, lady versifier until March, 1913, when she spied Pound's Imagist principles in *Poetry*. She had dashed off an Imagist poem, and set out for London. She arrived there in the summer of 1913, armed with her contribution to the Imagist movement and a letter of introduction from Miss Harriet Monroe.

Pound was not impressed by Miss Lowell's Imagist poem, but he charitably agreed to include it in the anthology he was then compiling. The new recruit was soon chafing at the bit, and she found an ally in John Gould Fletcher. Both Fletcher and Miss Lowell were annoyed by Pound's brusque manner, and also by his refusal to spend his time in that age-old amusement of poets, that is, sitting down and reading their poems to one another. Pound had no time to spend in listening to poets read their verse. He usually snatched the manuscript from the hand of the genius, glanced over it, scribbled a suggestion or two, blue-pencilling the most soaring lines, and handed it back. What really sensitive soul could bear such treatment?

Amy Lowell was seeking a sympathetic listener who could appreciate her verse. She invited Fletcher to visit her in her sumptuous suite at the Berkeley, and the two poets discovered that they had much in common. They were accustomed to paying their way, that is, footing the bills for the publication of their poems, and they saw no reason why they should endure further insolence from Ezra. They read aloud their immortal lines, and found that their depth of perception was surprisingly similar. Fletcher tells us, in *Life Is My Song,* that he was amazed when Amy Lowell declaimed,

> The loud pink of bursting hydrangeas

and he immediately responded with his own

> In the green gardens of my soul
> The crimson peonies explode.[14]

Amidst coronae of gaily-bursting flowers, Amy Lowell and Fletcher sat down to plot the overthrow of the literary dictator and up-start, Pound. Fletcher complained that Pound had loudly dis-approved of the exploding peonies, and Amy Lowell replied that he had been unable to appreciate her volatile blooms. A blow for freedom would have to be struck. The most readily available weapon was money. Fletcher suggested that Amy Lowell offer to contribute a large sum of money to *The Egoist,* with the stipu-lation that Miss Weaver get rid of Pound, but his mode of attack was too direct.

Fletcher was a person of unstable loyalties, and he mentions his "own peculiar bad temper." A prey to increasing depression, he finally drowned himself in a little pond in Arkansas. His alli-ance with Amy Lowell, like most of his relationships, was short-lived. He later wrote,

"Had I been wise enough with that wisdom which comes only to the intellectually mature, I would have seen in Miss Lowell's fresh arrival in England the opening attack in a carefully-planned and long-sustained literary campaign; a campaign, in fact, which only ended on the day of her death, and which, I am convinced, she enormously enjoyed. . . . Between the time of her first trip in 1913 and her second she had become transformed from the obscure amateur of 'A Dome of Many-Coloured Glass' (an early book of her poems) to the professional leader of the new poets. . . . From one included in the first Imagist anthology only for the sake of filling up space, she had already grown so important as to be able now to successfully dispute the leadership of the group with Ezra Pound."[15]

Indirectly, Ezra was responsible for the strength of Amy Lowell's challenge. He had included her little poem "In a Garden" in his anthology; if this was not done for the sake of filling up space, as Fletcher declares, at least it was done out of kindness. When *Des Imagistes,* was published by Albert and Charles Boni in New York in April, 1914, it caused a sensation. Ezra had modestly said nothing in the book about his role in putting it together, and American reviewers got the impression that Amy Lowell was solely responsible for it. After she returned to the United States, her disclaimers, if any, of this honor were inaudible. Soon she was convinced that she really was the leader of the Imagists.

Once more she sailed to London, this time on a voyage of conquest. She tried to lure the young poets into her camp with a bait to which they were peculiarly susceptible. She did not offer them bribes, but she suggested that she get out another Imagist anthology, at her own expense. The poets would see more of their work in print, but Amy, and not Ezra, would be the editor.

Surprised by this approach, but not very upset by it, Ezra countered with the proposal that she make better use of her money by financing an international review. Amy decided that this suggestion was a Fort Sumter. On September 15, 1914, she wrote indignantly to Harriet Monroe, complaining that Ezra had asked her to put up five thousand dollars a year for this enterprise.

"Like most people of no incomes," she raged to the independently wealthy Miss Monroe, "Ezra does not know the difference between thousands and millions, and thinks that anyone who knows where to look for next week's dinner is a millionaire, and therefore lost his temper with me completely, although he never told me why; and he accused me of being unwilling to give any money towards art."[16]

In the course of this lengthy denunciation (reprinted in what must be the longest biography of any modern poet, a life of Miss Lowell consisting of 773 pages compiled by S. Foster Damon), she mentions that Ezra had modified his demand for five thousand dollars, suggesting instead that if she wished him to cooperate with her on a new Imagist anthology, she should donate two hundred dollars to some indigent poet. She termed this "blackmail" and said that Ezra had demanded of the Aldingtons that they choose between him and Miss Lowell.

"The truth is," she continued in her plaint to Miss Monroe, "Ezra has ducked and draked his reputation with his last work. His poetry is too indecent to be poetical, and even when it is not indecent, it is too often merely vituperative . . . He looks very ill, and has a bad cough, and I'm afraid he is tuberculous. It has even been hinted that this may have attacked his brain. No one knows anything about it, and this is merely surmise."[17]

Amy Lowell's fears about Ezra's health have not been corroborated elsewhere. There is reason to suppose that the hint of brain damage was hinted only by herself. As she says, "no one knows anything about it," although this is no reason to suppress the rumor. She knew that the story would be circulated in Chicago, thanks to her letter to Miss Monroe, that Ezra was ill and perhaps insane, and that this tale would lower resistance to her capture of the Imagist movement. Her letter, which is quite an instrument of intrigue, rambles on for many pages, replete with such items as "Ezra has always thought of life as a grand game of bluff."[18]

Unable to resist the prospect of again appearing in print, the Aldingtons, Flint, and Fletcher turned over their manuscripts to Miss Lowell, and she sailed back to America, to bring out the first of several anthologies entitled *Some Imagist Poets* (1915).

Ezra was already preoccupied with another movement, Vorticism, when Amy held a victory celebration in London. His Vorticist group gave a dinner at the Dieudonne Restaurant on July 15, 1914, to hail the appearance of Wyndham Lewis' *Blast*. Amy Lowell gave a dinner there two evenings afterward, on the 17th. The Pounds, the Aldingtons, John Cournos, John Gould Fletcher, F. S. Flint, Gaudier-Brzeska, the Hueffers, Allan Upward, and Miss Amy Lowell's companion, Mr. Harold Russell, were the guests.

After the dinner, the poets were asked to stand up and give a brief personal statement about their understanding of the term "Imagist". Aldington was the first to speak, and he launched into an impassioned defense of Miss Lowell. He was soon interrupted by Pound's impetuous friend, Gaudier-Brzeska. As the two

opponents shouted at one another, Pound slipped out of the room.
The waiters stood grinning expectantly, for they had been let in
on the secret. In a few moments, Pound returned, bearing on his
shoulders an old-fashioned round tin tub. He set it down, and
declared that he wished to announce the formation of an important
new school of poetry, not Imagiste, but "nageiste". He then quoted
the line from Amy Lowell's Imagist poem "In a Garden",

> not the water, but you in your whiteness, bathing.

Everyone laughed, and even Miss Lowell smiled, albeit grimly.
"Ezra must have his little joke," she said, and the celebration
was ended.[19]

Her publishers now advertised Miss Lowell as "The foremost
member of the 'Imagists'—a group of poets that includes William
Butler Yeats, Ezra Pound, Ford Madox Hueffer—."

On October 19, 1914, Ezra wrote to Miss Lowell concerning
this advertisement, "In view of the above arrant charlatanism on
the part of your publishers, I think you must now admit that I
was quite right in refusing to join you in any scheme for turning
Les Imagistes into an uncritical democracy with you as intermediary between it and the printers. While you apologize to Richard,
your publishers, with true nonchalance, go on printing the ad in
American papers, which we would not see, save by unexpected
accident. I think you had better cease referring to yourself as an
Imagiste, more especially as The Dome of Glass certainly has no
aspirations in our direction. I don't suppose anyone will sue you
for libel; it is too expensive. If your publishers of 'good standing'
tried to advertise cement or soap in this manner they certainly
would be sued. However, we salute their venality."[20]

Ezra's opinion of American publishers, low as it is, nevertheless is based upon experience rather than upon theory. In the
course of helping T. E. Lawrence to find avenues of publication,
he wrote to him on April 20, 1920, "In sending copy to America,
let me caution you to use an incognito as well as a pseudonym.
Thayer is, I think, quite decent (he is the *Dial*), but I trust an
American publication about as far as I would trust a British government; my bright compatriots are quite capable of printing an

article by Mr. Smith and then printing a leetle note at the end of the number saying 'The article by Mr. Smith is really written by the distinguished Sheik-tamer and Tiger-baiter etc. who for reasons of modesty has concealed himself 'neath the ridiculous name of Smith-Yapper.' "

Amy Lowell got out two more volumes in her series of *Some Imagist Poets,* before she gave up. She offered Margaret Anderson one hundred and fifty dollars a month toward the expenses of *The Little Review* on the condition that she be allowed to take over the poetry department. Although Miss Anderson was, as usual, in need of funds, she refused the offer. She knew only too well that Miss Lowell's offer was but the first step toward a seizure of power.

Miss Lowell now contented herself with contributing two hundred dollars a month to Harriet Monroe's magazine, *Poetry.* She and Miss Monroe had much the same tastes, so that it was not necessary to dictate to her. On July 7, 1919, Miss Lowell wrote to Miss Monroe, "I see by the current number (of *Poetry*) that Ezra has left the *Little Review* also. I think the truth is that the world has left Ezra. . . . Poor Ezra, he had a future once, but he has played his cards so badly that I think he barely has a past now."[21]

Miss Lowell was not the first to bury Ezra prematurely. His critics have been doing that for a half-century. Conrad Aiken attacked Pound in a romantic diatribe in the Boston *Transcript* that was reprinted in the New York *Sun,* May 9, 1915, of which the following lines are typical:

> Pound, though your henchmen now agree
> To hail the Prince in the Anarchist,
> Where in a score of years will you be,
> And the pale pink, dream blown mouths you kissed?

A score of years later, Pound was in Rapallo, working on his *Cantos,* and there too he was to be found more than two score years after Aiken's prediction. And Aiken? He is right where he was in 1915.

Aiken's reference to Pound's "henchmen" illustrates the theory, always popular among his critics, that he is usually surrounded by a gang of tough supporters, who protect the literary "dictator" from attack. In reality, Pound has almost always been alone. His furious activities as an unsalaried editor for various publications, and his campaigns as an unpaid press agent for many talents over a period of fifty years, would lead anyone to suppose that the recipients of these favors necessarily would form a phalanx about him. But this has never been the case. The editors of the periodicals for whom he has toiled have always been glad to see him ride off into the sunset, and the writers whom he has assisted, when they were not to be found among his detractors, were usually silent when he was attacked. His only "henchman" in his career has been his wife, Dorothy Pound.

Amy Lowell had wrested a prize from Pound, the leadership of the Imagist movement, but he did not consider it a loss. Indeed, the young talents of the Imagistes had begun to bore him, and he had sought more virile company. He found the Vorticists much more stimulating.

His rival insisted on the spoils of her triumph. She banned his name from her anthologies, but considering the quality of her selections, this was of indirect benefit to Pound. She refused ever afterward to mention him as a poet of consequence. In her long poem *A Critical Fable,* an imitation of Byron's lambasting of his contemporaries, she included Pound and Eliot as an afterthought. This work, published in 1922, praised enthusiastically the poems of Sandburg, Frost, H.D., Fletcher, and Hilda Conkling. Near the end of the poem, as though performing a painful duty, she wrote,

> Eliot fears to abandon an old masquerade;
> Pound's one perfect happiness is to parade.
> Eliot's learning was won at a very great price;
> What Pound calls his learning he got in a trice.
> Eliot knows what he knows, though he cannot digest it;
> Pound knows nothing at all, but has frequently guessed it.
> Eliot builds up his essays by a process of massing;
> Pound's are mostly hot air, what the vulgar call 'gassing.'
> Eliot lives like a snail in his shell, pen protruding;
> Pound struts like a cock, self-adored, self-deluding . . .[22]

The last line is an apt illustration of the effect that Pound had upon lady poetasters. This poem continues its "Night Before

Xmas" rhythm with several other references to the men whom she hated. She said of Pound and Eliot, "Each one is a traitor, but with different reasons."[23] This was an interesting prediction, for Eliot would later be attacked for giving up his American citizenship, and Pound would actually be indicted for treason.

Miss Lowell did include one grudging line of tribute to Pound in *A Critical Fable*. She wrote of him,

Few men have to their credit more excellent verses.[24]

In a long letter written on July 7, 1923, to May Lamberton Becker, listing the contemporary American poets whom she considered worthwhile, Miss Lowell listed a dozen or so whom she considered pre-eminent, including such names as Maxwell Bodenheim, but she did not mention Pound.[25]

In reviewing Pound's association with the Imagist poets, Eliot wrote in 1946, "If it had not been for the work that Pound did in the years of which I have been talking, the isolation of American poetry, and the isolation of individual American poets, might have continued for a long time. I am not forgetting Miss Lowell, but it seems to me that the work she did in putting over American poetry upon an American public, was on a lower level. She was a kind of demon saleswoman; and unless my memory of her methods is at fault (for it is a great many years since I read her Six American Poets) they were more enthusiastic than critical. If today it is a matter of course that London should take an interest in poetry published in New York and that New York should be interested in poetry published in London—not simply in the decorated reputations, but in the new verse—this is largely due to what Pound achieved for poetry."[26]

Pound now dubbed his former movement "Amygism". To parody what it had become in the hands of female versifiers, he wrote a satirical piece entitled "Papyrus", which is here reproduced in full:

> Spring. . . .
> Too long . . .
> Gongula. . . .[27]

The poem was taken seriously, and the irrepressible Pound included it in his collected works. Because the critics of what he terms "littachoor" know so little of his work, it was inevitable that they should attack "Papyrus" as evidence of his poetic weaknesses. Howling with the pack, as usual, is Robert Graves, who complains in his collection of essays, *The Common Asphodel,* that this poem is typical of Pound's obscurantism.[28]

In the final analysis, the conflict between Pound and Miss Lowell was a conflict of standards. He had set up definite boundaries of excellence for his little group, and he refused to publish anything that did not measure up. He also refused to put his name to any Imagist anthology unless he had the last word on what was to be included, for rightly or wrongly, he believed that his judgment was the most valid of the group. Time proved him right, for under Amy's leadership, poetry was published as "Imagist" that was even worse than her own.

V

OUND'S LAST effort with group participation in the arts, before he retreated to a position of individualism, was his association with the Vorticists in London. Although some of the principles advanced by this group had first been heard in the rooms of T. E. Hulme, its key figures were Pound, Wyndham Lewis, and Gaudier-Brzeska.

Hulme was not a joiner, and he preferred to watch them from a distance. A giant of a man, he once startled Wyndham Lewis by holding him upside down over the railings of Soho Square in order to emphasize a point. There were many quarrels and fierce rivalries in the London Bohemia, and Hulme had Gaudier-Brzeska make a brass knuckle-duster for him which he carried everywhere.

One of the characters prominently seen, and gawked at, during this period was a Cheapside tout named Hixen, who sometimes performed missions for the artists. He ran about the town like a Western road runner. Hixen suffered from a pronounced stutter, the result of his having been caught stealing from a church poor-box when he was about six years old. The priest had painted such a frightening picture of the torments of hell that the poor lad had gone into shock, and stuttered ever afterwards.

Pound was boosting the work of his various "discoveries" in every issue of *The Egoist*. These enthusiasms included Lewis, Gaudier-Brzeska, Jacob Epstein, and James Joyce. His closest friend during the Vorticist period was Wyndham Lewis, who later was to denounce him as an "instinctive". He studied in Munich, and was heavily influenced by the stark line of the modern German artists.

Writing of his early association with Pound, Lewis says, "It was scarcely our fault that we were a youth racket. It was Ezra who in the first place organized us willy nilly into that. For he was never satisfied until everything was *organized*. And it was he who made us into a youth racket—that was his method of organization. He had a streak of Baden-Powell in him, had Ezra, perhaps more than a streak. With Disraeli, he thought in terms of 'Young England.' He never got us under canvas, it is true—we were not the most promising material for Ezra's boyscoutery. But he did succeed in giving a handful of disparate and unassimilable people the appearance of a Bewegung.

"It was Pound who invented the word 'vorticist,' " continues Lewis, "it was Pound who introduced Joyce to Miss Harriet Weaver—indeed thrust him down her throat—and thereby made a great many things possible which would not have otherwise been so; it was Pound who tirelessly schooled and scolded Eliot (as the latter is the first to recognize) and his blue pencil is all over The Waste Land. Ezra was at once a poet and an impresario, at that time an unexpected combination."[1]

Lewis' affection for Pound was a vessel that encountered rough seas from time to time, but during his last years, he was a warm correspondent. He accepted Pound's *bon mot* for his residence on Notting Hill as the title of one of his last books, *Rotting Hill* (1951).

"This theatrical fellow," Lewis wrote of Pound, "as he first seemed to me, I find to be 'one of the best.' I still regard him as one of the best, even one of the best poets."[2]

Lewis met Pound for the first time in 1910 at the Vienna Café on Oxford Street. One of Lewis' friends promptly informed him that Pound was Jewish. "When Pound appeared I was mildly surprised to see an unmistakable 'Nordic blond' with fierce blue eyes and a reddishly hirsute jaw, thrust out with a thoroughly Aryan determination. But this moment of disillusion passed, I took no further interest in the cowboy songster, said to be a young sprig of the Kahal. I turned my back: I heard the staccato of the States: I 'sensed' that there was little enthusiasm . . . And when I rose to go back to the Museum he had whirled off—bitterness in his heart, if I know my Ezra. This was his first taste of the English. He had no luck with the English, then or at a later date, and was always in his country a fish out of water . . ."[3]

Lewis seems surprised that Ezra should have been angry at being snubbed by a bunch of "Brits", but his observation that Ezra would have no luck with the English was essentially true. In 1914, he was in his heyday there, but England became increasingly cold to him in the next few years.

Pound printed some powerful boosts for Lewis in *The Egoist*. He wrote, in the issue of June 15, 1914, "Mr. Wyndham Lewis is one of the greatest masters of design yet born in the occident. . . . The rabble and the bureaucracy have built a god in their own image and that god is mediocrity. The great mass of mankind are mediocre, that is axiomatic, it is a definition of the word mediocre. The race is however divided into disproportionate segments; those who worship their own belly-buttons and those who do not."

Pound also described Lewis as "Not a commentator but a protagonist. . . . He is a man at war . . . you cannot be as intelligent in that sort of way, without being prey to the furies."

In *Instigations,* Pound described Lewis' novel *Tarr* (1918), as "the most vigorous and volcanic English novel of our time."[4] This statement might seem to be an exaggeration, until one actually compares it with the English novels of the time. Pound later noted, in criticizing Lewis' *Apes of God* (1932), that it was somewhat limited by Lewis' "peeve".

Lewis' striking drawings of Pound are typical Vorticist productions. After viewing an exhibition of Lewis' work at the Goupil Gallery, the *Observer* critic wrote, in describing one of the Pound portraits, ". . . the synthetic reconstruction of personality in light and pure terms of art."

Pound's other cohort in the Vorticist movement was a young French sculptor, Henri Gaudier-Brzeska. In his biography of this artist, Pound describes their meeting:

"I was with O.S. [Olivia Shakespear] at a picture show in the Albert Hall (International, Allied Artists or something). We wandered about the upper galleries hunting for new work and trying to find some good amid much bad, and a young man came after us, like a well-made young wolf or some soft-moving, bright-eyed wild thing. I noted him carefully because he reminded me of my friend Carlos Williams.

"He also took note of us, partly because we only paused before new work, and partly because there were few people in the gallery, and partly because I was playing the fool and he was willing to be amused by the performance. It was a warm, lazy day, there was little serious criticism mixed with our nonsense. On the ground floor we stopped before a figure with bunchy muscles done in clay and painted green. It was one of a group of interesting things. I turned to the catalogue and began to take liberties with the appalling assemblage of consonants; 'Brzxjk—' I began. I tried again, 'Burrzisskzk—' I drew back, breathed deeply and took another run at the hurdle, sneezed, coughed, rumbled, got as far as 'Burdidis—' when there was a dart from behind the pedestal and I heard a voice speaking with the gentlest fury in the world, 'Cela s'appelle tout simplement Jaersh-ka. C'est moi que les ai sculptes.' And he disappeared like a Greek god in a vision."[5]

Richard Aldington, who was not present, tells a slightly different version of the meeting:

"During the Albert Hall exhibit of the Allied Artists in 1913, Ezra went round with his mother-in-law, Mrs. Shakespear. They came to a statuette, in what was then loosely called the Futurist style, and Ezra began capering at and making fun of it. Suddenly a gaunt, sharp-faced young man, with flaming eyes and long dark hair, rushed at him and threatened him with immediate personal violence. Ezra prudently declined the combat, and at once became a warm admirer of the young man's work. Thus we came to know Gaudier."[6]

Aldington gives us a more intimate description of Gaudier than does Pound:

"He was probably the dirtiest human being I have ever known, and gave off horrid effluvia in hot weather. One summer day he came to see us in our small flat; we prudently placed him on a couch at one end of the small room and ourselves retired to the other. Who should come in but Ford, who had been to a fashionable luncheon, and wanted to display his shining topper and formal morning clothes with a red carnation in the buttonhole! Unluckily he had to sit beside Gaudier, and soon left. The next morning Ford gave me a paternal lecture on my wildness in permitting such a

creature to be in the same room with H.D. It was, he said, not
done. However, as the weather cooled, Gaudier was frequently at
Ford's evenings; and eventually his phallic statue of Ezra was
erected in Ford's front garden, much to Violet's distress."[7]

In their respective memoirs, both Wyndham Lewis and Jacob
Epstein corroborate the fact that Ezra gave specific instructions to
Gaudier, when he commissioned the magnificent bust now in Italy,
that it should be symbolically phallic, as, indeed, good sculpture
should be. In *Let There Be Sculpture,* Jacob Epstein writes,

"I visited Gaudier at his workshop in Putney. He occupied one
of a large number of workshops that were constructed under the
railway arches leading to Putney Bridge. Gaudier was at the time
working on the portrait of Ezra Pound in marble. Pound has asked
him to make it phallic, and this Gaudier was endeavouring to do,
explaining to me the biological significance of the parts."[8]

Violet Hunt writes that the bust, which sank steadily in the soft
turf of her garden, was popularly supposed by the neighbors to
provide immunity from the Zeppelin raids over London during the
First World War.[9] They were convinced that Ford was the director
of an important spy ring, and that secret instructions for his
German contacts were cached nightly beneath the great statue.

Pound says that Gaudier was quite depressed at that time, for
he had few commissions. He intended to make the bust in plaster,
but Pound would not hear of this, and purchased a half-ton block
of marble for fifteen dollars.

In his book *No Enemy,* Ford has given us a brilliant description of Gaudier, on the occasion of the famous Imagist dinner at
the Dieudonne Restaurant. Miss Lowell's victory celebration is
characterized by Ford as a "disagreeable occasion of evil passions,
evil people, of bad, flashy cooking in an underground haunt of
pre-war smartness.

"I daresay it was not really as bad as all that," he continues,
"—but when I am forced to receive the hospitality of persons
whom I dislike, the food seems to go bad, and there is a bad taste
in the mouth, symbol of a disturbed liver. So the band played in
that cave and the head ached and there were nasty, foreign waiters
and bad, very expensive champagne. There were also speeches—
and I could not help knowing that the speeches were directed at

the Neutral's breeches pockets. The Neutral leaned heavily side-
ways at table, devouring the bad food at once with gluttony and
nonchalance. It talked about its motor car, which apparently
was at Liverpool or Southampton—somewhere there were liners,
quays, cordage, cranes; all ready to abandon a city which should
be doomed should Armageddon become Armageddon. The
speeches went on. . . . Then Gaudier rose. It was suddenly like
a silence that intervened during a distressing and ceaseless noise.
I don't know that I had ever noticed him before except as one
among a crowd of dirtyish, bearded, slouch-hatted individuals,
like conspirators; but, there he seemed as if he stood amidst sunlight, as if indeed he floated in a ray of sunlight, like the dove
in Early Italian pictures. In a life during which I have known
thousands of people, thousands and thousands of people; during
which I have grown sick and tired of 'people' so that I prefer the
society of cabbages, goats, and the flowers of the marrow plant;
I have never otherwise known what it was to witness an appearance
which symbolized so completely—aloofness. It was like the appearance of Apollo at a creditors' meeting. It was supernatural.

". . . So when I first noticed Henri Gaudier—which was in an
underground restaurant, the worst type of thieves' kitchen—these
words rose to my lips. I did not, you understand, believe that he
would exist and be so wise, so old, so gentle, so humourous,
such a genius. I did not really believe that he had shaved, washed,
assumed garments that fitted his great personal beauty.

"For he had great personal beauty. If you looked at him
casually, you imagined that you were looking at one of those
dock-rats of the Marseilles quays, who will carry your baggage
for you, pimp for you; garotte you and throw your body over-
board—but who will do it all with an air, an ease, an exquisite-
ness of manners! They have, you see, the traditions, inherited
knowledge of such ancient matters in Marseilles—of Etruscans,
Phoenicians, Colonial Greeks, Late Romans, Troubadours, Late
French—and that of those who first sang the Marseillaise! And
many of them, whilst they are young, have the amazing beauty
that Gaudier had. Later, absinthe spoils it—but for a time they
are like Arlesiennes."[10]

Ford disapproved of Miss Lowell, as all Englishmen disapproved of Americans from 1914 through 1917, because they were Neutrals. And there is no doubt that he disapproved of her manner at table, as he disapproved of most Americans in this regard. He wrote, in his *New York Essays,* of a man in Chicago, a considerable patron of the arts, that "He eats like a pike snapping semi-circular gobbets out of a corpse."[11]

During his London period, another friend of Gaudier's was Horace Brodzky, who says that for a time, Gaudier supported himself by working as a foreign correspondence clerk in the city. He occupied Railway Arch 25, beneath the electric trains that ran to Putney.[12]

Gaudier lived with an odd consort, whose name he had taken. She was a Polish lady twice his age, whom he had met while studying in Paris. She had come to that city to kill herself, and while waiting for an opportune moment (for it is very formal and exact ritual), she spent her time reading in the St. Genevieve Library, where Gaudier also was studying. They adopted each other, and went to London. Gaudier took her name, Brzeska, in order to have a more aristocratic appellant, for he had come from an humble French family. She ordinarily addressed him as "Pik" or "Zosik", and he called her "Mamus" or "Mamuska". They were an extraordinary pair, very poor, and, as Aldington has recorded, they seldom washed.

In a letter to his mother in 1913, Pound pointed out that Epstein had the same shortcoming. "Epstein is a great sculptor," he remarked. "I wish he would wash, but I believe Michael Angelo never did, so I suppose it is part of the tradition."[13]

Excited by the new work of Gaudier and Epstein, Pound wrote, in the February 16, 1914, issue of *The Egoist,* on "The New Sculpture":

"Humanism long had no chance in the occident, in life, I mean, save for an occasional decade which has been followed by some plot like the counter-reformation or Praise-God Barebones or the most estimable S. Webbs & Co. Humanism has, I was about to write, taken refuge in the arts. The introduction of djinns, tribal gods, fetiches, etc. into the arts is therefore a happy presage. The artist has been for so long a humanist! He has had sense enough to know that humanity was unbearably stupid and that he must try to disagree with it; but he has also tried to lead and persuade it; to save it from itself. He has fed it out of his hand and the arts have grown dull and complacent, like a slightly uxorious spouse. The artist has at last been aroused to the fact that the war between him and the world is a war without truce. That his only remedy is slaughter. . . . The artist has been at peace with his oppressors long enough. He has dabbled in democracy and he is now done with that folly. We turn back, we artists, to the powers of the air, to the djinns who were our allies aforetime, to the spirits of our ancestors. It is by them that we have ruled and shall rule, and by their connivance that we shall mount again into our hierarchy. The aristocracy of entail and of title is decayed, the aristocracy of commerce is decaying, the aristocracy of the arts is ready again for its service. Modern civilization has bred a race with brains like those of rabbits and we who are the heirs of the witchdoctor and the voodoo, we artists who have been so long the despised are about to take over control."

Some of these statements, which might be analyzed as indicating "undemocratic attitudes", were a sort of war dance that preceded the appearance of a Vorticist Manifesto through the medium of the magazine *Blast*. This was a large, puce-colored magazine printed on thick paper. It was about the size of a large city's telephone book. The first of two numbers was published on April 20, 1914, and contained many pages of large-type Manifestoes, Blasts and Damns, mostly in capital letters.

LONG LIVE THE VORTEX proclaimed the revolutionaries.

> BLAST FIRST (for politeness) England
> Curse its climate for its sins and infections
> Dismal Symbol, set round our bodies,
>   of effeminate lout within.
> Victorian Vampire, the london cloud sucks
>   the town's heart.

2. OH BLAST FRANCE
    1. pig plagiarism
    Belly
    Slippers

Poodle temper
Bad Music
Sentimental Gallic Gush

The Manifesto was signed by "R. Aldington, Arbuthnot, L. Atkinson, Gaudier-Brzeska, J. Dismore, C. Hamilton, E. Pound, W. Robers, H. Sanders, E. Wadsworth, and W. Lewis." Point No. 6 declared,

We are primitive mercenaries in the modern world.
Let us once more wear the ermine of the North.

Another declaration stated that "The human form still runs, like a wave, thru the texture or body of existence, and therefore of art. But just as the old form of egotism is no longer fit for such conditions as now prevail, so the isolated Figure of most ancient Art is an anachronism. Dehumanization is the chief diagnostic of the modern world."

Pound was represented in *Blast* by several poems, including one, "Fratres Minores", that shocked most of the purchasers, as well as his friends. Library copies now have the first line and the last two lines delicately marked out, but diligent researchers can decipher them. At any rate, the poem is reprinted unmarked in Pound's later edition of *Personae:*

With minds still hovering at their testicles
Certain poets here and in France
Still sigh over established and natural fact
Long since fully discussed by Ovid.
They howl. They complain in delicate and
    exhausted metres
That the twitching of three abdominal nerves
Is incapable of producing a lasting Nirvana.[14]

In commenting upon this poem, in *The Egoist* of July 15, 1914, Richard Aldington wrote, "As the uncleanness of his language increases to an almost laughable point the moral sentiment of his writing becomes more and more marked. I understand that some people are objecting strongly to certain words in one of Mr. Pound's poems in Blast; that, of course, is their affair, but the amusing thing to me is that this poem was obviously written with a strong moral purpose. It is not my business to abuse Mr. Pound—he gets enough of it from other people—and I shall probably be called all kinds of sad names if I say that his contributions to Blast are quite unworthy of the author. It is not that one wants Mr. Pound to repeat his Provencal feats, to echo the 90s—he has done that too much already—it is simply the fact that Mr. Pound cannot write satire. Mr. Pound is one of the gentlest, most modest, bashful, kind creatures who ever walked the earth; so I cannot help thinking that all this enormous arrogance and petulance and fierceness are a pose. And it is a wearisome pose."

In addition to a couple of very orthodox pieces by Ford Madox Ford and Rebecca West, *Blast* also contained some individual Manifestoes on the state of the Vortex. Pound wrote, in part, "The Vortex is the point of maximum energy. It represents, in mechanics, the greatest efficiency."

Gaudier-Brzeska's excellent definition of the Vortex has been reprinted in full in Pound's biography of him. It begins,

"Sculptural energy is the mountain. Sculptural feeling is the appreciation of masses in relation. Sculptural ability is the defining of these masses by planes. . . . The sphere is thrown through space, it is the subject and object of the vortex."[15]

A full page advertisement of the new magazine that appeared in *The Egoist,* June 1, 1914, hailed it with the motto "No Pornography, No Old Pulp, End of the Christian Era."

The *Morning Post* greeted *Blast* as "full of irresponsible imbecility," but the good grey *Times* was more sympathetic, saying "Blast aims at doing for the arts and literature of today what the Yellow Book did for the artistic movement of its decade."

The New York *Times* on August 9, 1914, devoted a full page to the Vorticists, referring to Pound as "the ex-American poet". The reviewer declared that the Vorticists were simply jealous of Marinetti and the strength of his Futurist movement in England, and that Vorticism was merely a native English version of Futurism. Pound referred to Marinetti, a well-known Fascist, as a corpse.

For a short time, *Blast* was the talk of London. Copies were sold briskly at the Rebel Art Centre, 38 Great Ormond Street, which was the Vorticist headquarters. Another favorite meeting-place was one of London's first night clubs, the Cave of the Golden Calf. The habitués of these establishments having been decimated by the years, and having left few records of their escapades, I wrote to Ezra and inquired whether the Rebel Art Centre and the Cave might not be the same establishment. He was not slow to correct me on this point, replying, on April 6, 1959,

"NO, HELL NO! ! ! Rebel Art Centre, was serious VORT centre. supported by the pure in heart.

       There the emissaries of Moscow came to gaze, and having listened to Ez-vort

              said sadly :

                      BUTTT ! ! you are

in - di-VID -ualists ! ! !

       Whereto , I ever imprudent , replied : Yes, what the hell do you expect?

       AND they departed sadly. And there was one notice in hroosian, conserved somewhere.

Whereas the Cave of the calf was started by Frieda.

  'And are you any connection of THE Strindberg' ?

responsus :

  Yesss, I ahm vun of his Wives.

and to me : 'I needt money . I haff therefore dagen upp brosstiDushun , in tdiss bardicular form.'

I , then in the heights of Whistler and the refinements of Debussy, was unable to appreciate Frieda.

/also missed Arnold Bennett   ,   in a totally different dimension. which WAS a serious loss.

       but refinements , and aestheticism

in callow years , can but be cause of repining in later maturity, or approx. IN fact, no two places cd/ have been MORE different, than 38 Ormond St , in high candour, vs /Roger Fry 'pinching the baby' and etc.

his organism resisting Sophie Suzzann's effort to give Gaudier marble to the S.Kensington

because IF they HAD sold it they wd/
have made a commission,
            which was jeopardized by the gift to the
S.Kensington AFTER it had been placed on sale with the (small)
Fry. and the Cave of the Golden Calf, probably also an outpost for
espionage.
   The celebrities given honorary membership, but
the income from guardsmen who might in cups have said something.
   Don't think it amounted to much as help to the enemy.
and was, nacherly, the only night club (one of the first in London)
which impovrished artists cd/ get into.
                              Middle european acumen
as to advertising value of Mr. Epstein, Frank Harris etc.
you cd/ even get eats for free if you took 'em at Frieda's table.
Vague rumor that she got copped in N.Y. , at any rate
spurloss verschwinden, during that first so surprising unpleasant-
ness. more brains than Gertie or Amy put together.
                        Augustus John Sd/ to have been
insulted when she suggested he take a bath /
                   principle of bagno
ante scortun,
            vs. scortum ante mortem.
Travel broadens the mind."

Frieda, who was the playwright's third wife, had gotten Epstein
to do some striking columns for her place, and Lewis painted some
startling murals for her. In a letter to his mother of November,
1913, Pound complained that "a bloody guardsman" had removed
his hat from the Cave cloakroom.[16] The Strindberg relict later
moved her club to Beak Street, and renamed it, less dramatically,
the Cabaret Club.
   Pound, always conjuring up new projects, announced in *The
Egoist* of November 2, 1914, that a new college of the arts would
soon open its doors. He listed himself, Gaudier-Brzeska, Wyndham
Lewis, and Arnold Dolmetsch respectively as heads of ateliers of
Poetry, Sculpture, Drawing and Ancient Music. But, as H. Glenn
Hughes comments, "Of course it was only a dream, born of full

fancy and an empty stomach."[17] The college never held a class, although one might suppose that this stellar faculty could have attracted some students.

The Vorticists received a serious setback when the most volatile of their number, Gaudier, aged twenty-three, was killed in France.[18] It had taken determination and a long campaign for him to get himself killed. Before the outbreak of the war, he had gone home, but according to the laws of compulsory military service in France, he had been listed as a deserter. He faced the death penalty for this. When he returned to defend his country, he was arrested as soon as he landed in Calais, thrown into jail, and told that he would be shot.

As the result of living on a sculptor's income, he was very thin, and during the night, he managed to squeeze through the barred window and escape. He returned to England, but the plight of his homeland continued to affect his conscience. He went to the French Embassy in London, told them his story, and they gave him a safe-conduct to France. He was enrolled in the army, and attained the rank of sergeant before being killed at Neuville-Saint Vaast.

Wyndham Lewis had been ill with septicemia, which prevented him from enlisting in the army, and also delayed the second issue of *Blast*. The magazine finally appeared with a sober khaki cover, in July, 1915, more than a year after the first number. Included was a last notice for Gaudier-Brzeska, written from the trenches: "WITH ALL THE DESTRUCTION THAT WORKS AROUND US NOTHING IS CHANGED, EVEN SUPERFICIALLY. LIFE IS THE SAME STRENGTH, THE MOVING AGENT THAT PERMITS THE SMALL INDIVIDUAL TO ASSERT HIMSELF."

This statement was surrounded by a black box, with the note, "Mort Pour La Patrie, killed June 5, 1915."

Earlier, in his book on Gaudier, Pound had written, "If the accursed Germans succeed in damaging Gaudier-Brzeska they will have done more harm to art than they have by the destruction of Rheims Cathedral, for a building once made and recorded can, with some care, be remade, but the uncreated forms of a man of genius cannot be set forth by another."[19]

Wyndham Lewis made a notable statement in this, the last issue of *Blast:*

"We are not only 'the last men of epoch!' . . . We are more than that. *We are the first men of a Future* that has not materialized. We belong to a 'great age' that has not 'come off.' We moved too quickly for the world. We set too sharp a pace. And, more and more exhausted by the War, Slump and Revolution, the world has *fallen back.*"

The following year, in a postscript to the now defunct movement, Pound wrote a letter to the editor of *Reedy's Mirror,* July 30, 1916, correcting a misstatement which had appeared in the journal:

". . . I am not 'the head of the vorticist movement.' . . . As an active and informal association it might be said that Lewis supplied the volcanic force, Brzeska the animal energy, and perhaps that I had contributed to certain Confucian calm and reserve."

The "Confucian calm and reserve" of which Pound speaks were hardly evident in *Blast,* one of the most daring publications with which he was associated. He made some pertinent comments on form in the letter to *Reedy's Mirror:*

". . . The great mass of mankind are ignorant of the shape of nearly everything that they see or handle. The artisan knows the shape of some of his tools. You know the shape of your pen-handle but hardly the shape of your typewriter. The store of forms in the average man's head is smaller than his meager verbal vocabulary."

VI

THE FIRST WORLD WAR was a great psychic shock to a Europe that had known many years of peace. The subsequent blood-letting removed France and England from the scene as world powers. As Pound has often pointed out, it also broke up a process that had been continuously at work since the dissolution of the Holy Roman Empire. A young, bewildered and pathetically ill-prepared America emerged as the heir of Western civilization, as so often happens after a regicide.

Pound also was deeply shocked by the war. Never again would he be content to be merely an artist. In a brief autobiography prefixed to the New Directions volume of *Selected Poems* (1949), he stated that "In 1918 began investigation of causes of war, to oppose same."

The English writers and artists, almost to a man, rushed into the fray. Pound remained in London, for American sentiment, we should remember, remained equally balanced between pro-German and pro-British sympathies, until George Sylvester Viereck's inept pro-German propaganda pushed the Americans into the British camp.

Wyndham Lewis, seriously ill with septicemia, had to wait nearly a year before he was sufficiently recovered to go off to the slaughter. Ford enlisted, after a farewell party given for him at South Lodge that ended badly.

102

Another of Pound's friends, the painter Augustus John, enlisted as a major and headed for the front. His striking resemblance to King George V caused consternation whenever his staff
car drove into a new area. As he was rather fond of the grape,
he sometimes wondered what all the commotion was about. One
of the wits of London, he had startled Oliver St. John Gogarty
when that worthy asked him what his hobby was. "Converting
Lesbians," John had replied.

Iris Barry reports that the young people of London were not
enthusiastic about the war.[1] They had grown up during a time
when war, though often discussed, had ceased to be a reality.
Now it was a reality once more, and uncomfortably near. One by
one, they were caught in its maelstrom.

Despite his dwindling circle of acquaintances, Pound was busy
as usual. He had written to his mother in November, 1913, ". . .
I seem to spend most of my time attending to other people's
affairs, weaning young poetettes from obscurity into the glowing
pages of divers rotten publications, etc. Besieging the Home Office
to let that ass K_____ stay in the country for his own good if
not for its."[2]

Later, in an article in *Esquire,* of January, 1935, Ford recalled
that Pound had once asked him to help young Harry Kemp, an
American who had gotten into some scrape in London and was
about to be deported. Together, they went to see the American
Ambassador, Walter Hines Page, who, after hearing their story,
hemmed and said that he would have to wait for instructions from
Washington.

As they left the Embassy, Ford remarked, "An English Ambassador wouldn't have done much, but he would have done
something." They went to the Home Office, where Ford was well-
acquainted, and Kemp was permitted to remain in England. He
later wrote books about being a tramp.

Pound spent much of his time on errands of this sort, and
when many Americans were stranded in London at the outbreak
of hostilities, he rushed around to get them lodgings and funds.
He also kept up his chores on *The Egoist,* although the cause of
suffragism no longer attracted much attention.

He contributed a column of amusing quotes, culled from the

Times, to each issue. Pound was fond of such gems as "It is no new thing to discover how much may be gleaned from well-harvested fields by a skilful and patient toiler." He described this activity in the British *Who's Who* of 1914 under the heading of "Recreation: Combing the *Times* for evidences of almost incredible stupidity." He later shortened this to "Recreation: the public taste", and so it has remained for many years.

Pound's enthusiasm for Miss Monroe's magazine, *Poetry,* had waned considerably. He was sufficiently disgusted to offer his resignation as foreign editor in 1913, but, as he wrote to Amy Lowell in January, 1914, "they axed me back."[3]

He encountered increasing difficulty in persuading Miss Monroe to print the poems of his "discoveries". She was relying more heavily on local talent, which was even more discouraging in 1914 than now. Pound sent her Eliot's "The Love Song of J. Alfred Prufrock" in October, 1914, with an enthusiastic note, "Hope you'll get it in soon."

Months went by and Eliot's poem did not appear, although Miss Monroe continued to print the dross of the Midwest. At last, Pound could no longer hold his temper, and in May, 1915, he sent her a sharp note which began with this comment on the April, 1915 issue: "My gawddd! This is a rotten number of Poetry!"[4]

The Eliot poem subsequently appeared in the June, 1915 issue.

By this time, Pound had become a legendary name in the United States. Although his books of poems had been sold in small numbers, and not very widely read, he was the most discussed poet of the time. Then, as now, many more writers and critics talked about his work than actually read it. Mention of his name was always good for a violent argument between his protagonists and his detractors, who at that time were about equal in number.

William Carlos Williams remained his steadfast friend during this period. He wrote to Miss Monroe on May 8, 1915, "You know, there are people who find Ezra Pound chiefly notable as a target—and yet they can't perceive his greatness. . . . One perceives, however, that it is knowledge and not Ezra Pound that is so held—the confusion is, of course, inevitable under the circumstances."[5]

On March 23, 1918, he wrote to Marianne Moore, "If there is one thing that stands out clearly above Ezra's other perfections, it is his unswerving intelligence in the detection of literary quality."[6]

H. L. Mencken blew hot and cold about Pound, as he did about most things. His remark on Pound was, "Ezra Pound?—the American in headlong flight from America—a professor turned fantee, Abelard in grand opera."[7]

Carl Sandburg made his position on Pound clear in the February, 1916 issue of *Poetry,* saying, in part, "If I were driven to name one individual who, in the English language, by means of his own example of creative art in poetry, has done most of living men to incite new impulses in poetry, the chances are I would name Ezra Pound."

Iris Barry has given us a very memorable picture of Pound in London, as she knew him there in 1916. She writes, "Pound talks like no one else. His is almost a wholly original accent, the base of American mingled with a dozen assorted 'English society' and Cockney accents inserted in mockery, French, Spanish and Greek exclamations, strange cries and catcalls, the whole very oddly inflected, with dramatic pauses and diminuendoes."

Of his wife, she says, "With him came Mrs. Pound, carrying herself delicately with the air, always, of a young Victorian lady out skating, and a profile as clear and lovely as that of a porcelain Kuan-yin."[8] Four decades later, Dorothy Pound still carries herself as nobly as she did when Iris Barry knew her in London.

Miss Barry describes others of the London circle, during what she terms the "Ezra Pound period"—Violet Hunt, who complained that one of her chores was to pick snails off the Gaudier bust of Ezra which was sinking in her garden; Miss Harriet Weaver, the publisher of *The Egoist,* who was as stiff and severe as a bishop's daughter (Iris Barry says that she could hardly think of her as the one who first printed Joyce's *Ulysses*); Mrs. Strindberg, the cabaret proprietor, with her little troop of pet monkeys; and the very civilized Edmund Dulac, who had a Chinese signature stamp for Ezra so that he could sign his letters in an Eastern mode.

Although the winter of 1915–16 was the last in which Pound fulfilled the role of secretary for Yeats, he was soon involved in another project. Yeats wrote to his father on March 5, 1916,

"I am handing the letters over to Ezra Pound, who is to make a small volume of selections for Lollie's press. I thought he would make the selection better than I should. I am almost too familiar with the thought, and also that his approval representing as he does the most aggressive contemporary school of the young would be of greater value than my approval, which would seem perhaps but family feeling. It will also enable me to have a new book for Lollie sooner than if I did the work myself, as I should be busy writing something else and my sight makes my work slow."[9]

The handsome little volume, *Passages from the Letters of John Butler Yeats to William Butler Yeats, Selected by Ezra Pound,* appeared under the Cuala Press imprint in 1917. A "collector's item", it is printed "on paper made in Ireland", in an edition of four hundred copies. Although a complete edition of the John Butler Yeats letters appeared a few years later, Pound selected so well that this smaller book contains the gist of his outlook. There are many such gems as the following:

"Nov. 1914. The war will last until the money gives out, and poetry and art will never cease while life lasts.[10]

"Aug. 27, 1915. Democracy *devours* its poets and artists . . . Religion is only a vehicle, a splendid or impressive machinery where a man can stage his thoughts.[11]

"Dec. 26, 1912. I see Americans as impulsive as schoolgirls and as changeable as an April sky, always attractive for that reason, yet constantly disappointing because without principle. . . . The Puritans made the momentous discovery that human nature was in itself bad and for its sins condemned to eternal death; after that came commerce. The merchant who did not adopt this dogma and believe all men bad would end in bankruptcy.[12]

"Jan. 6, 1916. In America they make war on solitude."[13]

John Butler Yeats made an interesting comment on Pound in a letter to "Willie", May 31, 1921: "Love striking back can be as fierce as the moralists—in fact having few friends and its situation desperate it will strike murderously—and be venomous and obscene—forgetting all prudence, be more anxious to find enemies than friends—and be in fact love in a temper and write like Ezra Pound and his friends, very shocking to their well-wishers, myself, for instance, who am old and timid."[14]

The friendship between Yeats and Pound continued until the older man's death in 1939. In 1917, Pound was best man at Yeats' wedding, just as Yeats had served him three years before. In the last chapter of his long passion for Maud Gonne, Yeats had pursued her to Paris. Rebuffed once more, he fell in love with her beautiful adopted niece, Iseult. Iseult was taken with Yeats, and considered accepting his proposal, but at last she refused him.

When Yeats returned to London, he was much in the company of the Pounds and their friend, Miss Georgie Hyde-Lees. He had known her since 1911, and she shared many of his interests, including his enthusiasm for spiritualism. He proposed and was accepted. He was fifty-two; his bride was twenty-six.

Dorothy Pound went with her friend to post the banns in London; she recalls that the usually poised young lady was extraordinarily nervous that day. During his honeymoon, Yeats wrote his occult work, *The Vision* (1925).

On August 1, 1921, Yeats wrote to Olivia Shakespear, "Have you been reading me in the *Mercury?* I am afraid Ezra will not forgive me for publishing there: he had recommended the *English Review* but I have just as fierce a quarrel with that periodical as he has with the *Mercury,* so what could I do?"[15]

At this time, Pound fell heir to a new publication in which he could air his more pronounced likes and dislikes. This was *The Little Review,* which had first appeared in Chicago in March, 1914. It was financed and edited by Margaret Anderson. The *Review's* motto was "A magazine of the arts, making no compromise with the public taste." Assisting Miss Anderson was Jane Heap.

When her father died, Miss Anderson found that his affairs

had not been in order. She was penniless. After selling her furniture, she continued to live in the bare apartment. Nevertheless, she was able to bring out the magazine on a more or less regular basis.

She moved to San Francisco, and in September, 1916, produced an issue with many blank pages, because she found nothing worth printing. This set an excellent example for her contemporaries, but none of them were moved to emulate it. The blank pages, she said, comprised a "want ad" to let able contributors know that she was in need of material. Such a gesture could not escape Pound's eagle eye, and in 1917, he became the *Review's* unsalaried foreign editor, having once again parted company with Miss Monroe. He suggested a new motto, which was immediately adopted—"The magazine that is read by those who write the others."[16]

With this new vehicle, which was now being published in New York, Pound got into print several projects that he had been planning for years. Among them was a special Henry James number, in homage to the master. He also brought out a French number, presenting the latest French poets in the original.

One of his first pieces appeared in the May, 1917 number, a parting salvo to an old alliance. *"Poetry* (magazine)," he wrote, "has shown an unflagging courtesy to a lot of old fools and fogies whom I should have told to go to hell tout pleinement and bonnement. . . . There is no misanthropy in a thorough contempt for the mob. There is no respect for mankind save in detached individuals."

This last sentence is especially important, inasmuch as the terrible accusation has been levelled against Ezra that he has been a practitioner of group prejudice. Yet here he is stating definitely that he accepts people only as individuals, not as members of a group, a flat rejection of stereotyped racial attitudes.

One of Pound's best short pieces, "Advice to a Young Poet", also appeared in *The Little Review*. He said, in part, "Mastering an art does not consist in trying to bluff people. Work shows; there is no substitute for it; holding one theory or another doesn't in the least get a man over the difficulty."[17]

Pound enlisted Wyndham Lewis and others of his circle as contributors to the *Review*. Lewis wrote some rather strong pieces for the magazine, and, in the October, 1917 issue, Pound noted that some objections had been raised:

"There was also a lady or mother who wrote to me (personally) from New Jersey, asking me to stop the magazine as Lewis' writings were 'bad for her milk.' (I'm afraid there is no way of softening her phrase for our readers.) Madame, what you need is lactol and not literature. You should apply to a druggist."

Lewis wrote a series of "Imaginary Letters" for *The Little Review,* and Pound was moved to disagree with some of his sentiments, and to answer him with a like series. Some of Pound's most edged statements are found in these letters, which were collected and published by Caresse Crosby in 1930, in Paris, under the imprint of the Black Sun Press. Excerpts follow:

"I. Walter Villerant to Mrs. Bland Burn.

. . . I am, with qualifications, Malthusian. I should consent to breed under pressure, if I were convinced in any way of the reasonableness of reproducing the species. But my nerves and the nerves of any woman I could live with three months, would produce only a victim—beautiful perhaps, but a victim; expiring of aromatic pain from the jasmine, lacking in impulse, a mere bundle of discriminations. . . .

"There is no truce between art and the public. The public celebrates its eucharists with dead bodies. Its writers aspire to equal the oyster; to get themselves swallowed alive, thus encompass it. Art that sells on production is bad art, essentially. It is art made to demand. It suits the public. The taste of the public is bad. The taste of the public is always bad. It is bad because it is not an individual expression, but merely a mania for assent, a mania to be 'in on it.' . . . Even the botches of a good artist have some quality, some distinction, which prevents their pleasing mass palates . . . this nonsense about art for the many, for the majority. J'en ai marre. It may be fitting that men should enjoy equal 'civic and political rights'; these things are a matter of man's external acts, of exterior contacts. (Machiavelli

believed in democracy: it lay beyond his experience.) The arts
have nothing to do with this. They are man's life within himself.
The king's writ does not run there."[18]

It is interesting to note that, although the king's writ does not
carry, or should not carry, into the realm of art, the writ of democracy makes no bones about plunging into this area. This explains
the fact that Ezra Pound has been the most persecuted artist of our
time.

"II. Walter Villerant to Mrs. Bland Burn.

My dear Lydia

We are surrounded by livestock. I enjoy certain animal contacts . . . without malice. I have a 'nice disposition.' I pat them
like so many retrievers . . . ebbene? I live as a man among
herds . . . for which I have a considerate, or at least considerable, if misplaced affection."

"IV. Walter Villerant to the ex-Mrs. Burn.

My dear Lydia

Stupidity is a pest, a bacillus, an infection; a raging lion that
does not stay in one place but perambulates. When two fools
meet, a third springs up instanter between them, a composite
worse than either begetter. We see the young of both sexes, and
of your sex which is the more fluid, sunk into amalgams, into
domestic and communal amalgams.

"I call on the sisters Randall, they are in the studio next to
their own, seeking companionship. I am deluged with a half-
hour's inanity, breezy, cheerful inanity, replies that were 'bright'
in '92, replies that are modelled upon the replies in short stories.
People imagine that to speak suddenly, and without thinking beforehand, is to be brilliant. It feels so, the elder Faxton wrote
stories that would have been daring, in the days of Ibsen's ado-
lescence. The Soeurs Randall return to their studio, a brace of
callers is waiting. I am deluged again with inanity, bright, cheery
inanity. I flee waving metaphorical arms like a windmill.

"Because of amalgams, Bohemias are worth avoiding, the poor

ones are like pools full of frogs eggs, and hordes of these globules perish annually. I mean they merge into suburbias."[19]

It seems that suburbias were already a problem, or at least a matter for discussion, in Europe four decades ago. This illustrates the time-lag of which Ezra speaks in comparing Europe and America.

"There is a certain propriety," Pound continues, "a certain fastidiousness of the mind. The old Slautzer used to mutter in the face of the British scrubbed-clean nutocracy. We accepted her because she had once lived with a certain Viennese artist. She even passed for, and may have been actually, one of his various wives. That was her passport. She must have had some intelligence or he would not have stood her a week. She mumbled, she was hard to understand. I, on the whole, have very little to tell of her, but I can still hear her saying, as she waved a guardsman away from her table: 'No, no, vot I say to dese people. Vot, I will sleep vit you. Yes, I will sleep vit you. It iss nossing. But talk to you half an hour? Neffair! Vun musst traw de line SOMMEFVERE! ! '

"This fastidiousness of the mind, my dear Lydia, is something which I will recommend to you. The old Slautzer did not attain it on all planes . . . notably on the plane of her fingernails. And she never opened a window, or permitted one to be opened, and she wore a greasy (but rich, very rich) fur-coat, indoors, out-of-doors, all the time.

"There were certain things in her favour. But for constant immersion in second-rate conversation there is no extenuation whatever."[20]

"No. VI. No, my dear Caroline
    Russians! Am I never to hear the last of these Russians! I have shut up the esteemed and estimable William, and now you take up the pillows.

"The Russian (large R. definite article, Artzibasheff, Busti-kosseff, Slobingobski, Spititoutski and Co. Amalgamated, com-munutated, etc.). 'The Russian,' my dear Caroline, is nothing but the western European with his conning-tower, or his top-layer, or his upper-story, or his control-board removed. As neither the governed French, nor Englishman (undermined by sentimentality, but still sailing on ballast), nor the automatic American, barge about in this rudderless fashion, one makes comparisons with the Russian 'elan,' Russian 'vigour,' etc.

"Civilized man, *any* civilized man who has a normal lining to his stomach, may become Russian for the price of a little mixed alcohol, or of, perhaps, a good deal of mixed alcohol, but it is a matter of shillings, not a matter of dynamic attainment.

"Once, and perhaps only once, have I been drunk enough to feel like a Russian. Try it, my dear young lady, try it. Try it and clear the mind, free your life from this obsession of Russia (if Lenin & Co. have not freed you). . . . I have fathomed the Russians."[21]

"No. VIII. My dear Imogene [On Baudelaire]
    The stuff looks more vigorous than it is. . . . As indeed bad graphic art often looks more skillful than it is. . . . Passions . . ."[22]

An excellent example of this is the work of Dylan Thomas, who used his bellows lungs to pump up miniatures of sun and wheat and sky until they seemed quite impressive. His name came up once, and only once in our conversations, and Ezra dismissed him as "a good third-rater".

As Pound began to exercise a dominant voice in *The Little Review,* the same criers of doom who had pursued him on *Poetry* took up his scent once more. By 1918, the letters of complaint were flowing in. One, who concealed herself behind the signature of "An old Reader", said, in part,

". . . . The Ezras know too much. Their minds are black, scarcely smoldering logs. They are yogis. . . . But it is Ezra who sprawls all over the Little Review and bedecks it with gargoyles."[23]

Now Jane Heap, no mean ally, took up the cudgels in Ezra's defense. She wrote, "Judging from reverberations a great many people suffer loudly and continually over Mr. Pound. Harriet Monroe isn't the first to tell us that the Little Review is under the dictatorship of Pound. Our idea of having a foreign correspondent is not to sit in our New York office and mess up, censor, or throw out work sent us by our editor in London. We have let Ezra Pound be our foreign editor in the only way we see it. We have let him be as foreign as he likes: foreign to taste, foreign to courtesy, foreign to our standards of Art. All because we believe in the fundamental idea back of our correspondence with Mr. Pound: the interest and value of an intellectual communication between Europe and America. If anyone can tell us of a more untiring, efficient, better-equipped poet to take over the foreign office, let us hear from him. I have had countless letters from Jews, Letts, Greeks, Finns, Irish, etc. protesting against Mr. Pound's ignorance and discrimination. I have answered that this is always true of mushroom nations: the fixed imperception of the qualities and cultures of all other nations."[24]

One of the more interesting aspects of running an off-beat, experimental, or radical magazine is that the editor is constantly besieged by protests from offended readers. This is as true in 1961 as it was in 1918.

Not all of the subscribers to *The Little Review* demanded Pound's head. Witter Bynner, one of Ezra's first boosters, wrote in to say that "Pound has a rhythm he can't kill."[25]

Lola Ridge contributed an interesting tidbit to the same issue called "Ezra's Mind", in which she said, ". . . There is something about Pound's vituperations that savors of not too remote gutters—and coal stalls and tongues akimbo and herrings obvious in a rising temperature. I've sometimes felt like saying something like this out loud but—I'm frugal! And then he's done lovely things and I admire his cold shining thin-glass mind through which so many colors pass leaving no stain—and then—my stone-arm balks at swinging in rhythm with the mob's."

Ezra was soon chafing at his inability to exercise more control over the magazine. Although Margaret Anderson was much more prompt in printing the gems that he sent her from Europe, she was little better than Miss Monroe when it came to judging the work of her American contributors. In a letter printed in the July, 1918 issue, Ezra wrote,

"My net value to the concern appears to be about $2350; of which over $2000 does not 'accrue' to the protagonist. It may be argued with some subtlety that I make the limited public an annual present of that sum for the privilege of giving them what they do not much want, and for, let us say, forcing upon them a certain amount of literature, and a certain amount of enlightened criticism. This donation I have willingly made, and as willingly repeat, but I can not be expected to keep it up for an indefinite period. . . . It is bad economy for me to spend a morning tying up stray copies of the Little Review for posting, or in answering queries as to why last month's number had not arrived. This function could be carried out by a deputy, almost by an infant. It is not that I desire to 'get' such a lot as that I decline to have my own work (such as it is) smothered by executive functions. And unless said functions can relieve me of the necessity of writing ephemeral stuff for other papers I shall be compelled to relinquish them. Or, still more baldly, I cannot write six sorts of journalism four days a week, edit the Little Review three days a week, and continue my career as an author. . . . So that, roughly speaking, either the Little Review will have to provide me with the necessities of life and a reasonable amount of leisure by May 1, 1919, or I shall have to apply my energies elsewhere."

Margaret Anderson published this letter in the hopes that some subscriber would see fit to underwrite a salary for Ezra, but none was forthcoming. In giving her almost a year to meet this ultimatum, Ezra showed that he was not so desperate for the money as he was annoyed by the clerical tasks and the difficulty in keeping the *Review* up to his standards.

The Egoist ceased publication in 1919; Ezra had finally severed relations with all three of his female-dominated outlets. As he mentioned above, he was busy with a few regular writing chores. Since 1912, he had been writing on economics for *The New Age,* a very advanced socialist newspaper, which printed some good things. This paper, published by A. E. Orage, was distinct from Fabian socialism or the other garden varieties, in that it proposed genuine reforms.

Orage later became an enthusiastic follower of Gurdjieff, and sat in on his classes in Greenwich Village, as did Henry Wallace.

This information reached Westbrook Pegler in somewhat garbled form, and he supposed that Ezra too had had something to do with Wallace's "guru" period, and that he had been locked up to keep from telling what he knew about the lunatic government officials in Washington. But Ezra had no connection with the "guru", nor with Orage during his Gurdjieff days. He did lunch with Wallace in 1939, when he came over to try to prevent the Second World War, but the "peace luncheon" failed in its purpose.

From 1917–20, Pound contributed a column, "Art Notes", under the pseudonym "B. H. Dias", to *The New Age;* from 1917–21, as "William Atheling", he wrote "Music", a review of events in the musical world. Those who sneer at his knowledge of music do not know that he was a respected music critic in England for four years.

Orage had come a cropper by printing a strong editorial on the Friday before England went into the war, in which he said that there positively would be no war. The threat of hostilities was simply a capitalist romp to play with the stock market. He later realized that a genuine war provides the speculators with even more opportunities to play with the stock market than the threat of one.

Pound also published an article in *The New Masses,* June 28, 1915. He has been called a Fascist because some of his writings appeared in pro-Fascist journals. Perhaps we should now call him a Communist because of *The New Masses* effort. This article, entitled "The damn fool bureaukrats", was the first public expression of his discovery that government officials are every whit as dangerous villains as are other stock types, such as bankers and munitions-makers.

As Wyndham Lewis had foreseen, Pound's luck was running out with the English. He had begun to look across the channel to Paris, where world attention had focused. The Great War was over, and the manipulators had gathered to commit a worse crime, which Ezra defines as "ending one war so as to make another one inevitable."[26]

Sisley Huddleston, later a member of Pound's Paris coterie, and Paris correspondent for the *Times,* soon dismissed Versailles as *"panem et circenses."* The victors paraded down the Champs

Élysées; Wilson arrived on the scene with a vacant grin already
tugging at his somber mouth; and the old order was suitably
buried. It was a schoolboy farce in which three precocious off-
spring of Europe capered about, sniggering at the gaucheries,
pretensions and hallucinations of their American classmate, while
the Germans sat impatiently in the wings, waiting for their cue to
come on stage again.

Pound's growing disaffection with the English was stimulated
by an incident over one of his pet dislikes, John Milton. Pound
considered Lascelles Abercrombie, of *The Times Literary Supplement,* a symbol of all that he opposed in modern poetry. Abercrombie was the leader of the Georgian group of poets, which had
grown steadily in influence, and had even enlisted D. H. Lawrence
in one of their annuals. Abercrombie started a magazine, *New
Numbers,* which proved very successful, and his successive anthologies of *Georgian Poetry* became best sellers. The reason was
simple. He had worked with Rupert Brooke, Wilfrid Gibson, and
other war poets who obligingly got themselves killed. An inevitable reaction to the horrors of modern warfare was a sort of
literary shellshock, a wallowing in sentimental slush, such as
inundated the United States during both World Wars (pass the
ammunition, Pops, or whatever!).

The mounting Poundian rage at this tendency, which was sweeping away his few accomplishments in England, was accelerated
when Abercrombie published an article in praise of Milton in *The
Times Literary Supplement.* He fired off a letter, challenging
Abercrombie to a duel.

There are several versions of the reaction. Ford insists that
Abercrombie, knowing that Pound was an accomplished fencer,
was genuinely frightened, and that he went to the police. Dueling
had long been outlawed, and the statutes now listed a challenge to
such an affair as engaging in conspiracy to commit a murder. The
police went to Pound, says Ford, and shortly thereafter Pound
removed to France.

Another and perhaps more accurate version (we should not
condemn Ford if he prefers the picture of Pound fleeing England
with Scotland Yard detectives in full pursuit) is that Abercrombie,

taking advantage of the fact that the challenged party has the choice of weapons, suggested that the two authors bombard each other with unsold copies of their books. In any case, Ezra, with invective suitable for the occasion, left the country where he had spent the last twelve years, and became a resident of Paris.

VII

ONE OF POUND'S most fruitful relationships was his work with James Joyce. In this case, he did little or no editing, and had few personal contacts with the writer. The connection consisted, essentially, of Pound's unflagging sponsorship of Joyce's work over a period of ten years, 1914–24. It was during this period that Joyce did his important work, and that his reputation was made.

In 1913, William Butler Yeats had called Pound's attention to some poems by James Joyce as being worthy of inclusion in the *Des Imagistes* anthology, which Pound was compiling. Pound liked the work, and entered into correspondence with the poet. Soon afterward, Joyce sent him the first chapters of *Portrait of the Artist as a Young Man* (1916). They were enthusiastically received, for Pound at once realized that the contributor was a writer who was trying to do a great deal; and in art, effort is half the battle.

Pound did not always accept Joyce's work as flawless in execution, particularly some parts of *Ulysses* (1922), and he balked at *Finnegan's Wake* (1939); but the mission had been accomplished. One of the most advanced, and most difficult, writers of the twentieth century had been launched.

In the January 15, 1914, issue of *The Egoist,* Pound devoted his weekly book review column to citing Joyce's ten-year struggle to get *Dubliners* (1916) printed. Joyce had found one publisher willing to bring out the book, but he had backed out, in violation of his agreement. Like most writers, particularly those of integrity, Joyce was plagued throughout his life by difficulties with publishers. The most fortunate writer is one who has a Jekyll and Hyde personality, and who, after doing his work, can slip into another personality, in order to deal with publishers on their own terms.

Ulysses was issued in a pirated and botched edition in New York by Samuel Roth, who has been a guest of the government at Lewisburg Prison. He was prosecuted unsuccessfully for his robbery of Joyce, but he has lost several other cases, the charge being one of sending "pornography" through the mails. In defense of Roth, it is worthwhile to point out that the material that got him his latest prison sentence, a tale from the classics, is not so obscene as the periodicals that can be purchased on any newsstand.

Pound began the serialization of *Portrait of the Artist as a Young Man* in the February 2, 1914 number of *The Egoist*. In the July 15, 1914 issue, he commented in a review of *Dubliners*, "Mr. Joyce writes a clear, hard prose . . . these stories and the novel now appearing in serial form are such as to win for Mr. Joyce a very definite place among contemporary English writers."

Just as Pound's "Henry James" number of *The Little Review* provided first serious recognition of that writer, and the basis for the development of the "James cult", so Pound's review of *Dubliners* constituted the first public recognition of Joyce, and the means for launching his career.

Whenever Pound began a campaign to promote a new writer, it was much like the advance of a medieval army, with colorful banners, salvoes of rockets, and great beating of drums. Despite the continuous fusillades, casualties were few, but the spectacle was enormously diverting. Pound employed devious strategies as well as frontal assaults in his endeavours to "put over" his candidates. Among the beneficiaries of such campaigns have been T. S. Eliot, Robert Frost, George Antheil, and many others.

In March, 1914, Pound wrote to Miss Amy Lowell that D. H. Lawrence and James Joyce were "the two strongest prose writers among les jeunes."[1]

In his introduction to *The Letters of James Joyce,* Stuart Gilbert writes, ". . . There is no question of the importance of the part played by Mr. Pound—and by *'The Egoist'* magazine with which he was so closely and dynamically associated—in bringing Joyce's work to the notice of the more literate public . . . In a letter dated Aug. 13, 1913, Mr. Pound informed Miss Harriet Monroe that he had taken charge of the literary department of the magazine. In December of the same year he mentioned in a letter to Mr. William Carlos Williams that the *'New Freewoman'* was now to go as *'The Egoist.'* The 'official' change of title took place Jan. 1, 1914. In the course of the year Miss Marsden asked Miss Weaver to take charge of the editing of the magazine, on the practical and business side, and thanks not a little to Miss Weaver's energy and enthusiasm, *'The Egoist'* made literary history in that eventful period 1914–19. Many years later, in a letter to Mr. John Drummond, May 30, 1934, Mr. Pound emphasized the importance of the part played by Miss Weaver in the literary activities of the magazine. He wrote, 'HW deserves well of the nation and *never turned away* anything good. Also the few articles she wrote were full of good sense. She amply deserves Eliot's dedication of whatever book it was (*Selected Essays 1917–32*).' "[2]

Learning that Joyce was hard-pressed for money, Pound decided to obtain for him a grant from England's Royal Literary Fund. The officials of such organizations seem to grant money to writers only on two conditions—first, that the supplicant does not need it, and second, that he will never write anything worthwhile. Not only did the case of Joyce violate both of these precepts, but Pound was already *persona non grata* at that agency.

Pound's strategy in this instance was to deploy himself behind three of England's leading literary personalities, approaching the unsuspecting victim in the sheep's clothing of respectability. He chose as his agents William Butler Yeats, Edmund Gosse, and George Moore. His awareness of the fine points of military action, those little details that so often decide the day, is illustrated by the manner in which he handled this sally. Realizing that a single appeal, signed by three men, however eminent, might not carry the day for Joyce, he approached each of them separately. The secretary of the Royal Literary Fund soon received, not one, but three individual appeals from important writers for the relief of James Joyce. The cleverness of this approach obtained for a largely unknown and little-published writer the sum of one hundred pounds in 1915, sufficient to support him for a year.

In this connection, Yeats wrote on July 29, 1915, to the secretary of the Royal Literary Fund, ". . . if more particulars are needed you could perhaps get them from Mr. Ezra Pound, 5 Holland Place Chambers, who has been in fairly constant correspondence with Mr. Joyce and arranged for the publication of his latest book. I think Mr. Joyce has a most beautiful gift."[3]

So intense were Pound's efforts on behalf of this new protégé that he was determined to run chapters of *Ulysses* simultaneously in *The Little Review* and *The Egoist.* However, this project was abandoned when no English printers could be found who were willing to set type for the *Ulysses* chapters.

In a full-page advertisement in her magazine, Margaret Anderson announced the receipt of the first three installments of James Joyce's new novel, *Ulysses:* "So far it has been read by only one critic of international reputation [Ezra Pound]. He says: 'It is certainly worth running a magazine if one can get stuff like this to put in it. Compression, intensity. It looks to me rather better than Flaubert.' This announcement means that we are about to publish a prose masterpiece."[4]

Immodest and suspect though any such statement might sound from an editor, Margaret Anderson was correct. *Ulysses* has been one of the most widely-discussed—if not read—novels of the twentieth century. Yeats wrote to Olivia Shakespear on June 28, 1923,

"I have asked Joyce to come and stay for a few days. If he comes I shall have to use the utmost ingenuity to hide the fact that I have never finished 'Ulysses'."[5]

The novel ran for three years in *The Little Review,* although the United States Post Office burned four issues of the magazine because of the book's alleged obscenity. Margaret Anderson and Jane Heap were arrested at the instigation of the Society for the Suppression of Vice, but failed to benefit financially by the free advertising.

Ulysses soon became the focal point of one of those waves of popular indignation that periodically sweep across the United

States, leaving shattered lives and homes in their wake. The inevitable profiteers moved in to take advantage of the publicity, and smuggled or pirated copies of *Ulysses* brought prices of two hundred dollars and three hundred dollars. One enthusiast paid a top price of five hundred dollars.

The basis of this inflation was the book's supposed pornography. Neither Joyce nor Pound received any profits in this trade. Despite the million dollars worth of free advertising (surpassed in American publishing history only by the artificial furor over a dull novel by Bore-us Pasternak), there were not many copies of the book available. When Roth published a hastily-edited and botched version of *Ulysses,* Joyce was unable to obtain satisfaction in the courts.

The New York *Times Book Review* refused to mention the book, and Burton Rascoe, editor of the New York *Herald Tribune Book Review,* later tried to squirm out of his guilt in banning mention of *Ulysses* by saying that he had understood that Margaret Anderson had printed an early version, and that he was waiting for the final draft to appear before criticizing it. As Margaret Anderson says in her autobiography, this is bosh.

England's dean of literary critics, the eminent Sir Edmund Gosse, now entered the lists against Joyce, perhaps in remembered anger that he had been "had" by Pound when he was persuaded to sponsor the grant from the Royal Literary Fund. On June 7, 1924, he wrote to Louis Gillet, editor of the influential Parisian journal *Revue des Deux Mondes,*

"I should very much regret you paying Mr. Joyce the compliment of an article in the *Revue des Deux Mondes.* You could only express the worthlessness and impudence of his writing and surely it would be a mistake to give him this prominence. I have difficulty in describing to you, in *writing,* the character of Mr. Joyce's morality. . . . he is a literary charlatan of the extremest order. His principal book, *Ulysses,* has no parallel that I know of in France. It is an anarchical production, infamous in taste, in style, in everything. . . . He is a sort of M. de Sade, but does not write so well. . . . There are no English critics of weight or judgment who consider Mr. Joyce an author of any importance."[6]

Sir Edmund neglected to add that the English critics of weight and judgment at that time consisted of Arnold Bennett, AE (George Russell), and himself. Of these three dictators, dead set against the tide in one of the most brilliant periods of literary history, T. S. Eliot wrote in *Horizon,* March, 1941, "None of them could lay claim to any authority as a critic."

By this he meant that not one of the three had written any body of work that stated a system or theory of literary effort. Gosse's reviews show a limitation of taste that is a parody of the term "Victorian" when used in its derogatory sense.

When Oscar Wilde was sent to prison, not only was Gosse among his loudest detractors, but he forbade his house to Robert Ross, one of the few Wilde acquaintances who refused to denounce his friend. Yet Gosse represented the final word in English criticism for many years. With his associates, AE and Arnold Bennett, he could make or break any writer. Pound saw that he was facing the same situation that had driven him from the United States, where *The Blue Flower* was the poetic gospel of the time.

Wyndham Lewis recounts the story of an expedition on which Pound sent him and Eliot in the summer of 1920. Eliot was entrusted with a mysterious bundle, heavily wrapped, which he was admonished to deliver personally into Joyce's hands, and to no one else. Although the emissaries were curious as to what the package might contain, they did not open it. When they arrived in Paris, and delivered it, they sat back impatiently while it was being unwrapped. As he delved through many layers of paper, Joyce was as mystified as the couriers. At last he brought up from the considerable debris a pair of dilapidated brown shoes, which Pound had thought he could wear.

At the time, says Lewis, Joyce was wearing a new pair of patent leather pumps, which had been polished to a mirror-like smoothness.[7] Despite his life-long poverty, he had expensive tastes, and whenever he obtained any money, he spent it on living well, a not altogether reprehensible trait. His reputation for extravagance sometimes hindered his friends from helping him, or at least afforded them an excuse.

From 1914 through 1924, Pound's name was mentioned in almost every one of Joyce's published letters. He wrote to Yeats on September 14, 1916, "I can never thank you enough for having brought me into relations with your friend Ezra Pound who is indeed a wonder worker."[8]

Pound often compared Joyce's use of language with the talent of Flaubert, one of his lasting enthusiasms. In the *Mercure de France,* of June, 1922, Pound sustained this comparison in a lengthy article, which did much to establish Joyce's reputation in France and to make it possible for him to live there.

Joyce wrote to Harriet Weaver on April 10, 1922, "Mr. Larbaud's article has caused a great deal of stir here and there will be another by Mr. Pound in the Mercure on the 15th instant. Mr. Pound has been engaged in a long wordy war with Mr. Shaw over Ulysses. They exchanged about a dozen letters in all. Mr. Shaw has now closed the correspondence by writing, 'I take care of the pence because the pounds won't take care of themselves.' "[9]

In addition to Harriet Weaver, whom Oliver St. John Gogarty credits with having established a one hundred and fifty thousand dollar trust fund for Joyce's grandchild, Pound also put Joyce in touch with John Quinn, a New York lawyer who assisted many writers of the period. In 1917, Pound persuaded Quinn to buy the corrected proof sheets of *Ulysses* for twenty pounds. Quinn also represented *The Little Review* in the court action brought by the Society for Suppression of Vice. He purchased the manuscript of *Ulysses* from Joyce for two hundred dollars, and later sold it to the book dealer, Dr. A. S. W. Rosenbach, for nineteen hundred and seventy-five dollars.

Apparently he intended to turn over part of this windfall to Joyce, but he suffered financial reverses. At Joyce's instigation, he was trying to buy the manuscript back at the time of his death. Gogarty says that Quinn had given the two hundred dollars to Joyce to pay for a desperately needed operation on his eyes, and that Joyce had let him have the manuscript as security. In one of his letters, Joyce quips that "Dr. Rosybrook bought a weatherbeaten timetable for $150,000 in London."[10]

Samuel Roth's pirated edition of *Ulysses* sold an estimated forty thousand copies in the United States, and he announced that he was following up this success with a new quarterly review, *Two Worlds*. With his customary brass, he claimed that it would be edited by Ezra Pound, Arthur Symons, and Ford Madox Ford. He also promised that it would feature more contributions from James Joyce. Roth had actually written to Joyce in 1921, proposing such a magazine, but Joyce had refused to answer the letter. Pound was not at all disturbed by the unauthorized use of his name in the prospectus for the magazine (it did not appear on the masthead when the first issue came out), and Symons actually did write for it.

Roth boasted to Hemingway that he had only used Joyce's name for a "draw", and that he had gotten ten thousand subscriptions on the strength of it. Now that he had his subscribers, he didn't want Joyce, he wanted more amusing stuff. Nevertheless, he continued to print, without authorization, Joyce's writings. Joyce tried to get Quinn's successor to represent him in litigation with Roth, using Pound's father as intermediary, but he was informed that since he had neglected to copyright the book in the United States, he had no grounds for action.

In a letter to Miss Harriet Weaver, May 31, 1927, Joyce notes that "Mr. Roth has made public a letter in which he states on the authority of Dr. Joseph Collins that I am really a Jew. Mr. Roth is up for preliminary examination today 31 floreal in New York City."[11]

On December 2, 1928, he wrote to Miss Harriet Weaver, "I had a cable from New York to say that the solicitors were arraigning the case and that Roth was again in jail but that he is execution proof."[12]

Despite the fact that his eyes were often adversely affected, and that he suffered terrible headaches afterward, Joyce often spent his evening in drinking considerable quantities of wine. During the years that he and Pound were in Paris together, from 1920 through 1924, they were not too often in each other's company, for Pound was not much of a drinker. A more congenial companion for Joyce was the hard-drinking Robert McAlmon.

After Pound had removed to Rapallo in 1924, Joyce sent him the manuscript of *Work in Progress,* which he was constantly revis-

ing, and which finally appeared under the title of *Finnegan's Wake*.
Pound replied on November 15, 1926,

"Dear Jim;

Ms. arrived this A.M. All I can do is to wish every possible
success, I would have another go at it, but up to present I make
nothing of it whatever. Nothing so far as I can make out, nothing
short of divine vision or a new cure for the clapp can possibly be
worth all the circumnambient peripherization."[13]

So much for Pound's views on obscurantism.

Joyce wrote to Miss Harriet Weaver, apropos of this opinion, on
February 1, 1927, "It is possible Pound is right but I can't go back.
I never listened to his objections to Ulysses as it was being sent
him once I had made up my mind but dodged them as tactfully as I
could. He understood certain aspects of that book very quickly and
that was more than enough then. He makes brilliant discoveries of
howling blunders."[14]

On December 2, 1928, he wrote to Miss Harriet Weaver, ". . .
the more I hear of the political, philosophical ethical zealot members of Pound's big brass band the more I wonder why I was ever
let into it with my 'magic flute'."[15]

Nevertheless, Joyce had earlier acknowledged Pound's role as
sponsor. The first number of a new Paris expatriate review, *This
Quarter,* dated Spring, 1925, which was dedicated to Ezra Pound,
featured the following letter:

"8 avenue Charles Picquet
March 13, 1925

Dear Mr. Walsh

I am glad to hear that the first number of your review will
shortly appear. It was a very good thought of yours in dedicating
this number to Mr. Ezra Pound and I am very happy indeed that
you allow me to add my acknowledgment of thanks to him to the
others you are publishing. I owe a great deal to his friendly help,
encouragement and generous interest in everything that I have
written, as you know there are many others who are under a similar

debt of gratitude to him. He helped me in every possible way in
the face of very great difficulties for seven years before I met him,
and since then he has always been ready to give me advice and
appreciation which I esteem very highly as coming from a mind of
such brilliance and discernment. I hope that your review, setting
out under so good a name, will have the success which it deserves.

Sincerely yours
James Joyce."[16]

Some years later, Pound repaid this endorsement by devoting
one of his broadcasts to a memorial to Joyce's career.

In later years, Pound spoke rather benevolently of "Jimmy",
whom he had once termed a "dour Aberdeen minister". A more
intimate view of Joyce has been given us by Oliver St. John
Gogarty:

"Joyce was an unloveable and lonely man; but he willed his
life. He was an artist deliberately and naturally, and for this he
sacrificed everything, even his humanity. . . . He had the wrong
idea of an artist when he dressed himself as a Rembrandt and
sent postcards with his portrait to his friends—or rather to his
acquaintances, for he would not acknowledge that anyone could be
his friend."[17]

VIII

"THERE WAS never a day so gay for the Arts as any twenty-four hours of the early 1920s in Paris," says Ford Madox Ford, in the opening sentence of his charming book of memoirs, *It Was the Nightingale*.

Because the Versailles Peace Conference was held there, Paris became the symbol of man's hope that there would be no more wars. From all over the world, people came to bask in the comforting glow of the rays of peace sent out from the City of Light. In this false light, a Renaissance of arts and letters took place.

After the Second World War, young writers and artists again flocked to Paris, to live as their parents had done. Only one thing was missing—talent. There were no Pounds, no Eliots, no Hemingways among the shaggy creatures who disguised themselves in secondhand GI clothing.

The cast of characters in the Bohemian drama "Paris—the 1920s" reads like a Who's Who of Eumerican arts. In addition to Pound, Eliot, and Hemingway, there were James Joyce, Gertrude Stein, Ford Madox Ford, Robert McAlmon, Peggy Guggenheim, Caresse Crosby, and many other fine talents.

Ezra's departure from England was not abrupt. Robert Graves recalls that he met Pound in Lawrence's rooms at that time. Graves himself characterized post-World War I England as being symbolized by jazz and mad dogs.

128

Ezra made a tour of Italy and France in the summer of 1920, before going back to England for his effects. In Venice, where he had published his first book of poems twelve years earlier, he began a semi-autobiographical work, *Indiscretions, Une Revue De Deux Mondes,* which opens on a typically Poundian note:

"It is peculiarly fitting that this manuscript should begin in Venice, from a patent Italian inkwell designed to prevent satisfactory immersion of the pen. If the latter symbolism be obscure, the former is so obvious, at least to the writer, that only meticulous honesty and the multitude of affairs prevented him from committing it to paper before leaving London."[1]

Pound returned to England on June 30, 1920, to wind up his negotiations with the English. He ceded the island back to them, and departed for Paris on October 29. According to John Gould Fletcher, as a parting shot at London, Pound said that England was only a corpse kept alive by maggots.[2] Although this thesis may be somewhat inaccurate from a biological point of view, there is much to be said for it sociologically, especially as concerns the olfactory sense.

When Ezra went to Paris, he was thirty-five years old. He had married well, had published a number of books (more than we care to count at the moment), had been listed in *Who's Who in England* for the past six years, and had built an international reputation as a poet and critic. His work with Yeats and Joyce was largely behind him; the Paris years were to be devoted to the careers of T. S. Eliot and Ernest Hemingway.

In February, 1921, Pound issued a clarion call for assistance in rescuing Eliot from Lloyd's Bank. He requested thirty annual subscriptions of fifty dollars each. Although Eliot was earning more than the fifteen hundred dollars which might be raised through the subscriptions, he was willing to accept a cut in pay to become a poet. Many of the expatriates were living in Paris on considerably less. Fletcher cites the case of Humberston Skipwith Cannell, whose poems Pound had managed to get into *Poetry,* and who lived on the Left Bank on a modest thirty dollars a month sent him by his relatives.[3]

The outcome of this new campaign was a fortunate one. In

July, Pound reported that twenty-two of the thirty subscriptions had been pledged. By this time, Eliot had placed himself completely in the hands of his mentor.

This sense of dedication Pound was often successful in passing on to those around him. Eliot flung himself into his writing, and a long poem began to take shape. He wrote, in 1946,

"It was in 1922 that I placed before him in Paris the manuscript of a sprawling, chaotic poem called The Waste Land which left his hands about half its size, in the form in which it appears in print. I should like to think that the manuscript, with the superseded passages, had disappeared irrevocably: yet, on the other hand, I should wish the blue pencilling on it to be preserved as irrefutable evidence of Pound's critical genius."[4]

Pound had described Eliot to Harriet Monroe in a letter dated September 30, 1914, ". . . He is the only American I know of who has made what I call adequate preparation for writing. He has actually trained himself and modernized himself *on his own*. The rest of the *promising young* have done one or the other but never both (most of the swine have done neither). It is such a comfort to meet a man and not have to tell him to wash his face, wipe his feet, and remember the date (1914) on the calendar."[5]

Two letters from Pound to Eliot concerning his editorship of *The Waste Land* are in print. The first, dated December 24, 1921, follows:

"Caro mio:
MUCH improved. I think your instinct had led you to put the remaining superfluities at the end. I think you had better leave 'em, abolish 'em altogether or for the present.

"IF you MUST keep 'em put 'em at the beginning before the 'April cruelest month.' The POEM ends with the 'Shantih, shantih, shantih.'

"One test is whether anything would be lacking if the last three were omitted. I don't think it would.

"The song has only two lines which you can use in the body of the poem. The other two, at least the first, does not advance on earlier stuff. And even the sovegna doesn't hold with the rest which does hold.

"(It also, to your horror probably, reads aloud very well. Mouthing out his OOOOOOze.)

"I doubt if Conrad is weighty enough to stand the citation.

"The thing now runs from 'April . . .' to 'shantih' without a break. That is 19 pages, and let us say the longest poem in the English langwidge. Don't try to bust all records by prolonging it three pages further.

"The bad nerves is O.K. now as led up to.

"My squibs are now a bloody impertinence. I send 'em as requested; but don't use 'em with Waste Land.

"You can tack 'em onto a collected edtn, or use 'em somewhere where they would be decently hidden and swamped by the bulk of accompanying matter. They'd merely be an extra and wrong note with the 19 page version.

"Complimenti, you bitch. I am wracked by the seven jealousies, and cogitating an excuse for always extruding my deformative secretions in my own stuff, and never getting an outline. I go into nacre and objets d'art. Some day I shall lose my temper, blaspheme Flaubert, lie like a _____ _____ _____ and say 'Art should embellish the unbelicus.'

". . . It is after all a grrrreat littttttterary period. Thanks for the Aggymemnon."[6]

The second letter, written in January of 1922, continues Pound's suggestions on *The Waste Land:*

"Filio dilecto mihi: I merely queeried the dialect of 'thence'; dare say it is O.K.

"D. was fussing about some natural phenomenon, but I thought I had crossed out her query. The wake of the barges washes etc., and the barges may perfectly well be said to wash. I should leave it as it is, and NOT invert.

"I do *not* advise printing 'Gerontion' as preface. One don't miss it at all as the thing now stands. To be more lucid still, let me say that I advise you NOT to print 'Gerontion' as prelude.

"I DO advise keeping Phlebas. In fact I more'n advise. Phlebas is an integral part of the poem; the card pack introduces him, the drowned phoen. sailor. And he is needed ABSolootly where he is. Must stay in.

"Do as you like about my obstetric effort.

"Ditto re Conrad; who am I to grudge him his laurel crown?

"Aeschylus not so good as I had hoped, but haven't time to improve him, yet.

"I dare say the sweats with tears will wait. _____

"You can forward the 'Bolo' to Joyce if you think it won't unhinge his somewhat sabbatarian mind. On the hole he might be saved the shock, shaved the sock."[7]

When *The Waste Land* appeared, Eliot dedicated it to "Ezra Pound, il miglior fabbro", the master worker, the term which Dante had used in veneration of his own master, the Provençal poet, Arnaut Daniel.

In subsequent years, Eliot had a more direct influence on American poetry than did Pound. That is, he had more disciples. *The Waste Land* inspired many imitators. Hart Crane was one of those who found it expedient to switch from Pound to Eliot.

These two poets have continued their friendship, despite Pound's political involvements. Although great pressure was brought to bear upon Eliot, he never repudiated Pound.

He did reverse himself concerning one of Pound's favorite dislikes, John Milton. In 1936, Eliot said, "He (Milton) may still be considered as having done damage to the English language from which it has not yet fully recovered."[8] But in 1947, Eliot characterized Milton as "the greatest master of free verse in our language."[9]

At the same time that he was editing *The Waste Land,* Pound was button-holing people in Paris and demanding that they read some stories written by a talented young newspaperman, Ernest Hemingway. John Peale Bishop recalls that in 1922, when he was in Paris, Pound told him of a journalist who was trying to do serious work. Soon afterwards, he brought Hemingway around for an introduction.[10]

Hemingway was then living in the room in which Verlaine had spent his last years. It was more romantic than convenient, for it had no heat or running water. The rent was very low, but Hemingway could have afforded better, as he was on a salary from the "Moose Jaw Clarion" or some such Canadian sheet.

Pound's first lesson for Hemingway was, as usual, Flaubert, whom he offered as an example of precision of working and for his employment of *le mot juste*. Although Hemingway learned to work, it is difficult to say whether he uses the "right word". The language is spare and clean, the tone is masculine, but one does not hear the particular thud of the bullet landing in flesh. It is Americanese, a language more fit for vituperation than for romance. Perhaps it is this to which Wyndham Lewis refers when he speaks of the "staccato of the States". If Hemingway had not been a city boy, he might not have been quite so impressed with the hunt. Boys in Virginia learn to shoot squirrels plumb through the eye with .22 rifles. The lesson is one in precision. As for bulls . . .

Malcolm Cowley says that Ezra read Hemingway's stories and blue-pencilled most of the adjectives.[11] In a letter to me, dated June 30, 1959, Ezra says,

"Hem re/Cowley , 1922 aprox ; on sight ; Kent yeh see the s____o____b____ in ten years' time, setting in an office; turnin' some good guy down?"

Hemingway later remarked, "Ezra was right half of the time, and when he was wrong he was so wrong you were never in doubt."[12] This is high praise, as most criticism merely adds to the general confusion.

In *The Apprenticeship of Ernest Hemingway,* Charles Fenton says, "It was from Ezra Pound's edicts about imagism, in fact, and from their application to his own verse, that Hemingway profited most strongly from the exercise of writing poetry."[13]

Although he was a successful journalist, and had won praise for his newspaper stories, Hemingway was quite modest in submitting his work to Pound for editing. He also went to another Parisian teacher, Gertrude Stein, who looked over his stories. The results of this process, or the advantages accruing to Hemingway, are in doubt. The statement, "You are all a lost generation," which was printed opposite the title page of his novel, *The Sun Also Rises*

(1926), is generally attributed to Gertrude Stein. The phrase was subsequently applied to the *expatriate* group in Paris, and to the youth of America as well.

Pound was not a member of the "lost generation"; he was not looking for anything. He had found his work, and if others had not, that was their problem. By 1925, the Paris group had been corrupted by the swarms of tourists, and by the favorable exchange rate, which allowed the young writers to drink as much as they liked.

Although Pound never referred to whatever assistance he might have rendered to Hemingway, Gertrude Stein was more possessive. She convinced herself that she was solely responsible for his subsequent rise to fame. Had she kept this opinion to herself, her own reputation might not have suffered as much as it has; but she insisted on telling everybody how she had "created" Hemingway. She even took credit for having introduced him to bullfighting, as though it were a sport on which she had a sort of Max Jacobs monopoly. When she became vicious, and called him "yellow", in her autobiography, it turned many people against her, for Hemingway had been wounded and decorated for bravery during his service on the Italian front. He was justified in terming her book "a palpable tissue of lies."

In an interview with John Hyde Preston, Stein continued her vendetta against Hemingway, but she made some interesting points. She said, in part, "He was not really good after 1925. In his early short stories he had what I have been trying to describe to you. Then—Hemingway did not lose it; he threw it away. I told him then; 'Hemingway, you have a small income; you will not starve; you can work without worry and you can grow and keep this thing and it will grow with you.' But he did not wish to grow that way; he wished to grow violently. Now, Preston, here is a curious thing. Hemingway is not an American Novelist. He has not sold himself and he has not settled into any literary mold. Maybe his own mould, but that's not only literary. When I first met Hemingway he had a truly sensitive capacity for emotion, and that was the stuff of the first stories; but he was shy of himself and he began to develop, as a shield, a big Kansas City-boy brutality about it, and so he was 'tough' because he was really sensitive and ashamed that he was. Then it happened. I saw it happening and tried to save what was fine there, but it was too late. He went the way so many other Americans have gone before, the way they are still going. He became obsessed by sex and violent death."[14]

We leave Miss Stein before she suggests some more interesting hobbies. In preparation for this work, I reread *The Sun Also Rises,* and it is a fine piece of work. Hemingway never wrote another book, but then, who does? He had an unsurpassed hero in the *castrato,* Jake, for this handicap raised him to the quality of a god, whose involvement in human affairs was necessarily tortuous, inconclusive, and important. Never again did Hemingway find such a symbol.

During Pound's Paris period, he was Gertrude Stein's only rival in the specialty of handling genius. She looked upon this bounty-jumper from the West with great disfavor. In *The Autobiography of Alice B. Toklas,* their meeting is described by Stein through the eyes of her consort, Miss Toklas:

"We met Ezra Pound at Grace Lounsbery's, he came to dinner with us and he stayed and talked about japanese prints among other things. Gertrude Stein liked him but did not find him amusing. She said he was a village explainer, excellent if you were a village, but if you were not, not. Ezra also talked about T. S. Eliot at the house. Pretty soon everybody talked about T. S. Eliot at the house."[15]

The "house" was at 27 rue de Fleurus, where the lisstrichous Miss Stein and her consort, Miss Toklas, held sway over a sea of Picasso paintings. According to the autobiography, Ezra came once more to the rue de Fleurus, and again talked about Japanese prints. In her anxiety to convince him that she was not a village (an error which anyone could make, as she talked like one), Gertrude Stein became somewhat vehement. She says that Pound was not invited back. He does not recall the incident, but, in any case, he would not have spent much time with her. On the only occasion I remember when her name was brought up at St. Elizabeths, he said, rather benevolently, that she was "a charming old fraud."

As soon as he had settled in Paris, Pound wrote to Joyce, who was then living in Trieste, and urged him to come and join the party. On July 1, 1920, Joyce wrote to Carlo Linati, "My address in Paris will be chez M. Ezra Pound, Hotel de l'Élysée, rue de Beaune 9."[16]

This move was an important step in establishing Joyce's reputation. In Paris, he met many people who became fanciers of his work, and the "Joyce cult" began to take shape. Sylvia Beach, whose Shakespeare Head Book Shop was the meeting place for the avant-garde, decided that *Ulysses* must be published in book form. Since no publisher would touch it, she and her partner, Adrienne Monnier, financed it and saw the book through arduous months of preparation. A few years later, other Paris admirers published Joyce's final work serially in *transition*.

One of the more important figures in the American expatriate group in Paris was Robert McAlmon. His autobiography, *Being Geniuses Together* (1938), is one of the best, and least-known, books on the period. McAlmon, one of the ten children of a Kansas minister who was hard-put to feed his brood, came to New York after serving in the Army Air Corps during the First World War. He became a model at Cooper Union Art School, in order to finance his studies there. One of the students, Winifred Bryher, fell in love with him, and they were married in February, 1921. To his surprise, the marriage created a sensation in the press. McAlmon discovered that his bride was really Winifred Ellerman, only daughter of Sir John Ellerman, the richest shipowner in England.

Sir John appears in *Who's Who in England* for the first time in 1905, as "proprietor of the Leyland Line of Steamers." The Leyland Line had been built up by Francis Leyland, patron of Whistler, and Ellerman had been his accountant. Now the Leyland Line was again patronizing the arts. Although Sir John had little inclination along those lines, as long as McAlmon was married to his daughter, some of the Ellerman money went to help young artists and writers. McAlmon commissioned some works from Wyndham Lewis, and he brought out some avant-garde works under the imprint of Contact Editions.

Winifred Bryher brought her handsome young man home to the Ellerman establishment in London, but as soon as Sir John learned this his son-in-law cared nothing for the business world, he lost all interest in him. The Ellermans also had a son, John, who was kept close to home, although McAlmon occasionally helped him to sneak out to a movie. He later married Esther de Sola, of the Montreal de Solas, without issue.

The young couple soon left the dreary London mansion, and settled in Paris. When McAlmon had lunch with Pound, the two did not seem to hit it off very well. A few days later, says Mc-Almon, the story was repeated to him that Pound had said, "Well, well, another young one wanting me to make a poet out of him with nothing to work on."[17] McAlmon was incensed by the story, and he avoided Pound for more than a year. The remark seems to have been invented, as one of those stories designed to add interest and tension to the tight little expatriate community, which had become one of those Bohemias described by Pound in *The Little Review* several years earlier. At any rate, McAlmon never did get down to work.

The character Dick Diver, in Scott Fitzgerald's *Tender Is the Night,* is based upon McAlmon, although the critics seem to have missed it. Diver is portrayed as a handsome and intelligent minister's son who meets a neurotic girl from a very wealthy family. He marries her, and abandons his career in order to traipse around with her. Because of the emptiness of his life, he eventually becomes an alcoholic, gets a divorce, and returns to America as a drunkard and a failure, having dissipated his life in a few short years.

While living with Bryher, McAlmon failed to do any significant work, although everyone expected great things from him. He became more of a dilettante, began to drink heavily, and asked her for a divorce in 1926. More than anyone else, his life typifies what has been described as "the lost generation". As such, he is one of the important figures of the Jazz Age. He wandered about Europe for the next few years, returned to America, and lived in Mexico for a while. In 1940, he found that he had contracted tuberculosis. His last years were spent as a traveling salesman for a surgical supply house, owned by one of his brothers, that was located in El Paso, Texas. He died in 1956.

McAlmon and Joyce became great friends and constant drinking companions. The major part of the manuscript of *Ulysses* was typed by McAlmon while it was being readied for the printer. He recounts that he arbitrarily changed some of the words, and that some of his typographical errors appeared in the final version. So it is with literature.

On one occasion, says McAlmon, a dinner party by the editors of *The New Review* in honor of Pound almost became a tragedy. A Maltese youth was seated between Pound and McAlmon, and across from them was an English youth who was the rival of the Maltese in some sort of an affair. The Maltese was under the influence of drugs, and he had come to the dinner party, not in the service of literature or because he was hungry, but merely to assassinate his rival.

As Ford Madox Ford arose to deliver an oration on the achievements of Ezra Pound, McAlmon saw the Maltese draw a stiletto from under his jacket, and lean across the table to dispose of his enemy. The English boy jumped out of the window, and the drug-crazed youth then turned on Pound. McAlmon seized his wrist, and managed to stop him. After the police had taken the Maltese away, McAlmon found that his coat sleeve had been entirely cut away by one pass of the knife. It had missed his artery by a fraction of an inch. The incident was hushed up, and the American papers published in Paris never mentioned it. And, says McAlmon, Ford never did get to make his speech.[18]

The ubiquitous Ford was on hand in Paris to chronicle Pound's doings. No longer Hueffer, he was now officially Mr. Ford. His change of name and active service in the British army had done nothing to convince Ford's neighbors in London that he was not a German spy, or that confidential documents stolen from Whitehall had not been cached nightly beneath the stern visage of Gaudier's Pound in the garden. After all, the neighbors reasoned, why wouldn't a German spy try to deceive people by enlisting in the British army?

One cannot reproach Mr. Ford for leaving England and seeking a more hospitable environment. As he points out, it was actually dangerous for an English veteran to live in England after the war, for the populace was filled with bitter hatred against the men who had saved them from the Germans. The perfect army (and I believe there was such a corps in the history of Greece) is one which, in the act of defeating the enemy, manages to get itself entirely annihilated, relieving the succored inhabitants of any necessity for gratitude or for reabsorbing the veterans into their society.

So, Mr. Ford:

"The story goes—and it is too good not to be true—that, to add to the harmony of the war years, Mr. Pound left England because he had sent seconds to a harmless poet of the type that writes articles on Milton on the front page of the London Times Literary Supplement. The poet asked for police protection. So Ezra went. To issue a challenge to a duel to a British subject is, by British law, to conspire to commit murder, and the British police model themselves on Milton.

"Anyhow," says Ford, "It is always good to come upon Mr. Pound in a new city. I never could discover that he had any sympathy for my writing. He wrote to me last week to say that eighty per cent of my work is rubbish—because I am an English gentleman. Patriotism is a fine thing!

"All the same, if Mr. Pound is in Caparnaum and I go there Mr. Pound leads me in procession incontinently to the sound of shawms around the city walls. You would think I was the infinitely aged mummy of a Pharaoh, nodding in senility on the box seat of Miss Stein's first automobile. And before the car Mr. Pound dances the slow, ceremonial dance that William Penn danced before the Sachems. Then when I have told the elders and the scribes that Ezra is the greatest poet in the world, Ezra goes and whispers into the loud speakers that beneath the bedizened shawls I have asses' ears. The drone is thus killed."[19]

In Ford's books of reminiscences (there are quite a few of them), he wanders from the green fields of England to the fields of Provence, or from Paris to New York, without visible transition in his prose. In one paragraph, we are sitting in the Brevoort; in the next, we are ensconced at the Café Dôme, and apparently we have been there for some time. It is a sort of magic carpet prose, rather pleasant, although somewhat bewildering. Ford himself has written somewhere, "My brain, I think, is a sort of dove-cote."

The real explanation of this curious mode of transition is that Ford is the last cosmopolitan; he is at home anywhere in western civilization. Whether he is observing the antics of a Fifth Avenue millionaire in New York or the exuberance of a carpet-dealer from Keokuk vacationing in Paris, he maintains the same polite smile. Perhaps this is the most that culture can do for a man, that is, to give him a layer of weatherfat, which can absorb the chilling improprieties of others without visible discomfort.

Inevitably, the proximity of Ford and Pound in Paris had to result in another magazine. It was entitled *transatlantic review*. Ford recalls Pound's lack of cooperation in genial terms:

"Ezra at that moment had become both sculptor and musician. Thus all his thoughts were needed for those arts. He had living above his studio in the rue Notre Dame des Champs a gentleman whom he suspected of being an ex-Enemy, a person obnoxious to himself. He had therefore persuaded Mr. George Antheil, who, besides being a great composer, must be the heaviest living piano-player—he had persuaded Mr. Antheil to practise his latest symphony for piano and orchestra in Mr. Pound's studio. This lasted all day for several weeks. When Mr. Antheil was fatigued, his orchestra played unceasingly—Mr. Antheil's own arrangement of the Wacht am Rhein. In the meanwhile, turning sculptor, Mr. Pound fiercely struck blocks of granite with sledge hammers.

"The rest of his day—his evenings that is to say—would thus be given up to the court of the local justice of the peace, rebutting the complaints of the gentleman who lived overhead. He had some difficulty, but eventually succeeded in convincing the magistrate that he and Mr. Antheil were two pure young Americans engaged in earning their livings to the greater glory of France, whereas the gentleman upstairs was no more, no less than the worst type produced by a lately enemy nation. So that fellow had to leave Paris.

"It was not to be imagined that with all this on his hands, Mr. Pound could be expected to give time to the conducting of a Review and there the matter rested."

Pound did have a studio, and he was quite busy with his music and sculpture, but he managed to give Ford the amount of time that he had been accustomed to spend in advising and editing little magazines. Ford says that "As a sculptor Ezra was of the school of Brancusi. He acquired pieces of stone as nearly egg-shaped as possible; hit them with hammers and then placed them about on the floor."[20]

It was Ford's misfortune to stumble occasionally over these works, as no English gentleman ever looks where he is going. Although bruised, Ford was no action-taker of the type described by Shakespeare, and he never sued.

With or without Pound's cooperation, the first number of the *transatlantic review* appeared in January, 1924. It was short-lived. Ford later said that the first number went fine, but that the second and third issues fell absolutely dead. Some of the failure to capitalize on the initial success may be laid to the unusual staff. The first assistant editor was a White Russian refugee, who departed in anger when he learned that Ford had had lunch with a Jew. He was succeeded by Hemingway, who was quite conscientious.

Ford's principle objection to Hemingway was his predilection for the poetry of a lady known as the Baronin Elsa von Freytag Loringhofen. One of the sights of Paris, she went about in a hat which was simply an inverted coal-scuttle. For a time, she was to be seen with shaved head, which she had lacquered vermilion, and wearing a black crepe mourning dress. Her poetry, which Margaret Anderson sometimes printed in *The Little Review,* was passable for the Jazz Age, but Ford refused to have it in his magazine. Hemingway would include it in the copy for each issue, and patiently Ford would take it out again.

At last, Ford had to go to New York to deliver some lectures, and he left the magazine in Hemingway's hands. The issue, which Ford found satisfactory in every other respect, contained some poems by the Baronin.

Ford supposed that he would be relieved of this cross when the Baronin approached him and asked his assistance in getting her a visa. In this instance, Ford was glad to be of service. He sent her to the British Embassy in Paris with his recommendation. For the occasion, the Baronin wore a brassiere of milk tins, which were strung together on a dog-chain. On her head was pertly perched a plum-cake. She was thrown out of the Embassy, and the officials indignantly cancelled the Empire's subscription to the *transatlantic review*.

Thwarted in her desire to go to London, the Baronin stopped

in at a café to console herself. She seems to have been in a bad mood, for, during the course of the afternoon, she took exception to an innocent lady at a nearby table, and knocked her cold. For this she was expelled from France. She finally died of starvation in Munich.

Ezra wrote of her in *Section: Rock-Drill,*

> & Elsa Kassandra, "the Baroness"
> von Freitag etc. sd/ several true things
> in the old days /
> driven nuts,
> Well, of course, there was a certain strain
> on the gal in them days in Manhattan
> the principle of non-acquiescence
> laid a burden.[21]

The Baroness' expulsion was not an unusual event. French officials are violently opposed to violence, especially when it is committed by "les gangstairs", that is, the Americans who pay so much for bad champagne in Paris. Another assistant editor of the *transatlantic review,* who often became quite belligerent after a few drinks, slugged a café proprietor. In the United States, the proprietor would have slugged him right back, but in France, "Gendarme!" The difference is that in the U.S.A., a saloon is only a saloon, and often something less than that, but in France a café is the castle of the arts, and its proprietor *le grand patron.* The editor was with difficulty rescued from jail, and during his hours of imprisonment, Ezra took his bassoon along, and sat outside the window, playing and singing the songs of Arnaut Daniel. Prison has its compensations.

The *transatlantic review* printed some serials of current works, among them Ford's fine novel *Some Do Not* (1924), and Gertrude Stein's too-long novel, *Making of Americans* (1925), which, some critics claim, does not describe the process.

Pound contributed various pieces on music, some cantos, and much advice. William Carlos Williams, E. E. Cummings, and Tristan Tzara also were represented during the short life of the *review.* John Quinn had guaranteed its financing, but he had some setbacks,

and could not make good on his pledge. Ford excused him by saying that he had come out badly in some litigation in Scandinavia.[22]
Only Ford could come up with a story like that, that an Irish
lawyer, practicing in New York, should lose all his money in
Scandinavia.

Ford says that he first came upon Hemingway in Ezra's studio,
where the young journalist was shadow-boxing with the statue of
a richly-dressed Chinese bonze. Hemingway later enlivened the
offices of the *review* by suddenly crouching and aiming at a supposed tree-leopard crouching on a balcony just above Ford's head.[23]
This could hardly have lightened the strain of editorship.

Ford was able to excuse this midwestern *élan*—he seems to
have had a weakness for Americans, and he wound up his days in
Greenwich Village. Hemingway later quarrelled with him about an
attack on Eliot which appeared in the *review*. Hemingway insisted
on printing it, but in the next issue, Ford ran an apology to Eliot.
After this, Hemingway refused to have anything further to do with
Ford or the *review*. Although they often were with the same
groups night after night, they refused to speak. This was not as
awkward as it might sound, as it is quite possible to have good
times in a café without speaking to one's companions.

There are several opinions as to Ford's effect upon young
American writers, and as to young writers' effect upon Ford.
Douglas Goldring claimed that long association with Ezra Pound
and his "troupe of cowboys" severely damaged Ford's literary
reputation.[24] Another view, advanced by Van Wyck Brooks in his
Opinions of Oliver Allston, was that "his (Ford's) mind was like
a Roquefort cheese, so ripe that it was palpably falling to pieces,
and I do not think he was a good mental diet for the young
Western boys, fresh from the prairie, who came under his influence
in Paris."[25]

Another of Ezra's Paris protégés was George Antheil, who has
termed himself "the bad boy of music." Mr. Antheil won a certain
amount of respect as a musician at his ultra-modern concerts in
Europe, by his quaint custom of placing a fully-loaded revolver
on top of the piano before he began to play. Besides identifying
him unmistakably as an American artist, the gun also served notice

on the audience that he would not tolerate the riots that had characterized his public appearances before he armed himself.

For a few months in 1923, Antheil lived in a room above Sylvia Beach's bookshop. He records that here, on a single afternoon, his casual visitors included James Joyce, T. S. Eliot, Ford Madox Ford, Ernest Hemingway, Wyndham Lewis, and Ezra Pound. Such was the concentration of talent in Paris at that time.[26]

Ezra's enthusiasm for Antheil's music frightened the young composer, and, while he and Jean Cocteau were organizing a special concert to present his work, Antheil took off for Africa with his lady of the moment. This halted Pound's efforts on his behalf.

Malcolm Cowley has recorded Ezra in his Paris habitat: "Ezra Pound, in red dressing gown and red beard walked back and forth in his studio as he talked . . . I pictured him as a red fox pursued by the pack of his admirers, he led them through bushes and into marshes; some of them gave up the chase but others joined in. At present, in the Cantos, he had fled into high and rocky ground where the scent was lost and the hounds would cut their feet if they tried to follow, yet I felt that they would eventually find him even there and would crowd around muzzle to muzzle, not for the kill, but merely for the privilege of baying his praises. Then with his weakness for defying the crowd, for finding crazily simple explanations and for howling eccentric opinions, to what new corner would the fox escape?"[27]

Cowley blew hot and cold about Pound. In *Exile's Return*, he quotes Burton Rascoe: "Ezra Pound; now Pound's a talent, but has he written more than one lyric?"[28]

By 1923, the pack was indeed crowding into Pound's studio. In addition to the daily visitors, such as Hemingway, shadowboxing with the bonze, and occasionally with Pound (Hemingway wrote to Sherwood Anderson that Pound habitually led with his chin and had the grace of a crayfish, but still he thought it quite sporting of Pound to risk his dignity in the role of sparring partner), the visiting firemen of letters began to consider the studio a "must" stop in the standard tour of the Left Bank. This tour began at the Café Dôme, moved to Sylvia Beach's bookshop, then to

Pound's studio. No wonder that Ezra felt the need to escape his admirers.

Not all of the visitors were merely tourists. Harriet Monroe arrived in 1923 to meet the man who had done so much to put her magazine on the map. Pound informed her that the poem he was then working on would take forty years to complete. By this estimate, the *Cantos* should be in their final form by 1963.

Margaret Anderson also came to Paris in 1923, to meet her ex-foreign editor. *The Little Review,* having lasted almost a decade, was now on its last legs. She was impressed with Pound's lovely garden studio, and she describes the poet as wearing a large velvet béret, with the famed emerald dangling from his ear, a flowing tie like an artist of the 1830s, and a high Rooseveltian (TR) voice. She noted his "robust red blondness" and his nervous self-consciousness.

With some irritation, she comments, "Ezra had become fairly patriarchal in his attitude to women. He kissed them upon the forehead or drew them upon his knees with perfect obliviousness to their distaste for these mannerisms. In fact Ezra ran true to form, as the academic type, in everything—as I had anticipated."[29]

One can only wonder what sort of academicians Miss Anderson had been accustomed to. She declared that Ezra had stayed away from his homeland too long, and had become "a typical expatriate, which results in an oriental attitude towards women."[30]

Ezra never failed to arouse conflicting emotions in the opposite sex. One of my first missions for him was to call upon a pair of aged spinsters in Washington, the originals of the "Soeurs Randall" of the *Imaginary Letters*. One of them said, with some asperity, that Ezra had gotten into trouble because he had failed to come back to the United States every couple of years. The elder of the two was eighty-seven, her little sister was eighty-four, but even here I felt they had a lingering feminine irritation with Ezra.

They were characters from a Henry James story, who lived in a charming Georgetown house, and the gulf between them and Ezra was simply the gulf between Henry James' characters and life. Ezra had not come back to the United States every couple of years, to refresh his roots in the Fountain of Youth, because he did not have the money for the trips. But Henry James' characters only go to Europe if they have means to travel back and forth as they please.

Paul Rosenfeld writes that Sherwood Anderson introduced him to Ezra and Mrs. Shakespear when he came to Paris. Strangely enough, Pound's name does not appear in Anderson's published memoirs or letters, although the two saw quite a bit of each other. At any rate, Ezra was becoming one of the sights of Paris, a sort of Eiffel Tower, and he knew it was time to move on, as Daniel Boone moved West when a man settled only ten miles from him.

Early in 1923, Pound and Hemingway made a tour of Italian battlefields, particularly Piombono and Ortobello, where Hemingway explained the strategy of the medieval soldier of fortune and great patron of the arts, Sigismondo de Malatesta, who, unlike Eisenhower, was not himself a painter. This trip convinced Ezra that he should settle in Italy.

The increasing tide of visitors prevented him from spending as much time as he wished with the true artists of Paris. He was an admirer of Brancusi, but was unable to see him as often as he liked. He tells an amusing anecdote of Brancusi. One day the sculptor saw sitting across from him, on a Paris bus, a very beautiful girl, whose classical head and neck attracted him very much. Just as he was about to speak to her, she reached her stop, and got off. Reproaching himself for his hesitancy, Brancusi determined to find her. For weeks, he rode that same bus, hoping to see her again, but he had no luck. He gave up his vigil, and some time later, by accident, he encountered her near his studio. He immediately spoke to her.

"Do you know," he said, "that I saw you several months ago on the bus, and ever since then I have been hoping we would meet."

The young lady was pleased that she had been so noticed, and they began a cordial conversation. It ended abruptly when, Brancusi having mentioned that he was a sculptor, she smiled brightly and replied, "Oh, how interesting! Do you know, I am a sculptor too!"

The parade in and out of Sylvia Beach's bookshop must have been a sight. Ezra usually wore a bizarre outfit of tweeds, with bright blue square buttons, which he had designed himself; Eliot would be dressed in his banker's suit; and Wyndham Lewis wore a suit of jet black, with tie and cape to match.

The expatriates led a rather narrow existence in Paris. They took the bus over to the Rive Droit only to pick up a money order or letters at the American Express or Lloyd's. Those who were more affluent would visit their bankers, which, for most of them, was Morgan, Harjes & Company, the firm with which Harry Crosby had been associated.

On certain occasions, the entire colony would turn out. The première of Ezra's opera, *François Villon,* was one of those evenings. The opera was given in the old Salle Pleyel, where the dying Chopin is said to have fainted at his piano. McAlmon records that the audience, having come to scoff, was pleasantly surprised at the excellence of the work. It has since been performed over the BBC, and one day may even be heard in the United States. McAlmon says that Eliot was the only one of the audience to leave before the opera was concluded.[31]

Another enterprise of Pound's in Paris was the Three Mountains Press. A journalist named William Bird, who had founded the Consolidated Press Association with David Lawrence in Washington (now *U.S. News & World Report*), had come to Paris to manage the European branch of the enterprise. A jovial fellow, he soon became an integral member of the expatriate community. He got out a book on wines, and decided to spend some money in printing avant-garde works. Then as now, Ezra had masses of unpublished material, and the two entered into a worthwhile collaboration, which was called the Three Mountains Press.

An impressive early edition of the *Cantos,* gotten out under this imprint, now fetches very fancy prices. Only ninety copies, with giant initial letters on each page, reminiscent of the Irish illustrated manuscripts, and drawn by the artist Henry Strater, were printed. Dorothy Pound had two copies of this edition in Washington, perhaps for a rainy day.

A less happy occasion when the quarter turned out was the funeral of R. Cheever Dunning. A poet in the classical tradition of the starving artist, or rather, the western tradition, Dunning lived in a tiny garret room, slowly dying of malnutrition and tuberculosis. Pound and other expatriates helped him as much as they could, but at last he died in his garret.[32]

McAlmon tells the story of another casualty of the Left Bank, a lively and brilliant young Japanese of samurai stock. For some months, Toda had been seen daily at the Café Dôme, the Rotonde, and other haunts of the expatriates. Then he disappeared, and none of his friends could find out what had happened to him. Finally they located him in a tiny room, dying of starvation. His money had run out, and either he could get no more from his family, or he had exhausted his inheritance. At any rate, he was too proud to let anyone know of his dilemma, and he went to his room to await death. When he was discovered, it was too late to save him.[33]

One of Pound's visitors in Paris was Alfred Kreymborg, who had published some of his poems in a magazine called *Others*. This "little magazine" had been published in Grantwood, New Jersey, on the Palisades. The first issue appeared in July, 1915, and it lasted for three years. After its demise, Kreymborg joined Harold Loeb in editing *The Broom*.

Despite Pound's outspoken opinions on the Russians, he seems to have been acquainted at the Russian Embassy, or to have had some influence there. While in Paris, E. E. Cummings decided that he should go to Russia and see the great experiment. At that time, he was rather liberal in his views. Nearly all writers who had not been to Russia were enthusiastic about the benefits which the new regime was bringing to the people. Those writers who actually made the trip, however, came back with contradictory attitudes. These ranged from the enthusiasm of Lincoln Steffens, who exulted, "I have seen the future, and it works!" to the disillusionment of André Gide, who left the party after he had seen Communism in action in Russia.

As Cummings was favorably impressed by reports about the "New Russia", Ezra joshingly addressed him as "Kumrad", a nickname which he has used ever since. But when Cummings went to the Russian Embassy to apply for a visa, he was turned down. He had set his heart on making the trip, and later that day, he complained to Pound about his disappointment.

"Oh hell," said E.P., "we'll fix dem Slavs!" He immediately called the Embassy, and made such a fuss that the visa was granted. It turned out to be an indirect misfortune for Cummings. He saw at first hand that the new regime was little, if at all, better than the old. Before the Bolshevik Revolution, Czarist Russia had been exporting ten million tons of wheat to European countries each year. Under the Soviets, at that time, the people were starving. Cummings wrote a book about his experiences, entitled *Eimi* (1933), which describes the Communist bureaucrats unfavorably.

One of Pound's chores during the Paris years was a monthly letter from the Left Bank for *The Dial*. When the Moscow Art Theatre came to town, he missed a great opportunity to make peace with the Russians. Instead, he wrote, in the issue of February, 1923, "The Rooshians, as presented by the Moscow Art Theatre, and Chekhov's Cherry Orchard, confirm one's deepest prejudices, and leave one wondering whether Lenin, or any possible series of revolutions and cataclysms, could possibly have *added* any further disorder to the life of that unfortunate race."

Although this review might have been interpreted as a rather indirect compliment to the Soviet officials, it was a slap in the face of the intellectual world of the 1920s, which maintained an unbroken phalanx of belief in the Russian experiment. The next issue of *The Dial* contained a further note on the Moscow Art Theatre, by Edmund Wilson, a wide-eyed rhapsody, which was probably designed to soothe the feathers ruffled by the irrepressible Pound.

Ezra recalls an interesting luncheon in Paris with that well-known patron of the arts, Otto Kahn, which may have had beneficent results for his fellow artists. Knowing that Kahn had been scattering some money about for young poets, Ezra suggested that he set up a permanent fund. Kahn's benefactions had been on a hit-or-miss basis—he sometimes gave Hart Crane as much as five hundred dollars—but Ezra outlined a plan whereby a Kahn Foundation would make such grants, to needy practitioners, on a sounder basis—that is, a sum that would support the writer for a year.

Kahn did not wish to become involved with anything so complicated, but when he returned to New York, he mentioned Ezra's idea to a friend named Guggenheim. This was the genesis of the

Guggenheim Foundation, which has given grants to so many of
Ezra's critics.

E. E. Cummings was one of the beneficiaries of these grants.
Malcolm Cowley says that the early Cummings was influenced
by Pound's "Hugh Selwyn Mauberley",[34] which characterized the
post-war period,

> the age demanded an image
> Of its accelerated grimace.

Another of Pound's works of this period, "Homage to Sextus
Propertius", has been described by John J. Espey as "That booby-
trap for the classicist who is also a pedant."[35] He mentions William
Gardner Hale's attack upon Pound in the April, 1919 issue of
Poetry, as adding to the confusion. The London *Times Literary
Supplement* still refers to the Propertius poem as evidence of
Pound's ineptitude at translation, despite Pound's notification that
the poem is not an exact rendering, but rather a poem designed as
homage to the Latin poet.

Most classicists are also pedants, and they have had a field day
with the Propertius poem. Pound says that his lack of a union
card—that is, twenty years of slow deterioration at Balliol or some
such place—rouses the academicians to fury whenever he presents
a translation. Of course, he has been just as hard on them.

It would be a mistake to suppose that all of the expatriates were
engaged in the production of serious works of art. Most of them
frequented salons or cafés where no work was done or even contemplated. Such were the establishments of Harry and Caresse
Crosby, and of Peggy Guggenheim.

Harry Crosby was a nephew of J. P. Morgan, and he maintained
an elaborate place in Paris. The Crosbys often entertained forty
or fifty people. He ended this regime by shooting himself in the
temple, in order to get nearer to the sun.

Peggy Guggenheim, being a woman, did not shoot herself when
she became bored. She simply changed husbands, a recipe which
the envious Caresse was not slow to follow. The Guggenheim autobiography, *Out of This Century,* is "must" reading for many

reasons, none of them literary. In describing the aftermath of her parties at the Boulevard St. Germain flat, which were distinguished by the guests' lack of concern for their hostess, she says, "After the guests would leave, I went around, like my aunt, with a bottle of lysol. I was so afraid of getting a venereal disease."[36]

It wasn't safe to lie down in the Guggenheim apartment. Her book also offers a delightful description of a sexual experience atop a Portuguese manure pile. The tome really has something for everybody, and we should be grateful to all purchasers of copper for having made Miss Guggenheim's charming autobiography possible.

After Ezra departed for Rapallo, Paris was left to the Crosbys and to the Guggenheims. If the quality of work declined, at least everybody had a good time.

With the demise of the *transatlantic review,* the expatriates had to read imported copies of Samuel Roth's quarterly, *Two Worlds,* for they no longer had a magazine of their own. This too was short-lived, for Roth was sent to prison for selling through the mails a four-hundred-year-old work on love by an Arab physician —or was it four-year-old work on a hundred ways of making love? At any rate, poor Roth, victim of innumerable prejudices, went to jail. The several issues of his quarterly had contained, besides the pirated Joyce, an early poem by Whittaker Chambers.

Luckily, the expatriates were not long without a voice. Eugene and Marie Jolas happened along, and so, years later, S. J. Perelman could quip, "D'ya ever see any of the old 'transition' crowd?" *transition* published serially Joyce's *Work in Progress,* and some Dada poems by Tristan Tzara, but taking up where Pound had left off was no longer a novelty. When *transition* folded, the voice of the expatriates descended to an area considerably below the diaphragm, when a typesetter for the Paris edition of the *Herald Tribune,* Henry Miller, became the heir of the tradition.

By this time, the life of the expatriates had become a saleable commodity. Wambley Bald's daily column, "La Vie de Bohème (As Lived on the Left Bank)," which appeared in the Paris *Tribune,* had built up quite a following. When his peregrinations kept him from his typewriter, he allowed Miller to write for him. Miller gloried in depicting the swaggering existence of the American in Paris, who sauntered along puffing on the *gauloises bleus,* the French workingman's cigarette, cadging a *vin blanc cassis* or a *café arrose rhum* from a friend who had money, with an occasional *fine à l'eau*.

Miller's columns attracted some attention, and he began to expand them into a book. He developed a peculiar, foaming, self-propelled prose to describe his adventures in the prone, and soon had sufficient pages for two books. They eventually appeared as *The Tropic of Cancer* (1931) and *The Tropic of Capricorn* (1939). The publisher was one Jack Kahane, formerly of Dublin. His outfit was called the Obelisk Press, and its chief claim to fame was the publication of Frank Harris' *Autobiography,* four or five volumes in which Harris monotonously recounts in detail his seduction of innumerable Amys and Lillies. These works were sold to tourists who had advanced beyond the "feelthy postcard" stage.

Despite the success of the Harris work, Kahane was very cautious, and he did not publish anything else as daring. The rest of the Obelisk list was composed of innocuous volumes by "Cecil Barr" or by "Basil Carr", which were Mr. Kahane's pen-names. Unlike bootleggers, dope peddlers, or pimps, publishers of pornography are usually shy, nervous fellows, and are as reluctant to publish books as their more respectable colleagues. Kahane virtually swooned from fear when he read the purple pages of Miller's books, but he could not refuse them. They made a fortune for both himself and the writer, mostly because of the Second World War.

When the Americans liberated Paris, a vast stock of the "Tropic" books was discovered, and Kahane's nephew sold them for fifty dollars apiece to the victors. Soon Miller had a nest egg of forty thousand dollars in a French bank, enabling him to retire in California like any professor emeritus of biology, which, perhaps, he is.

The editors of *transition* wound up their affairs in a blaze of glory. That is, they devoted themselves to a conscientious denigration of Gertrude Stein, who in her autobiography had devoted herself to a conscientious denigration of her friends in Paris.

The *transition* volume, *Testimony Against Gertrude Stein* (February, 1935), was published as a rebuke to the appalling amount of misinformation about unimportant subjects which she had included in *The Autobiography of Alice B. Toklas,* as Gertrude modestly titled her own confessions. Many of the people whom she had slandered did not realize their unimportance, and they hastened into print to correct Miss Stein's multitudinous imperfections of memory, which had incarnadined faces all over Paris.

Georges Braque (who is not unimportant) said that "Miss Stein understood nothing of what went on around her." This was strong criticism of one who had appointed herself mentor of the Cubist movement.

André Salmon was equally enlightening. He wrote, "Miss Stein's account of the formation of cubism is entirely false. . . . Miss Stein often mentions people whom she never knew very well, and so irresponsibly, in fact, that the reader is astounded. . . . And what confusion! What incomprehension of an epoch!"

IX

I N THE 1920s one of the places of refuge from the great cities of Europe was the charming seaside village of Rapallo, on the Italian Riviera. Once Nietzsche had stalked its shores, and in 1923, Ezra Pound arrived, to remove himself from the deadening influence of the twentieth century's mass man.

Perhaps in the future, we shall come to think of Pound's successive retreats as abnegations of the modern idea that everything can be packaged and sold. It was packaged people, who wrapped themselves in cellophane, who had gotten on his nerves, people who pushed up to one, peering for a name tag, and asking, "What group are you with?" It was this desire to turn life into a perpetual convention of properly labelled "Unpeople", as Cummings would call them, which galled the artist. And even more, Pound resented being forced into a group that termed itself "Artists".

This development was one of the consequences of the abdication of the aristocracy. For they did abdicate. Viereck tells the story of Prince Rupert, after the Bavarians had pushed him off his throne. They soon regretted having to rule themselves, and a delegation came to him and asked him back. He replied, "Clean up your own mess."

Ezra has written somewhere that it is the function of an aristocracy to select. Until European civilization collapsed in the First World War, the artist functioned with some aristocrat's seal of

approval. He might die of hunger before obtaining this seal, or
he might live to be quite affluent. When the artist could no longer
take his work to the library of the castle, he found a new development, the salon, where fellow artists could give him a sort of
recommendation, if they found his work passable.

The *fin de siecle* saw the last of the great savants' salons, and
cercles, which had degenerated into social clubs when Pound
arrived in London. The future belonged to the artist whose voice
was truly international, and who could speak to the entire world.
Paradoxically, the artist could only do so if he were to remain
true to his roots; that is, if he were "authentic".

Ezra Pound has now been recognized as such a one. I had
said, rather rashly, that Pound was the first really American poet,
and it was with considerable relief that I found this statement
supported by the most brilliant of the younger critics, A. Alvarez,
in his book, *Stewards of Excellence.* He writes, "But it is Pound,
more than Whitman, Emily Dickinson, or Eliot, who is the first
really American poet."[1]

The impact of Pound upon the modern world has been as re-
freshing as was the impact of Whitman upon the pre-Raphaelites.
The *Cantos* are an announcement that the artist has moved into a
new phase, beyond the reach of aristocrats, salons, government
bureaus, or any such agencies. The new artist has a world view
of which he is as much the product as the inventor. He senses
that he encompasses a world, and this inspires him; his is no
longer the traditional role of the artist as sight-seer—a painter
of postcards for tourists, and one who gazes at the world he tries
to depict.

The new artist is a biological part of the entity of art, not one
who merely is rolling balls of clay; he has little in common with
those who wish to go on painting, sculpturing or writing in the
tradition of the past. Technique is more important than ever, but it
is useless unless one realizes where one is. This feeling of being
placed gives the new artist his sense of depth, and once we have
entered his world, we can only regard the work of his predecessors
as historically interesting, albeit important.

Ezra had visited Rapallo several times before moving there in
1924. The year of 1923 was one of indecision and shuttling back

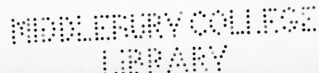

and forth between France and Italy, but at last he decided to give up his apartment in Paris.

In November, 1924, he wrote to William Bird, asking him to dispose of the studio and to sell its furnishings. He pointed out that the studio held a superior value because of the more favorable exchange rate. When he had first rented it, it had cost the equivalent of thirty dollars a month. Thanks to the vagaries of international exchange, in 1924, it rented for half of that sum.[2]

The lease was taken over by Yasushi Tanaka and his wife, Louise Gebhard Cann. "Paris was in one of its perennial 'crise de logemont,' " she recalls. "We lived in a furnished lodging that had to be given up within six months and the time was running out. We had been frantically seeking for a foothold on which we could get a lease so we could continue with our work but everything we looked at was tied up with a big premium, called a 'reprise' by the actual holder, a demand that could be met only by the rich. Mr. Pound could have made a similar stipulation. People with the means, and they were standing in line, would have paid almost any price to get the lease on his place, but we immediately saw that he was the kind of person who wouldn't even think of such a scheme. Quite as a matter of course he had performed what was then a miracle, opening the way for a destiny."[3]

On the third of December, 1924, Pound wrote exultantly to Wyndham Lewis, "I have never been converted to your permanenza or delayed dalliance in the hyperborean fogs, ma! ! Having rejuvenated by fifteen years in going to Paris and added another ten of life by quitting same, somewhat arid, but necessary milieu etc."[4]

Ezra's settling in Rapallo caused many of the international set to stop there who would have otherwise ignored it. Peggy Guggenheim relates that she and one of her husbands went down there to see Pound and to avoid Venice where they had been caught during the rainy season. "What a horribly dull little town it is!" she exclaims in reminiscence.

She says that she played tennis with Ezra every day while she was there, and fought with her husband every night. She recalls her tennis partner as "a good player, but he crowed like a rooster whenever he made a good stroke." Her current husband was not

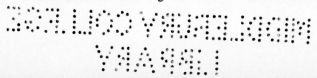

such a rewarding companion. He was Florenz Dale, who had
been known to a certain crowd in Paris as the "King of Bohemia".
Life with Peggy allowed him to drink heavily, and one evening
in Rapallo, he smashed an expensive twenty-seven piece tortoise-
shell dressing set, which she had just purchased. He then ran into
the cold sea with his clothes on. Afterwards, says Peggy, he sat
through a cinema in his wet suit, but suffered no ill effects.[5]

Such antics were nothing new to the natives of Rapallo. Most
of the visitors were people of means who, having been everywhere
else, at last had to stop at Rapallo.

For several centuries, Italy had been the playground of people
who go there to do things they would be arrested for at home.
Consequently, the townspeople of Rapallo were pleasantly surprised to find that Ezra had come there to work. No doubt it
took them some time to overcome their suspicions, but finally he
was accepted as visiting royalty, in a manner which Elizabeth
Delehanty later recorded, with amusement and frustration, in *The
New Yorker*.[6] On her visit to Rapallo, it seemed that everything
she reached for, including a beach umbrella, was reserved for
Mr. Pound.

The Italians extended him this sort of recognition because they
had had far too many residents such as Norman Douglas, author
of *South Wind*. Due to his predilection for boys, Douglas periodically left Italy in great haste, with a single suitcase, being
allowed to return only after the indignant parents had been molli-
fied. Lest this seem intolerant, it should be noted that the attitude
of the Fascist officials toward such customs was much stricter than
at the present time. Mussolini's "passion for order" included chas-
ing Mr. Douglas out of Italy, but he always got back in, and he
bore no scars. Visitors to Italy haven't been banned for these
practices since Mussolini was hanged by the heels in a town
marketplace.

As Mr. Pound did not wish to corrupt anyone, he spent a very
pleasant two decades with the townspeople of Rapallo, until the
soldiers took him away. George Antheil turned up, as did Richard
Aldington, William Butler Yeats, and others of Ezra's friends.
Lady Trowbridge came for a visit, accompanied by her companion,
Radclyffe Hall, who was then under indictment in England for her

book, *The Well of Loneliness* (1928), which deals with the problems of a lesbian.

Antheil noted that there was only one decent restaurant in the town, the café at the main hotel. There he sat at table one afternoon with two Nobel Prize winners, Yeats and the German playwright Gerhart Hauptmann. They were both fond of reading detective stories, so Antheil wrote one for them. It was published under the name of "Stacey Bishop" and was entitled *Death in the Dark*.

One day, Antheil fainted on the street. Pound picked him up and carried him to the doctor, who found that he was suffering from some sort of condition that would be improved by a stay on the Isle of Capri. This was the scene of some of Norman Douglas' scrapes with the law. Antheil departed for this romantic place, leaving Ezra to the companionship of his Nobel Prize winners and to such occasional visitors as Emil Ludwig and Franz Werfel.

Richard Aldington has recorded one of the most interesting *non sequiturs* in literary history, as follows: "William Butler Yeats and his wife once dined with me at my hotel in Rapallo. Spaghetti was served, and a long thin lock of Yeats' hair got into the corner of his mouth, while the rest of us watched in silent awe his efforts to swallow a bit of his own hair instead of the pasta. Giving up this hopeless task, in dudgeon he suddenly turned to me and said in a deep voice: 'How do you account for Ezra?' "

Apparently Aldington was unequal to the question, for he has not recorded his reply. He delivered this anecdote in a lecture to an American university audience, and later included it in his autobiography.[7] The story proves one thing—whenever one of the twentieth century literati comes upon something which he cannot swallow, he instinctively thinks of Ezra Pound. It is odd that Yeats, who used to introduce his friends to the ghosts who sat at his table, never considered Ezra as some sort of supernatural phenomenon; but if so, he never mentioned it. Probably he thought of Ezra as the most earthbound of men, and Ezra had little use for Yeats' "spooks", as he termed them.

Nevertheless, it was his friendship with Pound that drew Yeats to Rapallo for some of the most pleasant months of his life. He had been a Senator in Ireland for some six years, at a tax-free salary of three hundred pounds per year, a result of his work during the Irish Revolution, but now his health was poor, and he had been advised to seek warmer climes. His political service ended in 1928, and he came that summer to Italy.

In *A Packet for Ezra Pound,* he describes the little town where Ezra spent much of his life: "Mountains that shelter the bay from all but the strongest wind, bare brown branches of low vines and of tall trees blurring their outline as though with a soft mist; houses mirrored in an almost motionless sea; a verandahed gable a couple of miles away bringing to mind some Chinese painting. Rapallo's thin line of broken mother-of-pearl along the water's edge. The little town described in An Ode on a Grecian Urn. In what better place could I, forbidden Dublin winters, and all excited crowded places, spend what winters yet remain?

"On the broad pavement by the sea pass Italian peasants or working people, people out of the little shops, a famous German dramatist, the barber's brother looking like an Oxford don, a British retired skipper, an Italian prince descended from Charlemagne and no richer than the rest of us, and a few tourists seeking tranquillity. As there is no great harbour full of yachts, no great yellow strand, no great ballroom, no great casino, the rich carry elsewhere their strenuous life."[8]

In the winter of 1929, Yeats took rooms on the Via Americhe in Rapallo. On March 2, 1929, he wrote to Olivia Shakespear, "Tonight we dine with Ezra, the first dinner-coated meal since I got here—to meet Hauptmann who does not even know one word of English but is fine to look at—after the fashion of William Morris. Auntille—how do you spell him?—and his lady will be there and probably a certain Basil Bunting, one of Ezra's more savage disciples. He got into jail as a pacifist and then for assaulting the police and carrying concealed weapons and he is now writing up Antille's music."[9]

Hauptmann was a yearly visitor to Rapallo, spending part of each winter there. He had done well as Germany's leading dramatist, and his income from his work allowed him to maintain a magnificent place, "Der Weisenstein", near Dresden, as well as a summer home on the Baltic Island of Hiddensee. He would spend his autumns at a resort in the Alps, and then go on to Rapallo.

Yeats does not record whether he was able to exchange any conversation with Hauptmann, but they were almost the same age and had been successful for about the same number of decades. Hauptmann had received his Nobel Prize in 1912, while Yeats was a more recent winner, having been awarded this honor in 1923.

Yeats again mentioned Hauptmann in a letter to Olivia Shakespear of December 12, 1929: "Hauptmann has returned. He also has had blood-pressure. He uncautiously ventured to the doctor, enticed there by his son though feeling 'perfectly well.' The doctor said, 'Blood-pressure, produced by the strain of walking upright, you must become a quadruped once more,' and put him to bed for a month, depriving him of meat dinners and champagne. 'But why should anybody say I drink too much champagne? I only drink two or three bottles a day, and there are men who drink four.' Now he is out of bed and can't make out why he feels so extraordinarily vigorous but is quite certain that the doctor is a great genius, especially as he is now allowed to eat and drink as much as he likes. (It would have been no use telling him not to.)"[10]

The champagne regimen does not seem to have adversely affected Hauptmann. He lived on in good health until 1945, when the shock of seeing his home and the city of Dresden levelled by foreign bombers put him to bed, and he died soon afterwards.

Ezra's early years in Rapallo were enlivened by an amusing struggle between himself and his old Vorticist cohort, Wyndham Lewis. The battle, an international affair, was fierce; the weapons were magazines. Lewis began the fray in January, 1927, with the first issue of a periodical which he called *The Enemy*. Although the number contained an article by T. S. Eliot, most of it was taken up with the first section of a book by Lewis, *The Revolutionary Simpleton,* which later appeared under the title, *Time and Western Man* (1927).

The "revolutionary simpleton", of course, was none other than our Ezra.

Lewis wrote, "He [Ezra] was a born revolutionary, a Trotsky of the written word and the painted shape. Where he detected the slightest hint of fractious disposition, expressing itself in verse or pigment, he became delirious. He instructed the incipient rough-neck how to construct the infernal machine, he would spare no pains. I have encountered many a carbuncular little protégé of Ezra's who would produce from a vest pocket a packet of letters, full of instructions and admonitions—all typed in a violent-blue ink, and written in the most fantastic jargon. A most healthy destructive force, but more promiscuous than is permissible. I have called him a 'revolutionary simpleton.' I take this occasion of calling him that again."[11]

Lewis errs on the side of quantity when he only remembers the carbuncular protégés and ignores the writers who have derived positive benefit from Ezra's influence. He offers a rambling diatribe against the artistic Bohemians of the 1920s, whom Lewis in some way links with another of his dislikes, Oswald Spengler. He also tucks Gertrude Stein and Ezra into the same bed, which I am sure neither of them appreciated.

Despite its inadequacies, the book found an enthusiast in Yeats. After reading it, he wrote to Olivia Shakespear on November 29, 1927, telling her that he liked the book very much.[12] Again, in a letter dated December 12, 1927, he asked her to "Tell Wyndham Lewis that I am in all essentials his most humble and admiring disciple."[13]

Yeats wrote to Lady Gregory on April 11, 1928, from Villars-sur-Bex, Switzerland, "Have you read Wyndham Lewis? He attacked Ezra Pound and Joyce in 'Time and Western Man' and is on my side of the fence philosophically. My essay takes up the controversy and explains Ezra Pound sufficiently to keep him as a friendly neighbor, for I see that in the winter he must take Russell's place of a Monday evening. He has most of Maud Gonne's opinions (political and economic) about the world in general, being what Lewis calls 'the revolutionary simpleton.' The chief difference is that he hates Palgrave's Golden Treasury as she does the Free State Government, and thinks even worse of its editor than she does of President Cosgrave. He has even her passion for cats and large numbers wait him every night at a certain street corner knowing that his pocket is full of meat bones or chicken bones. They belong to the oppressed races."[14]

Ezra could not remain without a voice after such a biting attack, and he immediately started his own magazine, *The Exile,* in which he displayed his current disciples as a phalanx against Lewis' continued blasts. He did not answer Lewis directly; indeed, it would have been difficult to do so, as *The Enemy* had simply put its head down and charged. Modern art in its more extreme manifestations irritated Lewis, and, rightly or wrongly, he blamed Pound for Joyce, Stein, and perhaps even for Oswald Spengler.

During most of his life, Pound has been under attack as the symbol of something that somebody didn't like, whether it was Imagist poetry, Vorticist sculpture, or Fascism. The odd thing is that he is never praised for anything. If a critic likes an Imagist poet, he praises the poet without mentioning Pound; but if he dislikes Imagism, he dashes past Amy Lowell to get in a blow at Pound. In the same way, if someone has a good word to say for Fascism, he praises Mussolini, but if he dislikes Fascism, he ignores Mussolini and attacks Pound. This is due to Pound's predilection for sticking his neck out, and for drawing the erratic fire of various citizens and soldiers to himself. Usually, he is not seriously involved in any of these movements—his first and foremost concern has always been his own work, which has never owed its life to any of these schools—but he is the first target to draw fire.

At any rate, the initial number of *The Exile,* dated Spring, 1927, contained the work of Ernest Hemingway, John Rodker, Guy Hickok, and Richard Aldington. Ezra included part of his "Canto XX".

Hemingway's contribution was embarrassingly inept—a short work entitled "Neothomist Poem", which reads as follows:

> The Lord is my shepherd, I shall not want
> him for long[.]

With his usual biting humor, Aldington contributed a poem entitled, "Natal Verse for the Birth of a New Review":

> Let us resurrect the useful word Dick kopfig,
> Let us apply it to those it fits,

Above all let us apply it to ourselves.
But in any case let us apply it to Don Ezra,
Who, having secured at the prime of his life
A more than Horatian otium,
And having obtained more applause by his silence
Than ever he obtained by his not always negligible speech,
Now, in the eighth lustre of his career
When the libidinous itch for publicity
Should long ago have subsided into placid indifference
Madly casts away the only true felicity
For the ignominious servitude
And distracting toil
Of Editorship!
Let fall the blows upon his head—
For he will need all its thickness—
And let us regret the fall of this man
For he once had the courage
To be silent for several years.

Thus, far from attracting defenders, Ezra found himself in a nest of vipers. Aldington's contribution, no doubt, was meant to be good-humored, but it seems more malicious than otherwise. Perhaps he thought that Pound would not print it. Such a step would have been justified on the grounds of literary merit, but since the contributions that Ezra was able to cull for his new publication were not to be paid for, they were on the flippant side.

Pound injected a serious note in his editorial: "As to an editorial program: The republic, *res publica* means, or ought to mean 'the public convenience': when it does not, it is an evil, to be ameliorated or amended out of, or into, decent existence. Detailed emendment is usually easier, and we await proof that any other course is necessary. But in so far as America is concerned, we should like to know whether there is *any* mental activity outside the so-called 'revolutionary elements,' the communescents, etc.

"At present, in that distressed country, it would seem that neither side ever answers the other; such ignoring leading, in both cases, to ignorance. I should like a small open forum in which the virtues or faults of *either* side might be mentioned without excess animus. Both Fascio and the Russian revolution are interesting phenomena; beyond which there is the historic perspective. Herrin and Passaic are also phenomena, and indictments.

"The capitalist imperialist state must be judged not only in comparison with unrealized utopias, but on past forms of the state; if it will not bear comparison with the feudal order; with the small city states both republican and despotic; either as to its 'social justice' or as to its permanent products, art, science, literature, the onus of proof goes against it.

"The contemporary state will have to digest this concept; the state as convenience.

"The antithesis is: the state as an infernal nuisance. . . . The artist, the maker is always too far ahead of any revolution, or re-action, or counter-revolution or counter-reaction for his vote to have any immediate result, and his party program never contains enough of his program to give him the least satisfaction. The party that follows him wins: and the speed with which they set about it, is the measure of their practical capacity and intelligence. Blessed are they who pick the right artists and makers. . . . The American view is expressed in the Harding memorial postage stamp. . . . The American view as expressed by the leading American intelligentsia is that America is the most colossal monkey house and prize exhibit that the astonished world has yet seen; and that for this reason one *should* delight in the spectacle, and that as a spectacle it is unrivalled and diverting, not being a descendant of the Marquis de Sade, or a follower of the, I believe, Hungarian Massoch, I am unable to appreciate this form of pleasure."

This editorial presents one of Ezra's most revolutionary concepts, which sweeps all current "isms" into limbo. We must agree with Wyndham Lewis that he is revolutionary, but that he is a simpleton is not so apparent, unless one accepts as the definition of a simpleton, "one to whom all things are simple."

"Res publica, the state as convenience." These words should be carved in stone above our halls, or seats, of government. All of the modern concepts of the state treat this institution arbitrarily as a force whose arrogance must be absorbed by the citizens, the degree of oppression being greater or slighter, according to which "ism" you prefer.

Pound's suggestion is one that will strike fear into the heart of every bureaucrat and liberal. The bureaucrat sees the state as the god without whom he could not exist; the liberal sees the state as the only force that can implement his otherwise unpalatable desires. Even Trotsky pointed out that "Liberal principles can only be enforced by the police power." But Pound neutralizes these concepts with his axiom "The state as convenience." It is no accident that this idea should reach his homeland some three decades after he had advanced it, for he has often mentioned the thirty-year time lag in this country before serious work is noticed.

The basis of Ezra's struggle against bureaucracy—his "treason" if you will—is based on two fundamental concepts: "the state as convenience" and the tax system as "legalized robbery". It is no wonder that his captors put him in a madhouse for thirteen years. No doubt, he would have been shot had they not feared that this would only accelerate the circulation of his ideas. For they are *his* ideas. I fail to discover in Plato or Pascal anything so obvious, even though these abuses already existed, in a lesser degree, during their lifetimes.

Ezra once said to me, "I did not understand, until I read Confucius, the impact of one man upon another." He suggests that Confucius is the philosophical base for many of his ideas, as explained in the editorial in *The Exile* of Autumn, 1927:

"The dreary horror of American life can be traced to two damnable roots, or perhaps it is only one root: 1. the loss of all distinction between public and private affairs. 2. the tendency to mess into other people's affairs before establishing order in one's own affairs, and in one's thought. To which one might perhaps add the lack in America of any habit of connecting or correlating *any* act or thought to *any* main principle whatever, the ineffable rudderlessness of that people. The principle of good is enunciated by Confucius, it consists of establishing order within oneself. This order or harmony spreads by a sort of contagion without special effort. The principle of evil consists in messing into other people's affairs. Against this principle of evil no adequate precaution is taken by Christianity, Moslemism, Judaism, nor, as far as I know, by any monotheistic religion. Many 'mystics' do not even aim at the principle of good; they seek merely establishment of a parasitic relationship with the unknown. The original Quakers may have had some adumbration of the good principle. (But no early Quaker texts are available in this village.)"

Ezra's preference for Confucian principles is based upon his statement that "It is the only system which shows a concern with social order." This explains why he has devoted so many years to giving us the thought of Confucius in digestible language. In his translation entitled *The Unwobbling Pivot and the Great Digest of Confucius,* he says, "Finding the precise word for the inarticulate heart's tone means not lying to oneself, as in the case of hating a bad smell or loving a beautiful person, also called respecting one's own nose. On this account the real man has to look his heart in the eye even when he is alone.

"You improve the old homestead by material riches and irrigation; you enrich and irrigate the character by the process of looking straight into the heart and then acting on the results. Thus the mind becomes your palace and the body can be at ease; it is for this reason that the great gentleman must find the precise verbal expression for his inarticulate thoughts.[15]

"That is the meaning of the saying: If a man does not discipline himself he cannot bring order into the home.

"One humane family can humanize a whole state; one courteous family can lift a whole state into courtesy; one grasping and perverse man can drive a nation into chaos. Such are the seeds of movement . . . (semina motuum, the inner impulses of the tree). That is what we mean by: one word will ruin the business, one man can bring the state to an orderly course."[16]

These pithy excerpts, chosen at random from many such thoughts presented in Ezra's Chinese translations, explain what he wants to give to us. The greatest human problem, and the one most fraught with difficulties, is the problem of communicating with others, and here civilization is always put to the ultimate test. "The inarticulate heart's tone," that beautiful phrase for the melody of the being, depends upon not lying to oneself, a much more demanding precept than the conventional admonition that one should not lie to others.

We have seen in recent years the terrible truth in the Confucian saying "One humane family can humanize a whole state." Russell Kirk has written graphically of the decay of the great houses in

England and Scotland, those manifestations of a culture that now lie roofless to the weather, symbolizing the vanished glories of their builders as well as the present apathy of the village inhabitants. The strength of the shire, and its ability to produce people who emigrated to various parts of the world and distinguished themselves, notably in America, was centered in the "humane family" occupying the great house, and their humane influence pervaded the entire community. Now that good manners have been equated with tyranny, the villagers have returned to the graces of their cattle.[17]

The American South also has benefited by the influence of the "great house" and its humane influence. Now that most of its mansions are in decay, or restored and in the hands of "Yankees", the influence is hardly discernible, although traces of it linger in speech and minor courtesies.

Ezra's translations of Confucius were not widely reviewed in the United States because the first mention of the word "order" in contemporary intellectual circles is equivalent to the cry of "Fire!" in a crowded theater. Everyone dashes for the exits. Confucius states (and this is out of context) that "One man can bring the state to an orderly course." By this he means one "humane" man, not a Fascist dictator. Confucius treats of the "gentleman in government", not the egomaniac.

The history of modern Europe might have been quite different had Mr. Hitler been able to bring order into his thought, but he is seldom criticized on that ground, perhaps because many self-styled liberals think in the same irregular fashion that he did. Their minds proceed in a sort of Cinerama, at one moment whirling down the roller-coaster of psychoanalysis, and the next moment drifting in a balloon over Paris.

Fighting this trend, Ezra Pound was driven further and further from his homeland, geographically speaking, but at the same time, he was drifting closer to his roots. At least he came to an understanding of those Confucian gentlemen of the early Republic, Mr. Washington and Mr. Adams, whose *virtu* stemmed from the humane families of Great Britain.

In these editorials, Ezra was carrying on his battle with Wyndham Lewis, "the enemy", with his usual strategy. He presented his ideas in rebuttal of the other man's ideas in the belief that the best ideas should win. I do not say that they do, but they should. At any rate, after three numbers, *The Enemy* retired from the contest.

The second number of *The Exile* was published by Pascal Covici in Chicago. The first issue had been printed in Dijon by Maurice Darantiere, who had printed *Ulysses* and other avant-garde works. Ezra decided that he might find a larger public in the United States if he had the magazine printed there. Samuel Putnam put him in touch with Covici, who was willing to take a flyer on its prospects. He printed the second, third and fourth issues. The expected number of subscribers did not materialize, and that was the end of *The Exile*.

The Autumn, 1927 issue also contained a prose piece by Robert McAlmon, a description of the Paris Bohemia entitled "Truer Than Most Accounts". It had been written in 1922, and McAlmon gave it to Pound. He later asked that it be returned, but Pound held onto it, and five years later, was able to print it. Pound also included perhaps the only surviving chapter from Joe Gould's *Oral History of the World,* which had been sent on at the instigation of E. E. Cummings. Pound commented, "Mr. Joe Gould's prose style is uneven."

The third issue of *The Exile,* dated Spring, 1928, contained poems by William Butler Yeats, Louis Zukofsky and Pound. There was also the concluding chapter of a long story by John Rodker. On the magazine's title page was the bold motto "Res Publica— the public convenience."

Pound appended a long list of editorial suggestions, containing such pointed items as the following:

"3. All bureaucrats should be drowned. All interference in human affairs by people paid to interfere ought to be stopped."

"5. Le style c'est homme. Knowledge of this simple fact would have saved us from Woodie Wilson."

"6. All officials in the State dept. ought to be vacuum-cleaned."

Pound antedated Joe McCarthy's assault on the State Department by more than two decades. Despite this warning, no improvements were made until the lad from Wisconsin came onto the scene. As for Woodie Wilson, his style did not alert the American public against him, perhaps because no one ever read his dry historical writings.

In October, 1951, Ezra wrote me a note on Wilson: "From perusal of House's and Wilson's own writing it is difficult to form an estimate of their ethics, that is to say, they may have thought themselves honest. They did not believe in democracy or in representative government. Like all men who have respected Alex. Hamilton they believed in financial oligarchy and dictatorship. They played into the hands of international usury and control of that most vital 'instrument of policy' the issue of purchasing power. This they imposed on an unconscious public. There is not the slightest shadow of doubt that they knew their acts to be serious, vide House Memoirs, where the Reserve Board is considered (as) important as the Supreme Court of the nation. As an historian Woodrow is second only to Parson Weems, and shows no curiosity regarding the colonial period."

In order to compensate for the havoc wrought by his fellow American, Wilson, at the Versailles Peace Conference, Ezra Pound was trying to promote international peace during the 1920s. "Being in Vienna in 1928," he recently wrote, "and convinced that a character like Murray Butler would pay no attention to a communication from anyone not a millionaire or in high position I gave Mensdorf's secretary a few notes on the causes of war. Mensdorf being head of the local Carnegie contraption which had I believe no intention of doing anything useful, any more than Norman Angel or any of the professional exploiters of pacifist yatter, it seemed likely that a letter would at least be read by the N.Y. headquarters. Count Mensdorf took over the 1st/2nd and 3rd points of my summary, rejected 'dynastic intrigues' on grounds that as faithful servant he could not speak ill of the Habsburg, and I recognized at once that in any case Crowned Heads were no better than in J. Adams times and they had pretty well gone out of reality when all the swine in France, Bourbonist, Orleanist and Bonapartist ganged up on theirs who had got the banks by the scruff of the neck; had got their rate to government from 3% down to one and was going Jacksonian i.e. wanting to get rid of National Debt altogether.

"As I recall it Mensdorf's first suggestions included specific recommendation from reprint of Grotius and Puffendorf, but they seem to have got omitted, along with my 'dynastic intrigues.' In any case the Mensdorf letter got to N.Y., and was answered by an underling, as per enclosure which Dr. Matsih forwarded in copy to me in Rapallo, with ms/ note that it was copy of the Carnegie Endowment to Count Albert Mensdorf. (Das thust du nicht, Albert, in Canto whatever.)

"I take it the Endowment will not reply to a request from you to shed light on further actions, reactions or inactions, but can supply fotocopy of the two documents, along with the seal of Bundeskanzleramt, Republik Osterreich, Auswartige Angeleger, if required."

Ezra enclosed copies of the Count's letter to the Endowment and their reply. The points mentioned in the Count's letter are those suggested by Pound, and he also had them printed as an editorial in the last issue of *The Exile,* Autumn, 1928:

"From Albert Mensdorff-Pouilly-Dietrichstein, member of the Comite d'Administration, Minoritenplatz 3, Vienna 1, to Professor Nicholus Murray Butler, Chairman of the Executive Committee, Carnegie Endowment for Peace, 405 West 117th Street, New York City;

Sir,

"On page 67 of your Year Book of 1927 the wish is expressed for suggestions and collaboration of thought. This gave me the idea that I might venture to suggest certain points as worth while some study, considering the causes of war, which it might be perhaps more useful to go into carefully than to investigate the causes of war.

Some of these causes are:

1) Intense production and sale of munitions; the whole of the trade in munitions and armaments might be subjugated to contemporary, not retrospective investigation via trade channels.

2) Overproduction and dumping, leading to trade rivalries and irritation.

3) The intrigues of interested cliques.

All these are general and constantly active forces toward war. Further there are particular present subjects which might be clarified by Carnegie study.

1) The principles of international law as recognized by the decisions of the permanent international Court of Justice, should be studied and codified and summarised by clear statement.

2) We should be grateful for a clear explanation or study of the meanings of the reservations of the U.S.A. re adhesion to the permanent international Court of Justice.

3) And also for the interpretation of the Kellogg proposals for the outlawry of war and the war prevention policy of the U.S.A.

4) And for a further study of the attempt of the League of Nations to codify international law, if you are not already dealing fully with this matter.

> I remain very truly yours
> Albert Mensdorff
> per Matsih"

The Endowment's reply is as follows:

> "CARNEGIE ENDOWMENT FOR
> INTERNATIONAL PEACE
> 405 West 117th St.
> New York City
> July 26, 1928

My dear Count von Mensdorff,

In the absence of President Butler I have the honor to acknowledge receipt of your letter of June 18 which will be brought to his attention as soon as possible. In the meantime I am writing to Dr. Shotwell, Director of the Division of Economics and History advising him of the first three numbered suggestions in your letter. I am also writing to Dr. James Brown Scott, Director of the Division of International Law calling his attention to the last four numbered suggestions. In studying plans for work in the future we shall consider carefully all your suggestions and I beg to thank you cordially for giving us the benefit of your advice on the various subjects.

> Sincerely yours,
> Henry S. Haskell m.p.
> Assistant to the Director."

The letter was forwarded to Ezra by Count von Mensdorff, and that was the last that either of them heard from the Carnegie Endowment for International Peace. There have been several wars in the interim.

The Dr. Shotwell mentioned by Mr. Haskell has served long and faithfully with the Carnegie institution. He was named as the successor to Alger Hiss when the foundation's trustees, Dwight D. Eisenhower and John Foster Dulles, accepted Hiss' resignation from the Carnegie presidency, some six months after his indictment on two counts of perjury. Hiss had denied taking some papers from the State Department, which later turned up in a pumpkin.

Ezra's years in Rapallo were not devoted merely to promoting world peace, writing his *Cantos,* and developing young talents. He also had issue. Yeats wrote to Olivia Shakespear, September 5, 1926, "I hear that you are to be a grandmother and that the event is taking place in the usual secrecy. You are probably furious, but will find a grandchild a pleasing distraction in the end. It is an ideal relationship, for your business will be unmixed indulgence. I congratulate you upon it. Dorothy being doubtless still more furious will make an excellent mother. Motherly 'O God fill my quivers' mothers have made the world the disagreeable place it is. Your (grand) child—I am as you know a prophet—will grow up intelligent and revere your memory."[18]

Yeats proved correct, as Omar Shakespear Pound, the son who duly arrived, is following in his father's footsteps as a scholar.

Yeats and Pound continued to be close friends for some years in Rapallo. They went on a trip to Sicily to test the acoustics of the ancient Greek theatres, and Pound noted that Yeats was enjoying unusually good health at this time. Yeats went on alone to look at the Byzantine mosaics of Monreale and the Capella Palatine at Palermo. Pound was not then interested in the Byzantine. Later, because of his study of economics, he discovered that the Byzantine economy survived through twelve centuries, the longest period any civilization has endured in recorded history.

Yeats continued to have trouble with his lungs. While at Rapallo, he had another breakdown, and on March 8, 1930, he wrote to Olivia Shakespear, "Today I met Ezra for the first time—you know his dread of infections—seeing me in the open air and the sea air, he sat beside me in front of the cafe and admired my beard, and declared that I should be sent by the Free State as Minister to Austria, that Austria alone would perfectly appreciate my beard."[19]

He again mentioned Ezra's dislike of germs in a letter to Lady Gregory of April 7, 1930: "Ezra Pound arrived the other day, his first visit since I got ill—fear of infection—and being warned by his wife tried to be very peaceable but couldn't help being very litigious about Confucius who I consider should have worn an Eighteenth Century wig and preached in St. Pauls, and he thinks the perfect man."[20]

Yeats' conception of Confucius as an eighteenth-century preacher is an interesting one, not too far removed from the concept of the "humane man", and one can only wonder what Ezra's disagreement on this idea could have been.

Soon afterwards, Yeats rented his Rapallo apartment to Ezra's father, who had retired from the U.S. Mint and joined his son in Italy. At that time, the Steinach operation for rejuvenation of the glandular system was the rage, and Yeats underwent it. He said that he felt very fresh afterwards, but his health never showed any marked improvement.

He spent several months at Majorca with the Swami, Sri Purohit, correcting the English translation of that gentleman's version of the *Upanishads,* much to his wife's disgust. She felt that he should be putting in this time on his own poetry. The Swami's language was much too ornate and flowery for an English audience, and Yeats' work consisted essentially of what Ezra had done for him in 1914, that is making the style communicate something, rather than hang in the air like the swirling decorations for a parade.

Yeats wrote to Olivia Shakespear on March 9, 1933, "I wish I could put the swami's lectures into the Cuala series but I can not. My sisters' books are like an old family magazine. A few hundred people buy them and expect a common theme. Only once did I put a book into the series that was not Irish—Ezra's Noh plays—and I had to write a long introduction to annex Japan to Ireland."[21]

On his return visits to Rapallo, Yeats seems to have enjoyed his bouts with Pound, for their meetings were always, at this stage, verbal boxing matches. He writes in the preface to *The King of the Great Clock Tower* (1934), ". . . I wrote the prose dialogue of the 'King of the Great Clock Tower' that I might be forced to make lyrics for its imaginary people. When I had written all but the last lyric I went a considerable journey partly to get the advice of a poet not of my school who would, as he did some years ago, say what he thought. I asked him to dine, tried to get his attention. 'I'm in my sixty-ninth year,' I said, 'probably I should stop writing verse, I want your opinion on some verse I have been writing lately.' I had hoped he would ask me to read it but he would not speak of art, or of literature, or of anything related to them. I had however been talking to his latest disciples and knew that his opinions had not changed: Phidias had corrupted sculpture, we had nothing of true Greek but certain Nike dug up out of the foundations of the Parthenon, and that corruption ran through all our art; Shakespeare and Dante had corrupted literature, Shakespeare by his too abounding sentiment, Dante by his compromise with the Church.

"He said apropos of nothing 'Arthur Balfour was a scoundrel,' and from that time on would talk of nothing but politics. All the other modern statesmen were more or less scoundrels except 'Mussolini and that hysterical imitator of his, Hitler.' When I objected to his violence he declared that Dante considered all sins intellectual, even sins of the flesh, he himself refused to make the modern distinction between error and sin. He urged me to read the works of Captain Douglas who alone knew what caused our suffering. He took my manuscript, and went away denouncing Dublin as 'a reactionary hole' because I had said that I was re-reading Shakespeare, would go on to Chaucer, and found all that I wanted of modern life in 'detection and the wild West.' Next day his judgment came and that in a single word 'Putrid.' "[22]

Yeats sought other opinions, and finally published the play, which enjoyed a certain success. On August 7, 1934, he wrote to Olivia Shakespear, "Send the enclosed cutting to Dorothy to show to Ezra that I may confound him. He may have been right to condemn it as poetry but he condemned it as drama. It has turned out the most popular of my dance plays."[23]

Despite his gentle aversion to much that Ezra said to him, Yeats usually found him stimulating, and stimulation, after all, rarely comes cheaply. He wrote to his old friend T. Sturge Moore, veteran of their all-night wine and poetry sessions in London,

"Ezra Pound has just been in. He says 'Spengler is a Wells who has founded himself on German scholarship instead of English journalism.' He is sunk in Frobenius, Spengler's German source, and finds him the most interesting person. Frobenius originated the idea that cultures, including arts and sciences, arise out of races, express those races as if they were fruit and leaves in a preordained order, and perish with them; and the two main symbols, the Cave and the Boundless. He proved from his logic, some German told Ezra, that a certain civilization must have once existed at a certain spot in Africa, and then went and dug it up. He proves his case all through by African research. I can not read German so must get him second hand. He has confirmed a conception I have had for many years, a conception that has freed me from British liberalism and all its dreams. The one heroic sanction is that of the last battle of the Norse gods, or a gay struggle without hope. Long ago I used to puzzle Maud Gonne by always ultimately avowing defeat as a test. And our literary movement would be worthless but for its defeat. Science is the criticism of Myth. There would be no Darwin had there been no Book of Genesis, no electron but for the Greek atomic myth; and when the fire of criticism is finished there is not even a drift of ashes on the pyre. Sexual desire dies because every touch consumes the Myth, and yet a Myth that can not be so consumed becomes a spectre."[24]

In his old age, Yeats became quite philosophical, and the philosophy stated here is the one which is evolving from man's life in the twentieth century. As a Virginian, I knew defeat; therefore, I was able to know culture. Though his reference to "the last battle of the Norse gods" strikes terror into the hearts of the subhumans, it is the basic concept of modern life.

Frobenius became one of the principal contributors to Ezra's *paideuma.* One of his first efforts on my behalf was an attempt to get me a scholarship from the Bollingen Foundation, so that I could translate the works of Frobenius into English. Except for one or two earlier works, they have never been translated; the work of his *epigones,* such as Malinowski and Margaret Mead, is seen everywhere, and passes for basic anthropology in America.

In continuation of his stark philosophy of the later years—a sort of Greek bareness of rocks and sea, such as we find in the plays of John Millington Synge—Yeats wrote in one of his essays of the 1930s, "I think that profound philosophy must come from terror. An abyss opens under our feet; inherited conventions, the presuppositions of our thoughts, those Fathers of the Church Johnson expounded, drop into the abyss. Whether we will or no we must ask the ancient questions; Is there reality anywhere? Is there a God? Is there a Soul? We cry with the Indian Sacred Book: 'They put a golden stopper into the neck of the bottle: pull it! Let out reality!' "[25]

Despite his growing tolerance of terror, Yeats still found Ezra's poetry too much for him. He wrote to Dorothy Wellesley on September 8, 1935, "I'm tired, I have spent the day reading Ezra Pound for the Anthology—a single strained attitude instead of passion, the sexless American professor for all his violence."[26]

The anthology was *The Oxford Book of Modern Verse,* published in 1937. Yeats included Pound's "River Merchant's Wife", "Canto XVII", and excerpts from the Propertius poem.

The talks between Yeats and Pound at Rapallo must have been enormously interesting for them both. Each was secure in his reputation, and could afford to speak frankly. The relationship was no longer that of master and disciple, of Europe learning from America, or vice versa.

Ezra quotes Yeats in the *Cantos,* "Nothing affects these people / Except our conversation."[27] Certainly this communion of minds was fraught with all sorts of possibilities. Even today, two and a half billion people wait in fear of those two or three minds, now active, who will sooner or later inaugurate a new and an even bloodier struggle, by bringing forth a New Idea!

Ezra should not cavil at the revenge that the gods have wreaked on him, for he has done great damage to their hitherto secure Olympus. The mind of man is a force as violent as anything to be found in nature, and is not civilization too but an idea, the manifestation of man's idea of himself? Ah, protests Sadie Wetwash (better known in the peerage as Lady Hailstone) from the rear of the room, "Is not civilization really God's idea of man?" We acquiesce, but in self-extenuation, we quote the eminent Dutch philosopher, Professor J. Wetmaar Lieverlipps, who recently stated that God is only man's idea of God. In this arena which we call the world, the mind of man remains the primeval force, the only force still respected and feared by the "humanitarians!"

Yeats was an interested observer while Pound worked on the *Cantos,* and the *Packet* contains an excellent note about them. He writes, ". . . For the last hour we sat upon the roof which is also a garden, discussing the immense poem of which but twenty Cantos are already published. I have often found there some scene of distinguished beauty, but have never discovered why all the suits could not be dealt out in some quite different order. Now at last he explains that it will, when the last of the Cantos is finished, display a structure like that of a Bach Fugue. There will be no plot, no chronicle of events, no logic of discourse, but two themes, the descent into Hades from Homer, a metamorphosis from Ovid, and mixed with these mediaeval or modern historical characters. He has tried to produce the picture Porteous commended to Nicholas Poussin in 'Le Chef d'oeuvre Inconnu' where everything rounds or thrusts itself without edges, without contours—conventions of the intellect—from a splash of tints or shades, to achieve a work as characteristic of the art of our time as the paintings of Cezanne, avowedly suggested by Porteous, as Ulysses and its dream association of words and images, a poem in which there is nothing that can be taken out and reasoned over, nothing that is not a part of the poem itself. . . . It is almost impossible to understand the art of a generation younger than one's own. I was wrong about Ulysses when I had read but some first fragments, and I do not want to be wrong again above all in judging verse. Perhaps when the sudden Italian spring has come I may have discovered what will seem all the more, because the opposite of what I have attempted, unique and unforgettable."[28]

The *Cantos* have been Pound's most controversial work for his critics, because of their form, or what, to critics who are buried in the past, is considered lack of form.[29] Yet in his review of *A Draft of XXX Cantos,* an essay entitled "Ezra Pound's Golden Ass", Allen Tate points out that the form of the *Cantos* is very simple.[30] It is the form of conversation. When two people, or a group, meet and have converse, they form a relationship (really a new form), and their converse or intercourse takes place within that relationship. The *Cantos* take place within the interrelated aspects of man's existence, and as such, they can only puzzle those who are unfamiliar with that existence.

In one of the first comments on the *Cantos,* T. S. Eliot wrote, in 1917, "We would leave it as a test: when anyone has studied Mr. Pound's poems in *chronological* order, and has mastered 'Lustra' and 'Cathay,' he is prepared for the *Cantos*—but not until then."[31]

This suggestion still holds true. The reader should not approach the *Cantos* as his first step in discovering Pound. The necessity of familiarizing oneself with the body of Pound's poetical and critical work is not as painful a duty as it may sound, particularly to those who are not wedded for life to their preconceptions and prejudices. That work offers the only guide extant for young people who wish to write either prose or poetry; the rest of our contemporary writers have seen fit, for reasons best known to themselves, to shroud the creative act in mystery, or at least in Mother Hubbards.

The *Cantos* have served to excite much of that contumely that Pound, alone of present-day writers, seems able to arouse in the reader, the beholder, or the one who has merely heard his name. It is curious that Mr. Eliot and Mr. Yeats, no mean talents, have been unable to touch the wellsprings of fury in the populace as Mr. Pound seems able to do with his slightest work. Perhaps this is because Mr. Pound deals with realities, and realities are apt to touch us where we do not wish to be touched. As long as poets confine themselves to writing about how pretty the roses are, or praising or excoriating those currently managing the state, or wondering whether the Second Coming has come or gone, they do not really reach us. The discussion of such problems does not lead to the stake.

Richard Aldington stated in 1939 that "The proper place for Pound's Cantos is in D'Israeli's Curiosities of Literature, unless indeed it fits better into his Calamities of Authors. . . . Pound is really at his best in the penumbra of speech; where his reader is left just a little uncertain what the poet really meant to say and yet cannot help feeling that something rather beautiful has been said."[32]

In his later years, Aldington has busied himself with slashing attacks upon the writers whom he knew in his youth. He has written opprobrious biographies of Norman Douglas, D. H. Lawrence, T. E. Lawrence, and others. He can best be disposed of by remarking that as a critic he compares with Robert Graves.

In *The Saturday Review of Literature,* of January 19, 1935, John Crowe Ransom complained that he thought the *Cantos* were "missing the effect of poetry." Perhaps he should have qualified this by saying that the *Cantos* miss the effect of the poetry that he was accustomed to reading.

The New York *Times* carried a favorable review of *A Draft of XXX Cantos* by Roa Lou Walton, April 2, 1933. The critic said, in part, "Pound is a superb technician, perhaps the most important modern prosodist. He has contributed much to modern poetry by his many studies in rhythm. He has taught Eliot his technique. He has taught MacLeish a great deal about speech in poetry."

William Carlos Williams has made contradictory statements about the *Cantos.* He was quite impressed by the early ones, but has withdrawn somewhat from the development of the technique used in the later *Cantos.* He made an interesting comment on Pound in a letter to Kay Boyle, in 1932: "I don't think he has solved anything for us. His line is classic adaptation, no more."[33]

Ezra did not go unnoticed in the United States during his Rapallo years. *The Literary Digest* occasionally mentioned him. A photograph in the March 20, 1926 issue is entitled "An International Radical Literary Trio". The radicals are Ford, agape, on the left, a bored Joyce in the center, and a fierce Pound.

The Literary Digest quoted Pound in the January 14, 1928 issue as follows: "There will be no literate or educated party in American politics in our time; neither Mr. Sandburg nor I, nor even Mr. Ben Hecht, is like to invade the halls of Congress nor lead anyone over the barricades."

Yet we have lived to see Robert Frost's birthday commemorated by Congress, thanks to Sherman Adams; and that egregious Swedish hired hand, Mr. Sandburg, recently addressed a "hushed" Congress (the adjective is *Time*'s) on the occasion of somebody's birthday, but this is not a cultural revolution.

On February 24, 1925, Pound wrote to Simon Guggenheim, congratulating him on the establishment of the Memorial Foundation. He suggested Eliot, Antheil and Marianne Moore as possible beneficiaries of grants, and offered his fullest cooperation. Guggenheim did not avail himself of the offer.[34]

On December 25, 1927, the New York *Times* announced that Ezra Pound had been awarded the annual two-thousand-dollar prize given by *The Dial* for distinguished service to literature. The prize was then discontinued.

Ezra is described on one of his return trips to Paris, in 1930, by Caresse Crosby in a volume appropriately entitled *The Passionate Years* (1953): "We Parisians were ragged pale with winter, but Ezra arrived from Rapallo bronzed and negligé—there was a becoming saltiness to his beard."[35] He had made the trip to arrange for the publication of his *Imaginary Letters* by Caresse's Black Sun Press. They decided to do the town, and she tells us that Ezra danced a wild dance with a tiny Martiniquaise cigarette vendor.

Another of the little magazines, *This Quarter,* began in 1925 with a bold fanfare in honor of Pound, including an enthusiastic letter from James Joyce. The magazine's editors soon shifted their allegiance, as recounted in an editorial by Edward W. Titus in the August-September, 1929, issue of *This Quarter:*

"Arbiter Poetarium. . . . For clarity it should be recalled that the first issue of this quarter, dated Spring, 1925, bore the following eulogistic dedication: 'this number is dedicated to Ezra Pound who by his creative work, his editorship of several magazines, his helpful friendship for young and unknown artists, his many and untiring efforts to win better appreciation of what is first rate in art, comes first to our mind as meriting the gratitude of this generation.' Thus read the dedication, and let us say on our part that the qualities enumerated therein were understated rather than overstated. But in the interval between the first and third numbers of this quarter something had happened. Through the demise of her co-editor, Mr. Ernest Walsh, Miss Ethel Moorhead, having become sole editor, cancelled in the third number of *This Quarter* the dedication which the first number bore in honor of Ezra Pound, in a long editorial from which we abstract the following: 'I herewith take back that dedication. I have said before that Ernest Walsh was disillusioned about Ezra Pound before he died. We take back our generous dedication.' Now that reason which underlay the withdrawal of the dedication did not interest us then and does not interest us now, but the passion, the frenesie mystique, the courage, the moral fervor, the gesture, the utterly rectitudinous illwill and the unprecedented irregularity of it aroused our admiration. In the history of literary quarrels it is, as far as we know, unparalleled. 'Meriting the gratitude of this generation,' the Arbiter Poetarium,—as once the Roman populace hurled from the cliffs Eumolpus, the playmate of that other Arbiter, Petronius, wreathed in vervain and sacred garments,—was by the frail hand of brave little Ethel Moorhead thrown headlong from his eminence."

In 1931, Pound agreed to become a contributing editor for another little magazine, called *The New Review*. It was to be edited by Samuel Putnam, who had arranged for the printing of Ezra's magazine, *The Exile,* in Chicago. Putnam had been assisting Edward Titus, husband of Helena Rubinstein, in editing *This Quarter,* but, according to Alfred Perles, he quarrelled with the stingy Titus and started his own review. Perles describes Putnam as a "dried-up, dyspeptic scholar who translated Rabelais into Modern American."[36]

The New Review attained a total circulation of seventy-three subscribers. Putnam turned it over to Perles and Henry Miller for a few weeks while he was engaged in New York, and discarding a long story by McAlmon, they enlivened the issue with some of Miller's prose. When Putnam returned, he threw them both out. Pound's association with the magazine also was a short one. He intensely disliked one of the other editors, Peter Neagoe, author of *Easter Sun* (1934), and so he resigned. His place was taken by Maxwell Bodenheim.

In August, 1932, Olga Rudge was present when Ford Madox Ford came to Rapallo. She recorded the following conversation, which subsequently appeared in *Il Mare, Western Review,* and *Mood:*

"POUND: What authors should a young Italian writer read if he wants to learn how to write novels?

FORD: (Spitting vigorously) Better to think about finding himself a subject.

POUND: (Suavely, ignoring Ford's irritation) Well, suppose he has already had the intelligence to read Stendhal and Flaubert?

FORD: A different curriculum is needed for each talent. One can learn from Flaubert and from Miss Braddon. In a certain way one can learn as much from a rotten writer as from a great one.

POUND: Which of your books would you like to see translated into Italian and in what order?

FORD: I don't trust translations; they would leave nothing of my best qualities. Some writers are translatable.

POUND: What are the most important qualities in a prose writer?

FORD: What does 'prose writer' mean? The Napoleonic Code or the Canticle of Canticles?

POUND: Let us say a novelist.

FORD: (In agony) Oh Hell! Say philosophical grounding, a knowledge of words' roots, of the meaning of words.

POUND: What should a young prose writer do first?

FORD: (More and more annoyed at the inquisition) Brush his teeth.

POUND: (Ironically calm, with serene magniloquence) In the vast critical output of the illustrious critic now being interviewed (changing tone) . . . , you have praised writer after writer with no apparent distinction (stressing the word 'apparent' nearly with rage). Is there any?

FORD: There are authentic writers and imitation writers; there is no difference among the authentic ones.

POUND: Stick to literary examples.

FORD: Hudson, and Flaubert in Trois Contes. Not all of Flaubert, let us say the Trois Contes.

POUND: You have often spoken to me of 'fine talents.' Are some finer than others?

FORD: (Tries to evade comparison.)

POUND: Are there new writers on a level with Henry James and Hudson?

FORD: (After qualifying Henry James' talent at some length) Yes. Hemingway, Elizabeth Roberts, Caroline Gordon, George Davis. Read 'The Opening of a Door' and 'Penhelly.'

POUND: But as artists? If James is a consummate artist, is Hudson something else? He may be called a pure prose writer, not a novelist.

FORD: The difference between weaving and drawing.

POUND: Now for the term 'promising.' What makes you think a new writer 'promises'?

FORD: The first sentence I read. When two words are put together they produce an overtone. The overtone is the writer's soul. When Stephen Crane wrote, 'The waves are barbarous and abrupt,' he presented simultaneously the sea and the small boat. Waves are not abrupt for a ship. 'Barbarous and abrupt'—onomatopoeic, like 'Poluphloisboion' in Homer (when the Cyclops throws the rock).

POUND: (concluding) How many have kept their promises since the English Review was founded twenty-five years ago?

FORD: Stephen Reynolds is dead. Ezra has become hangman's assistant to interviewers. . . . I don't know what Wyndham Lewis is doing. Norman Douglas. D. H. Lawrence is dead, but kept on 'till the end. Rebecca West. Among the successors: Virginia Woolf; Joyce in 'The Portrait of the Artist as a Young Man'; the Hughes who wrote 'High Wind in Jamaica,' a dramatist's novel, not a novel writer's."[37]

Ford is the only critic who has defined the prose writer. The statement, "When two words are put together they produce an overtone. The overtone is the writer's soul", may be illustrated by quoting the opening of Chapter VI of Ford's novel, *Some Do Not* (1924):

"He let himself in at the heavy door; when he closed it behind him, in the darkness, the heaviness of the door sent long surreptitious whisperings up the great stone stairs."

Pound, we may note, is all poet—he seldom writes a complete sentence of prose. Ford is the greatest prose writer of his time because he represents an end product of Western civilization, the voice of the race, which wells up from its historic consciousness like the tones of a Delphic oracle.

Prose is, like architecture, a frozen music, and a final expression of a people, whereas poetry is international, because it can more readily employ rhythms from other races. The difference in the authoritative forward movement of the sentence may be perceived, by those who have the ear for it, in the statement "Prose is, like architecture, a frozen music." Compare this, for sound, with the manner in which most writers would render this sentence: "Prose, like architecture, is a frozen music." The juxtaposition of "Prose" and "is" sounds a monolithic overtone, whereas the second and more conventional rendering is merely conversational in tone.

As a poet, Pound could burst all the bonds of poetry (in reality, he returned it to more basic melodies which had been weakened by fatty degeneration) with his Imagist Manifesto of 1912, by demanding that the poet compose to the musical phrase, rather than to the metronome. Yet long ago, he went beyond that manifesto. The later *Cantos* are composed to the musical phrase of the idea, so that he may be termed the first poet of the Space Age.

Iris Barry remarked, in *The Bookman,* October, 1931, that "Pound himself is invisible, and, save for his own poetry, comparatively inaudible nowadays. He pontificates rarely, has few disciples, as though in the immense effort of his from 1912–1919 he had done all that (had in truth done more than) could be expected of anyone and were glad of the years from thirty-five onward to till his own plot."

Pound was not as invisible as Miss Barry supposed, for he was carrying on his accustomed vast correspondence. In July, 1931, he wrote to *Hound and Horn:* "Life wd. have been (in my case) much less interesting if I had waited until Joyce, Lewis, D. H. Lawrence etc. complied with what my taste was in 1908. Oh HELL, how shall I put it. My son, elucidate thine own bloody point of view, by its contrast to others, not by trying to make the others conform."

This is quite a plea for tolerance, but it is one which is beyond the capabilities of most editors or readers.

In recognition of Pound's services to the editors of little magazines, Gorham Munson wrote in *The Saturday Review of Litera-*

ture, March 27, 1937, a long tribute from which I quote: "Is there an editor of a little *tendenz* magazine who is not deeply indebted to Pound?—the elder who in the midst of composing his Cantos has read seriously the new publication, has taken the pains to pen his blessing, criticism and suggestions, has sent on writings of his own, and has even out of the straitened circumstances of a poet managed to make cash contributions to save the sinking ship? There is no explaining the time, the unwearying energy, Pound has expended on a succession of literary publications except to say that he is an aficionado."

One might suppose that with all this expenditure of effort, Pound would have built up a devoted clique in the United States, but this was not the case. Many of the editors of little magazines whom he had helped during the 1930s became his most bitter critics.

In 1933, Faber & Faber brought out a collection of work by Pound and his current disciples. *The Active Anthology* included William Carlos Williams, Louis Zukofsky, and T. S. Eliot. Pound included some portions of his *Cantos.*

In the *Prefatiio* to this collection, Pound stated, "Young men are now lured into colleges and universities largely on false pretences." It would be interesting to know if this statement were the inspiration for a suit recently brought against the trustees of Columbia for fraud, when a student charged that he had received no education there, after paying his tuition. The case was thrown out of court, because the plaintiff could not prove his ignorance.

When Pound brought out his *ABC of Reading* (1934), he again illustrated the gap between himself and the critical pack, by pointing out that "The great break in European literary history is the changeover from inflected to uninflected language. And a great deal of critical nonsense has been written by people who did not realize the difference."[38]

In 1935, Pound invaded the field of the American popular magazine. When Arnold Gingrich started *Esquire,* he decided to get the most famous avant-garde writers of the time for his publication. The masthead of the January, 1935 issue sports the names of Pound, Hemingway, Dreiser, Scott Fitzgerald, and Edgar Lee Masters. Pound contributed an article on Social Credit and the economic theories of Sylvio Gesell, but the effect was lost among the ads for gents' underwear and Scotch whiskey.

Gingrich's fad for the moderns did not last long, and he switched to cartoons and luscious photographs. A clever employee grabbed this idea, and now *Playboy* outstrips its immodest parent. Ezra has suggested that I go after Gingrich and try to get him back into the fold, but it is unlikely that he would choose to go back to literature at this late date.

Ezra founded a short-lived magazine in Italian, *L'Indice,* and advertised in the Genoese press for Italian writers, with little success. His efforts to rouse his countrymen from their seemingly hopeless state of mental torpor were not confined to the young. He wrote to his old English professor, Dr. Felix E. Schelling, at the University of Pennsylvania:

"Dear Doc Schelling,

As one of the most completely intolerant men I have ever met, the joke *is* on you if you expected to teach anyone liberality. As for my being embittered, it won't wash; everybody who comes near me marvels at my good nature. Besides, what does it matter to me personally? I don't get scratched by it, but the howls of pain that reach me from the pore bastids that are screwed down under it and who have no outlet, save in final desperation writing to someone in Europe . . . I have never objected to any man's mediocrity, it is the idiotic fear that a certain type of mediocrity has in the presence of any form of the *real*. And the terror of newspaper owners, professors, editors, etc. in the presence of *idea*. I have documents stacked high, from men in most walks of life. Proved over and over again. No intellectual life in the univs. No truth in the press. Refusal to look at fact. It is nonsense to talk about my being embittered. I've got so much plus work going on that I have difficulty in remembering what particular infamy I wrote you about. . . . What little life has been kept in American letters has been largely due to a few men getting out of the muck and keeping the poor devils who couldn't at least informed. . . . You ain't so old but what you wouldn't wake up. And you are too respected and respectable for it to be any real risk. They can't fire you now. Why the hell don't you have a bit of real fun before you get tucked under? Damn it all, I never did dislike you."[39]

James Laughlin, Pound's publisher, has described the Rapallo studio as a shadowy room in which many documents hung overhead, suspended on ropes. The poet was surrounded by stacks of papers and letters and books which he was using as the multitudinous references for the *Cantos*. He was determined to get in as much as possible.

Desmond Chute, who had first met Pound and Yeats in his London tobacco shop before the first World War, says that the Pounds "were living on the top floor of a cliff-like building facing the sea, in a narrow, pergola-like flat giving onto a vast roof terrace and chiefly remarkable for a wealth of works in various mediums by Henri Gaudier-Brzeska.

"I had come to Rapallo in 1923," continues Chute, "and the Pounds in 1924, soon followed by Ezra's parents. Homer L. Pound, despite his total lack of Italian, was much liked by the denizens of Rapallo, who seldom failed to describe him, in a phrase lifted from dialect, as 'una pasta d'uomo.' If Ezra owed to his father that disarming simplicity so inextricably woven with his own sophistication, from his mother he derived even more striking characteristics: a fine carriage, a springy walk, a sybiline poise of the head, an occasional wilfulness in not admitting or even seeing the other side. Not even a long and tedious year in the hospital could break Isabel Weston Pound's octogenarian determination never to allow the conversation to drop below a cultural level. Of course she and 'Son' held differing conceptions of culture. She would insist on reciting his 'juvenalia,' although two years had passed since T. S. Eliot had hailed him as 'il miglior fabbro' and the *Cantos* were already in spate. Any attempt to put in a word for the greater importance of his maturer work would be quenched with a glance while the early verses swept on to their Ninetyish close."[40]

Stella Bowen, one of Ford's later wives, came to see the Pounds in Rapallo. She described the situation in Paris, the occasion of their removal to Italy, as follows: "Their studio in the Rue Notre Dame des Champs had in any case become untenable for persons of their nervous and privacy-loving temperament. Being on the ground floor, they were at the mercy of anyone who chose to stroll in or knock. Hordes came. So when they got back from their winters in Italy, they would beg us to keep their return a secret for as long as possible. But in Rapallo, when we went to visit them, we found them in a sixth floor flat with a big *terrasse,* overlooking the harbor, and although the house was new, the lift was permanently disabled. Anyone who wanted to see them had six long flights to climb and with no guarantee that they would find anyone at home when they got to the top. This eminently satisfactory arrangement enabled Ezra to write his Cantos undisturbed and to devote himself to his immense correspondence, which consisted mainly of the wildest abuse of everyone who did not agree with him, conveyed in highly impressionist typescript. This gave him immense satisfaction, and meanwhile Dorothy applied herself to the composition of abstract water-colours. When disposed for conversation Pound would place himself on the quaiside *terrasse* of the cafe above which he lived, and conversation would come to him. It was an excellent system, which included one meal a day at the cafe-restaurant and the minimum of household chores."[41]

Pound's furious efforts on behalf of his fellow writers, artists, and musicians did not slacken during his years in Rapallo. In 1929, Douglas Goldring, whom he had met in London in 1909, at the office of *The English Review,* paid tribute to him as follows:

"Pound, like Ford, has a pure, passionate, disinterested love of good writing. He is one of the few men living who has a sense of team-work. So long as good literature continues to be produced, it does not so much matter to him who produces it or where it crops up. When I used to see a good deal of him, it seemed to me that he camouflaged extraordinary generosity of outlook in regard to other writers under a mask of rather amusing self-assertion. As a literary foster-mother Ezra has had few equals in our time. Let us look towards Rapallo and drink his health!"[42]

Of these years, Desmond Chute wrote, in 1955, "Had he not found here the freedom he sought: freedom to be a poet? (At Rapallo he was universally and spontaneously called 'il poeta': people still stop me in the street to ask for news of 'il Signor

Poeta'.) He saw himself, and was, a man of letters. What matter
if he looked the part so long as he lived it? On the Riviera of the
20s and the 30s, besides writing poetry he could work out un-
trammelled that vital and cultural synthesis which gave it con-
sistency. Here he could, with brusque delicacy, befriend promise.
Thus he provided one sculptor, Henges, with stone and the chance
to carve it; musicians with the possibility to be heard, poets to
write, talent to think. (So great indeed was his kindness of heart
that I still remember how distressed and generous he was over
local orphans lacking milk for breakfast, how outraged at the
spectacle of cats mutilated by traps.) Educative activities led
easily to a kindred discipline, which was also one of his main
interests: the anatomy of Culture. An element herein sticks in my
mind—Frobenius, to whom curiously enough Pound bore so
marked a somatic likeness. Another, the most important after
Poetry, was Music.

"Fanned by his disinterested and unflagging enthusiasm, rare
and unforgettable little concerts sprang up according to the frequency and incidence of performers. One remembers blocks of
music. *Block* in this context was a great word with Ezra; not only
did he insist at rehearsals on 'blocks' of light and shade in the
performance of old music, he also demanded integrated and consecutive programs. The Rapallo musical seasons started as weeks,
begun under the sign of Mozart, all of whose violin sonatas were
played at least once by Olga Rudge and Gerhart Munch. One
wonders when the whole series had last, if ever, been heard in its
entirety. There followed all Bach's and all Pergolesi's. In a similar
spirit, though more informally in a private house, Munch gave a
reading on three consecutive afternoons of the complete *Wolhtem-
perierte Clavier*. Meanwhile the weeks went on with Purcell's
Twelve Sonatas in Three Parts (with basso continuo, 1683) and
William Young's for strings and bass ('the first printed English
Sonatas, 1653'). For the latter, absolute priority of execution may
be claimed for Rapallo, actually in advance of the 'first' performance under the editor, W. Gillies Whittaker, at Oxford. In the
1930s Ezra Pound developed an intense interest in the vast unpublished output of Antonio Vivaldi, much of which, largely

thanks to Olga Rudge's research and to microfilm technique, has since been made available to the public. Some Vivaldi *inedita* were given at Rapallo. Particular interest attaches to Gerhart Munch's transcriptions of mss. embodying researches by the late Oscar Chilesotti into old music (e.g. Dowland, Jannequin, Francesco da Milano).

"The Bartok played here by the Hungarian Quartet, though published, was as yet seldom played and little known. As far as possible Ezra decided on local talent. Yet he was far from excluding good or excellent professionals on condition the program was not made up to show off the performers, but rather based on intrinsic musical worth. Nor was any discrimination ever made on grounds of race or nationality. Incidentally, the only aid received from the authorities was the loan of the hall. Besides the artists already mentioned, we heard Tibor Serly in Mozart's *Sinfonia Concertante* and *Sonata for Violin and Viola,* and some compositions of his own; Renata Borgatti in Bach, Haydn, Mozart and Debussy; Chiara Fino Savio singing *Arie antiche,* and Lonny Mayers, Hindemith. Lugini Franchetti and Giorgio Levi were due to come when war cut short so many things more important (but how few rarer!) than concerts memorable for music and innocent of banality and display."[43]

Stella Bowen says that these winter concerts afforded timely support for musicians who had been hard-hit by the depression. Ezra stood at the door of the hall and held out his slouch hat to the concert-goers. The proceeds were divided among the players.

During these years, Olga Rudge lived in a tiny villa above Rapallo. The house had no water or electricity, and she prepared her meals on a charcoal stove. The present vogue of Vivaldi's music in the United States and in other countries may be traced directly to the spadework that she and Ezra did on the work of the "Italian Bach" during the early 1930s.

When the war clouds were threatening, he realized that the priceless manuscripts of Vivaldi might be destroyed by an enemy attack. The practice of microfilming rare documents was then in its infancy, but he contacted Bottai, Minister of Information, and demanded that this cultural treasure be protected by the process of putting them on microfilm. Later, during the enemy invasion, many of the Vivaldi manuscripts were destroyed by bombing and by artillery fire. Today, musicians are performing from copies made from Pound's microfilms. He refers to this episode in *Section: Rock-Drill:*

> Bottai also phoned Torino
>   instanter, to dig out Vivaldi,[44][.]

Varied though Pound's interests might be, he always managed to link them in some way. Music, for him, was never very far from poetry. He has said, "Put words to music and you'll soon find out where you can whittle the words down."

In addition to poetry, music, and tennis, Pound's interest in economics, evident before the First World War, and accelerated by that catastrophe, had become more acute during the widespread misery occasioned by the Great Depression. Almost everyone in the world during the 1930s lived in the grim shadow of the Crash of 1929 and its aftermath. The Second World War was eagerly accepted by most people as an excuse to stop thinking about economics, but Pound continued to talk on the "Sale and Manufacture of War". As Renato Corsini wrote in *Il Seculo d'Italia,* May 4, 1955, "For Pound economics starts from justice, and the study of economics leads to the contemplation of justice."

Pound had been writing on economic problems since 1912, when he was a columnist for A. E. Orage's *New Age.* His only connection with the Fascist Party was based upon his hope, a groundless one, it turned out, that the party leaders would accept his economic doctrines. Desmond Chute writes,

"Economics, that was to cast so long and dark a shadow over the next period. Asked once why he was so patient of the regime (he never belonged to the party), he replied: 'as a platform for monetary reform,' convinced of having converted the Duce to the theories of Douglas and Gesell."[45]

As the basis of his contemplation of economic justice, Pound employed the Confucian ethic, which is divided into three parts— the axis; the process; and sincerity, the perfect word, or the precise word—as follows:

Metaphysic:

Only the most absolute sincerity under heaven can effect any change.

Politics:

In cutting an ax-handle the model is not far off, in this sense: one holds one ax-handle while chopping the other. Thus one uses men in governing men.

Ethics:

The archer, when he misses the bulls-eye, turns and seeks the cause of the error in himself.

Like many other writers and artists, Pound involved himself in the political enthusiasms of the 1930s. Most of his compatriots had gone to the left, because of the political alliance that the Roosevelt regime had formed with Soviet Russia in 1933. The Spanish Civil War in 1936 was the "moment of truth" for those whom Ezra termed "campus communists and millionaire Communards." His boyhood friend, William Carlos Williams, became chairman of the New Jersey Committee for Medical Help to Loyalist Spain. Hemingway donated forty thousand dollars to the Loyalist cause in Spain. He recouped this sum by the sale of newspaper articles about the Spanish war, and later, by the huge profits from his novel, *For Whom the Bell Tolls* (1940). Nevertheless, no one would ever accuse Hemingway or Williams of being a Communist. It was only a fad.

Years later, when Williams was offered the post of Consultant in Poetry to the Library of Congress, Washington bureaucrats dug up his connection with the Loyalist committee, which had been cited as a Communist front. It is useless to tell anyone in Washington that important Communist agents do not join Communist fronts. Hans Otto Meissner, German diplomat and expert on the Soviet Fourth Bureau, the most efficient and highly-trained espionage group in the world, has tried to make this point clear. He even warned us that no agent of the Soviet Fourth Bureau has ever been arrested in the United States. So much for members of Communist fronts. At any rate, Williams did not get the job.

Because Pound continued to live in Italy during the Fascist regime, the legend was spread by his detractors that he was a key figure in the Mussolini government, a sort of Rudolf Hess in Rome, apparently confusing him with Gabriele d'Annunzio.

Pound had only one interview with Mussolini, although he never gave up hope of converting Il Duce to his monetary theories. Due to his absence from his native land, Pound was not aware of the actual similarities between the Fascist system in Italy and the principles of the corporate state adopted by the New Deal. Westbrook Pegler has been the only American commentator to point out these similarities, with pungent remarks on the paradox that the loudest "anti-Fascists" in Washington were those who had secured the enactment of Fascist laws during the early years of the Roosevelt state. Rexford Guy Tugwell's work, *The Industrial Discipline, and the Governmental Arts* (New York, Columbia University Press, 1933) which was the handbook of that regime, urged the passage of many "fascist" laws, or principles of the "corporate state".

Pound was aware of certain coincidences between the state, which he was fond of terming *Italia irredenta,* and the early years of the American Republic. He had embodied these similarities in a book, which he wrote in 1933, *Jefferson and/or Mussolini, L'Idea Statale Fascismo as I have seen it* (London, Stanley Nott, Ltd., 1935; New York, Liveright Publishing Corporation, 1935). It was subtitled *Volitionist Economics.* The work was submitted to some forty publishers during the next two years. He comments that never before has he had such difficulty in finding a publisher. The book was ignored in Italy, nor was it circulated or subsidized by the Italian government. Despite the fact that Ezra had pointed out that he was not advocating a fascist system for the United States, the book has been criticized on that ground ever since, usually by people who have not read it.

Pound's only connection with the Fascist government, excepting his activity in getting Bottai to microfilm the Vivaldi manuscripts, was his friendship with a cousin of Ford Madox Ford, Signora Olivia Rossetti Agresti, a great-niece of Dante Gabriel Rossetti.

She edited a journal for the General Confederation of Industries in Rome.

While living as an American citizen in Italy, Pound conducted himself in much the same manner as he had done in England and France. He worked on his poems, studied, carried on a voluminous correspondence, and made a few public talks on his advanced economic theories. These theories were inspired by his hatred of war. Witter Bynner says that during the First World War, he asked Henry Ford how long the conflict would last. "Until the idlers have killed off enough of the workers to feel safe," Ford had replied.

Pound knew that great changes were needed. He had written editorially, in *The Exile,* "Quite simply, I want a new civilization."[46] In his *Polite Essays,* he had stated that "Civilization begins when people start preferring a little done right to a great deal done wrong."[47]

Pound had long been concerned about the anachronisms and injustices of monetary issue. In 1917, he had met Captain C. H. Douglas, an engineer who had formerly been in charge of international operations for the Westinghouse Corporation. Objecting to the nineteenth century mode of distribution, Douglas had worked out some improvements, which he termed "Social Credit".

A few years ago, I was asked at a trial in New York, "What is Social Credit?"

"Social Credit," I replied, "is a system which, in times of prosperity, not only discontinues the collection of taxes, but distributes surplus funds to the citizens in the form of a national dividend. It transforms the state from an organization whose motto is 'Always Take', to a government which is not a continuous misfortune borne by the citizens."

No doubt, Pound would disagree with this definition, since he would wish to get some of the fundamentals of the system before the public. His economic views have been widely misinterpreted, from malice as well as from ignorance. Horace Gregory, who had evidently not looked too deeply into the matter, commented in the August, 1935 issue of *Poetry,* "Like Douglas he [Pound] ignores the fact that labor is an integral factor in the denomination of money values."

Pound responded in the October, 1935 issue of *Poetry* by referring to his "volitionist economics" statement which begins, "If money is considered as a certificate of work done . . .", which disposes of the Gregory objection. He has pointed out that as soon as he mends his own trousers or prepares himself a meal, he escapes the entire cycle of Marxist economics, which, after all, is feudal in concept. It describes all labor as performed under duress for a master, and ignores the many persons self-employed, for self-employment, an aspect of individualism, is anathema to the Marxist.

This error was based upon Marx's lack of acquaintance with everyday life. Sitting in the British Museum, he decided that all work done was sweated from the worker by a greedy landowner or capitalist. He had never been on a farm or worked in a factory, but this did not matter. He became the great theorist of industrial labor. As Michael Lekakis has pointed out, "One always returns to the point from which he started, and, starting from a false premise, one always returns to that false premise."[48] Beginning with Marx's misconceptions of labor, Marxism attempts to force all workers and all work done into the maw of a single employer, the state. As Milovan Djilas says in his book, *The New Class* (1957), this system is a bureaucrat's heaven, in which the workers labor forever in the service of a parasitic elite.

In the confused world of the 1930s, there was no figure more bewildering than the Prince of Wales, or King Edward VIII, or the Duke of Windsor, as he was variously known. Pound refers to him a number of times, to the effect that "Eddie" gave the world three additional years of peace. Pound also has said, "They try to have a war every twenty years, so if you can postpone the damned thing a few times, that's one war they don't have."[49]

According to Pound, the cards had been dealt out in 1936, and the Second World War was all set to go. There was one last-minute obstacle—"Eddie" refused to sign the mobilization papers. He had been through the veterans' hospitals just after the First World War, and apparently he could not bring himself to send men into that kind of hell again. "That woman" rushed onto the scene, and "Eddie" was hustled out the back door. His family is still bitter towards him because at the moment he should have acted, he did not serve the purpose of a monarch. At any rate, there was no war in 1936, and there was one in 1939, after he had "abdicated".

Ezra tells another story about "Eddie", illustrating a thesis that certain members of the European aristocracy are apt to revert to type. That is to say, they sometimes like to bound about on all fours, especially late at night. He tells a tale to the effect that he was roused from his rest in a Riviera hotel one night by a woman's scream. He dashed out in the hall, just in time to see something or someone rounding the corner on all fours. Another lady was reassuring the frightened woman that "It's only our Eddie."

In January of 1939, Ezra's friend William Butler Yeats died, ending one of his longest and most stimulating associations. His mother-in-law had also passed away the previous year, and he decided that this was an opportune moment to revisit his homeland. As he tells it, in an interview after his release,

"In 1938 my wife's mother died and for the first time she had a little income and I was free of the responsibility for caring for her. I thought it was monstrous that Italy and the United States should go to war so I came here to stop it. For the first time I had money to pay for the trip. I took second class passage on the Rex . . . the ship was empty so they got me the bridal suite for $160. All I had was a suitcase and a rucksack so I spent nothing on porters. It cost me only $5 over the $160. Arriving in New York I entered as the poor boy making good."[50]

When Pound landed in New York, he was quoted in the New York *Times* of April 21 as saying that bankers and munitions-makers were to blame for the current unrest in Europe, rather than the heads of totalitarian states. On June 13, 1939, the New York *Times* printed an editorial congratulating him on his having been awarded a doctorate of letters at his alma mater, Hamilton College. The citation reads:

"Ezra Pound: native of Idaho, graduate of Hamilton College in the class of 1905, poet, critic, and prose writer of great distinction. Since completing your college career you have had a life full of significance in the arts. You have found that you could work more happily in Europe than in America and so have lived most of the past 30 years an expatriate making your home in England, France and Italy, but your writings are known wherever English is read. Your feet have trodden paths, however, where the great reading public could give you few followers—into Provencal and Italian poetry, into Anglo-Saxon and Chinese. From all of these excursions you have brought back treasure. Your translations from the Chinese, for example, led one of the most gifted of comtemporary poets (Eliot) to call you the inventor of Chinese poetry for our time. Your Alma Mater, however, is an old lady who has not always understood where you were going, but she has watched you with interest and pride if not always with understanding. The larger public has also been at times amazed at your political and economic as well as your artistic credo, and you have retaliated by making yourself—not unintentionally perhaps—their gadfly. Your range of interests is immense, and whether or not your theories of society survive, your name is permanently linked with the development of English poetry in the 20th century. *Your reputation is international, you have guided many poets into new paths, you have pointed new directions, and the historian of the future in tracing the development of your growing mind will inevitably, we are happy to think, be led to Hamilton and to the influence of your college teachers.* You have ever been a generous champion of younger writers as well as artists in other fields, and for this fine and rare human quality and for your own achievements in poetry and prose, we honor you."

Archibald MacLeish wrote an article about Pound which appeared in *The Atlantic Monthly* of June, 1939, and Pound had some interesting talks with him about literary matters, but he was not, at this juncture, much interested in literature. He had developed his ideas to the extent that he believed he could present them convincingly to his countrymen, and he hoped that by convincing them, he could avert the outbreak of the Second World War, or failing that, at least persuade the United States to keep out of it, and thus confine the conflagration to Europe. This was as vain and quixotic an undertaking as Ford's Peace Ship had been during the First World War, but this kind of optimism runs in the American grain. Some day, perhaps, Pound will be honored for this effort.

Pound hoped that his reputation as a poet might gain him an audience in the United States. A most serious voice in the conduct of American foreign policy at this time was that of Charlie Chaplin. Pound could not hope to compete with this clown on his own terms. His attempts to get radio time were rebuffed everywhere. After the initial *Times* interview, the press and radio newsmen closed their ranks against him. He was many months too early to get in on the non-interventionist movement in the United States, the "America First" group, which only began to function long after he had gone back to Italy.

He went to Washington, and had lunch with Henry Wallace, which, years later, caused Westbrook Pegler to suspect that Pound had been mixed up with Wallace's *guru*, Nicholas Roerich. Pound also conferred with Senator Harry Byrd. He says that he was mildly disturbed by that gentleman's blithe comment, "Oh, you can find anything in Jefferson!"

Pound had a chat with Senator Borah about Social Credit. The Senator had evinced considerable interest in this system a few years earlier, when Major Douglas had visited Washington. However, as Borah remembered the occasion, when he had persuaded a couple of Senators to listen to Douglas, the engineer failed to expound the theory lucidly enough to hold their attention, and they had drifted away.

Pound also talked with Senator Burton K. Wheeler, who would later become a leader of the non-interventionist movement. Wheeler said to Pound, "What do you expect me to do, when he's packed the Supreme Court so that they will declare everything he does constitutional?"

William Carlos Williams wrote to Robert McAlmon, May 25, 1939, "Ezra Pound is being mysterious about his comings and goings. Pound looks like Henry VIII of England. He was wrapped in sweaters and shirts and coats until I thought him a man mountain, but after a while he returned to normal measurements again —I think he was afraid of our damp spring weather!"[51]

Ezra could have not suspected in 1939 that he was to spend thirteen damp springs in Washington, or that he would contract bronchitis during one of those seasons.

He spent some time with an old friend, Congressman George

Holden Tinkham, who is referred to as "Uncle George" in the *Cantos*.[52] He had met Tinkham years ago in Europe, for Tinkham, the only bearded member of Congress, usually went abroad at campaign time and let his opponent talk himself into defeat. As a visiting Congressman, he had been allowed to fire the first American shot against the Austrians when the United States went to war against the Central Powers in 1917. Pound mentions in the *Cantos* that he and Uncle George tried to find the exact spot, years later, but the road had been blown off the mountainside.

A descendant of a Mayflower family, Tinkham represented the 11th Massachusetts District—including Newton and the fashionable Back Bay—from 1915 to 1943, when he retired. He was a colorful figure in Washington, and his office was filled with mementoes of his travels, including stuffed heads of game animals, African shields, and a picture of himself from a London newspaper. This last was an item listing the ten most prominent Negroes in America. Tinkham's name was among them, because one of his constituents had put him down as an honorary member of a Negro group in Boston. Tinkham found amusement in his visitors' reaction to this item.

Despite the fact that he enjoyed being a member of the ruling class, Tinkham accomplished some noteworthy acts during his terms of service. It was he who noticed the clause in the League of Nations bill that would have caused us to abnegate our sovereignty. He immediately rushed to Senator Henry Cabot Lodge's office, and told him about it. As Ezra describes the occasion in the *Cantos*, "and he knew there'd be one hell of a fight in the Senate." Lodge was subsequently memorialized as the man who led the fight against the bill and defeated it, winning for himself the title of the "founder of isolationism", or some such term.

Tinkham also made an amazing prediction in 1934, which was noted by the press, and quickly forgotten. He declared that Roosevelt's recovery program would be a complete failure, and that the President would have to take us into war in order to cover up his failure. As Herbert Hoover pointed out, after the event, in the third volume of his *Memoirs*, this is exactly what happened.

Tinkham did approve of one Roosevelt deed—repeal. He was one of the most steadfast fighters against prohibition.

Family investments in South African gold mines gave Tinkham a comfortable fortune. Ezra says that when "Tink" showed his letter of credit to the manager of an Italian bank, the man salaamed to the floor. And, to fix the situation in my mind, Ezra repeated the man's gesture of obeisance to money.

At Ezra's suggestion, I went to the Harvard Club in 1952 to see "Tink". With his typical enthusiasm for a campaign, Ezra had drafted no less than three letters to "Tink", the last of which had been signed by me, in order to set up the appointment. It had been decided that I was to write Tinkham's biography, which would be one of considerable interest, and that the wealthy old bachelor should finance the enterprise. "Tink" was easily the most interesting personality at the Club, openly contemptuous of the young Harvard men who were paralyzed at the sight of him. His beard was as raffish and his eyes as bright as they must have been when Ezra first set eyes on him.

We spent some pleasant hours together, but nothing came of the proposed book. Tinkham was not much interested in whether anyone knew what he had done for his country or not. He was then in his eighties, he had twenty million dollars, and he intended to live out his life as he had always lived it, enjoying it to the full.

Shortly after I talked with him, he went to Europe again. In 1956, he died, leaving only one survivor, a sister who was wealthier than himself, and who lived on top of a mountain in North Carolina. His money went to a children's home in Boston.

Pound's visit to America in 1939 was concluded by an evening at the Petitpas, in New York City, in homage to the late John Butler Yeats, who had spent his declining years at the boarding house of the Petitpas Sisters. This delightful restaurant was later operated by their younger brother, Nicholas Petitpas, and it continued to be a gathering place for artists and writers until 1954, when Nicholas retired, and the place was closed.

X

IN THE MIDST of one of the most destructive wars in the history of mankind, Ezra Pound remained true to his calling. While fifty million human beings were dying by violence, he went down to Rome and read his poems over the international wireless. And, as he had been doing all of his life, he interspersed his poetry with blistering invective against politicians and usurers.

He was the only Bohemian of the Second World War. In a world gone mad, he continued to cry out, "Stop it! Stop it!" He has never raised his hand against another human being.

Pound was duly indicted for treason, but the chief complaint against him seems to have been that he refused to take part in the slaughter. While so many millions were dipping their hands in blood, he asked only for peace.

His purpose was serious, although the result was disastrous for him. The fury against Pound, which is still unabated in many quarters, stems from the fact that he refused to become a barbarian. Almost alone of Western men, he has no blood on his conscience.

It was not a crime to remain a poet during the war, and, in its essentials, this is what he did. The war was characterized by the most brutal outrages against civilians ever recorded by civilized man. Pound was past the age of military service; as an American citizen residing abroad, he could have remained peacefully immobilized there throughout the war, as did his friend George

Santayana. He had stubbornly refused to give up his American citizenship, although he violently disapproved of the Roosevelt administration. His disagreement with the course taken by the Democrats since 1933 was no reason for him to renounce his heritage, and the rebuffs which he received during his 1939 visit to the United States only made Pound more determined to get his message across to his fellow citizens, who, he felt, rightly or wrongly, were being victimized by a political party bent upon war and a press that was a willing accessory to the crime.

The nature of the personality which could blithely fly against one of the most monolithic powers this country has ever known has been brilliantly analyzed by a friend of his London period, Phyllis Bottome, in her *From the Life:*

"In the history of twentieth century literature Ezra Pound may be known and valued more as a Portent than as a Poet. He was one of those unfortunate swallows who arrive early, but who don't make a summer. Yet I think he had in him the making of many summers. A quarter of a century ago he was saying to a predatory and complacent world what every young person and most intelligent older ones now [1946] automatically believe. Yet nobody believed the youthful Ezra when he first preached his creed of objective art, and urged the intellectual necessity of being as honest as you can be . . . he was as rigidly intelligent as a Plymouth brother; and as vulnerable as a sea-anemone. . . . Ezra always took every risk that came his way in his proclamation of truth . . . his courage was a touching and beautiful thing."[1]

When Pound returned to Italy, his duty was clear to him, and perhaps it will become clearer to subsequent generations of Americans. If the Congress was too impotent to stop Roosevelt's repeated and flagrant violations of his oath of office; if the system of checks and balances which had been set up in the Constitution was no longer functioning (because of excessive usurpation of power by the executive and the judiciary, leaving the legislative branch of the government as helpless as the Soviet Duma), then it devolved upon the citizen to act as an individual.

Pound received permission to broadcast from Rome, as an American citizen acting upon his own volition, unsought and unsalaried by the Italian government. In February, 1940, he was heard for the first time on the "American Hour", a program which Radio Rome beamed to the United States. In its March 17, 1941 issue, *Newsweek* noted that Pound was counselling the United States against providing aid to Britain. Some eighty-five per cent of the American public, at that time, felt the same way. This was the editorial policy of the Chicago *Tribune* and many other important newspapers outside of the Wall Street sphere of influence. It also was the program of a national-influential group, "America First", which opposed intervention.

Thus in 1941, according to national polls, Ezra Pound represented the sentiment of eighty-five per cent of his countrymen, and Franklin D. Roosevelt, determined to involve the United States in another European war, represented fifteen per cent—mostly those who had an ideological or business stake in intervention. At this point, it seemed that the representative system was not functioning.

Encouraged by the mushrooming isolationist sentiment in America, Pound tried to get a visa to return in the summer of 1941. The United States Embassy received him with bitter vituperation, accused him of being an agent of "Fascism", and would not issue him a visa. Confined to Italy, Pound continued his broadcasts from that nation. In a memorial broadcast to James Joyce, he defined his own position: "As a writer, I am given to no one and to all men."

Pound made about seventy-five radio broadcasts over Radio Rome, including one on December 7, 1941, before the advent of the United States into the Second World War. The Italian government, ever suspicious of his motives, then temporarily stopped him from broadcasting. The odd jargon and mixture of dialects that he employed had convinced the Fascist secret service, which was as prone to error as its American counterpart, that he was sending messages in code to the United States armed forces!

Prevented from continuing his broadcasts, Pound decided that he should return to the United States for the duration of hostilities. He and his wife settled their affairs, and prepared to leave Rome on a special diplomatic train early in 1942. American officials in Rome informed him that he was *persona non grata* with the United States government, and refused to let him board the train. According to the Washington *Post,* December 28, 1958, the State Department's passport file No. F-130 contained instructions that "Mr. Pound should never again be granted passport facilities by this government."

This was a clear violation of Pound's constitutional rights. He had never been charged with any wrongdoing; he was a citizen in good standing, and the State Department officials had absolutely no grounds for refusing him permission to travel. This was one of the more important reasons why the Department of Justice officials did not wish to prosecute Pound on a charge of treason. The charge could have been dismissed on the grounds that Pound had been denied a fundamental right of an American citizen, that he should be allowed to travel abroad and return without let or hindrance. The Supreme Court has repeatedly upheld this right.

William Rose Benét, in *The Saturday Review of Literature,* March 6, 1943, quoted Malcolm Cowley as follows: "He [Pound] tried to leave Italy a year ago on the train that carried our diplomats and newspaper correspondents, but by that time his record was so black that our government refused to give him a visa. . . . I now find it hard to believe that he is a fascist at heart, an apostle of racism or an enemy of his own country. It seems to me rather that a succession of literary attitudes and the habit of trying to amaze his readers have involved him in an utterly false and evil situation from which there is no retreat."

Just what was so black about Pound's record, Cowley does not say. Presumably he is referring to the pre-Pearl Harbor broadcasts from Radio Rome, which accurately reflected the prevailing American sentiment at this time. Even if Pound had been suspected of being an agent of Fascism, he could have been allowed to return to his country, and he could have been kept under surveillance, as many Americans are under surveillance twenty-four hours a day, even in the present era of relative peace. Pound was not then and has never been in the business of espionage, and such surveillance could have satisfied his detractors on that point.

The Radio Rome broadcasts contain much interesting biographical and philosophical material of Pound's which is not presently available elsewhere. Perhaps a volume of these broadcasts, which are of as great interest as his published letters, will be issued in the future. When I read some of the texts of these broadcasts, after having known Pound some five years, I was surprised at how much of this material continued to reappear during our daily talks. Perhaps two-thirds of the anecdotes, constitutional points, and literary references contained therein have been reiterated to me time and again in Pound's conversation. Some of the material appears in the *Cantos*. Consequently, I have selected from the transcripts available at the Library of Congress those items that are chiefly of biographical interest.

These transcripts comprise a very incomplete and inadequate collection of Pound's post-Pearl Harbor broadcasts. On some occasions, the transcribers failed to tune in until Pound's broadcast was almost over; on other occasions, poor shortwave reception made it impossible for them to understand what he was saying. The transcribers also had considerable difficulty understanding Pound's delivery, which was basically a Yankee "cracker-barrel" accent, interspersed with cockney, Flea Market, and other Continental accents. They seemed to be unfamiliar with artistic and literary matters—the transcripts are sprinkled with such errors as "money" for "Monet", "confusion" for "Confucian", and throughout one entire broadcast on the work of Louis Ferdinand Céline, the transcriber has put this name down as "Stalin", and even as "Ferdinant Stalin".

In order to make them readable, I have corrected the numerous misspellings of the transcribers and have noted where they occur in brackets. The following excerpts from Pound's broadcasts will be useful to students of Pound.

December 7, 1941:
"Europe calling. Pound speaking. Ezra Pound speaking, and I think I am perhaps speaking a bit more to England than to the United States, but you folks may as well hear it. They say an Englishman's head is made of wood and the American head made of watermelon. Easier to get something into the American head but nigh impossible to make it stick there for ten minutes. Of course, I don't know what good I am doing. I mean what immediate good, but some things you folks on both sides of the wretched ocean will have to learn, war or no war, sooner or later. Now, what I had to say about the state of mind in England in 1919, I said in Cantos

14 and 15. Some of your philosophists and fancy thinkers would have called it the spiritual side of England. I undertook to say state of mind.

"I can't say my remarks were heeded. I thought I got 'em simple enough. In fact, some people complained that several of the words contained no more than four or five letters, some six. Now I hold that no Catholic has ever been or ever will be puzzled by what I said in those Cantos. I have, however, never asked for any sympathy when misunderstood. I go on, try to make my meaning clear and then clearer, and in the long run, people who listen to me, very few of 'em do, but the members of that small and select minority do know more in the long run than those who listen to say, H. G. (Chubby) Wells and the liberal stooges. What I am getting at is, a friend said to me the other day that he was glad I had the politics I have got but that he didn't understand how I, as a North American United Stateser, could have it. Well, that looks simple to me. Things often do look simple to me. On the Confucian system, very few start right and then go on, start at the roots and move upwards. The pattern often is simple. Whereas, if you start constructing from the twig downwards, you get into a muddle. My politics seem to me simple. My idea of a state or empire is more like a hedgehog or porcupine—chunky and well-defended. I don't cotton to the idea o' my country bein' an octopus, weak in the tentacles and suffering from stomach ulcers and colic gastritis."

There were no further broadcasts until January 29, 1942, when Pound persuaded the Italian government to let him return to the air.

January 29, 1942:
"And then there was my old dad in bed with a broken hip. Lord knows who's going to mend it or when it is going to mend. So I read him a few pages of Aristotle in the Loeb [low, according to the transcription] Classical Library, as diversion to take his mind off it. Also to keep my own work in progress progressing; and because for some time I had in mind the need of comparing the

terminology of the Chinese and Greek philosophy and comparing that to the terminology of mediaeval Catholic theology.

". . . Every English friend I have got in the world has done his damdest to keep England from making such a golthunderer and abysmal ass of herself. As to my American friends, Senator Borah is dead, not that I knew him much save by letter, but I can still feel his hand on my shoulder just before he was getting into an elevator in the Senate building and I can still hear him saying a couple days before: saying to me, Borah saying to me, 'Well I am sure I don't know what a man like you would find to do here.'

". . . I don't think it is the citizen's duty to whitewash who blundered. I think the United States and even her British allies might do well to keep more in touch with continental European opinion. I don't think anybody is going to whitewash who blundered into the alliance with Russia. I think they will have some crimes that nothing can whitewash. [This was long before the Katyn Forest scandal.] I think an alliance with Stalin's Russia is rotten. I don't think the claim of even going through the motions of inviting [invading, according to transcriber] Russia to slaughter and kill all Eastern Europe is a necessary part of the program. Program of dissent. . . . I don't think that this was necessary. I don't think it is the function, even of the Commander-in-Chief of the United States Army, to dictate the citizen's politics. Not to the point of inviting [invading, according to the transcriber] Soviet Russia, Bolshevik Russia, to kill off the whole east half of Europe and ordering the citizens to approve of it. I don't think it is a lucky move. Even if Mr. Eden hopes to doublecross Russia, which nothing indicates [inducts, according to transcriber] that he does hope . . . If you can stop this Muscovite order, we will let by-gones be bygones. We will at least try to see half your argument. Instead of which, Hank Wallace comes up saying—No peace till the world accepts the gold standard. . . . Does look like there was a weakness of mind in some quarters. Whom God will destroy, he first sends to the bughouse."

February 3, 1942:
"Ezra Pound speaking, and the prospect of a thirty years' war is not one to arouse mirth and hilarity, even in . . . irresponsible

people such as the United States of Americans. You are in it and Lord knows who is trying to get you out. As the late Lord Rothermere, who was not much, as you might say, to write home about, finally decided that the English public was unteachable, wholly unteachable. Well, I don't know whether you can learn anything from history, I mean, I don't know whether you are even yet in a state of mind where you want to learn anything from history or from any other source whatever. A way to get yourselves out might be discoverable. It might be more discoverable if you first had a faint inkling or a curiosity as to how you get yourselves in.

". . . How well you can learn from the disasters of England I do not yet know. But I would lay it down as an axiom that empires do not get knocked apart from outside until they are plumb gone to rot in the middle. The laws of right government have been known since the days of You and Shun, old Chinese Emperors, and from the time of King Wong was a thousand years, and from Wong to Confucius was more than two thousand years ago.

"And those days when the policies of Chun and of Guan were slipped together, compared, they were as the two halves of a peel. Or it might be the two parts of a talley stick. And for nigh on to four thousand years I think no one has dodged the fate of those policies. Then from the time of Confucius, every dynasty in China has learned from Confucius—I mean he learned it from looking at history—talking of Chun and Guan. And after him whenever a great man learned it he started or upheld some sort of imperial order."

February 19, 1942.   Power:
"The President hath power. The president has no legal power to enter into serious and secret agreements with foreign powers. He has no legal power to cook up policies with Jones? Borkin? and sign the nation's name on the document. The United States treaties are valid when ratified by the Senate and not before. The President has no legal power to enter into condominiums with foreign governments for a misconduct of scandalous islands off the China coast or in proximity to distant Oriental or any other damn harbors. The President has no more legal right to do these infamies

than you have to sign my name on a check or I yours. There is no darkness save ignorance."

March 8, 1942. Gold:
". . . Arthur Golding's namesake and four generations over descendant, points out that even in the time of Queen Elizabeth, the Earl of Oxford was fallen. He was handing over his rents to some shyster in return for a fixed income. Ten thousand, or whatever it was, a year, and then the shyster had to squeeze what he could out of the peasants and out of men working the land. The return of the feudal system. Old Fordie used to talk about that. Liberty is not a right but a duty. Rot and laziness got men under, too lazy to function as lords and proprietors. The nobility sold out to the shysters. In my twelve years in London, how many people did I meet, I was meeting, as you might say, the flower of the writing class in your island. How many people did I meet who had read their own history? How many who had read Anthony Trollope?"

March 19, 1942. Time Lag:
". . . Now if American students will recognize that universities are there to prepare students for life in a given country, and in a given time and insist on finding out what will happen to life in that place and time, they can get their four years' work [worth?]. Nobody can do this for those students, they have got to do it for themselves. Ma Hopkins on one end of the log, and the students on the other. When Abe Lard [*sic.* transcriber] was kicked out of the University of Paris, five thousand students followed him out into the country. There were no dormitories or million-dollar gymnasiums. That is the sort of thing that builds the revival of learning, or intellectual re-birth."

March 30, 1942. Pattern:
"The place to defend the American heritage is on the American continent and no man who had any part in helping Franklin D. Roosevelt to spill out—get the United States into it—has enough sense to win anything. If Roosevelt were not below the biological level at which the concept of honor enters the mind, below the

biological level at which human beings can conceive of the existence of such a thing as honor, the liar would go out over the steps
of the American Capitol and commit hara-kiri, to atone for the
evils he has wrought upon the American people."

April 9, 1942.   Indecision:
"Sovereignty inheres in the right to issue money. And the
American sovereignty belongs by right to the people, and their
representatives in Congress have the right to issue money and to
determine the value thereof. And 120 million, 120 million suckers
have lamentably failed to insist on the obervation of this quite
decided law. . . . Now the point at which embezzlement of the
nation's funds on the part of her officers becomes treason can
probably be decided only by jurists, and not by hand-picked
judges hired to support illegality.
". . . The stock broker is not my ideal. He is not a sport.
A poker player plays with his own money. If he loses, he loses.
A man who buys a lottery ticket takes his chances with the other
purchasers of lottery tickets. Neither of them gambles with the
purse of the people. It's the old contempt for others, but a long
way back, there was still some perception of ethics and men were
supposed to look at the consequences of their act, before thinking
they were being both honest and clever.[2]
". . . The danger to the United States as a system of government is not from Japan but from jury."

Apparently Pound means from the "juridical" in this instance,
as he earlier cited "hand-picked judges hired to support illegality."
This is an interesting prediction in view of the postwar decisions of
the Supreme Court. Numerous bills have since been introduced in
Congress to limit the power of the judges to "make law".

April 13, 1942.   Question of Motive:
"I do not expect perfect and complete comprehension of these
discourses on the part of all of my audience. I should be content
if I get over one point of what I am driving at and why I am
driving. For over thirty years I have been driving at some of
these objectives, the same objectives. I thought in 1908 and before

then, that a nation's literature is important. Words, means of communication, literature, the most condensed form of communication, communication of the most basic and essential facts; ideas necessary for leading the good life registered in the best books. And man's duty as soon as he is fully a man is to keep those books and that tradition available. Keep it handy.

"And the public, American and English, but for the moment let me speak of the United States, the American public, rather like that lunatic in Paio's novel 'Mosquardino.' A chap in the gook house who just wouldn't believe that there could be enough microbes on the back of a postage stamp to knock a man cold. He thought it was doctor's fables, in fact he thought that the doctors had it from the other gooks in the asylum.

"Well, the Americans and the English just couldn't believe that it made any difference what a man or a nation put inside its head. . . . Hence I was supposed to exaggerate when I bust out against such dung heaps of perfumed pus as the Atlantic Monthly, and Harper's and Scribner's as they were in the year 1900, and ceased not essentially to be . . . Their stink of stale perfume contained deadly gases which finally poisoned. No language could quite cover the loathing I feel for a Sedgwick but it doubtless seems exaggerated. Later on, in London I did try to make a few people see why the printed matter on sale in that city would finally kill off the inhabitants. Witness Dunkirk.

"The 19th stinking century saw what is called an advance in science. People learned that bacilli can kill, and the concept of prophylaxis entered the general mind. But an older concept got knocked out of the popular mind. It has been possibly a good concept, but it decayed, it is what is or was called a biological concept. The age called the age of faith thought a wrong idea could bring evil. In the Middle Ages, they got a bit fantastic, dropped their eyes off the here and now and thought the bad idea would land a man in perdition, eternal flames, purgatory or whatever. Then something got tangled and people got fanatic and heretics were burnt and so forth. And Monsieur Voltaire tried to get that untangled; worked all his life against the cruelties of fanaticism, got himself called the atheist, which he was not.

"Now, I strongly suspect that almost no heretics were burnt, at least not at the beginning, except those who interfered with the usury racket, or those whose ideas were seen as inimical to that racket. But so far as I know, no research has ever been done along those lines. I am speaking of heretics proper; people who went into ideology, not talking about mere witch persecution.

"Well, the idea that a wrong idea could damage people here and now was, perhaps, not fully developed. The British theory was that free speech was a loophole. Let 'em talk and they will do nothing. Hyde Park Corner and so on.

"Well, Gus Flaubert and myself, and divers others, including, if you go back far enough, Confucius, saw something worse than just one bad idea, and that was the corruption of the whole and total means of communication of all ideas whatsoever; the corruption of language; the destruction of all precision in terminology, which destruction takes man back down to the status of beasts, or what beasts are supposed to be, namely, unable to communicate with each other. Yet even animals like the wolves and wild dogs do seem to understand each other and to collaborate. Very well, I sat there rooting around and gradually got some ideas as to combatting this universal gonorrhea of language, and this rotting of all printed sense of communication, monthlies, dailies, weeklies, publishing systems, all of which have been pretty well dished and ditched, the poor old Brit iniquitous [record stuck in Rome]. . . . And anyhow I am speaking to the United States of America.

"Forty years ago, Brooks Adams made quite a good study of England, foreseeing that she would bust up and part go to the U.S.A. and part to Germany. If I remember it right, Japan may be getting a look in. Naturally, very few people read Mr. Adams. I only know of one Englishman who has quoted him and I am not enamoured of retrospect. I ought to have been given Brooks Adams when I was having a shot at American History in the University of Pennsylvania, that, forty years ago, might have accelerated me and given him a little publicity. In fact, all history teachers in American universities ought to have got hold of Brooks Adams then, that is 1897, 1900, 1903, his best volumes.

"His weak and pingling brother Henry was not the man that his older brother Brooks was. Brooks seeing what had happened in history, seeing it pretty clearly, foreseeing what would happen in his time, but not seeing beyond that. He knew that an age-old faith, or ages of faith, had existed, but he did not foresee the next one. Living, as you might say, in his own phase, foreseeing the downflop of England, that is, of the Empire; noting symptoms of England's decline, which the English remained deaf and blind to, but not foreseeing the Italian rise. Not foreseeing the change of phase, from material to volitional. I will repeat that, not foreseeing the Italian rise, not foreseeing the change from material to volitional.

"Reading again John Quincy Adams' 'Judea: Home of Religion' I forget where he notes that, maybe in his preface to his book on New England. Anyhow, Brooks tried to figure out where John Quincy Adams, whom he greatly admired, had gone off the rail, not getting back to his great granddaddy, John Adams, the father of his country and inventor to some extent of General Washington.

"Well, I can't get it all into one discourse, but if there is still some campus . . . not wholly squashed under the dung floes of Wall Street and Washington, I suggest you start taking notes and figures. Figure out this affair of the ruin of language, the falsification of all reports in the well-paid magazines, the falsification of newsprint, and also the attack on historical knowledge. . . . Note when American history went out of fashion, when the kids in the lower grades heard of Lenin [Levin, according to transcriber] and Marx and Trotsky and not so much of Lincoln and Washington. Watch the gradual creep-up of obscurantism, the neglect from the start of John Adams, Van Buren and Johnson.

"Now there ought to be 700 students and 30 professors digging into these questions. Some day you will need to know, need to know more than you do at present, and Lord knows what will come to you fast. Old Ezra speaking. Pound speaking."

April 20, 1942. Aberrations:
"An Italian said to me yesterday, 'But so many people in England have no representation.' You could have a party of one million people in England and yet it might not have even one member in Parliament. . . . What congressional representation

or parliamentary representation have the professional classes had in the United States or in England since the beginning of their governmental system?"

April 26, 1942:

[Transcriber tuned in late; very poor reception, indicated by asterisks.]

". . . the publication of an art magazine called * * * [*Blast*] commonly explosion of dynamite, et cetera, but connected in the * * * and source of life, and this magazine or manifesto was in its way a harbinger. I am never quite sure about that word 'harbinger' but it does seem to be generally accepted as being a sign of something about to come. Well, the other war came after it had been planned as a periodical or annual publication. Got out a special number in 1917 [1915] * * * the sculptor having got himself killed in the interim. And that manifesto was the best we could do * * * what has now become known to the world or at least to the European continent as the crisis of the system. Crisis of, of the system. System, not merely [in the System].

"Now the particulars about the art movement in so far as it affects merely painting and sculpture may not much matter in themselves, we say, but the point is that these things only occur— changes like that in art and writing only occur when something moves deeper down, something is doing, something is working inside, and the live artist, as distinct from the exploiters and deadheads, tries to do something about it. Institute something likewise. Anyhow, it at last appeared and somewhere inside it or in some contemporary explosion, there was the live state of matter. Matter, when there is not a certain amount of intelligence inside it, decays and rots. I repeat that. Matter, when there is not a certain amount of intelligence inside it, decays and rots.

"It would have been a happier day for all England if all England had looked at that sentence, which marks the end of an era— marks the end of the nineteenth century, usurytocracy and mercantilism. Matter in which there is not a certain amount of intelligence, decays and rots.

"Profit motive, already known, two thousand five hundred years before BLAST, 2400 years before Marx halfswallowed Hegel.

. . . And the Ta S'ein, the Great Learning, first book of Confucian philosophy, ends; Profits do not profit a nation/ Lucre does not profit a nation/ The sense of equity/ sense of justice/ is that wherefrom a nation benefits. The whole of your ruling class has run plumb haywire on profits."

April 30, 1942:

". . . The era of biology in the nineteenth century was to split everything up into slivers. Get a man concentrated on a small enough field, microscopic area, and maybe you can prevent him from seeing what it has to do with the next field. Or with the national income, or with the health of a nation. I'm an authority on poetry, for example, any post graduate student can become an authority on something or other, and very good exercise too, if you don't get looped [roped?] and buffaloed. And if he don't lose all capacity to incorporate what it may apply, imply, that it may imply something or other.

"Just like the loss, the absolute loss of craftsmanship, the ceasing of the [Ben Nights?], the carving of the wood in the fan lights over London house doors, that implied something or other. Why did our Colonial architecture, what is called our Colonial architecture, go to pot? Wood-carving, Colonial cabinet-making, I mean furniture-making, digging holes and knots, why did that go to pot? American silversmiths' technique, why did it peter out? When do such things synchronize with other phenomena, such as usury, tolerance of usury?

"There is work for all sorts and kinds of humans, so long as the musician or glass-blower carries his idea deep enough into it. The picture painter, if he carries his idea deep enough into it, we find that he is not alone, not isolated, that he has something to do, some relations, vital relations, with the rest of humanity. Well, I guess that's enough for this evening."

On May 11, 1942, Pound delivered an excellent talk, "French Accents", on contemporary French writing. Another talk on this subject, "To Be Late", delivered on May 14, 1942, was concerned with the work of Louis-Ferdinand Céline, whom the transcriber identifies throughout the transcript of "To Be Late" as "Stalin".

Interestingly enough, three of the most powerful talents in Europe objected vociferously to the continued intervention of England and the United States in political affairs on the Continent during the Second World War—Céline in France, Knut Hamsun in Norway, and Pound speaking to his homeland, America. All three were indicted for treason. Céline was exiled to Denmark from his native France for a period of years after the war. Hamsun was placed in a mental hospital and his fortune confiscated, a fortune which he had built up over a period of years as one of the world's most important novelists.

Hamsun had bitterly criticized the destructive influence of England in Norway, which resulted in the nation's occupation by the German army. British influence on the Continent during the twentieth century was nothing short of suicidal, and as much detrimental to her own interests as to the nations whom she sought to destroy. The difficulty was that the British, flushed with their success in conquering and administering India, Malaya and other outposts of the Empire, tried to treat the inhabitants of other European nations as they did the wretches who lived in their colonies. The result was that England not only lost her influence on the Continent, but her "Empah" as well.

Nor could anyone say that she had not been warned. The gist of Hitler's message to Chamberlain, as he recorded in his *Table Talks,* was that if England insisted on going to war against Germany again, she would lose her Empire. Despite Mr. Churchill's assurances to the contrary, this is just what happened.

Although Knut Hamsun died in poverty and disgrace, the flags were flown over government buildings in honor of the centenary of his birth, in August, 1959, and a special thirty-three volume edition of his works was issued in commemoration of the event.

Céline is the most important modern novelist in France, although his impact has not yet been felt in America. And Pound too is just beginning to break through to the attention of his fellow countrymen, during an era when Edgar Guest, America's richest poet, sold a million copies of "A Heap O' Livin' ", earned one hundred and twenty-five thousand dollars a year, and maintained elaborate estates in Detroit and in Florida. Despite the efforts of Robert Frost and Carl Sandburg to imitate Guest's profitable folksiness, they have not yet ascended into his income bracket.

I mention these three men, Hamsun, Céline and Pound, because I am frankly puzzled that all three of them should risk their reputations and their lives to oppose further intervention by the democracies in European affairs. Since none of them had anything personally to gain, and everything to lose, it must have been a matter of conviction. All three were treated shamefully after the war, in complete disregard of their literary achievements and their reasons for having taken the position which led them into trouble. And, had the Axis Powers won the war, all three would probably have been treated just as shamefully, for the Norwegian patriot, the French patriot, and the American patriot would have been just as quick to criticize German or Italian injustice as they had criticized England and America.

To continue the excerpts from the broadcasts:

May 18, 1942. With Phantoms:

"Now every American or Englander of my generation or that before or after my generation knew and knows that we were up against a problem of be a slave or go free. Any man not born rich in our time, he had to mate late, breed late and breed few or else go into slavery. Curtis Moffett said to me that when he saw what would happen if he was a good boy, he decided on badness, that he would be a bad boy and float on top of the current. Well, I landed in Europe, as my incipient biographers have stated with justice, with eighty dollars, that is, eighty American dollars— pre-Morgenthau and my clothing. And that led me to a fresher view of some problems."

A talk on the work of E. E. Cummings was given on May 21, 1942, and repeated four times on subsequent evenings. It was included in a collection of five broadcasts made by Olga Rudge, "If This Be Treason", and privately published in Italy in 1948. The other four were "James Joyce—to his memory"; "A French Accent"; "Canto 45" and "Blast."

May 31, 1942. Braintrust:

"And the melting pot in America may have been a noble experiment, though I very much doubt it. At any rate, it is lost.

It is a failure, and the idea of breed was not always un-English. The mongrel may be clever. Varietism may be amusing and it undoubtedly claimed other empires which have decayed, why shouldn't we? But it says nothing to the morrow, absolutely it says nothing to the morrow. The brain monopoly will have to swear up to the race problem or perish.

"To hear 'em you would think the braintrust is interested in producing another sort of carcass that can support the greatest number of lice, namely, parasites, subhuman or other. The braintrust will have to face the problem of race, and you will have to face the problem of race, and you apparently dare not face it. Who are the Shoguns [Shotguns, according to the transcriber], I ask you?"

June 4, 1942.   As to Pathology and Psychosis:

"As to pathology and psychosis. Europe calling. Ezra Pound calling. Nebulous notions, fragments of messy-eyed girls, floating above a pea-soup of ignorance, dense impenetrable ignorance, ignorance of Axis, ignorance of the capacities of the American Navy, ignorance of the lower deck morale, and what causes that? Have you no pathologists in the country?"

June 8, 1942.   The Keys of Humor:

"Hired labor is cheaper than slave labor. And you don't really have to feed your employees, whereas if your stock is in slaves, you damn well have got to feed them.

". . . My heart doesn't bleed for my country. I would rather have my head work for my country. If you can't or won't think of the causes of your slavery; if this conducement of slavery of your children for ten generations—if you won't think of it—God help you. You are in for billions of debts and you have not got your own people's money to pay for it. And most of you have not got the groggiest idea of Lincoln—you don't know what he meant by it. Here are ignorance of coin, credit and circulation, said John Adams 80 years before Lincoln. Ignorance and of course greed—greed is your ruin, the lust of evil men to get labor for next to nothing, lust of a planter to get African labor. But then finds that they are not paying enough, the lust of the immigrant with no regard for national welfare, no regard to the race, no regard to keep up the human breed, just blind greed, blind hate to get in as much cheap labor as possible."

The references to John Adams and Abraham Lincoln in the above broadcast are elaborated in what Ezra calls the *Introductory Text Book—in Four Chapters* (a one-page throwaway) as follows:

"I. 'All the perplexities, confusion, distress in America arise, not from defects in their constitution or confederation, not from want of honour and virtue, so much as from downright ignorance of coin, credit, and circulation.' John Adams.

"II. '. . . and if the national bills issued be bottomed (as is indispensable) on pledges of specific taxes for their redemption within certain and moderate epochs, and be of proper denomination for circulation, no interest on them would be necessary or just, because they would answer to every one of the purposes of the metallic money withdrawn and replaced by them.' Thomas Jefferson in a letter to Crawford, 1816.

"III. '. . . and gave the people of this republic the GREATEST BLESSING THEY EVER HAD—THEIR OWN PAPER TO PAY THEIR OWN DEBTS.' Abraham Lincoln.

"IV. 'The congress shall have power . . . To coin money, regulate the value thereof and of foreign coin, and to fix the standards of weights and measures.' Constitution of the United States, Art. 1, Legislative Dept., Section 8, p. 5.

"Done in the convention by the unanimous consent of the States, Sept. 7, 1787, and of the Independence of the United States, the 12th. In witness thereof we have hereunto subscribed our names:

> George Washington
> President, and Deputy from Virginia."

The *Text-Book* was first printed in Rapallo in 1938. On May 12, 1939, in response to a request from Kunitz and Haycraft, compilers of *Twentieth Century Authors,* Pound sent them some material, including the *Text-Book,* stating that they would not be allowed to reproduce any of the material unless the *Text-Book* were included. They complied with this stipulation.[3]

June 25, 1942. That Interval of Time (on the twenty-year cycle of war):

". . . History is a very dangerous subject. . . . Beware of folks who lump different things, different kinds of things under one label, such as a plow and a mortgage and call both of them capital. Keep lands and hands separate in your mind, and remember that all capital does not come from labour.

". . . And of course you ought not to be in this war, even to cover up the grievous failure of the administration to govern the United States, let alone fixing up the affairs of Europe and Asia."

July 6, 1942:

"There is so much that the United States does not know. This war is born of such vast incomprehension, such tangled ignorance, so many strains of undoing, that I'm held up in a rage by the delaying needed to change a typing ribbon, so much is there that ought to be put in young America's head.

". . . Art, economics, pathology [this is transcribed as 'Art, economics, mythology' in the rebroadcast on July 7]—you need to know more about all of them, need to get out of this war, need to stay out and to prevent the next one, need to change the stinking old system. Rotten art, artists, pathology, university delays. How come class war? What is it the profs don't know? . . . No, let us start on something that has been discussed in America for 20 years, 30 years. Doctor looks at literature. All this silly talk about the diseased mind making a modern painting. It bored me like hell. It was mostly poor stuff, but the fault lay in its limitations and criticisms, not in the main what caused half-educated medicos to go into it. What was wrong in the criticism was its lack of proportion.

"Health is more interesting than disease: health is total. Beauty is more interesting than distortion. We have most of us been buffaloed, at any rate the intelligentsia is mostly an art not from having no brain but simply from partialism in the original sense of this word.

"Intelligentsia is mostly inducant because it runs on snobbism and fragments.

". . . In this day the conventional precision of line will give way, interesting details, suggestions of luxury will augment as people lose an ethical basis of life. As they lose passion for justice, as they lose the love of real distinction between one idea and another, this diagnosis will replace love, analysis will give way to quarrels. . . . Honest men, when a dogma or style has been falsified, will turn analytical. They will be partial.

". . . But what is temperament in a sound man becomes by the excess diseased in a weak man, unbalanced, hard to divide it at a certain point but if one drips with the courage, one grows tolerant first of weakness, then accustomed to weakness, and then flops into squalor.

"Mediterranean sanity and beauty, order—the world was saner when the cult [transcriber has this down as 'coat'] of ugliness did not engage the attention of anyone. . . . Any deflection of the aim is a vagrance. It is a false repining. It is green fruit going rotten.

"Beardsley was a sick man who knew he had to make a name quickly if he wanted to make it, personal wish, not believing in what art is or ought to be. When he had time to learn to paint, his youthful impulse was towards pre-Raphaelite beauty. His early drawings like Verne Jules. That's what he wanted, Yeats asked him why he hadn't stuck to it. Well, Beardsley was no slouch. He was a courageous invalid. He was a heroic invalid, up to the point of his force. He didn't lie to himself or his friends in private. He knew that beauty is so difficult. He said, Beauty is so difficult.

"We have all seen the cult of beauty turned and slapped. We have seen an artist who won't take pains, who will not face the work needed to paint a good picture or write a good novel or poem. All fragmentary, nothing total. In the great perversion, the great decadence, when the painting is made to sell, that's when it is, when the artist stops wanting to live, wears his hair long, must eat but it's secondary to his desire to paint or to make . . .

"The futurist rooms are always an affirmation of propaganda that could get along by itself without any painting whatever. I mean the line of futurist propaganda is an idea, the painting an adjunct. An adjunct that proves the idea has other dimensions that are merely ideologies. It is a good idea, it is not a whole idea. But it needs plastic expression. It has imperfect plastic expression which is a dawn of its force, but it does not arise from a plastic need.

"Health is cruel, or rather health is often accompanied by what seems cruelty to the bacillus. A man who is totally healthy don't worry about bacilli. Yet he is perpetually surrounded by patent medicine bottles and disinfectants. But, for God's sake, look at your art! When art is subordinate to the picture dealer, the museum in the United States gets what is left after the European connoisseur has taken the pick of it.

"Ezra Pound speaking. I know I haven't got very far in this talk, so wait for the next. Health, damnit! Think about that in the interim. Pound speaking."

In "Darkness", a broadcast on July 13, 1942, Pound suggested putting Congress on the air, so that the people would know what they were up to. This was one of his favorite themes during the years he was imprisoned in St. Elizabeths Hospital. He has also plugged for the sale of the *Congressional Record* on newsstands, and suggested that each tourist visiting the halls of government in Washington be given a copy as a souvenir, in the hope that he might read it. He continued in this vein,

"I'm telling you, I'm just telling you, as Jimmy Whistler said to the painter Chase, I say I'm not arguing, I'm just telling you. You can keep your Constitution, most of the sailors and land-lubbers no longer care. But as a technicality, if no more than that, I'm telling you, a lot of folks want to bust it, so as to fish in the troubled waters. Lots of folks want to keep it rusty and inefficient so's it won't interfere in their various rackets. I'm telling you how to oil up the machine and change a few gadgets, so it will work as the founders intended."

July 26, 1942.   Axis Propaganda:
In this broadcast, in order to illustrate the type of Axis propaganda that he used, Pound gave the following quotes:

" 'I believe that banking institutions are more dangerous to our liberties than standing armies.'—Thomas Jefferson.

" 'I have two great enemies, the southern army in front of me and the financial institutions in the rear. Of the two, the one in the rear is the greatest enemy.'—Abraham Lincoln.

" 'The money power preys upon the nation in times of peace and conspires against it in times of adversity. It is more despotic than monarchy, more insolent than autocracy, more selfish than bureaucracy; it denounces as public enemies all who question its methods, or throw light upon its crimes.'—William Jennings Bryan."

March 25, 1943:

"The true basis of credit consists in the abundance of nature and the responsibility of the whole people.

"A knowledge of the world that we were born into is requisite for the understanding of the events subsequent to our births. A deliberate attempt, as I believe, has been made to blot out the historic record. And that attempt I propose to combat. I have in fact been combatting it for some time, as did my grandfather before me. And my talks on the radio will eventually have to be judged by their contents. Neither the medium of diffusion nor the merits or defects of my exposition can be the final basis of judgment. The contents will have to serve as their basis.

"I have taken up one point after another, one bit of evidence after another, trying to explain the facts in the simplest possible terms, trying to catch and hold the attention of the individual hearer. Wars in old times were made to get slaves. The modern implement of imposing slavery is debt. I repeat that. The modern implement of imposing slavery is debt.

"Usury is an instrument for increasing debt, and for keeping the debtor in debt perpetually or at least for the longest possible period. And it is hypocrisy to prattle of liberty unless the liberty includes the freedom to keep out of debt. There are ample records available from the 'Agitations of New Tables,' 'Tabulas Novas,' the new account books in the time of Caesar, down to the present. The auditor or reader who wants to understand these things cannot excuse his ignorance on the grounds that there are no sources of enlightenment at his disposal."

In connection with the foregoing statement on credit, Ezra once said to me, "Credit is the future of money." He also defined it as "future-money." In an extensive study of economics, I never found credit defined so well or so succinctly.

In making these broadcasts over Radio Rome after the United States and Italy were at war, Pound, I believe, knew that he was laying himself open, technically at least, to a charge of treason, or of giving aid and comfort to the enemy in time of war. From my knowledge of him over a period of years, and after a study of these broadcasts, I have come to the conclusion that he deliberately invited this charge, in the expectation that he would eventually be tried and that he would then have an opportunity to discuss openly his economic ideas. It may seem incredible to anyone living in the twentieth century that a character sufficiently quixotic to lay his head on the block in order to get his ideas discussed could still exist, but I do not think anyone who knows Pound will quarrel with this conclusion.

March 26, 1943.   Money:

". . . I took a banker's opinion about money the other day, he replied, 'Money is the statement of a government's debt to the bearer, meaning it's how much the government owes to the bearer.'

"I should have preferred him to say the state or the community owes to the bearer. I'm perfectly aware that I might as well be writing Greek or talking Chinese with a foreign accent, so far as making the statement clear as far as the hearer or reader is concerned. And the public can most certainly not be blamed for this. You can read a hundred books, by no means despicable books, on economics, without finding any hint that such an idea about money is possible.

"The only statement in even an approximately similar form that I can recall at this moment was made by a Congressman back in 1878 [T. C. Pound]. He said that an amendment offered by him to a bill about silver coinage had been an attempt to keep some of the non-interest bearing national debt in circulation as currency. As a definition, he called his amendment an attempt to keep some of the non-interest bearing national debt in circulation as currency. And in quoting that statement, I might just as well be talking Chinese or Tibetan, as far as the average reader is concerned. Money is a means of exchange. It is called upon to circulate the goods, a measured vane. It is both a title and a measure.

"The use of measured quantities of metal for this purpose should be considered as barter. Powdered gold was still being used in India when Kipling wrote Kim. He described the gold brokers dipping a wet slide into the gold dust and popping it into a box, the adherent dust being their commission on the exchange. . . .

"The sovereign power over issue of money can, or could of course, be used for maintaining justice. A study related to flagrant injustice. Thousands of men have become indebted in cheap or depreciated currency, and then been forced on more than one occasion to pay these debts in money worth twice or much more than the money wherein they had been contracted. In Brooks Adams' opinion, this was not by accident. He thought it was the fruit of design. He cited a great deal of conclusive evidence in support of his views.

"Now supposing Adams' view correct, would it not be interesting to pursue the subject further? Would it not be of interest to know whether the same banking firm had indulged in this little practice several times over? And let us say after the war of Napoleon, after the great and terrible Civil War in America, and after the dictate of Versailles. Ezra Pound asking."

How many times have I heard Pound say, "Keep some of the non-interest-bearing national debt in circulation as currency." The meaning of this statement eluded me until I had heard him say it perhaps some fifty times, over a period of years. It was almost impossible for me to conceive that a dollar bill in my pocket was not simply cash, but that it was part of the national debt and, as such, was drawing interest for the benefit of a private stockholder. Cash is not cash. The idea is a frightening one.

Jefferson had touched upon the idea of non-interest-bearing national debt in circulation as currency. Lincoln had done it, issuing greenbacks, not bottomed on debt, in order to finance the Civil War, and had gotten himself assassinated for it. Congressman Thaddeus Coleman Pound had dwelt upon it, but I do not believe the idea was quite as obscure in the nineteenth century as it is today. Perhaps we have now so accepted the idea that all currency is bottomed on national debt that we cannot understand any other sort of issue.

Pound also broached another of his basic ideas in this broadcast of March 26, the idea that paper money shows a higher state of civilization than metal. I would not have said, "The use of metal for this purpose is barter," but now that Pound has said it, the idea is worth considering. Can a modern society be built upon a concept of monetary issue which goes back to walled cities in the desert, the idea that all money, paper or no, must be based upon a quantity of metal buried somewhere, which can be, but seldom is, brought out and shown to the sceptical, like a Byzantine icon? Where is the madness or treason in this case?

March 28, 1943:

"An Italian Admiral said to me, 'Oh, he's one of those Hitler jugend, he doesn't smoke or drink.' He took a glass of Vermouth as a concession so as not to be stiff to foreigners. I can see the shudders of horror in Mayfair. What is the world coming to? What place has this new world for Churchill? And we do not believe the Atlantic Charter.

"Disorder in the American and British is as we see it reflected in crime waves in the need of more belief. Look at the police blotters on the two sides of the battle line. I'll repeat. Crime here has pretty well died out, a few 'crimes passionelles,' an age-old custom, but very few. There are a few cases of violations of food regulations but what does that mean? It does not mean the breakdown of the old but the imperfect establishment of a whole new frontier. A new sense of civic order, of cooperation. Considering that a whole new concept of a good citizen has been set up, still there is surprisingly little said against it. Now compare that with

the howls about rising crime and especially juvenile crime from
America. It may seem a trifle but if you cannot keep order in your
own house, how do you expect the world to believe that you could
keep it abroad?

". . . War is the maximum sabotage."

The anecdote, "He doesn't smoke or drink," was one of Ezra's
favorite stories. And certainly he was premature about criticizing
the wave of juvenile crime in America, for if he considered this
problem in 1943, what would he think of it in the sixties? Some
cynics say it is better for boys to be killing one another instead of
their parents, but such have always been with us.

March 30, 1943:

"Ezra Pound speaking. Brooks Adams observed that after
Waterloo, the battle of Waterloo, no power had withstood the
power of the usurers. We will try to mention, as distinct in our
own minds, the difference between the production system, the
system of actual goods, and the wangles or corruptions of account-
ancy, or the money wangles that corrode both the system of production and the system of exchange.

"The phase of the usury system which we are trying to analyze
is more or less Patterson's perception that the Bank of England
could have benefit of all the interest on all the money that it
creates out of nothing.

"The quite exquisite spirit of illegality and treason, these manifestations of a usurer, should need no comment. It takes five million dollars to start a daily paper of any size in the United States.
One should have ten million to date with any chance of getting the
paper going. It is hardly safe to attempt it without twenty million.
And in that case you would have to be willing to consider the
views of your advertisers, hence the totalitarian state, hence Fascism, and the national socialist revolution.

"Now the American citizen can, of course, appeal to his Constitution, which states that Congress shall have power to coin
money or regulate the value thereof and of foreign coin. Such
appeal is perhaps quixotic."

April 4, 1943:

"I am opposed. I believe that no American should kill or be killed in order to maintain the fetish value of metal, of any metal. The pattern of crime is known, the patterns of various component parts of a major crime are known. They have been witnessed time after time. . . . Has no one ever examined the Reconstruction Period, the period after the American Civil War, from this angle? The more people are ruined, the more bankruptcies, the more bankrupt concerns can be snapped up by the owners of loan capital. With race or without race, examine it. The more energy goes into destroying goods, the less will go into making them. The more energy goes into goods intended for immediate destruction, the less will go into goods made for use. The faster you destroy goods, the faster superfluous money will mount up. Unless you employ a bomb or similar mechanism to destroy the money as fast as the goods are blown to hell or sunk in the ocean. Well brother, that means inflation. That is a dollar worth seven cents of potatoes. And debt is already upon you."

April 18, 1943:

". . . War is his only out, as an experienced American politician [George Holden Tinkham] put it of Roosevelt. He continued: 'Most of the golden world is in the United States and the British Empire and in Russia. I reckon any attempt to diminish the power of them that have it will meet with pretty serious resistance.' The voice of experience, that, not of theory.

". . . Churchill, a blind alley * * * a target for metaphor. The position of the laborers as part from the labor-ites, the pie in the skies, the pie at the end of the next century, the known and unknown possibilities of abundance in the United States before Mr. Roosevelt's war started.

". . . And men in America, not content with this war, are already aiming at the next one. War with Russia. The time to object is now."

April 20, 1943:

"The United States once this war is over must be strong enough to bear Russia. The United States had a chance to maintain her prestige and unique position by staying neutral. Neutral, while other powers exhausted themselves. And she did not. Who are the lunatics? Was there a deliberate plot? That is what should concern you."

It is amazing that Ezra Pound, in 1943, should have been able to predict so accurately the postwar situation. Was it treason for him to warn his native land that she "must be strong enough to bear the strength of Russia" in the postwar world? Churchill said it in 1946, at Fulton, Missouri, but Ezra Pound had already said it in 1943. He continued in this vein with subsequent broadcasts.

April 27, 1943. Preparing Another:
"Oh, yes, another ten- or twenty-year war, between the United States and Slavic Russia. It'll start just as soon as this one shows signs of relaxing.

". . . I quote Jefferson. 'But with respect to future debts would it not be wise and just for the nation to declare in the Constitution that they are forming, that neither the legislature nor the nation itself can validly contract more debt than they may pay within their own age, or within the term of 34 years.' "

May 2, 1943:
". . . The artist does not need to own property, it usually bores him, bores him, but he wants to own his tools. No, not even that, he wants the right to use the tools of his craft."

May 4, 1943:
". . . Just why the campus Communist, the starry-eyed idealist Communist, or realist Communists . . . should suppose that Stalin is leading to a world revolution, instead of playing power politics on the old Romanoff model, I'll leave to you."

May 8, 1943:
" 'Religion, the opium of the people,' said Lenin. The late William B. Yeats countered that by saying, 'Science, opium of the suburb.'

". . . And Russia's contempt for the present pawnbrokers' regimes in London and Washington is even more vigorous than that of the Axis."

May 23, 1943:

"The moment calls for realism of a kind more real than you are accustomed to. Let us take down the stage set. It is very easy to fall into rhetoric; it is very easy for people to be swayed by clichés. No one is immune from that danger, least of all men who write in a hurry."

June 5, 1943:

"Your Russian allies are slaves of an infernal state, got life sentence. You have pretty nigh got a life sentence. . . . It is not, and has not been my purpose in these talks to speak of this war as an isolated phenomenon, as a bit of meteorite fallen from some other planet. My function is to arouse a little bit of curiosity about such profits. War is part of a profit. Some men should want to know what part of a profit it is, and what profit it is part of."

June 12, 1943:

". . . The German revolution a revolution of the home brothel against the American, mammas have not thought of it that way. And the intelligentsia has had 150 years of propaganda for the bordello. Disguised as Romantic literature, and disguised as a falsification. At first the Romantic literature was something sane. Then it got rotten. It began with a return to nature. Purity of nature as against the rottenness of artful society. How come it went rotten? Oh, one thing leads to another. False standards of Puritanism lead to revolt, quite properly.

"It is now very hard to touch upon such subjects at all without sounding like a Methodist elder or killjoy. All I can say is that nobody with a knowledge of the facts can claim that I have passed my life in gloom and without a fair share of the pleasures. This is not a Salvation Army meeting. I hereby maintain that I have seen more pleasure loosed on the evening air at a marshmallow roast than in any Cafe de Nuit in Montmartre.[4]

"Dreary cafes, with a few wornout bags and the usual staff

sitting around, hoping against hope that something will come in from outside and spend some money; and hope dies hard. Hoping somebody will come in and entertain them or introduce a little variety."

June 19, 1943:

"That text is known to them that have patience to read it, possibly one one-hundredth of one per cent of the denizens. They forget it, all save a few Western states. I think somebody in Dakota once read it. The Constitution.

"However, I don't mean that a new amendment would get enough publicity to prevent a vast movement to suspend the amendment in favor of Trilby. Yes, his middle name is Trilby. He writes it Franklin D. Roosevelt. However, the removal of one hypnotized lunkhead for the sake of inserting another hypnotized lunkhead or rabbit, might not bring sudden salvation.

"And prosperity was just around the corner. And now it is out guarding Persian railroads. Iran used to be Persia. Now it is part of Soviet Russia, with American troops guarding the railways, in order to bring the good life to Arkansas.

". . . No American boys will be sent to die on foreign fields. O Mother, Oh American Mother. Did you hear your beloved Franklin Trilby sing that operetta? Now I repeat it to you. I go on repeating it to you."

June 22, 1943:

". . . There really seems to be little doubt as to Stalin's direction. His mind appears to be remarkably clear."

June 26, 1943:

"An idea is colored by what it is dipped in. Take, for example, the more or less Teutonic idea of materialism—Marx and Engels just fooling around with Hegel's philosophy or something, and evolved, or developed what is called Marxist Materialism, and it got toted off into Russia and after 25 years, what do we have? We have those howlin' Slavs gone off on a purely metaphysical, typically Russian crusade, as crazy as any excess of the Middle Ages, trustingly oblivious of the material trend."

July 4, 1943.   On the Postwar Situation:

"Perhaps you will be able to get some employment but that isn't necessary. You are used to not being busy so that will not disturb you. You will not have to think about anything. That will be a comfort to your penury. You never did like to think about anything."

July 6, 1943:

"John Adams won the American Revolution as a law case before the peculiarly venal and squalid government of England at that time had recourse to arms.

"If a man appeals against economic aggression, he appeals to economic justice. Or at any rate he takes grounds from which appeals to economic justice must be eventually made. Now, what is economic justice? Is it based upon property? Do the Communists answer that in the negative? Is economic justice material justice? In modern society I think the answer must be, economic justice means an equitable distribution of purchasing power. It means a living wage for all labor in all places where the means of subsistence exists."

July 17, 1943:

"I reckon my last talk was the most courageous I have ever given. I was playing with fire. I was openly talking about how the war may be prolonged, by fellows who were scared that the war might stop. I mean they're scared right out of their little gray panties, for fear economic equity might set in as soon as guns stop shooting or shortly thereafter. The stage scenery fell with a flop, simultaneously with some anti-Axis successes.

"Mr. Welles trod on delicate ground, but he did make a step forward. I mean when he spoke of economic aggression. How can you prevent economic aggression inside a nation? If you can't prevent it inside a nation, how do you expect to prevent it on the world base? How do you expect to prevent it on the international scale if you can't prevent it internally?

"Inside the territory already crushed and defiled by the plutocracy, by the usury system, by the rump end of the mercantile system, which has been diseased and worm-eaten by the cancer of usury, at sixty per cent. And by the wheeze of varying the purchasing power of the government's money at the every whim of the financiers. And if you won't, or if a given gang of profiteers, sometimes called politicians, would not even try to prevent it inside their own countries, how the Sam Hill do you expect the rest of the world to do anything about preventing it outside the boundaries of their own oppressed and unhappy countries?

"London slums and the rest of it is proof of Churchill's misanthropy, and his contempt for all social justice, his loathing of the ideas of justice and equity. Of the three . . . Churchill, Roosevelt and Stalin, conscious or unconscious, Stalin is the more open. I think he has never tried to deny his hand in mass murders, assassinations and so on. He'd argue that it is just part of his business. Roosevelt would try to say that a murder today is committed in the hope of preventing your being murdered by your greatgrandchild's nephew.

"Mr. Churchill, who is an arrant . . . and clever scene-shifter, has never faced or answered questions. Is there any difference between slaying a man with a sword and killing him with a system of government? Hence the pink popularity of Bolshevist propaganda amongst Lord Professor Keynes' students in Cambridge, England.

"Well, part of the world prefers local control of their own money, power and credit.

". . . But I should like them to preserve a few art works, a few mosaics, a few printed volumes. I should like to store or bring to peace what is left of the world's cultural heritage, including libraries, and architectural monuments, to serve as models for one who constructs them.

". . . But there is no accounting for the peculiarities of the American people or for their lack of coherence. They seem to like spending their money on war, destruction and inedible metal. Perhaps the biosophites or some other American votaries of the infinite will, in time, produce some sort of diagnosis of the neurosis of the American sweetheart."

On July 25, 1943, the last of the talks was transcribed in Washington, and an indictment for treason returned against Ezra Pound. Of the seven broadcasts specifically cited in the nineteen-count indictment, only four are to be found in the Library of Congress transcripts. None of them are to be found in the file of the case, in the United States Court House in Washington.

Of the four broadcasts cited which are available, one, on March 19, 1943, had as its subject Henry Adams and the equation of the acceleration of the historical process. The transcriber notes that much of this broadcast was not taken down because of poor reception and unintelligibility. The other three that are available—May 12, 1943, May 14, 1943, and May 15, 1943—all deal with the same subject, an exposition of Acting Secretary of State Sumner Welles' Toledo speech on economic aggression.

The indictment reads as follows:

"par. 1. That Ezra Pound, the defendant herein, was born in Hailey, Idaho, October 30, 1885, and that he has been at all times herein mentioned and is now a citizen of the United States of America and a person owing allegiance to the United States of America.

"2. That the defendant, Ezra Pound, at Rome, Italy, and other places within the Kingdom of Italy and outside the jurisdiction of any particular state or district, but within the jurisdiction of the United States and of this Court, the District of Columbia being the district in which he was found and into which he was first brought, continuously and at all times beginning on the 11th day of December 1941 and continuing thereafter to and including the 3rd day of May, 1945, under the circumstances and conditions and in the manner and by the means hereinafter set forth, then and there being a citizen of the United States, and a person owing allegiance to the United States, in violation of said duty of allegiance, knowingly, intentionally, wilfully, unlawfully, feloniously, traitorously and treasonably did adhere to the enemies of the United States, to wit; the Kingdom of Italy and the military allies of the Kingdom of Italy, with which the United States at all times since December 11, 1941 and during the times set forth in this indictment, have been at war, giving to the said enemies of the United States aid and comfort within the United States and elsewhere, that is to say,

"3. That the aforesaid adherence of the said defendant, Ezra Pound, to the Kingdom of Italy and its military allies and the giving of aid and comfort by the said defendant Ezra Pound, to the aforesaid enemies of the United States during the time aforesaid consisted

"(a) of accepting employment from the Kingdom of Italy in the capacity of a radio propagandist and in the performance of the duties thereof which involved the composition of texts, speeches, talks and announcements and the recording thereof for subsequent broadcasts over short-wave radio on wave lengths audible in the United States, and elsewhere on ordinary commercial radio receiving sets having short-wave reception facilities; and

"(b) of counseling and aiding the Kingdom of Italy and its military allies and proposing and advocating to the officials of the Kingdom of Italy ideas and thoughts, as well as methods by which such ideas and thoughts could be disseminated, which the said defendant Ezra Pound believed suitable and useful to the Kingdom of Italy for propaganda purposes in the prosecution of said war;

"That the aforesaid activities of the aforesaid defendant, Ezra Pound, was intended to persuade citizens and residents of the United States to decline to support the United States in the conduct of said war, to weaken and destroy confidence in the Government of the United States and in the integrity and loyalty of the Allies of the United States, and to further bind together and increase the morale of the subjects of the Kingdom of Italy in support of the prosecution of the said war by the Kingdom of Italy and its military allies.

"4. And the Grand Jurors aforesaid upon their oath aforesaid do further present that the said defendant, Ezra Pound, in the prosecution, performance and execution of said treason and of said unlawful, traitorous and treasonable adhering and giving aid and comfort to the enemies of the United States, at the several times hereinafter set forth in the specifications hereof (being times when the United States were at war with the Kingdom of Italy and its military allies), unlawfully, feloniously, wilfully, knowingly, traitorously and treasonably, and with intent to adhere to and give aid and comfort to the said enemies did do, perform and commit certain overt and manifest acts, that is to say . . ."

Nineteen counts follow from which I excerpt, in part, as follows:

"1. . . . September 11, 1942 . . . the said defendant asserted, in substance, that the war is an economic war in which the United States and its allies are the aggressors.

"2. On or about December 10, 1942, the said defendant Ezra Pound, for the purpose of giving aid and comfort to the Kingdom of Italy and its then allies in the war against the United States, spoke into a microphone at a radio station in Rome, Italy, controlled by the Italian Government, and thereby recorded and caused to be recorded certain messages, speeches and talks for subsequent broadcast to the United States and its military allies, and that the purport of said messages, speeches and talks was to create racial prejudice in the United States.

"3. . . . February 4, 1943 . . .

"4. March 19, 1943 . . . purpose . . . cause dissension and distrust between the United States, England and Russia.

"5. . . . May 12, 1943 . . .

"6. . . . May 14, 1943 . . .

"7. . . . May 15, 1943 . . ." (These seven are the only talks specifically cited.)

Counts 8 through 19 deal with the over-all offense, as witness Count 17:

"Between December 11, 1941 and May 3, 1945, the said defendant Ezra Pound, for the purpose of giving aid and comfort to the Kingdom of Italy and its then allies, in the war against the United States, on a day and date to these Grand Jurors unknown, accepted and received payment and remuneration from the Kingdom of Italy in an amount to these Grand Jurors unknown, for compiling and recording messages, speeches and talks for subsequent broadcast to the United States and elsewhere from a radio station in Rome, Italy."

Count 16 names the amount received as seven hundred lire; Count 18, three hundred and fifty lire. Pound stated in an interview on April 30, 1958, "I got three hundred lira for writing and three hundred and fifty lira when I registered them. When I left Italy I had twenty dollars in occupation currency. The [broadcast] money barely covered my necessary expenses."

Pound had accepted no payment for the broadcasts until 1942, when his modest funds from England and the United States were cut off. He then accepted payment that would cover the expense of his train fare to Rome and his return to Rapallo.

The indictment concludes:

"The defendant Ezra Pound, committed each and every one of the overt acts herein described for the purpose of, and with the intent to adhere to and give aid and comfort to the Kingdom of Italy and its military allies, enemies of the United States, and the said defendant, Ezra Pound, committed each and every one of the said overt acts contrary to his duty of allegiance to the United States and in the form of the statutes and constitution in such cases made and provided and against the peace and dignity of the United States (Sec. 1 U.S. Criminal Code)."

The indictment was signed by Albert V. Llufrio, Foreman of the Grand Jury, and Theron L. Caudle, Assistant Attorney General. Caudle was later to win fame as "Mink Coat Caudle" in one of the most astounding scandals of the Truman regime, a scandal which played a considerable role in sweeping the Democrats out of office in 1952.

Since the case was never brought to trial, the indictment is now of historic interest, but one can only wonder how the government officials could have prosecuted it successfully. In one comment upon the indictment, Westbrook Pegler wrote that an attempt "to create racial prejudice in the United States," as cited in Count 2, violated no statute of the United States. It would, indeed, be almost impossible to prove that the broadcast had created racial prejudice in the United States. The curious idea that criticism of one member of a group creates prejudice against the entire group has not yet been codified into the U.S. Criminal Code.

And one can only wonder how the government officials could have proved that Pound's broadcasts exhorting his fellow citizens to live up to their Constitution could "increase the morale of the subjects of the Kingdom of Italy," as charged in Count 3. One broadcast was devoted to the career of James G. Blaine—only Ezra could have involved Blaine in the Second World War.

"Pound distinguishes between American government *de jure* and *de facto*," writes Professor Giovannini, "and the attack is directed at a *de facto* government which, as he understands it historically, has been since the Civil War in the hands of public servants who, more in ignorance than in malice, failed to realize the social and economic principles of the Founding Fathers. They failed, he argues, to implement the article in the Constitution giving Congress the absolute power to issue money and 'regulate the value thereof.' To Jefferson and John Adams the meaning of this Congressional power was clear: by it the nation's sovereignty is assured. But in Pound's view the meaning was subsequently blurred, and the power passed from Congress."[5]

As pointed out in *Esquire,* February, 1958, "No one familiar with Pound's work or his politics would fail to recognize the broadcasts as his own. Every year brings the correctness of his views more closely into focus. The idea that an American poet would be able to capture an enemy microphone and put it to his own use will no doubt escape the notice of those unable to distinguish Italians from Germans. Many people even today recoil from the suggestion that Pound was able to achieve a degree of freedom of speech—free radio speech—that was not available to him in this country under the Roosevelt administration."

Since 1945, many persons have sought refuge in the Constitution, particularly when accused of Communist espionage activities within the United States, but Pound's espousal of its principles over Radio Rome was not an appeal for himself. Unlike the Communists, he was not hiding behind it—he was urging his countrymen to use it, or at least to read it.

In November, 1956, the Washington *Star* printed a letter from the scholar, Professor J. C. LaDriere of Catholic University, which made the point that many people suppose "Pound was employed by the government of a nation with which we were at war to broadcast its propaganda against our country. . . . it is important to observe the following facts (all of which are fully available in many published sources, though mostly foreign): Pound was never a member of the Fascist Party or in any way affiliated with it . . . Pound was not invited to give the broadcasts in question; he sought the opportunity. The Italian authorities did not welcome, but were persuaded to tolerate, this eccentric and to them incomprehensible gesture of the distinguished American poet; to the last there remained distrust of him in high places, and suspicion that perhaps his broadcasts were in fact code messages for the benefit of the allies. Pound exacted assurance from the Italian authorities that his allegiance as an American citizen should not be compromised; he spoke as an American patriot, 'for' the United States of America and its Constitution which he conceived to be imperilled by the Roosevelt government. He was broadcasting for some time before we entered the war; the day after Pearl Harbor his broadcasts stopped. It was some time, Pound says, before he was able to get himself back on the air." Pound had recently published a pamphlet, *America, Roosevelt and the Causes of the Present War,* which concluded,

". . . Roosevelt being in all this a kind of malignant tumor, not autonomous, not self-created, but an unclean exponent of something less circumscribed than his own evil personal existence; a magistrate with legally limited jurisdiction, a perjurer, not fully aware of what he does, why he does it, or where it leads to. His political life ought to be brought *sub judice.*"[6]

Pound's main criticism of Roosevelt was not the man's personality, but the fact that he perjured himself when he took the oath of office and swore to uphold the United States Constitution. Pound merely recommended that Roosevelt be brought *sub judice,* before the law, as is done with any criminal.

When he learned that he had been indicted, Pound wrote to Attorney General Francis Biddle, on August 25, 1943, "I have not spoken with regard to this war, but in protest against a system which creates one war after another, in series and on system. I have not spoken to the troops, and have not suggested that the troops should mutiny or revolt. . . . At any rate, a man's duties increase with his knowledge. A war between the United States is monstrous and should not have occurred. And a peace without justice is not peace but merely a prelude to future wars. Someone must take note of these things. And having taken count must act on his knowledge, admitting that his knowledge is partial and his judgment subject to error."[7]

Biddle made no reply, and the indictment continued in force.

When Pound was mentioned in literary periodicals, he was now condemned as a "Nazi", although he was *persona non grata* with the German government. He had publicly criticized Hitler as being "too hysterical", and at no time was he on good terms with any official of the Nazi regime. This was proven when the German government, reflecting the widespread distrust of him, refused to grant him a visa to travel to the scene of the Katyn Forest massacre.

Katyn was one of the great scandals of the Second World War. Stalin had determined to end Polish resistance by classical Communist means, that is, by eliminating the educated classes who were capable of leading a resistance movement. Several thousand Polish prisoners in this category, including doctors, professors, and army officers, were taken into the Katyn Forest, despatched by small-arms fire, and buried in mass graves. When the Germans recaptured the area the following spring, peasants led them to the scene of the atrocity. Hoping to show the Americans what their Soviet allies were really like, the Germans invited Red Cross representatives and newsmen and writers from various countries to visit the scene. When Pound applied for a visa, he was refused.

The official United States propaganda agency, the Office of War Information, took its lead from Radio Moscow throughout the war. Moscow attempted to cover up the crime by claiming the Germans had massacred the Poles, and Elmer Davis, head of the OWI, echoed the Communist line. After the war, a Congressional investigating committee proved decisively that the Russians had committed the massacre.

Pound was the first American ever indicted for treason for opinions aired on the radio. Government officials long hesitated to bring him to trial, for, perhaps, if they were to lose the case, an important precedent would have been set, and it would have been difficult to obtain convictions against others who aired their opinions. In any event, his radio broadcasts would have had to be examined in the light of their effect.

Pound's appeal to his countrymen to get out of the war was even more quixotic than his request that they look to their Constitution. Many in England and the United States who were suspected of being lukewarm about prosecuting the war were put in a concentration camp. Thousands of native-born citizens, as well as "enemy aliens", spent the war years in these camps without trial. Most of them lost their property. A refugee from the Nazis, whom I knew for some years in New York, told me that the English took no chances with anyone; they even put the refugees from the Nazi concentration camps into their own camps for the duration of the war.

The New York *Times* of September 8, 1943, noted an announcement by Radio Rome that "Ezra Pound was not and had never been in our employ. He began transmitting before America entered the war. Yes, we gave him permission to use our microphone with the stipulation that he should not be asked or expected to say anything contrary to his conscience or contrary to his duties as an American citizen."

This was an unusual stipulation, but it was observed by both parties. Nevertheless, Pound's position in Italy was not a comfortable one. According to Carlo Scarfoglio, in *Paese Sera,* June 16, 1954, the Italian government seized Pound's bank account as an enemy alien, kept him under observation, and questioned his friends. Camillio Pellizzi, onetime president of the Institute for Fascist Culture, reported in *Il Tempo,* March 20, 1953, that Fascist secret police repeatedly questioned him about Pound, asking whether he thought the broadcasts might not be code messages to the Allies.

Pellizzi also stated, "I had many occasions to be in contact with Mr. Ezra Pound through his cultural activities and also because of my personal friendship with him, and I can assure you that he was never a member of the Fascist party."

This statement was corroborated in a letter written by the Mayor

of Rapallo and signed by sixty citizens of the town, which was
sent to Professor Giovannini, October 18, 1948:

". . . It is not true that he took part in Fascist activities in
this city. There is no record of his presence at local meetings, nor
was he a member of Fascist organizations. He was always considered an American citizen, a friend of Italy, openly sympathetic
with certain Fascist principles of a social economic nature and
with the struggle against communism which he believed was a
danger to the United States themselves. During the war Mr.
Pound continued to reside in Rapallo, and from his mode of life
it was evident that he did not enjoy privileges, but that he suffered hardships and economic privations. Since it is an evident
fact that he never acted from motives of profit, he was able to
keep the respect of even those neighbors of his who disagreed
with his political opinions. During the long years of residence in
Rapallo, Mr. Pound's activity was always artistic and cultural, as
illustrated in his writings in literary criticism and political economy. He always conducted himself properly and never engaged
in anti-Semitic activity."[8]

The fact that Pound was not acting from motives of profit was
undoubtedly the cause of much suspicion. George Sylvester Viereck told me that when he was conducting a pro-German propaganda organ in New York in 1915, two government agents
visited him and examined his books. They were satisfied that he
was being paid a salary for his work, and this seemed a great
relief to them. One of them told him, "We had heard that you
were doing this because you believed in it, but so long as you
are just doing it for pay, it's all right."

The New York *Times* noted on March 8, 1944, that the National Institute of Arts and Letters, which had accepted Pound
as a member in 1938, refused to expel him until he had been
convicted of the charge against him: "Mr. Pound, like every
other citizen of the United States when indicted for a crime,
must be presumed innocent until proven guilty after a fair and
impartial trial in which he is entitled to benefit of every reasonable doubt arising from the evidence. The Institute, as a national
organization, stands for ideas expressed in the Bill of Rights.
Until and unless Mr. Pound is convicted by a jury of the charges

against him, his relationship to and his privileges in our organization cannot be impugned."

Mr. Pound is still a member in good standing of the National Institute of Arts and Letters.

The charge of treason made against Ezra Pound lumps him with those hirelings who spied against the United States for foreign powers both in peace and in war. Whatever Ezra Pound has done has been done in the light of day, broadcast to the world and signed with his name. There were no secret meetings, no assumed names, no ideological twistings and turnings to suit the needs of the moment or the orders of superiors.

"Only the most absolute sincerity under heaven can effect any change whatsoever." Pound's broadcasts were made in conscience, fulfilling his duty as a citizen of the United States as he saw it, and informed by his understanding of the Confucian ethic.

Did Pound advocate fascism for the United States? He wrote, in *Jefferson and/or Mussolini,* that he did not advocate fascism for America. When he came to the United States to lecture against war in 1939, he said, in an interview which appeared in the *Capitol Daily,* May 9, 1939, "The corporate state is an elaborate and un-American organization."

Ezra often said to me, "Knowing what I knew, I would have been a cad not to speak up."

After his release, Ezra published an article on one of his later discoveries, Sir Edward Coke. The subject was "Coke on Misprision". "Misprision," wrote Ezra, "is what I would have been guilty of had I not made the broadcasts."[9]

According to Coke, he would have been guilty of misprision of treason, had he not gone on the air to warn his fellow citizens against Roosevelt's plan to involve the United States in a world war. Ezra's position has been substantially borne out by Professor Charles Callan Tansill's *Back Door to War* (1952), Morgenstern's work on the Pearl Harbor massacre,[10] the several Congressional investigations of that atrocity, and numerous other books and articles.

In deliberately exposing himself to a charge of treason by making the broadcasts, and risking a possible death penalty, Ezra was acting in accord with the stern New England sense of duty that informed the Founding Fathers, and which Professor de Piña Martins has characterized as "excessively puritanical and rigid." It is a vanishing spirit, but one occasionally encounters it still in seeing some elderly gentleman resolutely marching along in the chill of a Massachusetts winter, wearing scarf and gloves, but no overcoat. It is a sense of duty that is incomprehensible to today's "practical" or "modern" Americans, but it is the spirit that built this nation.

Time commented on the broadcasts on January 26, 1942: "Those best qualified to judge thought him the master verse-maker in English of his generation. He lived in a decaying palazzo in Rapallo, on the Mediterranean shore near Genoa." *Time* also noted that after the United States had declared war on Italy, Radio Rome announced that "Dr. Ezra Pound, the well-known writer, retired to continue his study of Chinese philosophy." This was during the period when the Italian government refused to allow Pound to continue his broadcasts, from December 7, 1941 to January 29, 1942.

Some Americans residing in Italy, like Giorgio Nelson Page, gave up their American citizenship and became Italian citizens. Pound not only refused to give up his American citizenship, but went to a great deal of trouble to retain it.

Some years ago, he wrote to Hubert Creekmore, "Am I American?. . . . Yes, and bugger the present state of the country, the utter betrayal of the American Constitution, the filth of the Universities and the . . . system of publication whereby you can buy Lenin, Trotsky (the messiest mutt of the lot), Stalin for 10 cents and 25 cents, and it takes seven years to get a set of John Adams at about 30 dollars."[11]

Far from advocating fascism for America, Pound had said, "I think the American system *de jure* is probably quite good enough, if there were only 500 men with guts and the sense to use it, or even with the capacity for answering letters, or printing a paper."[12] Pound's optimism concerning the future of fascism depended on whether or not its officials would adopt his monetary reforms; he was never as enthusiastic about its achievements as were many business and political leaders in England and the United States. Typical was Winston Churchill, a fervent admirer of Mussolini and the Fascist system during the 1920s. It was not Pound, but Churchill, who termed Hitler the "George Washington of Europe", and who heaped praise on Mussolini. In a press conference in Rome, as reported in the London *Times,* January 21, 1927, Churchill said,

"I could not help being charmed, like so many other people have been, by Signor Mussolini's gentle and simple bearing and by his calm and detached poise in spite of so many burdens and dangers. Anyone could see that he thought of nothing but the lasting good, as he understood it, of the Italian people, and that no lesser interest was of the slightest consequence to him . . . If I had been an Italian I am sure that I should have been wholeheartedly with you from start to finish in your triumphant struggle against the bestial appetites and passions of Leninism."

One of the leading British journalists, Lord Rothermere, publisher of the *Daily Mail,* expressed this sentiment about Mussolini in March, 1928: "He is the greatest figure of our age. Mussolini will probably dominate the history of the twentieth century as Napoleon dominated that of the early nineteenth century. I am proud of the fact that the 'Daily Mail' was the first newspaper in England, and in the world outside Italy, to give the public a right estimate of the soundness and durability of his work."

Pound never had any such extravagant ideas about Mussolini's prowess. He envisioned Mussolini as the leader of an *Italia irredenta,* but in his eyes the Fascist never achieved this goal. Pound was not interested in Mussolini merely as one who could make the trains run on time, and meet the interest payments on Italian bonds held in London and New York vaults.

Far from being the advisor to the Italian government, as charged in Count 3b of the indictment, Pound had little contact with the regime. Anyone high in the councils of the party could hardly have suffered such want during the war as Pound endured. Ezra wrote to me in 1959 that he certainly would have advised Mussolini if he had been able to reach him, and during the second *decennio* of the regime, he had protested against Il Duce's break with the *Risorgimento,* that is, the hoped-for Renaissance of

Italy. He made one last effort to persuade the Cisalpine Republic to issue Gesellite script, but he was ignored.

The Chief of the Fascist Ministry for Popular Culture, who was in charge of Pound's broadcast efforts, was also an American expatriate, George Nelson Page. He was the son of Thomas Nelson Page, former U.S. Ambassador to Italy. Born in France, young Page became a great admirer of Mussolini, took out Italian citizenship in 1935, and changed his name to Giorgio Nelson Page. The Nelson Pages are "old Virginia", with the family estate, I believe, near Amherst. I recall a visit there in 1947, and I suppose it is still in the family.

On July 16, 1944, Page was arrested by American forces as they entered Rome. He could not be charged with treason, as he was an employee of his own government. Had Pound taken out Italian citizenship, as Page had done, no charge could have been lodged against him. Nevertheless, as an official of the defeated regime, Page was kept in a concentration camp at Padua for many months after the war. He wrote a book about himself and the thousands of others who were imprisoned there. No charges were ever brought against them, and they were finally released.

The New York *Times* (July 16, 1944), noting Page's arrest, said that "Ezra Pound, who retained his American citizenship while broadcasting for the Fascists, and is therefore wanted on a treason charge, has not been apprehended and presumably is in northern Italy."

Pound's greatest danger in 1944 was not the possibility of arrest by the United States armed forces, but the possibility of execution either at the hands of the Gestapo or of Communist partisans. He had shielded a number of Jews from the Nazi exterminators, several of them Jewish musicians whom he had hired to play at the Rapallo concerts during the 1930s. The death penalty was automatically incurred for hiding Jews.

A rabbi who had fled the Nazi terror in Budapest also came, seeking aid, and Pound sheltered him for three weeks. The Gestapo searched his rooms twice during this period, but he had been warned aforetime by friendly townspeople, and the rabbi was sent to hide in the butcher shop. The disgruntled Gestapo officer took away some of Pound's letters and papers, but noth-

ing incriminating was found. Pound says that the papers were
returned in "good order" the following week.

He left Rome the day before Allied forces entered the city.
He says that it was a tremendous experience to witness the collapse of an entire civilization before one's eyes. He managed to
get on a train, paying a premium to get a seat by the window,
but he was appalled by the overcrowding. When an old man
standing in the aisle keeled over for lack of air, Pound gave him
his seat, and got off the train.

He decided to walk to the north, a decision that saved his
life. A band of Communist guerillas, led by the notorious Genoese pimp, Sbarbero, had been informed that he was on the train.
They halted the train in true Jesse James style, and searched the
cars, for there was a price on his head. Had he been found, he
would have been shot immediately, as many victims were murdered on the spot by the Communists.

Sbarbero continued to search for Pound during the ensuing
weeks, calling for him at the hotel in Rapallo, while Pound was
hiking through the hills. As soon as he learned that American
forces were in the vicinity, he went up to a patrol and said, "I'm
Ezra Pound. I hear that you're looking for me."

He was fortunate to have survived Italy's reign of terror, when
more than one hundred thousand anti-Communists were murdered by the partisans. As the Allied forces liberated Italy, the
Mafia once more took over the cities, and the Communist guerillas ruled the provinces.

Mussolini had crushed the Mafia organization by stern measures—that is, by shooting them. Those gangsters who survived
escaped to the United States, where they became loyal supporters
of the big city political machines. Now the American Army, accompanied by Lucky Luciano and his friends, came as liberators.
The police officials who had driven them from the country were
slaughtered in terrible scenes, and once again the Mafia ruled
unopposed. They were now "political refugees" who had been
persecuted by "Fascist beasts".

The Mafiosi contented themselves with hanging and shooting
police officials, but the Communist guerillas who ruled the provinces were more ambitious. They wanted some massacres like

those of the Bolshevik Revolution in Russia. Anyone who owned property or a business was fair game. The ensuing reign of terror has been described by Luigi Villari, former lecturer at the University of Virginia and official of the Italian Foreign Office, in *The Liberation of Italy*. He quotes Carlo Simiani's *"I giustiziati fascisti dell'aprile 1945"*:

"The first days in Milan were terrible. Many citizens talked of the probability that a new reign of terror was being prepared. . . . Executions were carried out in double-quick time. Firing squads were rare; machine gun volleys were simpler. . . . No one troubled about illegality. People's courts existed, but in many cases only in name. . . . Quick and cruel forms of justice produce morbid effects on simple minds in times of revolutionary frenzy. . . . Murder reached its culminating point after the slaughter of Mussolini and the other Fascist leaders. . . . In many cases the murders were the result of love affairs, or vendettas, without a shadow of a political motive; poor wretches meeting with an unscrupulous commander were put to death. There were cases of persons seized merely in order to extort money from them, after which they were released even if deserving punishment.

"Thousands of persons were put to death without having undergone any form of trial, without any possibility of appeal, nearly always without religious rites. Very rarely were they allowed to send farewell messages to their families. . . . A foreign official stated that at Sesto San Giovanni (near Milano) 4,000 persons had been killed, while a French paper put the number in that town as high as 10,000.

"Any attempt to arrive at the truth is impossible, as all witnesses are afraid of speaking out.

"When the German and Fascist authorities had disappeared, innumerable armed brigades and armed bands of partisans arose, searching for a nonexistent enemy. The older and authentic partisans were flabbergasted, but could do nothing. At first, the partisans were very few, but now they were innumerable. It was a hodgepodge of uniforms, ranks and weapons of all kinds. . . .

"Many industrial experts, engineers, et al., all excellent men, were murdered, such as Ugo Gobbati of the Alfa Romeo, Siliveri, manager of the Marelli Company, a man esteemed by everyone, and many others who had taken no part in politics, Giacomo Grazoli, head of the Grazoli plant and a pioneer of industry, Scoloni and Mazzoli, engineers of the Breda works at Sesto, Weber of Bologna, Vischi of the Reggiane at Reggio Emilia, were all murdered.

"The moderating orders of the CLNAI existed merely on paper.

"In the province of Como, 1,200 persons were murdered, in that of Varese 300, in that of Brescia 1,700, but when, later, the Fiamme Verdi (partisans consisting of regular officers and men) arrived, order was restored. In the province of Bergamo, there were 53 murders, in that of Mantua 1,500, at Lecco 37, in all Lombardy 10,000!"

"These atrocities were nearly all committed by men who had become partisans *after* hostilities had ceased."[13]

The effect of the "liberation" can be compared to a situation in the United States if all the prisons were to be opened, and exiled criminals invited back to shoot the police who arrested them. The "liberation of Italy" deserves the closest study by Americans, for it is an accurate description of what would take place here if the Communists succeed in seizing power.

In France, Communist partisans were murdering Frenchmen during this same period. In the Ardennes Forest, a vast area is still closed to tourists, because Frenchmen who had opposed Communism were slaughtered and buried in mass graves during the "liberation" of France. They were nearly all businessmen, educators and engineers of the upper middle class, the same classes which the Soviets had murdered at Katyn Forest.

Sisley Huddleston, former Paris correspondent of the London *Times,* fully documented this massacre of the French middle class in two books, *Terreur 1944,* and *France; The Tragic Years, 1939–47.*[14] These massacres of anti-Communists in France and Italy have few parallels in the history of Europe.

Although Ezra Pound escaped certain death at the hands of the partisans by surrendering to United States forces, as far as he knew, he was to have been sentenced to death by his captors. The New York *Times,* May 6, 1945, carried the headline, "EZRA POUND, WANTED FOR TREASON, / Seized by American

Forces NEAR Genoa in Italy." One might suppose that Pound had been a major military objective. The item noted that "Pound left America at the age of twenty-two and returned in 1939 after an absence of thirty-one years. In 1942 he tried to get back to the United States but was left to continue unwillingly his thirty-three year exile."

Thus the New York *Times* corroborates the fact that Pound had been left in Italy against his will, and in violation of his rights as an American citizen. This was important evidence in his favor, and it explained why the government was not anxious to bring the case to trial.

Six terrible months began for Pound. Few men could have survived his ordeal, and younger, hardened soldiers, kept in the same environment, suffered nervous breakdowns or tried to commit suicide. Although he was nearly sixty years old, Pound was sent to a brutal concentration camp then operating in Europe, the United States Army Disciplinary Training Center near Pisa, Italy.

After the war, there were a number of Congressional investigations of these "D.T.C." units, as they were called. The commander of the one at Litchfield, England, was punished. A D.T.C. in Africa was run by a master sergeant who had been a professional torturer for the Communist Party during the Spanish Civil War. The one at Pisa, where Ezra Pound was imprisoned, was the most notorious of these camps.

Government officials have never advanced any explanation as to why Pound was kept for six months in the Pisa D.T.C. As Pound points out, in a letter to me dated June 24, 1959, "D.T.C. Pisa solely for american soldiers guilty of anything from mild inebriety, AWOL, to murder, high-jacking, or sending home $15,000 in one week, origin of same unaccounted for."

There was no looting by American forces in Italy. At any rate, the D.T.C.s were operated to punish members of the U.S. Armed Forces, and Ezra Pound did not fit into this category. The only possible explanation for placing him in the Pisa camp was the fact that in addition to the rapists, hijackers and murderers imprisoned there, a number of "political unreliables" also were serving indefinite terms. These were American soldiers who had been reported for making criticisms of Roosevelt or Stalin, or who had said, during typical barracks' discussions, "When we git to Berlin, we ought to keep right on goin' and mop up that crowd in Moscow too." As Russia was the official ally of the United States, such statements were reported as high treason, and the soldiers were sent to prison.

Even Pound's most steadfast detractors fall silent when the point is made that he was denied the right to a speedy trial, which is guaranteed us by our legal system. The six months' imprisonment at Pisa made it certain that, even if he were convicted of the charge against him, an appeal on this ground would free him. It would seem that he was sent to Pisa for only one reason, that is, to break him, so that even if he were to survive this "cruel and unusual punishment," he would be in no condition to defend himself.

When the Provost Marshal at Pisa was informed that Pound was being sent there, he had a squad of men working all night with acetylene torches to construct a special cell for him in "Death Row". This was a row of iron cages for men who were awaiting execution. Since Pound had not even been tried, this seemed somewhat premature.

Metal airfield stripping was cut up, and the sides of the cage reinforced with this material. A special squad was detailed to guard the cage twenty-four hours a day. The prisoners and the military police at Pisa were warned that they would be severely punished if anyone were caught speaking to Pound. This warning, coupled with the elaborate security precautions, convinced the personnel and prisoners that he was a very important man. None of them had ever heard of him or his poetry, but they regarded him with great respect.

During those months in the death cell, Pound was exposed to the broiling Italian sun during the day, and forced to sleep on the damp ground at night. For weeks, his only covering was some newspapers, which a kindly prisoner had tossed into his cell, and at last, he was issued a blanket. He obtained a few books, but it was difficult for him to read because of an inflammation of the eyes. The death cells were close to a military highway, and the constant dust, as well as the glaring sun, affected his sight.

From time to time, men in the cells next to his were taken

out and executed, and he supposed that his own turn might come any day. For awhile, he had as a neighbor a Private Till, who is referred to in *The Pisan Cantos* as "St. Louis Till". Pound wrote,

> and Till was hung yesterday
> for murder and rape with trimmings[15] [.]

Till, a Negro soldier, had raped two Italian women during a drunken orgy. He finished the party by slashing them to death with a bayonet knife.

All about Pound was the stuff of tragedy during that terrible summer of 1945. He writes in *The Pisan Cantos,*

> As a lone ant from a broken ant-hill
> from the wreckage of Europe, ego scriptor.[16]

His old friend Gerhart Hauptmann, the Nobel Prize-winning playwright, had died of shock after seeing his home and the cultural city of Dresden levelled by Allied bombers, an attack in which forty thousand women and children, fleeing the onrushing Communist hordes, lost their lives.

Pound's wife had not been informed where he was, and did not know if he was alive or dead. To this day, she has never received any official notification of her husband's whereabouts from the government.

It seems probable that Pound suffered a sunstroke, or a mild stroke, as a result of prolonged exposure. The poet Alan Neame, writing in *Blackfriars, the English Dominican Review,* in May, 1951, notes that Pound was "exposed to the variations of the Italian climate and to the ill treatment of . . . guards who used to while away their time tormenting him with their bayonets."

By autumn, his physical condition had deteriorated alarmingly, and the camp commandant informed Washington that he would have to have medical care. He received no answer to this message. A guard made Pound a wooden platform, so that he no longer had to sleep on the ground. This kind deed is referred to in *The Pisan Cantos,*

> "doan yu tell no one I made it"
>   from a mask fine as any in Frankfurt
> "It'll get you offn th' ground"[17][.]

One afternoon, eight of the prisoners, driven almost mad by the harsh treatment, tried to make a break for it. As they dashed past Pound's death cage, they were mowed down by automatic rifle fire. The guards continued to rain bullets into them as they lay helpless on the ground, only a few feet from Pound. The horror of this scene had a lasting effect upon him. "After that," he said, "I needed a five-year rest cure. But I didn't bargain for a life sentence."

On the evening of November 17, 1945, two lieutenants took Pound away. He supposed that, at last, he was being led out to be executed. Instead, they put him in a jeep and drove him to a landing strip, where he was put aboard a C-54 Army transport. The next morning, under heavy guard, he was taken from the plane and lodged in the District Jail in Washington, D.C.

Two days later, Omar Pound, who was serving in the U.S. Army in Germany, arrived in Pisa to see his father. He had heard from a fellow soldier, a former inmate of Pisa, about the old man in the cage ("he had the same name as yourn"), and obtained an emergency furlough.

The District Jail held many critics of Franklin D. Roosevelt during the two years previous to Pound's incarceration there. Two other poets, George Sylvester Viereck and Ellis O. Jones, accused of sedition, were still locked up there when Pound arrived. Viereck asked permission to visit with him, but he was refused.

During his months of captivity in Pisa, a blackout had been placed on news of Pound. Not only his family, but his friends as well, were unable to find out what had happened to him. T. S. Eliot finally discovered that he was imprisoned in the D.T.C., and wrote some indignant letters to the authorities. He also contacted some of his fellow writers, and asked them to protest. Robert Graves wrote a sneering answer which was typical of the responses. He said, "I never interfere with the domestic affairs of another nation." Yet many of these same writers who refused to help Pound leaped to the defense of the Communist poet Boris

Pasternak when he was involved in a squabble with other Communists in Moscow.

A brief note in the New York *Times* of September 5, 1945, mentioned that "The Justice Department said it did not plan to drop treason charges against Ezra Pound, American writer held by the U.S. Army in northern Italy. A spokesman said the Department recently had received a memorandum on Pound from military authorities in Italy and added that his case is being studied 'intensively.' A Rome dispatch recently suggested that Pound might be released for lack of evidence."

The memorandum referred to was the commandant's request to permit Pound to receive medical treatment, and to learn what disposition was to be made of him. Roosevelt might be dead, but his spirit was marching on. Many people supposed that Pound would be reprimanded for having made the broadcasts, and then released. No one who had heard the talks supposed that he would actually be prosecuted for treason. William Carlos Williams was approached by Federal Bureau of Investigation agents and asked to testify against his friend, but the agents never came back.

The New York *Times* reported on November 19, 1945, that Pound had asked Henry Wallace, Secretary of Agriculture, and Archibald MacLeish, Assistant Secretary of State, to be subpoenaed at his trial. He said that he had conferred with them in 1939, and that his purpose then was "to keep hell from breaking loose in the world." Pound had only twenty-three dollars, and he asked that he be allowed to serve as his own defense counsel. The judge replied that this could not be permitted on such a serious charge.

In describing his appearance, the *Times* said, "Pound, one-time Paris dandy, appeared tired and disheveled in court. He wore a dirty GI undershirt, a pair of baggy trousers, and GI shoes that were too large."

In a lengthy story in the Sunday edition of November 25, 1945, the New York *Times* repeated Pound's request to subpoena Wallace and MacLeish, and noted that counsel had been obtained. The story, which was subtitled "His Purpose", said that Pound had told Judge Bolitha J. Laws that he wished Wallace and MacLeish to verify his statement that he had come to the United States in 1939 on a mission "to keep hell from breaking loose in the world." The *Times* reported that "Striving to assure victory in this crucial case, Department experts believe they have the necessary proofs, and by their tactics can jump the legal barriers created by precedents, such as that laid down by the Supreme Court in the treason trial of Anthony Cramer. . . . Much work has been done on the case here and abroad. . . . Incriminating statements have been obtained from Pound."

There are some odd phrases in this news story, such as "crucial case". What was so crucial about it, except that the Department of Justice might at last be able to obtain a "Guilty" verdict against one of Roosevelt's critics, after having failed in thirty-two previous cases? The experts planned to "jump the legal barriers created by precedents." Why not shoot him outright? And finally, "incriminating statements have been obtained from Pound."

Here we come to the crux of the matter, and the position Pound took that landed him in St. Elizabeths for thirteen years. He has told me on a number of occasions during the past decade that the government lawyers refused to try him for a very simple reason— namely, that he insisted he would stand by every statement he had ever made over Radio Rome. He would repeat his statements about Roosevelt before a packed courtroom and newspaper reporters. Obviously, the government lawyers did not want this to happen.

On November 26, 1945, the New York *Times* announced that seven Italians who said they had seen Pound make anti-Allied broadcasts from Rome and from Milan had flown to the United States "voluntarily" two weeks earlier. On the following day, Pound was arraigned, and his attorney, Julian Cornell, entered a plea of "Not Guilty".

Newsweek noted Pound's reappearance in the issue of December 3, 1945: "Behind him in Italy, Pound left a wife, a mistress, two sons and an eighty-six-year-old mother." Pound had only one son, who was serving in the U.S. Army.

In its issue of December 10, 1945, *Time* spoke of him as "the ragbaggy old darling of the U.S. expatriate intelligentsia," and made a very interesting comment: "Jurists, who anticipated the most sensational case of its kind since the trial of Aaron Burr, wondered just how the U.S. proposed to convict its disaffected poet."

Time's query was soon answered. The U.S. did not propose to try to convict its disaffected poet. There were too many precedents for Pound in American history of prominent men who risked their necks in order to express political dissent. One of the most notable was Pound's mentor, John Adams, who has been described by Russell Kirk as "a man censorious, practical, ironic and heroic, a man not afraid to risk hanging for the liberties of Massachusetts, not afraid to plead for Captain Preston after the Boston Massacre, not afraid to denounce the Gallic enthusiasm raised by Citizen Genet."[18]

Like John Adams, Pound always opposed the mob, because the mob will never discuss the questions. They can only riot. As Adams said when running for the legislature, "No democracy ever did exist or can exist." The answer of the offended American people to Pound's criticism of them was not a defense, but a subterfuge. Instead of trying him, and allowing him to air his arguments, as he had anticipated doing, the government officials put him in an insane asylum. He was removed to Washington's Gallinger Hospital, the temporary stopping place for dope fiends (many of them prostitutes) and other citizens who are due to be committed to St. Elizabeths Hospital.

The file in the United States Court House in Washington, D.C., "Criminal No. 76028, United States vs. Ezra Pound, charged with violation of Section I, Title 18, US Code (Treason)", is now marked "Case Closed". The chronology of the case is scrawled on the file cover in pencil and ink, with the following notations:

"Nov. 26, 1945. Presentment and Indictment Filed.

"Nov. 27, 1945. Defendant waives reading of the indictment and stands mute. Arraigned. Plea 'Not Guilty' entered by the Court. The motion for admission to bail is continued for further hearing until Dec. 14, 1945.

"Dec. 21, 1945. Motion for admission to bail is further argued and by the Court denied. Order directing deft be sent to St. Elizabeth's Hospital for treatment and examination filed.

"Jan. 18, 1946. Motion for a formal hearing to determine deft's mental condition heard and granted. Hearing calendared for Jan. 30, 1946.

"Jan. 30, 1946. Sanity hearing continued indefinitely.

"Feb. 13, 1946. Lunacy Inquisition—Jury sworn. Verdict—respondent is of unsound mind.

"Jan. 29, 1947. Deft's motion for bail heretofore argued and submitted is further argued and by the Court denied.

"4-18-58 Motion of deft to dismiss the indictment heard and granted. Order dismissing indictment recorded."

The psychiatrists who made the preliminary examination of Pound at Gallinger's Hospital made their report to Judge Bolitha J. Laws on December 14, 1945, representing the Federal Security Agency:

"The undersigned hereby respectfully report the results of the mental examination of Ezra Pound, now detained in Gallinger Hospital . . . for observation from the District Jail on a charge of treason . . . the defendant . . . was a precocious student, specializing in literature . . . He has long been recognized as eccentric, querulous and egocentric . . . He is abnormally grandiose, is expansive and exuberant in manner, exhibiting pressure of speech, discursiveness, and distractability . . . He is, in other words, insane and mentally unfit for trial, and is in need of care in a mental hospital.

Respectfully submitted,
Joseph L. Gilbert, M.D., Marion R. King, M.D.
Wendell Muncie, M.D., Winfred Overholser, M.D."

Dr. Wendell Muncie was a psychiatrist from Johns Hopkins University. King was an official of the United States Public Health Service, a career bureaucrat since 1922, who would hardly have been expected to defy the administration. Dr. Overholser, superintendent of St. Elizabeths Hospital, also was a career bureaucrat who had been in government service ever since his graduation from the University of Chicago. Although no one could blame the administration for being well-represented in a case that was regarded as extremely crucial, it did seem that the deck was stacked.

Amazingly enough, the government psychiatrists' report on Pound, with the exception of the statement "was a precocious student", was an accurate description of Pound's long-time enemy, Franklin D. Roosevelt! Pound was described as "eccentric, querulous, and egocentric"—one would need only to add the noun "megalomaniac" to bring any Washington correspondent to his feet with the exclamation, "Why, that must be FDR!" "Abnormally grandiose, expansive and exuberant in manner": the analogy is too close to be accidental.

During the early years of the Roosevelt regime, one of his advisers was the highly respected historian W. E. Woodward, the only American historian, so far as I can find out, who claims that Wilson suffered his mental breakdown *before* he went to Versailles. Pound was in correspondence with Woodward, and occasionally suggested items that he might pass on to the President. Hence this passage in *Rock-Drill:*

> "Don't write me any more things to tell him
> (scripsit Woodward, W.E.)
> "on these occasions
>
> # HE
>
> talks." (End quote)[19]

When Pound was released, the Chicago *Tribune* printed a brilliant editorial entitled "Who's Crazy Now?" The editorial pointed out that although Pound had been examined by psychiatrists, no clinical study of Roosevelt's mental condition had ever been made. The writer suggested that Roosevelt's costly crusade to save Soviet Russia from the German armies may have been due to mental illness, rather than to deliberate treason, a very charitable conclusion.

The testimony given by the government psychiatrists at the Lunacy Inquisition on February 13, 1946, fills more than one hundred pages. Most of this testimony consists of verbal fencing on the part of the psychiatrists. The following excerpts contain the gist of their statements concerning Pound's mental condition:

Dr. Wendell Muncie testifying—

"Q. Will you state what symptoms you found in Mr. Pound?

"A. There are a number of things which attracted my attention in examining Mr. Pound, and these are essentially the items that appeared to me:

"He has a number of rather fixed ideas which are either delusional or verging on the delusional. One I might speak of, for instance, he has been designated to save the Constitution of the United States, for the people of the United States.

"Secondly, he has a feeling that he has the key to the peace of the world through the writings of Confucius, which he translated into Italian and English, and that if these had been given proper circulation the Axis would not have been formed, we would be at peace now, and a great deal of trouble could have been avoided in the past, and this becomes his blueprint for world order in the future.

"Third, he believes that with himself as a leader, a group of intellectuals could have gotten together in different countries, like Japan, for instance, where he is well thought of, to work for world order. He has a hatred of bureaucracy which goes back a long way, and one may conclude that his saving of the Constitution draws a clear distinction between the rights of the people and those who govern the people . . . In addition to that, he shows a remarkable grandiosity. He feels that he has no peer in the intellectual field, although conceding that one or two persons he has assisted might, on occasion, do as good work as he did.

"Q. Did you at any time ascertain whether he understood the nature of the offence?

"A. Whether he understands the meaning of treason, or not, I do not know. He categorically denies that he committed anything like treason, in his mind, against the people of the United States.

"Q. Were you able to discover whether any other mental difficulties had occurred in his previous life?

"A. Well, all we know is from the record that he went through an unusual mental experience in a concentration camp in Italy, which, by all the records, must have been a profound emotional experience amounting, I suppose, to a panic state, but to suggest it may be described technically, I don't know, but it was rather a severe emotional crisis he went through, at which time he was seen, I think, by the psychiatrists.

"Q. Before that did you examine sufficient of his writings and so on, to be able to determine whether or not there was a question of this condition in his early life?

"A. I have read a great deal of his writings in connection with preparing this case, and it is my idea that there has been for a number of years a deterioration of the mental processes . . . I would say in ordinary language he has been a peculiar individual for many, many years, and that on top of that, in recent years, I don't know how long back, he has been engrossed in these things I have talked about as neurotic developments [the three points cited earlier]. For statistical purposes we would call this a paranoid condition.

"Q. By paranoid condition I understand that involves delusions and self-aggrandizement?

"A. Yes."

According to Dr. Muncie, Pound's insanity consisted of three things—his passion for the Constitution, his espousal of the Confucian ethic, and his desire for world peace. The use of the phrase "his blueprint for world order" by Dr. Muncie suggests that Pound desired to set up a totalitarian state along Confucian lines, although no one else has ever mentioned that Pound entertained such an idea. Dr. Muncie also blithely states that Pound's writings show a "deterioration of the mental processes" over a number of years. Oddly enough, he was not asked to cite a single passage to bear out this contention, nor was the matter referred to again in his subsequent testimony. The gist of Dr. Muncie's analysis is that Pound is "peculiar".

Dr. Muncie stated that he saw Pound twice, and was with him about five hours. He continues his testimony as follows:

"Q. How did you find his memory?

"A. His memory, as far as I could find, was material, and that

I knew about, was all right, except that for a good period in the concentration camp where there appears to have been a blackout of memory.

"Q. That would not be unusual, in your opinion, Doctor, that stress or strain?

"A. It is unusual when related to that emotional panic which he experienced there at that concentration camp, and to which concentration he was not used to.

"Q. Don't you think it is rather normal for a person subsequently arrested for a charge of treason to be under great emotional stress?

"A. I wouldn't know, Mr. Metlack [Isaiah Metlack, government prosecutor]. I might suppose that would be an incentive to keep your thoughts about you. The answer is, I don't know."

Dr. Marion R. King testifies:

"Q. How much have you read of his literary output?

"A. Very little of his poetry. I have seen one of the Cantos, and samples of poetry that have been reprinted from others . . . He was very much concerned with political, economic and monetary problems, as time went on his enthusiasm became greater, and there is no question but what he has a lot of sudden, emotional feeling in connection with these hobbies . . . I am convinced he glorifies in his rebelliousness rather than disguising it, and that again is indicative of a paranoid condition or paranoid state . . . I consider him to be a sensitive, eccentric, cynical person, now in a paranoiac state of psychotic proportions which renders him unfit for trial.

"Q. What classification would you state for Mr. Pound's mental condition according to your classifications pertaining to mental illness?

"A. I would say that would fall in two categories or paranoid states, sometimes called paranoid conditions. That is not a very satisfactory term because it is part way between so-called paranoid schizophrenia and dementia praecox, paranoid type, and true paranoia, and there are all types or gradations at different extremes, and it is my opinion that he falls in between these two extremes.

"Q. Does he have a split personality?

"A. No.

"Q. Just what is it that makes you place him in that category?

"A. He does not have the clear, well-defined, systematized delusions of the paranoiac type; neither does he have the disassociation, the personal hallucinations or delusions, the disordered delusions that go with the dementia praecox, paranoid type, and the other extreme, but he does have a rather diffuse paranoid reaction which falls somewhere between those two fields, and that is the reason I would not classify him as a dementia praecox patient, or a case of true paranoia.

"Q. What is his qualification, or what is his I.Q.?

"A. Very high . . . There has been no impairment of the intelligence over the years. That again is a characteristic of the disorder we are describing. Paranoids are very apt to develop, whereas the schizophrenia is more likely to occur in individuals with low I.Q."

Dr. King's statement that "There has been no impairment of the intelligence over the years" might seem to conflict with Dr. Muncie's previous statement a few moments earlier that "there has been for a number of years a deterioration of the mental processes." The attorneys did not notice the discrepancy.

Dr. Winfred Overholser's testimony:

". . . He has a very high degree of intelligence . . . he speaks in bunches of ideas.

"Q. Would you state by referring to them what the records show as to his present state of mental health?

"A. It is a rather bulky record, as you see.

"Q. Can you summarize it?

"A. Essentially it is that there has been very little change in his condition since he came in [to St. Elizabeths Hospital]. A summary of the case from the time he came in is pretty much in line with what I said this morning, and the whole staff has seen him. There has been some discussion about him which has not been formal; in fact, there has been no formal diagnosis they have made as yet.

"Q. No formal diagnosis?

"A. No."

If a formal diagnosis were ever made, neither I nor any of Pound's acquaintances ever heard of it. In 1948, when I specifically asked the nurse who saw his records at the hospital about the diagnosis, she could not recall if there had been one.

Dr. Overholser also was asked about the Pisa episode:

"Q. When they said he was not psychotic, that means he was not insane? [referring to his examination by psychiatrists while incarcerated in Pisa].

"A. That he was not suffering from a major mental disease. That was their impression. How long they saw him, I don't know, or what their experience was.

"Q. Would you say that the incident known now as the Pisa incident was the result of one of those blow-ups?

"A. Yes. Apparently he had been held incommunicado in an uncovered garage of some kind out in the yard, and had apparently developed a neurotic state out of that."

After this expert, if somewhat conflicting and inconclusive, testimony by the psychiatrists, the jury returned a verdict of "unsound mind", and Pound was committed to St. Elizabeths Hospital. The jury consisted of Benjamin Abramson; William T. Berry; Thomas H. Broadus; Ethel M. Christie; Carroll K. Jenkins, Sr.; Raymond M. Lawrenson; Frank A. Marceron; Edward T. Martowicz; Edward A. Mohler; Leonard W. Morris; Jesse W. Missear, and George E. Polen, presumably all from the District of Columbia, or its environs.

Since Pound did not testify, it is doubtful that they could venture any further opinions on the matter if questioned today. Shortly after presiding over the hearing at which the charge of treason was dismissed more than twelve years later, Judge Bolitha J. Laws passed away.

XI

THOSE INNOCENT of the intrigues of the literary world might suppose that Ezra Pound's imprisonment, as well as his alleged insanity, would influence his critics in his favor, but any creative talent that has swum too near the piranha-like jaws of the liberal book reviewer knows too well that such is not the case. The parasite prefers that its host should not defend itself, and the waters of the literary world are constantly boiling as the body of some new writer is torn to pieces and the stripped skeleton slowly sinks to the bottom.

Ezra Pound was one of the few talents of the twentieth century who survived every attack of these creatures. These half-hearted talents have burrowed into the muscles of every literary journal in the western world, in the approved manner of the trichinosis worm, and from these vantage points they have steadily sickened and paralyzed the healthy development of our literature.

It is too kind to explain their conduct by merely saying that they had to project their sickness into their surroundings, and it ignores the fact that the community has the right to protect itself against any harmful influence, whether it be a rapist or a literary critic who has allied himself with the forces of destruction. They gained a certain strength through placing themselves in the hands of the new Moloch, the monolithic power of the post-Rousseauian madmen.

Henry Seidel Canby, editor of *The Saturday Review of Litera-ture,* displayed the characteristic accuracy and grace with which our leading "litteratti" treated their historic enemy, Ezra Pound. He wrote editorially in the issue of December 15, 1945, "The false scholarship, the excessive eccentricity, and the confused thought of much of his poetical work show something less than greatness . . . He was a traitor . . . Pound of the broadcasts, the prose pamphlets and private letters, was a muddled and mediocre mind, easily deluded by childish fallacies in government and economics."

Canby set a standard for the vituperation of Pound that was difficult for his successors on *The Saturday Review,* Norman Cousins and Harrison Smith, to maintain, but they did their best.

Pound continued to work on his *Cantos* while he was imprisoned at Pisa, and the ones completed there were published as *The Pisan Cantos.* A recent news story states that this book is now one of the texts at the Aspen Institute, where such as Adlai Stevenson improve their minds. It would be interesting to observe the effect on these business and political leaders of lines such as,

> and if theft be the main motive in government
> in a large way
> there will certainly be minor purloinments[1][.]

The sponsor of former President Truman's political career was Boss Pendergast of Kansas City, who stole forty million dollars and died in jail.

Television viewers are familiar with Mr. Bennett Cerf as the witty and urbane judge on the program "What's My Line?" He has not always been so poised, notably when he considered the case of Ezra Pound. Although he had made a fortune from his Modern Library series, Mr. Cerf found the Second World War a harrowing experience. The grim hand of Nazism came perilously close to his comfortable book-lined den on Madison Avenue, where he sat tormenting his brain into devising more effective ways of defending democracy.

He was particularly aware of the menace to civilization as he had known it, as presented by the personage of Ezra Pound.

Even after Pound had been shut away, Mr. Cerf continued to sound the tocsin against him. He exhibited raw courage in 1946, when he deleted twelve poems by Pound from an anthology that Conrad Aiken had compiled for the Cerf firm of Random House.[2] Some of Cerf's friends thought this might be going a bit too far, and protests against this quaint Madison Avenue custom of "book-burning" were heard from W. H. Auden, Max Lerner, and Robert Linscott of Cerf's own office.

Some months earlier, Cerf had suggested to the editors of *The Saturday Review* that he would like to write a weekly column of chit-chat for them. He had long been one of their heaviest advertisers, and they were more than delighted by his offer. He used his column, "Trade Winds", to air his perplexity over the problem of disposing of Pound and his work. In the issue of February 9, 1946, stung by Lewis Gannett, book editor of the New York *Herald Tribune,* who had called him a book-burner and akin to the Nazis, Cerf printed his reply:

". . . The war is not over. . . . You say I am being emotional about this. Of course I am!"

Cerf appealed to his readers for support. In the March 16, 1946, issue, he reported that readers had sent in 289 opinions on his deletion of Pound's poems from the anthology. He said that 142 opposed the inclusion of Pound's poems, 140 approved, or wished that he had included them, and several respondents said that they hadn't been able to make up their minds. Despite the remarkably even distribution of opinion on this very controversial matter, 142–140, Cerf admitted that the omission of Pound's work was "an error in judgment, to be rectified as soon as possible." He added, "I still think that Ezra Pound and men like him are the scum of the earth, and must be fought without quarter and without cease. In this particular issue, however, I went charging off on the wrong course."

Cerf then printed several pages of excerpts from the opinions of his readers. These are priceless, but we can only reprint a few of them, and they, after all, represent but a small number of the 289 that Cerf said he received.

Norman Rosten wrote, "Mr. Pound is a traitor and he should

be shot and I would be the first to join the firing squad for that purpose."

Robert Hillyer wrote, "I said there was no question that Pound should be omitted from the anthology. Of course, I never considered Pound a poet of any consequence. . . . For years he had been a foolish mountebank."

One of the last letters written by the heavily-ulcerated Harry Hopkins praised Cerf for omitting Pound's poems. He ordered a copy of the anthology to be sent to the hospital, but he died three days later without reading it.

Clyde Brion Davis wrote, "Years before he officially turned Fascist the work of this articulate lunatic impressed me as valuable chiefly as a clinical case record."

Gordon Young wrote, "Ezra Pound is not only a traitor but—like all who are stuffed with megalomania—a thorough faker." After continuing in this vein of invective for several paragraphs, Mr. Young suddenly weakened his statement by concluding, "I am merely a writer of pulp stories, and what can a pulper know of poetry?"

Roberta James wrote, "A traitor such as Pound, far from having his name perpetuated, should be shot, buried and forgotten as quickly as possible."

Gail Russell (is this the movie star?) wrote, "Having heard the vile mouthings of this traitor I am whole-heartedly in agreement with your position."

Captain Paul H. Elmen wrote, "I lost my leg outside the town of Gleiderkirck—You say that he (Pound) is crazy . . . You say that he was a Nazi. Obviously he was."

Cerf's most impressive testimonial for his book-burning escapade was a letter that stated, "We heartily agree with you, in the exclusion of Ezra Pound's poetry from 'An Anthology of Famous English and American Poetry.' " It was signed "The Senior Class of Houston High School". Is it possible that someone played a joke on Mr. Cerf?

Cerf, fighting to the last, said that he would include Pound's poems in future editions of the anthology, but that he would prefix this note, "Here he is, Pound the man we consider a contemptible betrayer of his country."

Pound's lawyer, Julian Cornell, immediately wrote Cerf that this was a clearly libelous statement, and demanded a retraction. Cerf replied that he would retract the statement "only over my dead body."

With their position on Pound clearly defined, Cerf and the editors of *The Saturday Review* waited for Pound's next move. They had to wait several years, and even then the action was not initiated by him, but by a quasi-governmental body, the Fellows of American Literature at the Library of Congress.

Pound's work had received little recognition in the way of prizes. He had been awarded a fellowship from the University of Pennsylvania in 1906, such as are given to "bright" students, and in 1927, he had received the annual "Dial" award, but the Guggenheims and their imitators had ignored him when it came to passing out the cake. In 1949, however, he was awarded the Bollingen prize of one thousand dollars for "the best poetry published by an American citizen during the year in the United States." The award was given for his *Pisan Cantos,* and the New York *Times* headlined the front-page story, on February 20, 1949, "POUND, IN MENTAL CLINIC / WINS PRIZE FOR POETRY / PENNED IN TREASON CELL".

The implication of the headline was that Pound was not only continuing to write his "treasonable" works, but that he was being praised for them. The award was given at the recommendation of the Fellows of American Literature, a group that had been organized four years previously to function in coordination with the Library of Congress. They had been asked to serve in this capacity at the suggestion of Allen Tate. At the time of the Pound award the group was composed of Leonie Adams, Conrad Aiken, W. H. Auden, Louise Bogan, Katharine Garrison Chapin, Robert Lowell, Archibald MacLeish, Katharine Ann Porter, Allen Tate, Willard Thorp and Robert Penn Warren. Thus it included a good cross section of the leading American poets of the 1940s.

Paul Green was a member of the Fellows at this time, but he abstained from voting for Pound. Tourists may recall that he writes outdoor dramas that are staged in public parks. Theodore Spencer also was a member, and he cast his vote for Pound, but he died before the prize was awarded.

There was a flurry of interest over the fact that Pound, indicted for treason and incarcerated in a madhouse, had won a prize for his work, but the New York *Times* soon went on to other things. During that spring, several well-known writers received proofs of two articles by Robert Hillyer, an academic poetaster much loved at *The Saturday Review of Literature,* whose work had been ignored by the "new school".

In the issue of June 11, 1949, the first of these articles, "Treason's Strange Fruit", appeared. The second, "Poetry's New Priesthood", came out in the June 18 issue. The gist of these virulent outpourings was that Paul Mellon, the sponsor of the Bollingen prize, Dr. Carl Gustav Jung of Switzerland, and a mob of poets led by T. S. Eliot, had combined in a worldwide "fascist" conspiracy, involving, among other persons, the proprietors of an outfit called Pantheon Books. The purpose of this "fascist" conspiracy was to give Pound an award for his poetry, and Hillyer was now warning the democracies that this objective had been achieved. It was obvious that he considered himself to be a Paul Revere of modern literature, sounding the tocsin against the forces of Pound and Eliot.

In addition to the numerous distortions, inaccuracies and mis-statements that marred these two items of prose, we must consider the background in which they appeared. *The Saturday Review of Literature* had long since given up any pretensions of serious literary criticism. It was simply a trade publication, which announced new books, with brief reviews contributed by the hewers of wood and drawers of water in the literary world, the university professors, newspaper copyreaders, and retired high school teachers who could write for the magazine's high school and small town library audience.

The Saturday Review also conducted a highly profitable "Personals" column, which accounted for a considerable portion of its revenues. There had been a growing demand for entertainment after the war, and almost any peccadillo found a ready audience. The editors of *The Saturday Review* found that the more unusual advertisements they printed, the more they received, and the "Personals" column steadily grew.

These advertisements might sound suspiciously like invitations to participate in various amusements, to anyone more sophisticated than *The Saturday Review*'s editors, although many of them were geared to what might be called "normal needs". The June 11, 1949 issue, in which Hillyer's first article appeared, contains a number of such advertisements as the following:

"Job worn young professional, uninhibited, likes the unusual, invites female correspondence."

"Young male, weary college senior, seeks gay, stimulating, distracting correspondence."

No doubt some interesting literary relationships resulted from these ads.

The June 18, 1949 issue, including the second of the Hillyer outbursts, contained the following notices:

"Versatile young male seeks position with gentleman as facto-tum-companion. Travel anywhere."

The editors must have been looking the other way when some-one slipped the following advertisement into the June 25, 1949 issue of the magazine: "Male desires male secretary-companion position. Offers youthful, energetic services, gay personality, vivid imagination."

In this context, the glaring inaccuracies of Hillyer's articles no longer seem quite so disturbing. Obviously, the entire magazine could not be a series of "Personals" columns, and something had to be used to fill up the white space in the front pages. An editorial introduction to "Poetry's New Priesthood" in the June 18 issue declares that Pound had been arrested in May, 1944, instead of the correct date of May, 1945. Hillyer quotes two lines of Pound and makes five errors in so doing:

> Summer is icumen in
> Lhude sing goddamn[.]

Pound's original reads,

> Winter is icummen in,
> Lhude sing Goddamn[3][.]

The July 2, 1949 issue contained a number of retractions by the editors in regard to Mellon, Jung, the Bollingen Foundation, and virtually everything else that Hillyer had said. Pantheon Books, which he had suggested was part of the fascist conspiracy, was actually run by two refugees from the Hitler regime! Nevertheless, letters again poured in from loyal readers, supporting Hillyer and the editors in every one of the distortions and falsehoods. Such is the flexibility of the liberal mind! Dixon Wecter wrote,

"Congratulations on publishing Robert Hillyer's inquiry into the Bollingen award to Ezra Pound. Whether that moth-eaten faun deserves the noose or merely the straitjacket I don't pretend to judge . . . a shabby charlatan from the start . . . a thirdrate hack. . . . His snobbery has always been cheap and vicious, but only within recent years has his genius—fructifying in the Pisan Cantos now crowned by the bays of the Library of Congress—been compounded by senile dementia."

The July 2 issue also contained a letter from a lady in Milan, Michigan: "I'm just a housewife but this Ezra Pound case has me incensed. I just sent off a letter to Senator Vandenberg to say so." Vandenberg made no statement on the Pound case, perhaps because he was too busy with the British Secret Service agent whom Ruth Montgomery, Washington newspaperwoman, gives credit for reversing Vandenberg's stand against the United Nations.

The more intellectual members of the United States Congress, that is, the readers of *The Saturday Review,* were not slow to sense the immorality of the Fellows' decision to award Pound a prize for his poems. The Hon. James T. Patterson reprinted the two Hillyer articles in *The Congressional Record,* on July 19, 1949. Oddly enough, the editors of *The Saturday Review* refused permission to the compilers of *A Casebook on Ezra Pound*[4] to include them in that collection, the only such instance of a refusal from the editors of newspapers and magazines who allowed use of the material for this "textbook".

The Hon. Jacob Javits, the present U.S. Senator from New York State, inserted material in *The Congressional Record* on

August 2, 1949, to the effect that fascists were taking over the Library of Congress. Throughout the controversy, Luther Evans, Librarian of Congress, was as unhappy as a trapped bear. His bureaucratic career depended upon his maintenance of his reputation as a "liberal", yet he was being accused of being a "fascist". He wrote a letter to the editors of *The Saturday Review,* which appeared in the July 2, 1949 issue. He said, in part,

"That Mr. Paul Mellon has through some diabolical and perverted motivation tried to influence the decision of the Fellows, is an insinuation which I believe to have no foundation whatever . . . I am deeply disturbed by one point of view which you and Mr. Hillyer seem to share, and that is that poetic quality must somehow pass a political test."

In *The Triple Thinkers* (1938), Edmund Wilson has pointed out that "The leftist critic with no literary competence is always trying to measure works of literature by tests which have no validity in that field."[5]

On August 19, 1949, Senator Theodore Green of Rhode Island announced, as Chairman of the Library Committee, that the Library of Congress would give no more awards of any kind. He informed a New York *Times* reporter that "We are opposed to the Government discriminating between individuals in the matter of taste. There are no standards to apply, only personal opinions." (*Times,* August 19, 1949.)

In blithely dismissing all standards of artistic and literary judgment, Senator Green announced to the world, as an official of the United States government, that such standards are never exercised in this country, and that statements on the merits of a poem or painting are merely "personal opinion". Luckily, the European press ignored his remark.

The nation's press had a field day after the Hillyer articles appeared. Modern poetry, as well as the "crazy traitor" came in for some rough, if good-natured, jibing. As Ezra once remarked, "Americans tend to turn everything into a bean feast." The Bollingen controversy was the greatest American literary bean feast of all time.

After a sobering interval, some writers began to suspect that

serious damage had been done. A lucid statement was made by
Malcolm Cowley in *The New Republic* of October 3, 1949:

". . . I confess to being less excited than others by the
public implication of his [Pound's] disloyalty. The London Times
Literary Supplement was not altogether frivolous when it said that
his worst crime was not his broadcasts for Mussolini but his
translations from Sextus Propertius. [Pound had repeatedly informed the *Times Literary Supplement* that the Propertius poems
were not literal renditions.] The broadcasts were silly and in-
effective. They did not succeed in persuading American soldiers
to desert or malinger—the GI's weren't even amused by his thirty-
year-old slang. —nor can I believe that his anti-Semitic outbursts
caused the death of a single Jew among the millions who perished
. . . The little American republic of poetry is under attack by
pretty much the same forces as those to which the Russian
writers have already yielded: that is, by the people who prefer
slogans to poetry, and national self-flattery to honest writing.
Hillyer has gone over to the enemy, like Pound in another war
. . . Worsted in a struggle among his colleagues and compatriots,
he has appealed over their heads and under false colors to the
great hostile empire of the Philistines."

The New Republic, in its October 7, 1949 issue, printed two
letters excited by the Cowley article, one from William Rose Benét,
upholding Cowley, and one from David Weissman, attacking him.

The Saturday Review of Literature crusade to save the United
States from Ezra Pound provoked two books of dissent, one by
Archibald MacLeish, entitled *Poetry and Opinion* (Urbana, Uni-
versity of Illinois Press, 1950) and *The Case Against the Saturday
Review of Literature,* published by *Poetry* in 1949.

MacLeish defended Pound in a dialogue between "Mr.
Saturday" and "Mr. Bollingen". *The Case* revealed that *The Saturday Review* had refused to publish letters in defense of Pound that
had been sent the editors by Archibald MacLeish, Mark Van
Doren, William Meredith, Ivor Winters and many others. *The
Saturday Review*'s own poetry editor, William Rose Benét, was
quoted as describing *The Pisan Cantos* as "extraordinarily fine
and sensitive poetry."[6] John Berryman had written in the *Partisan
Review* of the "marvelous pages of the 'Pisan Cantos.' "[7] And

Robert Gorham Davis, also writing in *Partisan Review,* had attributed to *The Pisan Cantos* a "new humanity, tenderness, maturity, with no loss of lyric beauty or wit."[8]

Allen Tate contributed a "Personal Statement on Fascism" to *The Case,* saying, "I have no clear idea of the meaning of Fascism when the word is applied to conditions in the United States. At intervals since 1933 I have been accused of 'Fascism' by persons who were either Communists or affected by Marxist ideas. In the literary world such charges have little real political significance; they are used against anti-Communists as demagogic weapons. The Marxist policy has held Fascism to be a 'reactionary' movement, or return to tradition."[9]

Tate is one of the few American writers to recognize a fact that is widely known in Europe, that is, that the accusatory word "Fascist" simply means one who is opposed to Communism. The word is rarely used except by Communists or apologists for Communists. There has never been a group known as the Fascist Party in the United States, and there is no legitimate use of the term "Fascist" in our political debates.

The Saturday Review attack on Pound coincided with the trial of Alger Hiss. The chronology is as follows:

June, 1947—Alger Hiss receives an honorary degree from his alma mater, Johns Hopkins University.

May, 1948—John Foster Dulles and Dwight D. Eisenhower, trustees of the Carnegie Endowment for International Peace, appoint Alger Hiss president.

August, 1948—Whittaker Chambers makes public charges, that Hiss is a Communist agent.

December, 1948—Hiss is indicted.

June, 1949—*The Saturday Review* unleashes an attack on Pound.

January, 1950—Hiss is convicted.

After being convicted for perjury on two counts, Hiss served three years and eight months, and was released with the promise of a Federal pension. Pound served thirteen years without trial, and was released without compensation for his sufferings. Where was justice in this case?

One of the excuses offered by politicians for their failure to speak up for Pound was the charge that he was "anti-Semitic", and that the wrath of the Jewish community would fall on any politician who tried to help him. Walter Winchell, Bennett Cerf, Karl Shapiro and many others waged virulent hate campaigns against Pound on the grounds that as Jews they were bound to attack anyone who was anti-Semitic. Karl Shapiro stated quite frankly that he could not vote for *The Pisan Cantos* because he would not support anyone who was "anti-Semitic", regardless of the merits of the work.[10]

The editorial page of the *B'nai B'rith Messenger* of April 8, 1955, carried this note: "TALKING ABOUT unsavory characters, you might be interested in the fact that Ezra Pound, the poet who joined Hitler and Mussolini in the campaign of extermination of Jews is well taken care of in the St. Elizabeths Hospital for mental diseases, in Washington, D.C."

This was typical of the allegations that were hurled against Pound throughout his imprisonment. This was the gratitude that was offered him for the forty years during which he helped Jewish poets, and shielded them from the death cars of the Gestapo. Pound had publicly criticized Hitler, was *persona non grata* with the Nazi government, as proven by their refusal to grant him a pass to Katyn, and had met Mussolini only once.

After the war, a public ceremony of thanksgiving was held in Florence, Italy, in honor of Dr. Gerhard Wolf, the German wartime consul, who had saved hundreds of Jews from the Gestapo, openly defying that organization in many instances. It is to be hoped that Ezra Pound's work on behalf of the Jewish artists will likewise be recognized.

Throughout his life, Pound sponsored Jewish writers and artists who were beginning their careers. In a letter to his mother, written in November, 1913, he said "Epstein is a great sculptor." In the March 16, 1914 issue of *The Egoist,* he wrote an enthusiastic review of Epstein's work. Another of Pound's enthusiasms was Ben Hecht, at that time a promising young avant-garde writer. In the June, 1918 issue of *The Little Review,* Pound wrote, "He (Hecht) alone, of the few bards with whose work I am acquainted, preserves an exquisite balance in the current of his own emotions." Pound also wrote, "Ben Hecht is an asset. . . . He is trying to come to grips."

Hecht later became a highly-paid Hollywood scenario writer, but kept up his literary associations, especially with Sherwood Anderson. Anderson wrote to Roger Sergel, December 25, 1923, "The rest of them in Chicago, except Ben Hecht, now and then, when he isn't being a smarty, are just talking. The smartiness will perhaps defeat Ben. It may have already."[11]

On October 13, 1936, Anderson wrote to Laura Lou Copenhaver, "Had a long talk yesterday with Ben Hecht, who has gone sour on the movies. You know we were once great friends in Chicago. His old mother was killed in an auto accident, in Los Angeles, and the last thing she said to him was that he should have stuck with me and gone with me on my road."[12]

John Cournos, of Russian Jewish background, wrote of his acquaintance with Ezra in London, in his autobiography, as follows: "Ezra, as I had cause later to find out, was one of the kindest men that ever lived. Ezra . . . was the ideal missionary of culture."[13] Cournos also stated that "Ezra Pound divined my loneliness and went out of his way to get me acquainted."[14]

Another of his protégés was the poet Louis Zukofsky, who wrote, in a contribution to Charles Norman's *The Case of Ezra Pound,* "I never felt the least trace of anti-Semitism in his presence. Nothing he ever said to me made me feel the embarrassment I always had for the 'Gentile' in whom a residue of antagonism to 'Jew' remains. If we had occasion to use the words, Jew and Gentile, they were no more nor less ethnological in their sense than 'Chinese' or 'Italian.' "[15]

In 1938, Pound dedicated his book *Guide to Culture* to Louis Zukofsky, an individual Jew, and Basil Bunting, an individual Quaker. On February 18, 1932, Pound wrote to John Drummond of the need for "some place where men of good will can meet without worrying about creed and colour etc."[16]

During the years that he was aiding these Jewish artists, Pound was writing the *Cantos,* which contain supposedly "anti-Semitic" passages. At the time that the Jewish artist Modigliani died, he was very little known, but Pound, in response to a query from John Scheiwiller, contributed the following statement, on November 29, 1929: "Premature death of Modigliani removed a definite, valuable and emotive force from the contemporary world."[17]

It has been noted that the more cultured members of minority groups seldom have a chip on their shoulder about their ethnic origin, but less educated members are quite aggressive on this point. Race is the hobgoblin of little minds, and my Jewish friends have often expressed their embarrassment at the antics of self-styled "defense" organizations, which pretend to speak for the entire Jewish community. Stephen Spender, the English poet, and of Jewish origins, is typical of the more civilized strata among the Jews. On December 5 and 8, 1955, the Yale University radio station, WYBC, broadcast an hour-long program, "A Tribute to Ezra Pound", in which Spender said,

"Today I would, in greeting Ezra Pound, like to thank him, to thank him for the tremendous example he has been to other poets as a technician and as a translator, and to thank him for the hundreds of acts of generosity by which he has been able to help other poets. Without this great generosity of his, without this great illumination, the whole situation of English literature today would be quite different."

Spender is one of many Jews who visited Ezra during his thirteen years of imprisonment. In citing the number of Jews whom Pound aided in one way or another, I should not like to convey the impression that he ever helped anyone because he was Jewish or because he was not Jewish. When Pound was considering the merits of young artists, their race, color or creed simply did not enter into the picture.

I suggested to E. E. Cummings in 1950 that because of the impression of Washington political figures many Jews favored keeping Pound in prison, Jewish intellectuals could strike an impressive blow for freedom by starting a drive to release him. Such an effort would have reflected great credit on the Jewish community, at no risk or cost to themselves, and would have been a small token of gratitude for Pound's assistance to Jewish artists. The suggestion was passed on, but nothing came of it, because the artificial flames of hate were still being stoked, years after the end of the Second World War.

Typical was the statement in *Partisan Review* by its editor, William Barrett, that Pound's lines in *The Pisan Cantos,*

> Pétain defended Verdun while Blum
> was defending a bidet[18][.]

"Express a vicious anti-semitic lie."[18] My understanding of "anti-Semitism" is that it is an expression of hate or prejudice against the Jews either as a group or as a race. Yet the Jews are not mentioned in these two lines. When I read them, I had no knowledge that Blum was Jewish, and only my curiosity as to what Barrett was driving at led me to check into it. Because he had called my attention to the fact, I became aware that Blum was a Jew, yet it was Barrett, not Pound, who had mentioned it. Now, who is spreading anti-Semitism by bringing up the Jewish issue in connection with these two lines? It is not Pound, but Barrett, who forces us to consider the Jewish question, and thus brings in the issue of "anti-Semitism".

Peter Viereck, whose logic compares favorably with William Barrett's, wrote in *Commentary,* April 1, 1951, "Is it anti-poetic and philistine to feel rather violently about the 'Pisan Cantos' and other influential neo-fascist revivals when one hears of an ex-Nazi official boasting this year in Frankfort that, when Jewish mothers asked him where their missing two-year-old babies went, he replied, 'Up the chimney!' "

In contrast to this sort of hysteria, Babette Deutsch, the eminent Jewish poet and critic, has made one of the most sweeping comments on Pound's influence as a teacher, in *The Yale Literary Magazine,* December, 1958, saying, "The major poets of the twentieth century have acknowledged publicly their debt to Pound, the teacher."

Perhaps Peter Viereck modestly does not include himself in this category. Frederick Morgan, publisher of *The Hudson Review,* injected a note of sanity into the furor about Pound's "anti-Semitism" in the Spring, 1951 number of his magazine:

"In recent discussions of Pound, his anti-Semitism (for reasons that are in one way understandable; it *is* a live issue and one that carries a tremendous emotional charge) has been magnified out of all proportion with the place it actually occupies in his work. William Barrett, for example, in the editorial which inaugurated 'Partisan Review,' symposium on the Bollingen award, quoted seven lines from the 'Pisan Cantos'—and the only ones out of 118 pages that could possibly be interpreted as anti-Semitic—as though they were representative of the entire sequence. . . . On the basis of these seven lines, and with entire disregard of the courage, the humility, and the love which animates, for the rest, these Cantos, he proceeded to the assumption that the matter of the poetry as a whole is 'ugly' and 'vicious!' It is hard to conceive of a more complete distortion."

Ezra Pound had pointed out some decades before that his critics would "use any stick to beat me," and the issue of anti-Semitism in his work is merely one of the desperate measures to which the liberals resort in their ceaseless efforts to discredit him. In a number of cases, literary periodicals that defended him were quickly put out of circulation! He contributed an article to an intellectual magazine, *The European,* citing Coke on misprision of treason. That was the last issue of that publication. Hayden Carruth wrote a rather favorable essay on Pound for the Summer, 1956 issue of *Perspective, U.S.A.* This was the last issue of this periodical, which had been subsidized by the Ford Foundation. At the first kind mention of Pound, the entire project was abandoned.

He once sent me a telegram to come to Washington and edit a new magazine called *The Spectator.* I arrived there, only to find that *The Spectator* was no more. Ezra had written an editorial for the previous issue that referred to Eugene Meyer in rather strong terms. *The Spectator*'s principal source of revenue was the back page, which had been taken by the radio and television station, WTOP. Eugene Meyer owned station WTOP.

Ezra has had the same experience with literary awards. Scofield Thayer established *The Dial* annual award of two thousand dollars in 1921, for distinguished service to literature. The first recipient was Sherwood Anderson. The award was given to various of Pound's students, and finally, when he could no longer be overlooked, he was given *The Dial* award in 1927. This was the last time it was given.

No doubt Ezra will be given the Nobel Prize at some future date, and that will be the end of that famous award. The Bollingen story is but one in a long list of such incidents. When Pound was awarded the Bollingen prize, that was the last time it was awarded under the auspices of the Library of Congress. He told me that just before the outbreak of the Second World War, he had been commissioned to write an article for a Japanese newspaper. He sent them the article; not only was it never printed, but the ownership of the newspaper was promptly changed!

In 1959, I suggested Pound for the annual five thousand dollar award of the American Academy of Poets, which to celebrate its twenty-fifth anniversary, was awarding an additional five thousand dollar prize that year, but the suggestion was ignored. This was the more surprising because the prize had been set up by the Bullock family with a view to counteracting the excessive influence of the leftwing critics. Pound would have been a logical recipient; both the literary merit of his works and the donors' leanings (which considerably influence all such awards) were in his favor.

This brings us to another aspect of the Pound question. A visitor once questioned him concerning the most difficult thing he had ever attempted. Without hesitation he replied, "Trying to get the rich to do something useful with their money."

Nevertheless, few critics have been sufficiently honest to see that *The Pisan Cantos* is one of the few good things to come out of the horror of the Second World War, and courageous enough to say so. In reviewing *Section: Rock-Drill* for the New York *Times* on December 16, 1956, Archibald MacLeish said,

"For forty years the curious structure of the Cantos has been rising, figure by figure, out of the disorder of the time, like a coral reef out of shattering water, and as the book completes itself, one sees what it is, a true book, true dissent from the dead assumptions, but not dissent for its own sake—dissent for the sake of the ideal of order in men's lives."

Many American critics have been somewhat less enthusiastic. Louise Bogan, poetry editor of *The New Yorker*, said, in reviewing *Section: Rock-Drill,* in the issue of September 1, 1956, "At present, Pound has no direct imitators. The contemporary generation writing in English has learned from him, it is true; the rules he formulated for the Imagists, more than forty years ago—directness, naturalness, and precision—still hold. The actual form of the Cantos, however, now seems slightly fossilized—praiseworthy of note as origin and as process but with no truly invigorating aspects."

Donald Stauffer said of the *Cantos,* in *The Saturday Review,* March 22, 1947, "Pound's Cantos cannot win many readers because the images and rhythm, faultless in themselves, are not sufficiently attached to significant thought."

Perhaps the "significant thought" is not stated simply enough for Mr. Stauffer, for it is certainly there. The clarity of this line, which is repeated in *Rock-Drill,*

Our dynasty came in because of a great sensibility.[20]

seems to escape this type of critic, to whom it is as incomprehensible as the Chinese characters that accompany it.

Some of his critics like Pound's poetry but shrink from his crisp style of literary criticism. Yet Horace Gregory, in reviewing Pound's *Literary Essays* in the New York *Times,* July 4, 1954, said of this book, "It represents a 'maker' of contemporary criticism and if since 1900 a better book of its kind has been written, the world has yet to learn of its publication."

Despite such enlightened criticism, his work still meets with much of the same old "sour grapes" that have been his lot since the beginning of his career. Robert Graves is typical of the "sour grapes" school of criticism. He commented on Pound's revival of Provençal poetry as follows:

"I don't claim to be an authority on Provençal, but Majorcan, which my children talk most of the time, and which I understand, is closely related to it. When my thirteen-year-old boy was asked to compare a Provençal text with Pound's translation, he laughed and laughed and laughed."

This type of criticism might be passable at a literary tea, but amazingly enough, it comprised part of a lecture that Graves delivered at staid old Trinity College, England, and was one of the supposedly scholarly Clark lectures given at that school. These talks were published under the title of *The Crowning Privilege* in 1955. One can only wonder how the faculty and students at Trinity College received the news that Pound's poems had been judged for all time by a thirteen-year-old boy who spoke a dialect related to Provençal. It seems that literary criticism in England has abandoned the sober scholarship of T. S. Eliot, and is now the playground of thirteen-year-old boys.

Graves himself has always puttered about in the classical world like an ancient country squire stalking about his garden. His standards of criticism, depending as they do upon the intellectual support of a much younger generation, leave much to be desired.

Pound ignores such snide approaches to his work. After all, scholars like Robert Graves use their intellects as most men use their stomachs, that is, to digest things for which they have a preference. They react with acute indigestion when attempting to absorb something that is not part of their regular diet. It is not out of place to observe that such scholars practice a sort of intellectual nudism, and parade about in the world of ideas clothed only in their ignorance. The spectacle is not a classical one.

Ezra has been sustained all these years against this type of critic by what may best be described as insouciance. In *Blast,* in 1914, he announced that he was going to be around for a long time, much to the dismay of his enemies. He entitled this declaration "Salutation the Third":

L ET us deride the smugness of "The Times":
                GUFFAW!
            So much for the gagged reviewers,
It will pay them when the worms are wriggling in
    their vitals;
These are they who objected to newness,
Here are their tomb-stones.

> They supported the gag and the ring:
> A little BLACK BOX contains them.
> So shall you be also,
> You slut-bellied obstructionist,
> You sworn foe to free speech and good letters,
> You fungus, you continuous gangrene.
>
> Come let us on with the new deal,
> Let us be done with pandars and jobbery,
> Let us spit upon those who pat the big-bellies for
> profit,
> Let us go out in the air a bit.
>
> Or perhaps I will die at thirty?
> Perhaps you will have the pleasure of defiling my
> pauper's grave;
> I wish you joy, I proffer you all my assistance.
> It has been your habit for long
> to do away with good writers,
> You either drive them mad, or else you blink at their
> suicides,
> Or else you condone their drugs,
> and talk of insanity and genius,
> But I will not go mad to please you,
> I will not flatter you with an early death,
> Oh, no, I will stick it out,
> Feel your hates wriggling about my feet
> As a pleasant tickle,
> to be observed with derision,
> Though many move with suspicion,
> Afraid to say that they hate you;
> The taste of my boot?
> Here is the taste of my boot,
> Caress it,
> lick off the blacking.[21]

There is something prophetic, as well as biological, about this declaration that Ezra intended to stick it out. Also, the type that he defied is certainly a biological manifestation.

This poem could have provided the Roosevelt administration with one of its key phrases. Perhaps one of the great man's speech writers happened upon a copy of *Blast* while looking up some reference at the Library of Congress, and snatched the phrase "new deal" for wider distribution. If so, no credit was given to Ezra Pound.

XII

FOR SOME forty years, Ezra Pound had been regarding the antics of his critics with mild amusement. The furor over the Bollingen award, which took his native land by surprise, was nothing new to him. He continued to work in his dreary cell, his only recreation the daily visits of his wife and his friends.

On summer afternoons, the Pounds created a little world of their own as they looked down from their height upon the wedding cake dome of the United States Capitol. Usually they sat near a giant Japanese pine, but because of the ban on taking photographs, I was never allowed to take a picture of Ezra standing beneath this rugged tree, which was so much like him.

Whenever they emerged from the ward, carrying their chairs, their string bags bulging with odd lots of food, books and letters for the visitors, their pet blue jays always set up a great screeching, wheeling above them as the chairs were arranged. Then the squirrels would come skipping down from nearby trees for their daily treat. Ezra would lure them up onto a bench with a peanut tied to a string. He taught them to take the nut from between his fingers, a practice that I considered reckless.

During these afternoons, Ezra's manner was that of a deservedly popular professor at a small but highly-regarded school, who was having some of his star students in for tea. His *bonhomie* was always perfect for the occasion; he was a benevolent Socrates who as

285

yet had no intention of drinking the cup of hemlock which his fellow citizens had offered him. Dorothy Pound was also as apt and self-effacing as a professor's wife, as she poured tea, murmured "Shush" when the bluejays became too noisy, and produced little paper bags for the shells of hard-boiled eggs, so that we should not litter the lawn.

I never failed to experience a thrill of excitement and anticipation as I disembarked from the bus and strode across the broad campus of St. Elizabeths. Despite the elevation, the ground was often swampy, but I preferred crossing it to following the more circuitous route along the concrete walk. If it were a summer's day, I knew that Ezra and his wife would be waiting on the lawn, near a clump of bushes that partially shielded them from the buildings. After shaking hands with them, I would go on to the administration building to report and perhaps bring back a Coca Cola from the machine or a cup of coffee for Ezra and his wife.

When I had returned, Ezra would be occupied with the first business of the day, my lunch. My writings had not as yet brought in a financial return, and Ezra was pleased to be able to renew his lifelong role of assisting the careers of writers and artists, even while locked up by his government. He brought down leftover hard-boiled eggs, salami and other food, some of which was slightly stale, but under the circumstances most of it was rather good. As someone has said, "Americans are the greatest consumers of stale food in the world." Certainly I have consumed my share of it.

There was a plentiful supply of dry white bread, much better than that produced by our commercial bakeries; tea, which had been stored in mayonnaise bottles; and the hospital doughnuts, which also were good.

Later, we would enjoy for dessert some of the specialties that had arrived from his admirers in various parts of the world. Although there was never a flood of these delicacies, they arrived steadily, so that there would often be a choice between a Port du Salut from a Trappist monastery in Canada, a banana sweet from the Philippines, or ginger from Hong Kong. Edith Hamilton always brought out a box of exquisite chocolates on her visits, which were far too infrequent. They were in a plain box, and after

Dorothy Pound had repeatedly tried to find out where she bought them, she finally confessed that her cook made them.

While I would eat lunch, Ezra would be sorting out various papers and letters that he wanted me to read or to answer. He would be dashing off the addresses of people whom he wanted me to contact, and titles of books that I should consult at the Library of Congress. Although he carried on a heavy correspondence, he occasionally farmed out letters for his friends to answer, especially if he thought they might have more direct knowledge on points contained in the letters. His manner during this period was usually one of furious haste, as though he wanted to make the most of this brief daily interlude away from his cell. If, during our conversation, the name of someone else came up whom he thought I should contact, he would immediately jump up and make the long trek back to his cell to get the address.

There was no significant change in the nature of his correspondence during his years of incarceration. To the best of my knowledge, he never contacted anyone with a request to aid him in seeking his release, although some of his friends were active in this regard. His letters were filled with advice to young writers, exhortations to old friends, such as Eliot and Cummings, and correspondence with other political prisoners, such as Admiral Sir Barry Domvile in England.

Many people who met me during the years I was visiting Pound would ask, "Is he really crazy?" Usually they knew that he was continuing his work (he published some eight books during his period of confinement), but perhaps they supposed that he was lucid for an hour or two each day, during which he would hastily write some poems, and then relapse into madness until the following day. My answer was always the same: "Come out and talk to him. You can decide for yourself. He receives visitors every afternoon, and converses freely with them about many subjects. If he really were crazy, could he carry on these rational conversations, day after day?"

I never heard Ezra make an irrational statement, nor to my knowledge, did any of his other visitors. The most widely-encountered impression among people who knew something of Pound's situation, but who did not visit him, was that he was being foxy. They supposed that he either feigned insanity to avoid a treason trial and a possible death sentence, or that he acquiesced in the government's move to declare him insane in order to avoid a trial.

Such suppositions are not only false—they are grossly unfair to Pound, and contradict everything relating to his character, which is apparent throughout his work. The Pound who would have done that would not have insisted on retaining his American citizenship while broadcasting to the United States. He would have protected himself against retribution by taking out Italian citizenship, as he would certainly have been justified in doing, since he had lived there longer than he had lived in the United States.

Conversation with Ezra was not a static affair. If we were sitting on the lawn, he would jump up every half hour or so and stride about to keep from getting stiff, for it was damp there on any but the hottest afternoons. On occasion, particularly if I stopped by unannounced after I had moved from Washington, he would insist on going back to the ward to get mail or addresses for me. If I brought out something that I thought he would be interested in reading, as I usually did, he would switch his various pairs of glasses back and forth until he got the one with the proper focus. All of his movements were made with great energy, or rather with great expenditure of energy, as if to illustrate his theories of the prodigality of Nature.

He was a splendid pantomimist. His youth in America had coincided with the great period of vaudeville, and he could imitate almost any accent, using a profusion of them while relating a single story.

In a recent book about the Paris expatriates, *The Way It Was*, by Harold Loeb, the author mentions that Ezra was apt to leave a group at a café without warning and without saying goodbye to anyone.[1] Such unceremonious departures are common to busy people in many countries, although the practice must have been irritating to the dilettantes of Montparnasse.

The late Secretary of the Navy, James Forrestal, developed the habit of speaking to everyone whom he wanted to see at a Washington cocktail party and leaving within fifteen minutes. I suppose that Ezra had learned this trick from Henry James, for he once acted out for me a pantomime in which he illustrated James' slow but steady progress toward a side door while attending a fashionable party in Mayfair. Ezra reincarnated James' pontifical but gracious manner as he paused before one guest after another, dropping a few words here and there as he moved nearer and nearer the exit with each acknowledgment. Suddenly (and here Ezra made a jump to one side), he was gone!

The most striking thing about the Pounds at St. Elizabeths was that their manner bore no recognizable relationship to their grim surroundings. A few feet away, a madman might be standing with his naked body pressed against the barred window (William Carlos Williams has recorded seeing this spectacle); and armed guards always stood between them and freedom. A psychiatrist would undoubtedly describe Ezra's blithe overriding of his bleak and sordid home as advanced schizophrenia. It must have been frustrating to them as they watched him resolutely refuse to be overcome by the atmosphere that turned most men into shells and robots within a matter of days.

What other modern writer (say, for instance, the Prophet of the Swamps, William Faulkner) could continue to produce under the pressures that were forced upon Ezra Pound for thirteen years? Calling upon the seemingly inexhaustible resources of his character, he carried on his work, his teaching and his philosophy without being visibly affected.

What psychological crutch could Ezra's contemporaries lean upon to sustain themselves in such trials? Many of them became dope addicts, alcoholics, manic-depressives and suicides, even though they won greater fame and the financial rewards that were never his. Hart Crane was one such suicide, and the laws concerning libel make it impolitic to list the names of writers who became alcoholics or dope addicts, since some of them are still with us and fiercely protect their vanished virtue.

Of them all, E. E. Cummings alone has shown as much strength as Ezra. He too has a touch of John Bunyan in him, and he if he were again locked up, might produce another *Pilgrim's Progress*. He wrote a fine book, *The Enormous Room* (1922), after a youthful term of imprisonment as a suspected spy. Being an idealist, Cummings had volunteered to serve the French Army as an ambulance driver. Since all governments distrust idealists, he was thrown into a dungeon for some months.

Ezra said to him, during one of his visits to St. Elizabeths, "How fortunate you were to have served your imprisonment while you were still young!" He was referring to the fact that since the young have no independence, and are always bound out in one form of servitude or another until their maturity, it is not such a great sacrifice for them to be imprisoned; whereas an older person who has won a sort of independence, feels very cruelly its deprivation.

One of the more interesting aspects of Ezra's daily activities was his manner of handling individual visitors. If he were bored, or saw no possibilities in the newcomer (a rare decision indeed for this incurable optimist!), he would maintain a discreet silence, letting the conversation drift at random. Bores generally excluded themselves out of decency, for the small talk that won them a reputation as scintillating wits at Washington cocktail parties fell rather flat at St. Elizabeths.

There were always three or four people present, and sometimes as many as a dozen might drop by during the course of an afternoon. We sat on ordinary park benches, painted the usual dark green, which we pulled up close to the aluminum camp chairs occupied by the Pounds. Their chairs, which were very light, were folded and carried back to the room each afternoon. Because of the arthritic condition of his neck vertebrae that he had suffered ever since the imprisonment at Pisa, Ezra could not sit in an ordinary chair for very long. He had acquired an aluminum chair that could be extended, so that he maintained a semi-recumbent position during most of the afternoon.

Ezra's eagerness to get outside and enjoy a few moments' respite from Bedlam almost cost him his life in the spring of 1953. Washington weather is quite treacherous in March, and one afternoon, when a pale sun had lured him outdoors, he became badly chilled. He developed serious bronchial trouble, and his son and daughter were summoned to his bedside. Fortunately, he soon recovered.

This crisis afforded me the opportunity of meeting his daughter, the Princess Mary de Rachewiltz of Schloss Brunnenberg, Italy, who has presented Ezra with several lively and intelligent grand-

Portrait of Ezra Pound, taken in 1958 by Eustace
Mullins on the lawn of St. Elizabeths. Pound con-
siders this the best likeness ever made of him.

The author Mullins, and painter Sherri Martinelli, another member of the young avant-garde that visited Pound during his imprisonment.

Ezra and Dorothy Pound, and poet Dallam Flynn, on the lawn of St. Elizabeths (October, 1951).

The three portraits of Pound on this page were taken by Mullins in the home of Dr. J. C. LaDriere of Catholic University, where Pound spent several days following his release.

Dorothy Pound at the door of her Washington apartment, just a few blocks from the hospital (upper left). (Right) Pound, just after his release (May 12, 1958). (Below) Ezra Pound, Eustace Mullins and another young friend of Pound's, Marcella Jackson.

children. I had already met his son, Omar Shakespear Pound, who, as Ezra explained, was so named to build up to a crescendo. He was really entitled to all three names by inheritance. Ezra's father was Homer Loomis Pound, which Ezra employed in the older form, Omar; and his wife's maiden name, of course, was Dorothy Shakespear.

The visitors who saw Ezra in the ward were not so anxious to come out again, for the surroundings were too grim. Some charitable soul had contributed a dozen used television sets to the ward in 1952, and this created a genuine Bedlam. For some reason, viewers of television often try to correct a bad picture by turning up the volume. The pictures on those old sets were usually but flickering shadows, and to compensate, the inmates would steadily increase the noise. I have often wondered if American television programs were created with the demented in mind as the ideal audience, and seeing them in the madhouse, even from a distance, confirmed this impression. Sitting there with Ezra as we tried to talk against the blaring comedians and commercials, the dim shadow of the picture flickering in the distance, I was reminded of Plato's cave, in which the prisoner is shut off from life, and sees only its reflection, which he comes to accept as reality.

Visitors who only saw Ezra outdoors received an opposite impression and imagined that Ezra was quite fortunate to have such a pleasant resort in which to live out his declining years. They described to their friends, and in print, the sweep of green lawn, the great trees (many of them prize specimens, for the grounds were originally designed as an arboretum), and the sun-bathed benches, on which his disciples and friends could sit and listen to an exuberant Pound. This impression gave rise to the legend that Ezra was ensconced in luxurious quarters with many comforts, and ignored the fact that he would enjoy this sunshine, which, after all, cost the government nothing, for only a couple of hours each day during a few months of the year. The preponderance of his hours were spent in the gloom of the ward.

The poetasters of Washington, violently in disagreement with his political and economic views, but aware of his importance as a poet, had discussed various means of making life more bearable for "poor Ezra", as they generally referred to him. This group was dominated by Katharine Garrison Chapin, a poetess who also was the wife of Francis Biddle (Biddle had been Attorney General of the United States when Ezra was indicted for treason). When a member of her group, Inez Boulton, suggested that a small house be erected on the grounds of St. Elizabeths, to be paid for by private subscription so that Ezra could carry on his work during his incarceration, the project was immediately endorsed and dubbed "the Biddle hut". The idea was that it later would be consecrated as a shrine. Ezra would still be under guard within the walls of St. Elizabeths, obedient to the terms of his commitment and not posing a threat to the government, so that there seemed to be no valid objection to the idea.

Nevertheless, one was found. The story was circulated that "poor Ezra" was too mad to be allowed to occupy his little hut, for he might wander out into one of the roadways that traverse the grounds of St. Elizabeths and be struck down. None of the poetasters in Mrs. Biddle's circle had ever bothered to visit Ezra, who often strode about the grounds of the hospital, much more alert, keen and vigorous than the shambling, dejected members of the staff. The objection was accepted, and the project was abandoned.

Dorothy Pound told me that soon after her arrival in Washington, she was invited to an "evening" at the Biddles'. She took in the crowd, in her mild way, and was startled to see an exceptionally fierce pair of eyes glaring at her from across the room. The protruding orbs belonged to none other than Justice Felix Frankfurter, one of her husband's most determined ideological opponents. Dorothy Pound took her leave, nor did she visit the Biddles again. As she remarked, she didn't care to be in the same room with "such people".

Perhaps Ezra had encouraged her to accept this initial invitation, for he was quite interested in that family. Nicholas Biddle had been the American sponsor of the Bank of the United States, although the real influence behind it was a European family. Ezra often quoted to me a passage from the published correspondence of Nicholas Biddle, which was not brought out until a century after his death. The item was from a letter to Tom Cooper, dated May 8, 1837, in which Biddle boasted, "and as to mere power, I have been for years in the daily exercise of more power than any President habitually enjoys."[2]

This was Dorothy Pound's only visit to the *haut monde* of America. I believe that her stay in the United States was a liberal education for her. She was puzzled by the strange types who came to visit Pound, not only the early beatniks, anarchists, and cranks of one kind or another, who were attracted by his legend, but also by the vagaries of the "average American", who is an unnecessarily complicated individual. She was glad that I was often on hand to see her home in the afternoons, not only because I was a cousin of sorts but a Virginian as well.

She never quite knew what to make of America. Of our cities, she saw only Washington and Philadelphia, which should only be visited on safari. Despite their great history, these cities today are but vast slums, and one meets in the halls of Congress persons who should be seen only by social workers.

Like most persons from the British isles, Dorothy Pound believed that the area west of the Appalachians was still unsubdued, which was true, after a fashion, and she marveled whenever she met anyone who had dared to travel there. Our movies have done little to offset the widely-held belief in Europe that America consists of some Eastern seaboard colonies whose inhabitants occasionally journey upriver to trade for furs or to dig for gold.

Consequently, Europeans were not surprised to learn that the poet Ezra Pound was a captive in America. Most of them supposed that he was being held for ransom by Indians, or by Al Capone. They did not understand that the United States government was the villain in this case. Although some editors tried to explain the situation to their readers, they were unable to figure it out for themselves.

For Dorothy Pound, America was a primitive wilderness which surrounded a madhouse. Perhaps Pound may be forgiven his comment that "The insane asylum is the only place I could bear to live in, in this country." Seen in context, his statement means that he could not stand to participate in the mass insanity of modern America, and that he preferred the relative quiet of the madhouse.

I am proud to say that I was able to bestow an additional privilege upon Ezra Pound while he was at the hospital—that is, the privilege of drinking wine. It has been said that man turned to alcohol as consolation for the loss of his freedom when he abandoned the life of an itinerant hunter and settled for the advantages of civilization. However this may be, it is certain that wine has brought considerable amelioration to the life of the plowpusher and the clodhopper as well as the townsman. Few scholars seem to know that Gutenberg got his inspiration for the mechanics of the printing press while watching the operation of a medieval wine press.

The rules at St. Elizabeths, as at all mental institutions, strictly forbid giving any alcoholic beverage to a patient. I thought this was an uncivilized situation, and on my third or fourth visit to Pound, I brought him a bottle of white Graves, 1945. It was the first wine he had been offered since his arrest almost five years before, as none of his other visitors had wished to defy the regulations.

He insisted on uncorking the bottle himself (this was in the gloom of a ward afternoon), and after the corkscrew had done its work, he jerked it out with a tremendous "Pop!" while Dorothy Pound and I looked on aghast. We were sure that the noise would summon an attendant, but none appeared. Our bottle contained a very pleasant white wine (there has been some criticism of James Joyce for drinking white wine, which was supposed to be bad for his eyes, instead of red). We had nothing to drink from but little paper cups, which did not interfere materially with the flavor. After several quaffs, Ezra became quite mellow.

This was the first of many such bottles, always smuggled in and drunk without permission. I do not wish to convey the impression that Ezra became an alcoholic; generally, there was but one bottle of twelve per cent wine for three or four of us, which was consumed over a period of three hours. We usually insisted on Ezra draining the bottle, and it is pleasant to think that some of the later *Cantos* were penned in the afterglow of a few paper cups of Graves.

After I had been bringing wine to him for several years, the Flemings decided to risk a libation to celebrate the publication of the *Confucian Odes*. (This is the classic anthology defined by Confucius, translated by Pound, and published by Harvard University Press in 1954.) They took the precaution of decanting the wine into a thermos bottle before leaving home so that the guards would suppose they were bringing their usual tea; but since half the fun was to uncork the bottle on the premises, it was not such an exciting afternoon. It is the only time I can recall having drunk wine from a thermos bottle.

It was early in 1950 that I made the acquaintance of Elizabeth Bishop, who was then Consultant in Poetry at the Library of Congress. This post is held for one-year periods by various poets who are in good standing with the current administration. No revolutionaries need apply.

Elizabeth was a lady, from the Back Bay of Boston. There was a fortune somewhere in the background (Eaton paper or something of that order), and she dressed with excellent taste. She had a mellifluous voice, and it was always a delight to hear her read her poetry. Some of these readings are now available on records. Also, she kept an excellent sherry on hand at the Library, the only Consultant who has shown such consideration for visitors.

Elizabeth wished to go out and see Ezra, but she needed moral support. At any rate, she would never go out unless I accompanied her. I mentioned the wine problem, but did not enlarge upon the attitude of the hospital authorities. Whenever Elizabeth went out with me, she brought not one but two bottles. Furthermore, these were more costly than those I had been able to provide. Usually she brought one German and one French variety, a good Moselle or a Liebfraumilch, and perhaps an Haut Sauterne.

Despite the reinforcement of the wine, Elizabeth was never comfortable in Ezra's presence. I think that she looked upon him as a sort of naughty old grandfather whose habits are somewhat questionable, but who, after all, is one's ancestor. She insisted that the way in which he twisted the ends of his beard gave him a quite diabolical appearance. One afternoon, when the conversation lagged, Elizabeth volunteered the information that she was studying German. Ezra looked up and said, "Humph! That won't be much help to you!" The inference was that Elizabeth was beyond any sort of assistance, and she sank into a glum silence.

Although she visited the hospital as a filial duty, Elizabeth occasionally suggested to her literary friends that they go out. She made it known that I was available as a "white hunter" with whom it was safe to visit "the zoo".

One morning, when I stopped at the Library to see her, she introduced me to the critic Lloyd Frankenberg and his wife, the painter Loren MacIver. Later that day, she called me to say that Frankenberg was anxious to visit with Ezra if I would go out with him the next day. As an additional request, she asked that I clear this with Ezra beforehand. Although Ezra always demanded to know ahead of time what visitors were coming out, I was the only one who consistently violated this rule. He rarely objected, since most of the people I brought out were rather interesting characters.

Since Frankenberg was rather nervous about the prospect, I decided that I had better get in touch with Dorothy Pound and let her know about him. The next morning, I called and asked if I should bring him. She seemed rather surprised, but told me it would be all right. When I went to the Library to pick up Frankenberg, Elizabeth told me that he had changed his mind about making the visit, and had gone back to New York.

I went out to the hospital and related my story. Dorothy Pound then said that she was amazed that Frankenberg would even think about coming out, as he had said some unpleasant things about E.P. Even so, they were willing to receive him. Their tolerant attitude was in striking contrast to that of the liberal critics, most of whom seemed willing to blast away at Ezra from a safe distance, but who would under no circumstances face him.

When Elizabeth had served her allotted stint at the Library, she was replaced by Conrad Aiken, who, of course, was looked upon with high favour by the ritualistic liberals. Ezra suggested that I call upon him, not to request that he come out, but to let him know that if he wished to visit at St. Liz, he would be welcome.

Aiken was rather guarded with me, and looked as though he wished he had had a chance to put away the silver before I came in. When I suggested that he come out to see Ezra, he seemed nervous. At that time, I knew nothing of the difficulty he had had with his publisher, Bennett Cerf of Random House, when he included some poems by Pound in an anthology and Cerf, in a flagrant example of book-burning, took them out. Aiken sat stroking his chin. Eventually he said that he didn't think he would go out to see Ezra "just yet". In so far as I know, he never did go out to see Ezra during his term at the Library.

When I informed Ezra of this response, he said that Aiken had come to call one afternoon, in 1947, being supported on one side by Allen Tate and on the other by Robert Lowell. Apparently he had no desire to come out alone or even with me to beat the brush for him.

Those who visited Ezra at my instigation provided very interesting company for him. During the first couple of years of my visits, there were few arrivals, and I was free to bring along whomever I could persuade to make the trip, without giving Ezra prior notice. One afternoon, I saw a typical American teen-ager in Army uniform, loafing along "F" Street, looking very bored, as people are apt to look in Washington. I was about to get on the bus for the hospital, when, obeying a rascally impulse, I asked him to come along. Since he had nothing better to do, he agreed. I told him I was going to see a friend of mine, but nothing more.

If Ezra was surprised to see him, he concealed it from me. The soldier turned out to be an interesting specimen. His conversational gift was limited to two short sentences, "We're all in the same boat!" and "Well, THAT's something!" The youth had no idea who Ezra was, but he found him fascinating company, which bears out Donahoe's contention that Ezra would be a great success on American television.

The following day, I explained my prank to Ezra saying that I wanted to keep him in touch with his homeland. In reality, Ezra has never seen anything of America during his years here except two universities and an insane asylum, which may explain his comment when he landed in Italy in 1958, "All America is an insane asylum!"

I had been a professional photographer and possessed a very fine camera, which had the finest lens in the world. I was very anxious to focus this instrument in Ezra's direction, but at first he abruptly refused. Dorothy Pound informed me that it is against the law to photograph any patient in a mental institution, a regulation designed for their protection, as most of the patients could be snapped in attitudes which would be shocking for them to see later on, if they should be released.

Nevertheless, I continued to bring my camera out, slung concealed under my jacket like a pistol in a shoulder holster. Seeing that the attendants would not notice the camera, Pound decided one afternoon that I could take a few quick snapshots. He judged the resulting portrait (reproduced on the dust jacket of this book) to be the best photograph ever taken of him—high praise indeed, for he had been shot by the best. He informed me that he had not had to pay for having his photograph taken during the past fifty years.

I made a number of copies of this portrait and gave them away to friends, with the result that I have only one left. The picture was reprinted in the Italian press in 1955, and did much to convince the Italians that he was being wrongly held as a madman. The person depicted is a man in possession of all his dignity and power, with none of the visible attributes of the mentally ill. This photograph turned out so well that he never let me take any more until he sat for me after his release in May, 1958; that series proved most satisfactory to both of us.

Ezra was often ebullient during the afternoons on the lawn, and with reason. Not only did he have a circle of faithful friends and young men who hung on his every word—the sincerest flattery—but almost every day's mail brought some announcement of new recognition abroad. There would be an exquisite volume of his poems in Swedish, Japanese, Hindustani, Arabic or German. His daughter Mary was translating his *Cantos* into Italian. And there were many feature stories about him in the European press, reciting those triumphs with which his countrymen were largely unfamiliar, since newspapermen in America were not encouraged to interview him lest sentiment be aroused in his favour. Despite the fact that his publisher continued to bring out his books during his years of confinement, Ezra himself was never considered "news", and such recognition as he attained appeared almost exclusively in the Continental press.

On one occasion, the Flemings brought out a lute. They frequently appeared in Greek plays around Washington, and the lute served as a prop for one of those affairs. Ezra seized the instrument, stood up and began strumming upon it with great passion, singing a lyric from Sappho. It was a splendid and moving sight, but the lute was not built for Ezra's exuberance, and its strings began to zing, and then broke one by one until it gave a last despairing twang and died.

One of Pound's regular visitors when I first came upon the scene was "Big Swede", the poet Charles Olson. He was about seven feet tall, and had a diminutive wife named Connie. He had received a Guggenheim fellowship for his fine work on Melville, and he cultivated a cryptic style of correspondence much like Pound's. During the war, he had had some sort of position with the Democratic administration, and his politics were the reverse of Ezra's. Despite this area of disagreement, Ezra liked him, and he came out over several years. They finally had a violent quarrel, and Charlie was seen no more.

Charlie's protégé, Frank Moore, continued to maintain a regular schedule of visits to Ezra for several years afterward. Like most of Pound's visitors, Frank disagreed with him on everything. He finally became impossible, and went the way of Charlie Olson.

One of my friends whom I introduced to Ezra later played a key role in his release. He was the well-known Washington newspaperman, Rex Herbert Lampman. Rex had had a nervous breakdown, due principally to the chaos that Cissie Patterson had left behind her when she died. She bequeathed the Washington *Times Herald* to seven of her employees, and so multiplied by seven the amount of confusion that she had been able to engender while still alive.

Rex was confined in a violent unit of St. Elizabeths known as the Male Receiving Ward. This department of Bedlam was located about a mile from Chestnut Ward, and I was puzzled as to how I could visit both Ezra and Rex on the same afternoon. However, Rex was soon allowed out of his ward and given permission to sit out in front of the building without a guard, since he was not a political prisoner. I went up and got him, and brought him back to Ezra. Thus I was able to visit with them both, making the most of the limited time that I was allowed to spend with the many brilliant minds confined at St. Liz.

It was a very serious violation of the hospital rules for patients to visit other wards. The reasons for this rule were obvious. The staff was barely able to outwit the madmen in one ward. If the patients were allowed to visit afield and create conspiracies in other wards, the doctors would soon be encased in their own strait-jackets, as has been so delightfully depicted in a story by Edgar Allan Poe. It is possible that Poe was inspired to write this story after visiting some institution like St. Elizabeths, although that particular Bedlam was not standing in his own day. I was re-minded of this tale whenever I went out there, and I avoided looking at the doctors, lest one of them should turn out to be a madman in disguise. Anyone planning to visit a madhouse should avoid reading the Poe story.

I said nothing to Ezra about Rex's status, as I wanted them to enjoy each other's company, and I knew that Ezra would be upset by any new infraction of the rules. They were two of a kind, hav-ing known and viewed the world's great with a jaundiced eye. Rex's taste in poetry had never advanced beyond George Sterling, and he said that although Pound seemed sane enough, the *Cantos* were certainly crazy.

Soon Rex began to visit Pound every afternoon. He was able to tell many inside stories about Washington between the wars. His story of Henry Morgenthau's campaign against the pigeons on the Treasury Building is one of the great sagas of Sodom on the Potomac. He is quoted in "Canto 97" of *Thrones:*

> And he, the president, is true to his caste
> "and that caste," said old Lampman, "the underworld."

This passage is followed by a comment on the early career of another great American president:

> "I am sorry,"
> Said the London judge, "that this has been brought as a civil
> and not as a criminal action."[3]

The reference here is to a sixty-million-dollar theft, which set off the Boxer Rebellion in China.

One afternoon, Rex brought along another friend of his, a Panamanian palmist. Like most people in Washington, the Pana-manian had come there to recoup his fortunes at the expense of the Treasury. He had almost lost the sight of one eye as the result of some sort of accident while working on the Panama National Railways. Of course, our government ought to pay for this, as the government of Panama has no money. The case dragged on for some years. He could have gotten an award at once, but he did not have the necessary cash to expedite matters.

I had hoped that Ezra would let this dark little man, who was nearly blind, tell his fortune, but he would not. I had practiced palmistry myself, but I had never been able to grab Ezra's paw and see what was written there. The Panamanian was also an authority on diet. He informed Ezra that when a person drank orange juice and ate eggs for breakfast, the resultant combination of chemicals lit a slow fire in the intestines, which burned for about three days. I am inclined to believe this, and, no doubt, most of our superior "drive" stems from just such fires. We are, so to speak, jet-propelled.

I am ashamed to admit that, like so many of my close friends, Rex has caused serious embarrassment to the government. I do not refer to his part in freeing Ezra, but to an earlier escapade. In 1948, Rex was still employed by the Washington *Times Herald*. He was undoubtedly the best-liked person in that collection of misanthropes, even though his tips on the horses were sure death.

Among Rex's acquaintances was a gentleman who was engaged in the business of charity, which is a very good business. We will call him Major Villrey, and his organization the Soldiers of Misfortune. The Major had had a quarrel with his superiors—the inevitable disagreement over money—and he had struck out for himself, or rather, I should say, for charity. At this time, he was holding forth in modest quarters on Pennsylvania Avenue.

Like most newspapermen, Rex was very interested in charity, and he always crossed the street in order to hand a beggar a quarter. He felt that the Major's divine work of saving wrecked bodies should have greater support from the populace, and he persuaded his city editor to run a small item describing the work being carried on by the Soldiers of Misfortune.

As chance would have it, an old Negro, lying on his deathbed, read the story in the *Times Herald*. With his last bit of energy, he scrawled out a will, leaving Major Villrey title to a building he owned. He then died, and the Major found himself the proprietor, as well as the landowner, of a very valuable property, thanks to the efforts of Rex. As a token of his gratitude, he promptly gave Rex twenty dollars, and the Soldiers of Misfortune were in business.

But one public relations stunt breeds another, and he needed additional funds to keep the building going. As usual, Washington was filled with people looking for a handout. What could have been more natural in this environment than Rex's suggestion that the Major start a breadline? The Major accepted the idea with enthusiasm, as he accepted everything. He cadged soup and bread from local grocers and other men of good will, and within the week, a block-long line of chow hounds could be seen waiting outside of his building.

Now, had Rex let well enough alone, this would not have been such a good story. He sent over some *Times Herald* photographers to take pictures of the bread line in our nation's capital city. The pictures caused a sensation, and were reproduced in *Life* the same week that the government announced the Marshall Plan to feed the hungry peoples of Europe. Upon such unhappy coincidences does the expenditure of billions of dollars depend. Nevertheless, the Truman administration insisted on sending its billions to Greece and Turkey with not one cent appropriated by Congress for the bread line in Washington.

Luckily, our foreign friends were not so heartless or cold-blooded as Mr. Truman. Eva Peron, never one to pass up a public relations gesture, promptly organized a drive in Argentina to aid the poor *gringos* of the North. As the politicians gathered on the dock in New York to send off the first boatload of Marshall Plan goods to Europe, at the next pier the stevedores were unloading the largesse of Eva Peron for our own poverty-stricken people. But the politicians shunned this cargo as though it carried the plague, which, in a sense, it did, for the stevedores were unloading food and clothing for our needy ones. The consignment was duly deposited before the Major in Washington, and I could only marvel at Rex's ability to cause the best-laid plans of politicians to go agley.

One of Ezra's pre-war friends who had settled in Washington was Ivan Stancioff, a former Bulgarian diplomat who had been stationed in Rome. After the war, Stalin incorporated Bulgaria, including the considerable Stancioff estates, into his Socialist paradise, as a gift from Roosevelt and Truman. Luckily, Stancioff had married an American girl whose father not only built bridges, but owned some of them. This nest egg enabled the Stancioffs to purchase a place in Urbana, near Washington, which had formerly been General Jubal Early's headquarters during the Civil War. It was a magnificent old house, set on an elevation that allowed General Early to see if the Yanks were coming. Unlike his Northern counterpart, General Sherman, he did not burn it when he left.

Ezra occasionally farmed out some of his disciples to the Stancioff place, and one of his protégés, the painter Sheri Martinelli, spent much time there. She had perfected a jewel-like tone in her painting, much like the ancient Persian painting, which was very effective. At the time of Ezra's release, Sheri had gone on to San Francisco, so that she was not present to welcome him on regaining his freedom, an event which all of his friends had anticipated for so many years.

I was present when Edith Hamilton and Ezra had such a stimulating talk that I took notes on it. The company had been criticizing the annoying habit of young people today of regretting everything they did, and the following excerpts are indicative of the way the talk flowed at the madhouse:

"EDITH HAMILTON: I'm eighty-four years old, and I have never regretted anything I have done.

POUND (with gusto): It's just as well. If they didn't stop to regret it, they would be doing something worse.

(He shows Miss Hamilton one of the Confucian ideograms.)

POUND: This ideogram means respect, the root of respect, respect for the kind of intelligence which enables the cherry tree to grow cherries. Now, this other ideogram represents the man carrying a lance and the spoken word from the mouth, meaning the crusade to find the rightly-aimed word. Yeats said to me that if they knew what we thought, they'd do away with us. They want their poets dead.

EDITH HAMILTON: A Chinese friend of mine was told in the

examination halls at Nanking of a great Confucian scholar, such a scholar that he wrote a letter, and there was only one man in all China who could understand it. That is not very democratic, I'm afraid. That is aristocratic, like you, Mr. Pound.

POUND: But it is democratic as long as it provides that any one may have the opportunity to learn enough to read that letter.

EDITH HAMILTON: You always puncture my balloons, Mr. Pound.

POUND: You haven't been out since my latest theory that Dante was a real democrat and Shakespeare a bloody snob.

EDITH HAMILTON: I'm no Shakespearian, Mr. Pound, but I must quarrel with you there. I don't believe Shakespeare ever had that fixed an idea.

POUND: In the Inferno, Dante doesn't pay any attention to the class from which the characters sprang.

EDITH HAMILTON: But he didn't have any common men in his Inferno. They were all important people. He didn't portray the torturing of the common man.

POUND: Shakespeare was propounding this idea of a limited monarchy in his twelve histories.

EDITH HAMILTON: I don't think so. I think he was too careless a man to do anything like that. And I think that Mr. Dante was more aristocratic than Mr. Shakespeare. (She quotes Hamlet's Soliloquy). The soliloquy was Mr. Shakespeare coming through— the only time I know where he really came through. By the way, is that Rousse translation of Homer a good one?

POUND: It doesn't have the movement or the sound or any approximation of one. Edwards in the Hudson has done the best translation, but it hasn't got the right quantities in it.

EDITH HAMILTON: Is anyone doing a good translation?

POUND: There are probably fifty or sixty people doing bad translations, and I know of five or six incompetent young men doing better translations that will not be good enough, but they are trying to make a good translation.

EDITH HAMILTON: Mr. Pound is such a naughty fellow (to Mrs. Pound). What do you do with him when he's like that? Does scolding do him any good?

DOROTHY POUND (laughs): Oh help, I gave that up long ago. (Pound grins, pleased at having amused the ladies.)"

In retrospect, it seems that tape recordings of such conversations would have found a ready market, but Pound's circle was never much concerned with markets. Over each of those afternoons, sometimes light-hearted, sometimes depressing, hung the ever-present cloud of his situation, and the awful thought that he might never be released from his sordid dungeon.

At the end of each afternoon, we helped Ezra carry his things to the ward. The grim door would swing shut behind him, and Dorothy Pound and I would wait on the lawn until he appeared at the tiny window of his cell. *"Ciao!"* she would bravely cry out, and he would wave in response. Then we would turn away, leaving him to another night in that hellish place. It was a difficult and a shameful thing to do, and it is no wonder that some of his visitors became revolutionaries.

XIII

EZRA'S VISITORS were divided into two groups, those literati, such as Huntingdon Cairns and other semi-official personages, who came to visit him out of a sense of duty, and the young men who realized instinctively, as there were no advertisements to that effect, that they would find at the madhouse the consideration and instruction (inspiration, if you will) that they needed.

One literary figure has bemoaned the fact that so many "immoral rightwing beatniks" were numbered among Pound's regular visitors. This impression has probably stemmed from the publicity attendant upon the exploits of John Kasper and a few other reckless young people who were attracted by the Bohemian legend of Pound. He rarely turned away a young visitor. He liked expounding his theories to the young, and the groves of St. Elizabeths became an academy which may produce America's leader of the future, although the thought is enough to cause a wave of suicides among our liberal intellectuals.

Pound had no way of investigating the background or personal habits of his visitors. On several occasions, I recall that he refused to believe revelations about the characters of some of his circle. He seemed to attribute these stories to the jealousy among the intimates, who maneuvered to get the positions closest to him, and certainly such jealousy was evident.

One of Pound's most frequent visitors for several years was the

poet Dallam Flynn. Dallam bore a startling resemblance to the
Ezra Pound of some forty years ago. He had the identical piercing
eyes, red beard and mustache, as well as the flowing, wavy blond
hair. Ezra said that it was quite interesting to sit and contemplate
himself as he had looked in his youth, but he remarked that it was
sometimes disconcerting.

Dallam had published a magazine called *Four Pages,* which
had originated in Texas, as had Dallam himself. The similarity to
Blast caught Ezra's eye, and he sent for the young editor to come
to Washington. For several years, this modest literary journal (it
was only four pages long) was Ezra's principal outlet, other editors
having deserted the "mad traitor", as they preferred to speak of
him. His contributions were usually anonymous, and filled about
half of each issue. Occasionally, he signed them as "E.P." The
September, 1950 issue carried a note from "E.P.", announcing
one of his important discoveries, and still one of his great enthusiasms, the work of Alexander Del Mar.

"If Del Mar was not, as some have claimed, the father of modern historiography," Pound wrote, "it is nevertheless quite certain
that a new historiographic phase is present in his work that was not
present in Mommsen and that Del Mar's vast and exact erudition
enabled him to correct Mommsen on various points. Mommsen's
great merit as a teacher resided in his demonstration that the
stability of the Roman Empire, in contrast to the various Mesopo-
tamian despotisms, lay in Rome's planting its veterans in home-
steads, as distinct from mere raids of pillage."[1]

In the summer of 1950, Ezra noticed an announcement of a
book by Del Mar in the yellowed back pages of an early work by
Louis Agassiz, who was also a current enthusiasm. The title, *History
of Monetary Systems* (1903), immediately attracted him, and his
wife was able to borrow the book from the local library (despite
his fame as a scholar, he had to get his books like any housemaid
seeking a novel for entertainment).

He found the book very informative, and asked me to find out
what I could about this unknown author. I discovered that Del Mar
had occupied almost half a page in *Who's Who* until his death in
1926, shortly before his ninetieth birthday. From 1865 to 1869, he

had organized and directed the United States Bureau of Commerce, Navigation, Emigration and Statistics, which later became the separate departments of Commerce and Labor. Although he founded these important offices, his name is little known in Washington today, because of his opposition to some of the monetary policies of the New York bankers. He had represented the United States at the Hague Conference, and was later United States Commissioner to Russia.

Ezra realized the importance of Del Mar's contribution, and began to publicize his work. He wrote letters to his friends, urging them to read Del Mar's books on money. A Del Mar Society was formed in London, and the firm of Kasper and Horton in Washington began to publish small paperback editions of Del Mar's books. This was the beginning of the Square Dollar series, which is still handled by T. David Horton. Stacks of unsold copies of Del Mar began to pile up in Horton's rooms, and Kasper decided to retire from the firm.

A shy, thin, long-legged fellow, Kasper had turned up as a visitor from New York City in the autumn of 1950. Because of his desire to get some things into print, Pound thought him very useful. Kasper later went South in search of amusement, and wound up in Clinton, Tennessee. Pound had nothing to do with the subsequent riots, the calling out of the troops, and the surrounding of the schools with tanks and bayonets. This is merely part of the American educational system, which is largely due to the excessive concern of the progressive Deweyites with melodrama.

Frederick Morgan, publisher of *The Hudson Review,* sometimes visited Pound. He published some of Ezra's work in 1950, and he also brought out another of Pound's enthusiasms, Jaime de Angulo, a California anthropologist who lived among the Pit River Indians.

Ezra made few if any demands upon the young men who came to him seeking instruction. He never asked where they had been to college, which would have been a waste of time, as they were all starved by the same diet. On my first visit, he leaned back and looked at me, asking sharply, "What languages do y' read or speak?"

"Just American," I answered.

"Too bad," he said. "I was going to suggest that you read Flaubert's *Bouvard et Pécuchet,* but I guess you can get it in a translation."

Flaubert was always his only "Penelope", the first lesson in Pound's course, but Flaubert's exacting search for the "right word" is somewhat lost in translation. Certainly no translator could afford to spend the time that Flaubert lavished on the original.

Some of the young people who were regular visitors formed the habit of addressing Pound as "Grampaw", although my Virginia background prevented me from taking such a liberty. He never seemed to object to this designation, and even used it in referring to himself. After I had been visiting him about six years, I began to address him as "E.P.", as did his wife, but I used the salutation scrupulously.

He also referred to himself as "Ol Ez," and at various periods during his life, he contemplated an attempt to reach the American people through the medium of a native cracker barrel philosopher as a sort of Will Rogers or Doc Rockwell. It was this desire that finally culminated in his series of broadcasts from Rome, in which he used an exaggerated Yankee accent.

The poet Wade Donahoe writes in a letter to me of May 21, 1959, that "One thing that has long puzzled me about the public reception of the Ol Ez character is that no one has taken him up except a few writers, a few appreciators, and that is all. The late Frank Lloyd Wright, for example, was admired by the millions as a genius who always spoke loudly. When he castigated his profession, or took a shot at a politician, everyone cackled and said what a Genius he is b'god. There are all sorts of witty sayings and bright quips in the Ol Ez scrapbook, but nobody gets it out to take a look.

"Whereas any bright young literary man will tell you what a wit Bernard Shaw was, had Pound been able to take on that role of eccentric genius, he would be drawing down a hundred thousand a year from TV appearances on the Men of Genius series. Instead, they took him dead seriously and, of course, found out all those madnesses common to us critters. I suppose satire, as opposed to "humor" is harder to take. A man of good quality should change his name every ten years and have a go with plastic surgery."

One reason for Pound's inability to get any articles or short pieces into print during his years of incarceration was his well-known opinion of American publishers. In 1939, he wrote to Kunitz and Haycraft as follows:

"The printing centre for live writing in the English or American language was shifted to New York in 1917 or 1919. After that war the muckers of the American publishing swamp did nothing and London again took over the lead in this field. America once again gets her stuff after London has had it."[2]

American publishers during the 1930s did little more than print some "social protest" novels by the hack writers on *The New Masses*. In the 1940s, they printed a great deal of poor stuff, mostly war propaganda. One might suppose that war propaganda would be exciting, but this material was not. In the 1950s, they began to unmire, and now it seems that a few good things will be printed. It is interesting to note for the record that the best avant-garde periodicals during the years 1948–1955 were those that Ezra inspired from the madhouse. He was still keeping the banner flying, just as he had done in 1912 with *Poetry;* in 1917 with *The Little Review,* and in 1927 with *The Exile.*

These little publications were sometimes printed on hand presses by members of Pound's circle. T. David Horton was printing *Mood;* Dallam Flynn was printing *Four Pages;* William McNaughton was printing *Strike;* and I was printing *Three Hands.* And there were others. In Provincetown, Paul Koch was printing some good items.

The editorial tone of these "little magazines", which achieved very little in the way of circulation, was often as gruff as Ezra himself had been in his writing and such broadcasts as his exhortation on the work of E. E. Cummings, when he demanded of his audience, "well dam you read Cummings if you won't read Brooks Adams/ or better read both of them and try to find out what has been done to you/ what is being done to you/ conducive to material/ spiritual and intellectual RUIN."

Pound was outraged when President Truman seized the steel

mills, and praised Judge David Pine when that official put Truman back where he belonged—with "his caste", as old Lampman would say. For a time, Pound approved of George Sokolsky's daily pontifications. Not long afterwards, he began to distrust Sokolsky, whose references to the free enterprise system are uneven, and are apparently based on a sort of tribal collectivism.

In the August, 1955 issue of *Strike,* Ezra contributed a note on current Congressional investigations. He had followed these hearings with great interest, for he regarded them as a feeble attempt by the Congress to regain some of its lost powers, which had been gradually usurped by the executive and the judiciary branches. In this sense, the investigations aimed at restoring the system of checks and balances among the three delegated powers, the executive, the legislative and the judiciary, which had been so carefully set up by the framers of the Constitution.

The examination of the Morgenthau diaries by the Senate Internal Security Subcommittee was a crucial part of these investigations. Ezra wrote,

"MORGENTHAU DIARIES: 1—These records, covering 'almost entirely' Henry Morgenthau Jr.'s activities as Secretary of the Treasury, 1934–45, are being examined by the Senate Internal Security Subcommittee:

" 'A special meeting to promote Harry Dexter White, December 8, 1941. H.M. Jr. What I wanted to tell you people is this. . . . I want to give Harry White the status of an Assistant Secretary. I can't make him an Assistant Secretary. I want to give him the status just as though he were and he will be in charge of all foreign affairs for me. See? . . . (Edward H.) Foley (Jr., Treasury General Counsel) will continue as chairman of his committee, but if it is a foreign matter or something like that he wants to know about, he will discuss it with Harry and Harry will come in to me with Foley. In other words, the way it is now, nobody knows everything that is going on except me and I don't always know. . . . I want it in one brain and I want it in Harry White's brain.' "

The significance of this date on the memorandum, December 8, 1941, is that the commissars were openly assuming power over the war machine, now that we were in it on the side of the Soviets.

Rex Lampman had been in the public relations department of the Treasury Department during the 1930s. He says,

"Men who had been in the Treasury Department all their lives were suddenly shunted aside and stripped of their power. We were told to clear everything with new officials, such as Harry Dexter White, people who were brought down from New York, and some who were sent in from China and Russia. Who were these people? Some of them we still don't know. They had a different name every time we cleared something with them."

White, or Weiss, as he was sometimes known, was in charge of this strange task force in Washington. He turned over U.S. Government printing plates for currency to his Soviet bosses, was named as a Communist agent, and supposedly committed suicide when he was due to testify before a Congressional committee. A body was hastily buried, and he has since been reported in Uruguay.

Ezra continued his comments in *Strike:* "Mr. Morgenthau (Henry Jr.) has stated that he did not know what Dexter White was up to. If his claim contains the slightest fragment of truth, we recommend that the government trade young Henry for any of the less-qualified persons it has recently clapped into homes for the mentally deficient. The government has twice put this product of degenerate nepotism into a witness stand for the sole purpose of paying him public praise."

During the time that White functioned as an unofficial Assistant Secretary of the Treasury (he dared not accept an official appointment, for fear that the necessary Senate confirmation might expose his position as second-in-command of the Soviet Fourth Bureau—top-level espionage unit operating in the United States), he carried out many important missions for the Soviet government. Not the least of these was the occasion when he turned over the Treasury printing plates for German occupation currency to Moscow. The Russians printed billions of German marks, which we had to redeem.

When the scandal could no longer be concealed, we changed our plates. In an attempt to stop the issue of the new marks, the Russians blockaded Berlin, and this strategy resulted in the first battle of the cold war, the Berlin airlift. General Lucius Clay, the hero of the airlift, never explained publicly what the disagreement between the American and the Soviet Military Governments in Germany was about.

As Henry Hazlitt, economist for *Newsweek,* has often pointed out, White also committed the United States to postwar monetary agreements that have cost us many billions of dollars. It would have been much cheaper for us to have given him a pension of a million dollars a year and sent him back to Lithuania, the country in which this shadowy figure is reputed to have originated.

In the September, 1955 issue of *Strike,* Pound wrote, "TRAVEL NOTE. Two zones have been located INSIDE Gunther. (1) the torcellian vacuum. (2) the vacuum absolute."

During the years that I knew him, Ezra's sole lapse into bad taste was an occasional interest in American politicians. Self-respecting persons pretend that these characters do not exist. He contributed this note to the October, 1955 *Strike,* "EDITORIAL —If a few Republicans were ready to repudiate Roosevelt, they might even win the election next year."

This issue of *Strike* also contained his review of a novel: "There has been no adequate advertisement of a novel called *'Liberty Street.'* It is badly written but it does deal with a useful topic, to wit, the grease in burocracy. The type of well-dressed illiterate who has never done anything but annoy the ill-starred members of the public who fall under his detailed control. This is not a local problem, all countries produce this type of vermin, which should provide material for whole flocks of aspiring historians."

In another passage, he dealt with our propaganda machine, which, like our intelligence network, was made up principally of malcontents who wished that they could live in Moscow: "CHINA AND 'VOICE OF AMERICA'—'A square li covers nine squares of land, which 9 squares contain 900 mau. The central square is the public field, and eight families, each having its private hundred mau, cultivate in common the public field. And not until the public work is finished, may they presume to attend to their private affairs. This is the way the country-men are distinguished.'—Mencius, Book III, Part I, Chapter 3.

"We ask 'Voice of America' if they are making full use of this idea in the fight against Communism in China. Bolshevism started off as an attack against loan-capital and quickly shifted into an attack against the homestead. The nine-field system stimulated Lung to say, 'Nothing better than share, nothing worse than a fixed tax,' and it has been part of the Chinese mind for 3000 years."

In 1957, I informed Ezra by letter that I was starting a new poetry magazine in Chicago. He responded with some advice on October 31, 1957:

"Poetry of Kishago, Harriet's nose rag always DEAD cause tried to separate poetry from language/ ONLY use for ploot mag of poetry/ IF concentrated on meaning of words/ ploot COULD be induced to print great literature /i/e/ Coke and Blackstone as such. The Duke of Hamilton het up to reprint fine edtn/ Blackstone

"but nex think u know, is found stiff on floor of his club and rushed to Swiss clinic/ unapproachable since then, must be 3 years ago

"that I never shd/ have seen Coke text till yester. is enough to make me want to assassinate all the pore fat heads who participated in giving me a better educ in 1902 than yu pore bastids can get the tenth part of now after the spew deal and 50 year brain wash."

Coke is one of Pound's more recent passions. He was notably irritated because his educators did not refer him to the legal basis of Anglo-Saxon civilization, but he overlooked the fact that they probably would have referred him to it, if they had known about it.

Coke was a much more important influence on the framers of the Constitution than was the Magna Carta, but scholars prefer the Magna Carta because it is shorter and much easier to read than the works of Coke. The ignorant public does not know that most scholars are abominably lazy—the works of "history" that they produce please everybody because they include so few facts, and refer to so few sources. A genuine contribution to knowledge, such as Dr. Pitirim Sorokin's brilliant thesis on the importance of the contract in our economic and social structure, is ignored, although he identifies (or perhaps *because* he identifies) the degeneration of modern society with the erosion of contractual obligations during the twentieth century by the advocates of Rousseau's "social contract".

The references to "ploot" (plutocracy) in Ezra's letter were occasioned by my wistful desire to attract some of the gold in Chicago, one of the wealthiest cities in the world, to the support of a useful magazine of modern poetry. As he suggested in his reply, something always intervenes to prevent the plutocracy from doing anything useful with their money, on the rare occasions when they evince a desire to do so.

A first glance at a letter from Ezra is sufficient to convince anyone that the writer is indeed a madman. He throws in words, symbols, abbreviations, obscure names and references, with much more freedom than he does in the *Cantos*. Since he carries on an immense correspondence, all of which is intended to edify the receiver, he does not bother with punctuation, sentence structure, or other amenities of polite communication. Nevertheless, he communicates, as witness the howls of rage from some of the recipients of these letters. His outspokenness has always offended the plutocrats, as well as his ability to get things done without basing everything on an expenditure of money.

On the several occasions when I tried to interest plutocrats in his work, they shocked me by dismissing him as "obviously mad". The first time this occurred was at the estate of one of the more august names on Wall Street. My host said, "Your friend can very well remain where he is."

The intense dislike that Ezra has engendered in the foundations and the millionaires who support them is not accidental. After all, his career consistently downgrades most of the folktales without which they suppose they cannot continue to exist.

He once told me that the wealthy were always intensely irritated by the fact that he could do things without money, such as starting literary movements, founding magazines, and instructing his disciples. There is a type of plutocrat who regards wealth and power purely as force, as Aristotle's "prime mover". He does not expect personal obeisance as much as he expects homage to his millions, to the capital or reserve energy that he controls. And on this ground, the artist always offends him, or should offend him.

His favorite hobbies which currently are socialism, psychiatry, and the superior attributes of money—these shibboleths came under Pound's merciless scrutiny. Instead of socialism, Pound suggested a Confucian society in which men respect one another and one another's property; instead of psychiatry, he suggested love; and instead of money, he suggested art.

His years of exile were due to the flight of intellect from money, for the two are incompatible, as witness the operation of any great American corporation. Money reduces everything to quantity; intellect, performing a selective function that is necessary to life itself, sternly insists upon quality. The very existence of an Ezra Pound negates the theory of quantity. How many Ezra Pounds are there? Such men compel us to deal in unities of one, instead of escaping into the never-never land of socialist numbers, which deal only in billions and trillions.

In a letter from Italy dated March 18, 1959, Ezra suggests that I append this comment on contemporary literary criticism: "The freudian approach to literature: not which the author has managed to get onto the page; but : did he wet the bed as a child."

It was no accident that the rich adopted Freud, for he was as vain and useless as the idlest millionaire. Who could foresee that justice would be wreaked by the gods, and that this foul-mouthed creature would spend the last eighteen years of his life suffering the Dantean punishment of the lower half of his face slowly rotting away?

With the gods of Marx and Freud being raised over the United States like funnyfaces painted on giant balloons for a college football rally, it is no wonder that Ezra remarked to me, "the only place I could stand to live in this country is the madhouse." He often said that the company of the eight thousand in St. Elizabeths might not be so unbearable as that of the "160,000,000 crazier ones outside."

Ezra Pound helped others without thought for himself; he wrote poems without worrying about who would pay him for his work. This set him off too jarringly against the mainstream of American life. Consequently, he was able to look at his countrymen with an objective eye, nor was he insensitive to their appearance.

During the 1956 elections, he called to my attention the commissar or foetus type of public official that seems to have been produced by the modern state. It is characterized by a round head, usually bald, a petulant mouth, and the formless features of a newly-born baby. In July, 1959, he wrote to me,

"Look up Lavater, 1741–1801, 'inventor of physiognomic studies,' esp. criminal TYPES.

"my impression that he set almost at lowest level the foetus type . . .".

I promptly did some research, and found, to my surprise, that a number of great leaders in recent years could be classified as the foetus type, or those who have not been fully formed in the womb. Such people seem capable, indeed fated, to cause great harm to others. These atavistic types are characterized by slight development of the pilar system, low cranial capacity, great frequency of Wormian bones, early closing of the cranial sutures, and a lemurine appendix. The type is round-faced, with slightly protruding eyes and a vacant grin.

Ezra's interest is purely anthropological, and he shows no personal animus, even though he endured six years of imprisonment during the Eisenhower regime, and seven years under Truman. There was definitely a bi-partisan policy toward Pound. He is in possession of a critical estimate of Eisenhower as a military leader, contained in a personal letter from one of the leading British authorities on strategy, which I leave to him to make public. He did venture a passing comment on Eisenhower in 1952. We were sitting in the madhouse, listening to the results of the Republican convention, when he remarked, "Well, if this doesn't finish off the Republican Party, nothing else will."

Although Ezra was conscious of the importance of representative government, he had his lighter moments concerning our servants. One afternoon, a visitor in the ward asked why the flag over the Capitol was being flown at half-mast. Another visitor gravely informed her that one of our Congressmen had passed on to that bourne from which no traveler returns. Ezra leaned back in his chair, his eyes dancing with impish lights, as he exclaimed, "What the heck—we've still got 497 of 'em left, haven't we?"

As one of Pound's early critics wrote in *The Little Review*, "The Ezras know too much." The shibboleths by which the press and the public maintain their existence are unimportant to him. He once remarked to me, "There are always two sets of lies—one for the people who will believe anything, and another for the people who like to think they are sceptics and can't be fooled. An 'inside story' is usually fed to the latter set of fools."

At one point, I became enthused about the possibility of persuading Ezra to make some recordings of his *Cantos*. On occasion, he would read a passage to some of his closest friends, and he often read aloud the witty letters of Sir Barry Domvile and other correspondents. Despite repeated blandishments, he had refused to make recordings for the Library of Congress poetry collection.

The difficulty could easily have been resolved had Ezra been allowed to go to the Library of Congress (as a madman under heavy guard, of course) and make the recordings as his colleagues had done. Instead, the bureaucrats insisted that they could bring the equipment out to the hospital. Not even for such a desired gift to his nation could Ezra be allowed to leave the grim prison for a few hours.

While she was Consultant in Poetry at the Library of Congress, Elizabeth Bishop urged me to use my influence in this matter. I did so, and received a patient refusal from Ezra, while his wife looked somewhat askance at me, as though I had been recruited to the other side, as indeed I had in this lone instance. I then realized the incongruity of it, and said no more. When the next Consultant, Aiken, again requested me to get Ezra to make the recordings, I delivered the request without comment. He never bothered to come out and personally discuss it. Such requests, and there were many of them, usually exposed the fact that Ezra was resentful at being cooped up in the "Hellhole". He said, "Some caged birds sing. I don't."

After I had been visiting Pound for several years, I was urged by many of my acquaintances to write something about him. At every mention of such a project, he emphatically refused. "Hang it all," he would say, pounding the rickety arm of his aluminum chair for emphasis, "it's a waste of time for people to read about me! Just get 'em to read which I've got to say!"

In retrospect, I think that Ezra had always exercised his influence as a teacher at such a personal level that he had lost sight of the fact that he could exercise a much greater influence if people knew about him as a person. There have been very few people in his lifetime who have been privileged to know him and work with him as I have. It was only right that this knowledge should be used to serve as his introduction to all those who wished to benefit by his work. I was convinced that Pound, a necessary guide to students of writing, needed a map so that newcomers to his thought could steer their course into the *Cantos* through the Scyllae and Charybdae of Imagism, Vorticism, and various other "isms", real or imaginary, with which he is said to have been associated.

It was principally due to our conversations at the ward that I had gone so deeply into his work, and I resolved to lay out a chart of the essential Pound so that other students would not overlook it. Few of his visitors had read the complete Pound, nor did he expect it. It was a rare occasion when he directed some student to read one of his books. He was always more interested in which he termed the "agenda" than in his past work.

Many "literary" visitors who came out to the hospital with the expectation that they would be treated to priceless reminiscences of duels with Gaudier, lunches with Joyce and parties with McAlmon, went away disappointed. Invariably, Ezra talked about his current social, political and economic studies, the material of the *Cantos*. If the visitor insisted on returning the conversation to these sight-seeing tours in the Bohemias of the past, Ezra would fall silent and patiently gaze past the offender.

One of the few who succeeded in getting any anecdotes from him was Virginia Moore, who included these stories in her biography of William Butler Yeats. Others who brought up something that Ezra had said four or five decades ago would brusquely be told, "All that stuff is in my books. I'm too old to go over it again." But he was never too old, or too tired, to discuss his current interests for hours at a time.

He always remained on the alert for anything that one of his "students" might turn up in additional researches, and at times, there were four or five of us with permanent desks in the Library of Congress as we carried out our assignments. These included the entire works of Alexander Del Mar, Louis Agassiz, John Adams, Thomas Jefferson, and, for those who could read German, Frobenius. One of the weaknesses of present-day scholarship is the practice of referring to only one or two volumes of the output of an important thinker. We never went to an author without ordering his

entire output, not only his books, but his articles, letters and references to him in other places. "Total research" is the only key to a
man's thought, and this makes it necessary to live near a great
library, of which there are only a few in the world, and but two in
the United States, the Library of Congress and the New York
Public Library.

Pound was sometimes abrupt with those who were looking for a
place to begin their education. "I put all that in *ABC of Reading,*"
he would say. "I don't want to go over it again." One might suppose that a prospective visitor would at least read one of his
volumes of criticism, *Instigations,* or *Pavannes and Divisions,* before visiting Pound, but most of the curious were not at all abashed
by their lack of familiarity with his work.

On a few occasions, I produced a small notebook, but Pound
would wave it aside. "You'll be able to remember what is worth
remembering," he said. I usually scribbled the day's notes on scraps
of paper as I left the hospital on the bus.

Neither he nor his wife ever mentioned the influence he had
exercised on so many of his contemporaries through direct association. His friends and admirers rarely discussed the role of teacher
that he had fulfilled for so many twentieth century poets. As I
delved into the careers of such writers as Yeats, Joyce, Eliot, and
Hemingway, I began to realize how much he had done to develop,
guide and correct the maturation of these fine talents.[3]

Occasionally, some visitor would ask Pound about his relationship with Joyce or Yeats. I noted that Dorothy Pound would smile
a quietly contented smile, and Pound would mention these absent
luminaries with fond recollection. His reticence about his aid to
these writers has caused some of his critics to discount his effect
upon them. Babette Deutsch gave the final summation of Pound's
role as teacher in *The Yale Literary Magazine,* December, 1958:

"The major poets of the twentieth century have acknowledged
publicly their debt to Pound, the teacher. Not all have been as
explicit about it as the author of *The Waste Land* (and how much
the rest of us could learn from the blue pencillings on the 'sprawling chaotic' first draft of that poem by the 'miglior fabbro!'). In
any event, makers as diverse as Eliot, Yeats and William Carlos
Williams were tutored to some degree by this ruthless critic, this

generous friend. And since Wallace Stevens spoke of Eliot as one of his masters, he must be counted among the many who profited indirectly from Pound's teachings. Indeed, there is no poet writing in English, and few writing in the other Western languages, who has not learned from this craftsman. There are, of course, also those who show the strength of his influence by rebelling against it.

". . . There have been earlier teachers: among them, Horace, Lu Chi, Coleridge, who gave similar good advice. It remained for Ezra Pound to give it in the language of our time to the poets of our time, so that, if civilization survives the militant madness now rampant, readers in later centuries will rejoice."

To this generous tribute from Miss Deutsch, one is obliged to add that the influence of Pound upon Wallace Stevens was not only indirect through Eliot; it was also direct through the impact that Pound's lyrics had upon Stevens' work.

Eliot himself commented in his essay, "Isolated Superiority",

"I cannot think of anyone writing verse, of our generation or the next, whose verse (if any good) has not been improved by a study of Pound. His poetry is an inexhaustible reference book of verse form. There is, in fact, no one else to study."[4]

As Eliot points out, most of what Pound has to offer young writers can now be found in his work, and he is the only one whom beginning poets and prose writers can study with profit. It is possible to read Hemingway and then write a more sparse prose, while sacrificing richness of language; it is possible to read Eliot and improve one's knowledge of the uses of poetry, but the result is usually unfortunate. The difference may be that Pound first gives the correct example, and then inspires one to think for oneself. To expose the student's undisciplined mind to the undisciplined mind of a Crane or a Faulkner is not only folly—it is criminal.

In 1951, Ezra scribbled a note on the back of an envelope. We had been discussing moral guides, and he hastily scrawled for me the Four Tuan of Confucius:

love 1
duty 2
propriety 3
wisdom 4

Perhaps his success as a teacher lay in the fact that he never tried to teach his students one thing—he always tried to teach them everything. In his earlier years, this meant that he furiously exposed Yeats and Eliot to Provençal and Chinese poetry, the Noh plays and Walt Whitman. Later, the student could not get poetry without economics, or history without poetry.

He confirmed the gloomiest predictions of Dr. Overholser that he would never "improve" when he issued the following manifesto a few days after leaving the madhouse:

"Notes on this and that, May, 1958

1.

"Towards a new bill of rights: Any man, even a lousy pinko or a putrid Spew Dealer has the right to have his ideas examined ONE at a TIME.

"The skunks use package words to prevent all communication of fact and intelligence.

2.

"The map of Washington having been elucubrated by an idiot, that it be federal offence if any house owner fail to put his house number in VISIBLE position

numerals 8 inches high

"That numerals on corner house be illuminated after twilight.

"That NO fund be allocated to the apes on the District Board until the STREET signs, on ALL streets, be printed 12 inches high, and VISIBLE from opposite corners, whether N.S. or E.W.

"And god DAMN the bastards who put street names in HALF the size of the present lettering on some of the street signs.

3.

"That the poor kids be told what is SOVEREIGNTY.

4.

"That a sane bill re / college entrance exams be brought into Congress not only for service academies, but for land grant colleges.

"NOT coercion from the central govt. but ADVICE.

5.

"That the Jacobites be driven; in this case COERCION is needed—that the Jacobites be driven back to CONSTITU-TIONAL government.

"AS formulated in the clear language of the Constitution as written and not as beshat under the reigns of Wilson the Damned and Roosevelt the putrid.

6.

"That all men left over from the era of F.D.R. be considered guilty until proven clean.

"This does not imply that they can be legally punished. The term 'considered' to mean at this point merely the hypothetical mental attitude of the examiners.

"They should be proved legally guilty before being sent to the electric chair, or compelled to LOOK at some of the remnants of that unfortunate era. Notably certain faces."[5]

Despite Pisa and St. Elizabeths, Pound has never faltered in his campaign against the tax system. In one of his broadcasts, he uttered the treasonable statement that "Debt is slavery." He moved on to the economic proposition that "The tax system is infamy." His latest memorandum on this subject is as follows:

"What should a tax system be?
"What are desiderata? Are they net:
"Cheapness in collection / no! Let us start with justice:

1.

"Justice of the tax. As from Mencius : a percentage of the product, not a fixed charge.

2.

"Minimum cost of collection.

3.

"Convenience of collection, let us say a manner of collection that does not permit dodging.

4.

"That it should encourage production, not sabotage it.

5.

"That it should NOT create crimes, i.e., turn simple mercantile utility into contraventions of statute."[6]

Perhaps some scholar will eventually make a study of the coincidence of confiscatory rates of taxation and the decline of a nation. Americans pay the highest rates of taxation ever suffered by any citizens, including those of Soviet Russia. Tax rates less than half those presently levied against our people have caused bloody revolutions in the past, notably the Rebellion of '76.

Some observers of the literary scene have suggested that Pound as a teacher will finally outweigh Pound as a poet, but such a prediction depends largely upon the supposition, or the hope, that an epic poem greater than the *Cantos* will be written in our time. Pound's preeminence as a teacher and a poet is based upon his concern with essentials and his impatience with trivialities. The talent that breathlessly flung aside the dusty drapes of the Victorian era in search of "the real thing" has come into its own.

XIV

I N 1955, Ezra Pound had already suffered ten years of imprisonment, under conditions that would have crushed most men, both physically and mentally. Rex Lampman says of St. Elizabeths, "If you're not crazy when they bring you in here, you will be nuts within three days."

I was frequently told that Pound did not deserve to be housed in such comfort as he enjoyed at St. Elizabeths. The persons who said this were those who had never gone out to see him, and who had heard this observation from other people who had never gone out to see him. The propaganda that Ezra occupied luxurious quarters, where he could entertain guests and carry on his work, made it difficult to interest influential people in his release.

Robert Hillyer wrote in *The Saturday Review* that Pound's comfort "may with just indignation be contrasted to the crowded wards in which are herded the soldiers who lost their minds defending America, which Pound hated and betrayed."[1] Mr. Hillyer is so accustomed to flinging about his fallacies—most of which, I am sure, he himself believes—that he is probably impervious to debate.

St. Elizabeths was begun as a veterans' hospital, and the majority of its patients are veterans of our two world wars. Pound was offered no comfort at the hospital that was not given to these veterans, and during his incarceration in Howard Hall, he suffered the most primitive conditions of this Bedlam. As for Mr. Hillyer's charge that Pound hated and betrayed America, no other expatriate has shown the love for his native land that he has displayed throughout his life. Henry James and T. S. Eliot became British citizens, but Pound risked a death penalty to retain his American citizenship.

Frequently, when I suggested that Pound might like to leave St. Elizabeths, I would encounter the most annoying and incredibly naïve arguments. "But he's very comfortable there, and well taken care of," someone would say. "Why does he want to get out?" I believe that I would go mad if I had to spend a night in the room that was Ezra's home for so many years. It was really a large closet, a narrow cell furnished with a very narrow cot, taking up two-thirds of the floor space. The rest of the room was filled by a small bureau and a little table, which served as his desk. The room was illuminated by a high, narrow window, of leaded glass, with a heavy metal screen locked over it. This was a considerable improvement over the open-air death cage at Pisa, and it was somewhat quieter than Howard Hall, but that was the most that could be said for it.

Dr. Overholser maintained that Pound enjoyed "special privileges" while he was imprisoned at St. Elizabeths. Drew Pearson, in his column of December 28, 1958, which appeared in the Washington *Post and Times-Herald,* quotes a letter from Overholser to Pound's lawyer, Julian Cornell:

"It remains a fact that Mr. Pound is under indictment for the most serious crime in the calendar and that he has at the present time far more privileges than any other prisoner in the hospital. In spite of his being a well-known author, I question whether I should put myself in the position of giving unusual privileges to him over and above those which he already enjoys."

Although I was visiting Pound every day, I had no idea that he enjoyed any extra privileges, and since Dr. Overholser does not enumerate them, I have no idea what they were. The initial restrictions at Howard Hall, where his visitors were limited to fifteen minutes' talk with him in the presence of a guard, were more severe than those at Chestnut Ward. Other prisoners were allowed to sit on the lawn without hindrance, but to ensure that Pound would not escape, his wife was bonded for his safety. If he had left the grounds, she would have been arrested.

It was this fact alone that prevented me and some other hot-heads from bundling Pound into a car and taking him out of the hospital in 1950. Other patients were given daily passes into the city when they were adjudged to be in Pound's "quiet" condition.

I wrote to Overholser's superior, Mrs. Oveta Culp Hobby, who was at that time Secretary of Health, Education and Welfare, requesting that Ezra be allowed to attend the Sunday evening concerts at the National Gallery of Art. This reached her during the hectic period of the Salk vaccine imbroglio, when a number of children died from spoiled vaccine, shortly before her resignation. She did not reply, and I addressed a similar request to Dr. Overholser. He answered with a polite "No", explaining that the hospital had no personnel who could guard Pound during such an excursion. Since his wife was responsible for his custody, this struck me as an obvious evasion. To add insult to injury, he noted that Luther Evans still hoped that Pound would make some recordings for the Library of Congress!

The only "privilege" that Ezra may have enjoyed was the absence of hospital censorship of his letters. These were taken along by Dorothy Pound each afternoon. However, this custom was practiced by many visitors, and it could hardly be termed a special privilege that she was not stopped and searched when she left the hospital.

The reason for hospital censorship of letters written by mental patients is a curious one. It is done to prevent the sane public from being victimized by such letters. It is an interesting observation on contemporary American life that a sales letter, request for charity, or some similar scheme sent out by a mental patient draws, on an average, a higher percentage of paying returns than sales letters sent out by supposedly sane organizations. Jealous businessmen have imposed a rigorous censorship on madmen, but even so, these ingenious fellows smuggle out their appeals and cause a great deal of confusion. Housewives, grammar school students, and university professors will put ten dollars in an envelope and write, "Please send me at once your exciting offer!"

Soon after meeting Pound, I had begun to investigate the possibility of freeing him. George Stimpson, founder and former president of the National Press Club, conducted a series of coffee seminars at various cafeterias each day. Rex introduced me to him, and he was very interested in the Pound case. He told me some behind-the-scenes stories about it that cannot yet be set down, and promised to make some inquiries.

George occupied a unique position in Washington. The most respected newspaperman in our capital, as *Time* Magazine termed him, he exercised great influence, and had obtained positions for Lincoln White, State Department press officer; William Hassett, White House press officer, who was with Roosevelt when he died, and many others. For thirty years, George's hobby had been Congressmen. His closest friend was Sam Rayburn, and he had helped Tom Clark, Fred Vinson and Lucius Clay when they first came to town.

At my behest, George asked Clark and Vinson about the Pound case. They both said that nothing could be done, and that any move at that time would generate tremendous counter-pressure. Of the two, Vinson, who was then Chief Justice of the Supreme Court, was the more optimistic. He thought the heat would be off in about five years. It actually took eight years. Clark told George that it was hopeless, and that Pound could never be released from St. Elizabeths because of political pressure.

I said nothing to Pound about these gloomy predictions, but continued my efforts. At George's suggestion, I went over to see a member of his "breakfast club", crusty Congressman John Rankin of Mississippi. I mentioned Pound's name with jaunty assurance and was shocked when he said that he had never heard of him. When I told him that Pound was locked up in St. Elizabeths, he launched into a reminiscence of his early days in Washington.

During his initial term as Congressman, just after the First World War, he received a complaint from a constituent that her son was being illegally held in St. Elizabeths. Rankin checked the story, and found that it was true. A crooked lawyer had formed a conspiracy with a policeman and a judge to arrest veterans. If they were receiving any sort of pension for wartime service, the judge would promptly commit them to St. Elizabeths. He would then appoint the lawyer as their power of attorney to receive their monthly checks, which were split three ways.

When Rankin looked into the case, he found that the lawyer had been serving as power of attorney for forty patients at St. Elizabeths, all war veterans receiving as much as two hundred dollars apiece. He was able to free thirty-eight of them, but despite the flagrancy of the case, he was unable to have the lawyer disbarred.

This revelation was of little benefit to Ezra, and I continued to trudge around Capitol Hill for some months before it finally dawned on me that neither he nor I had any representation there. My efforts soon brought retribution of a sort. One evening, I heard a light rap on my door, and opened it to see my mousy little landlady standing there. She was one of those frail old things who inhabit our cities and who whisper through the parks before noon like dried oak leaves pushed by the wind.

"Oh, you're home!" she said.

"Yes, I am," I replied.

"There's some gentlemen here wanted to see you," she stammered and fled. Behind her I saw lurking two dark figures, like assassins. She probably had brought them up to go through my things, supposing that I had gone out for supper, as I usually did at that hour.

The two men pushed into my room, looking contemptuously at its cheap secondhand furniture, which the landlady had picked up from the Salvation Army. There was only one chair, so I could not ask them to sit down. They glared at me and simultaneously flipped open their wallets, exposing some sort of badge like the ones that children get from breakfast food companies.

"EFF BEE EYE," said one of them ominously. His companion nodded sagely, confirming his statement.

"You the fellow that goes out to see Pound?" one of them asked.

"Yes," I said.

"Know anything about him?" asked the second man sharply.

"He—he writes poems," I gasped.

"Very dangerous man," said the first agent. "Whaddya go out there for?"

"You been stirring up some trouble," said his companion

sternly. "Who's putting you up to go around talking to these Congressmen about getting him out?"

"Getting paid pretty well for it, aren't you?" said the first agent. This barrage continued for some minutes without my being able to edge in with a word of response.

"We'll be back to see ya in a couple of days," the first agent said. "Meanwhile, better be careful." I took this to mean "Stay away from Pound." I decided against reporting this incident to him, and during a lull the next day, I casually asked Dorothy Pound if she were bothered much by F.B.I. agents.

"Well, I really don't know," she answered with her charming laugh. "There's all sorts of queer people hanging 'round my place."

One of my fellow students at the Institute of Contemporary Arts was a nephew of Senator Robert Taft. I took the nephew out to see Pound in order to convince him that he was sane and should be released. The nephew then took me to see the Senator. At that time, Taft was contending with Eisenhower for the Presidential nomination, and he was afraid to speak up for Pound. He promised to do something later on, but he never did.

I then brought in an attorney from New Jersey, Edward A. Fleckenstein, who had been prominent in German relief work after the war. He had been deported from Germany only a few months before, on a charge of making a speech in which he favorably mentioned Senator Joseph McCarthy. The action was taken at the request of the U.S. High Commissioner to Germany, James Conant. This ubiquitous "liberal" was one of the advisors who persuaded President Truman to drop the atom bomb upon a Japan that was already suing for peace, thus paving the way for a self-righteous Russia to drop one upon us at some future date.

Pound was not pleased at the intervention of Fleckenstein. For the first time, he told me that he was not interested in obtaining a writ of *habeas corpus,* and that he no longer wished to see the case tried. I was amazed to hear him say that the government should drop the charges of treason, paving the way for his immediate release from St. Elizabeths. It seemed incredible, after hearing Vinson's and Clark's inside view of the case, that this development could ever come about. Four years later, the government met Pound's demands.

The following year, while in Chicago, I tried to interest Ellen Borden Stevenson in the Pound case. She had lurked on the fringes of what few intellectual circles were active there, and she did go so far as to refer me to her lawyer. He promptly informed her that Pound was "anti-Semitic", and refused to have anything to do with the case.

It was now obvious to Pound and his friends that the government would never try him. During his imprisonment, one of the most persistent voices calling for his release was that of Dr. Frederic Wertham, a psychiatrist who was also a self-taught expert on comic books. Wertham stated that Pound was not insane (although he had never talked to him), and demanded that he should be removed from St. Elizabeths and tried for treason.

This could have been done at any time. The fact is that the government officials never dared to try him.

The case against Pound, open and shut though it seemed to the lawyers on the poetry magazines, would never have stood up in court. In an article entitled "Ezra Pound, Traitor and Poet", appearing in the *Kansas* Magazine, 1951, Earle Davis commented upon the transcripts of Pound's "treasonable" broadcasts. "One can hardly blame the authorities for dodging a trial in which this material would have to be presented to a jury as proving treason. In fact, as broadcasts, these transcripts are generally unbelievable." This critic, who was hardly friendly to Pound, as witness the libelous title of the article, took it for granted that it was the government, rather than Pound, that was avoiding an open trial.

I was always puzzled as to how anyone could believe, and repeat this belief, that the government was doing Ezra Pound a favor by keeping him imprisoned at St. Elizabeths without trial. I certainly hope that no government ever does me the favor of throwing me into a brutal concentration camp for six months and then shutting me up in a sordid Bedlam for an additional twelve and one half years!

Ezra served such a long imprisonment, and under such terrible conditions, because most Americans had either never heard of him, knew little of the case, or supposed that he was really insane.

The flood of articles about him in the European press during the early 1950s, and the devoted few who spoke up for him here constituted a growing tide of criticism, which the government officials could not withstand. He was released by the same cowards who had imprisoned him, and because of the same cowardice through which a few "liberals" could use the might of the State against an individual citizen, who was also a poet.

Pound knew what powerful subterranean forces he was defying when he made his broadcasts, but I believe that he did so deliberately, putting himself to the test, as heroes have done since the beginning of time. Lest the reader think that I wax unduly enthusiastic, or that such men are no longer among us, there is a note that he contributed to the August, 1955 *Strike* that is enlightening:

"EARLY ENGLISH PROSE—From Ford Madox Ford's *March of Literature:*

" '. . . And if you have not read the *Morte d'arthur* you will not know the quintessence of recklessness and the rareness of chivalry. You will not merely be a different man after you have read for the first time the letter of Sir Gawain to Sir Launcelot:

" 'I send thee greeting and let thee have knowledge, thou flower of all noble knights that ever I saw or heard of by my day, that this day I was smitten on the old wound that thou gavest me afore the city of Benwick and through the same wound that thou gavest me I am come to my own death day wherefore I beseech thee, Sir Launcelot, to return again into this realm, and see my tomb and say some prayer more or less for my soul!' "

To which Ezra added the comment, "—but you will become acquainted with a firmness of approach between man and man that has vanished from our world—aided by Cervantes!"

It is no accident that the "debunking" movement was coincidental with the rise of "modern literature", wherein all saints stink and all knights have syphilis. Pound has mentioned the "glorification of the brothel," which became the goal of the Romantic movement.

I quoted this note from Ford because it contained the adjective "reckless". Ezra once admitted to me, during one of his rare references to his broadcasts, that he had been "reckless" in making them, and it is a recklessness that would not be out of place in a modern *Morte d'Arthur*.

It was obvious that most of Pound's visitors accorded him the homage due to a *natural* aristocrat, one who had "arrived" through deeds rather than through inheritance, although, in a larger sense, he was the heir of the world's culture. Edmund Wilson's *Apologies to the Iroquois* (1960) echoes D. H. Lawrence's view of the natural aristocracy of the American Indian. The Iroquois chief does not need to identify himself by living in a mansion or surrounding himself with a fawning entourage, nor do the other Indians need such aids to the eye in identifying him. The weakness of parliamentary democracy is that it destroys the natural aristocracy, and eventually devours itself. The natural aristocrat needs above all to retain his inherent dignity and integrity, and he cannot do this by crawling through the sewers to the polling place.

The poet Dallam Flynn was commissioned to go to Europe and organize a committee of intellectuals who would petition for Pound's release. Ezra was optimistic about the possible formation of such a committee, because of the favorable press that the Continent afforded him. The outcome of Dallam's efforts was to increase considerably the number of Ezra's enemies in Europe.

Dallam had no luck with the Europeans, but the seeds were sown, and several years later, a committee was formed in Italy. It was headed by Giovanni Papini, who, although aged and blind, and in the last year of his life, still commanded great respect because of his widely-circulated *Life of Christ* and other religious writings. The second-in-command of the committee was the Mayor of Florence, Georgio La Piro, who was famed for his piety and his work among the poor.

The influence of this committee was soon felt. On March 30, 1954, the Vatican Radio broadcast an appeal by Duarte de Montalegre, the pen name of Professor Jose V. de Piña Martins, of Rome University. This talk was later broadcast by the Italian Radio, and appeared in printed form under the title, *Prometheus Bound*. He said, in part,

"Eight years have now gone by. And Ezra Pound, the greatest poet of the United States and one of the greatest poets of the world, is still detained in a prison in his country, a prison of which the inmates are dangerous lunatics; he, the artist, the man of culture, the messenger of the spiritual value of knowledge, the 'priest of uncreated beauty,' to use Holderlin's definition of the poet. It may be said of this great poet, and supreme artist, or craftsman, as Eliot calls him without further qualification, that he is paying the penalty for teaching men the road by which to reach the divine ideal: the ideal of truth unblemished, without artifice, without hypocrisy. Prometheus Bound!

"Unanswerable evidence has now been produced that Ezra Pound never spoke or wrote against America, never urged his compatriots to be enemies of their country, whose democratic principles and whose noblest traditions he extolled to the utmost. Camillio Pellizzi has furnished undeniable proof of this aspect of his mental outlook. Ezra Pound has always remained faithful to the ethical and juridical principles of the American Constitution; indeed, he had laid such stress on the classical form of the typically American conception of liberty as one would hardly expect to find in a humanist of the broadest outlook whose all-embracing mind soars to the highest and freest flights in the world of history and culture.

"In our own opinion, speaking as a disinterested reader and critic, we would say that the great purpose of his ethical and economic teaching is revealed by his uncompromising stand for the principles of Jefferson, John Adams and the American Constitution; it is in the light of this objective that his criticism of 'usurocracy' should be considered.

"In this he seems to us to adopt an attitude that is excessively puritanical and rigid, but it is an attitude based on the most scrupulous respect of a perfectly coherent conception of morality and civic duty. All the rest is secondary. His attacks on Roosevelt are incidental. The poet was fully entitled to hold his own opinions. What we must do is to obtain a grasp of the whole economic and moral philosophy of Ezra Pound, though we might be asking too much if we expected the verity of his poetry in all its vital and psychological aspects to be fully understood.

"From other quarters Ezra Pound has been accused of racial prejudice and antisemitism. But those who make such absurd charges forget that the very logic of the broad humanistic culture of a poet and thinker like Ezra Pound makes racialism or anti-semitism impossible. They also betray an ignorance of the writer's personal relationships, in which he assisted Louis Zukofsky and other Jews in their artistic and literary careers. They forget that in the *Cantos* (XXII and LXXVI) themselves he speaks of Jews with admiration, and that Jews such as John Cournos have spoken of him with interest and admiration in their biographies. It is a charge that should be supported by proof, and up to the present this has never been done. Facts, not words, should be produced.

"In October, 1945 Ezra Pound wrote to his lawyer: 'I was not sending axis propaganda but my own, the nucleus of which was in Brooks Adams' works 40 years ago, and in my own pre-war publications.' It may be said that the time chosen by Pound to set forth his personal views was not the most opportune, but this only shows his sincerity and his high conception of the freedom of speech. By so doing, he was, in a certain manner, keeping faith with the traditions of his great country. The *Mercure de France,* in April, 1949, was able to adduce irrefutable evidence that the Poet had never betrayed either his conscience or his country.

"The essence of Ezra Pound's teaching may be summed up in these words which appeared in an article published in the newspaper *Il Tempo: 'He inveighed against usury.'* This is why so many people believed him to be an antisemite, erroneously identifying a vicious practice with a whole race. Once this misunderstanding has been removed no serious grounds for the accusation remain.

"The time has now come, therefore, to set free the Prometheus Bound, to give Ezra Pound his liberty again, for he would have nothing to fear from a trial, having always loved his country and all that there is and has been in it of the purest and the best. To liberate a poet is not only an act of universal justice; it is above all an act of homage to world poetry which has in Pound one of its greatest exponents. The Poet is the freest creature in the universe. The very essence of poetry is freedom! Pound belongs not only to the United States but to the whole of humanity. Roosevelt, whose economic policies Pound attacked, was only a man. Men die, but poetry lives forever. Beauty and culture are the highest values that a nation can make its own, for their nationality is universal, their nation the Universe, the country common to all mankind.

"While from this microphone many words of historic importance have been pronounced, by men of great authority, by the highest spiritual authority in the world, it is now a humble writer of this harassed and suffering Europe of ours who raises his voice in defense of a poet. And to speak in defense of a poet such as Pound is to defend the principles of human liberty and dignity, and the supremacy of spiritual values—principles and values which the United States recognizes as her own, and of which she justly proclaims herself the pioneer."

We have reproduced only a portion of Professor de Piña Martins' fine speech, but the entire tribute is worth reading. Interestingly enough, *A Casebook on Ezra Pound,* edited by William Van O'Connor and Edward Stone, is subtitled "Pro and Con Selections". However, the "Pro" items, of which this is only one, are notable by their omission. The Vatican broadcast was widely circulated in printed form, and it is odd that it did not come to these editors' attention. Perhaps the iconoclastic reference to Roosevelt as "only a man" offended them. We remember the abortive efforts to enshrine him as a risen god in 1945, and it is satisfying to note that the Democratic Party avoids reference to him as much as possible, due to the revelations of his guilt in the Pearl Harbor massacre, and only tolerates the occasional exhibition of his relict.

De Piña Martins emphasizes Ezra's allegiance to the American Constitution, which indirectly calls attention to the fact that all of his constitutional guarantees were suspended when he was arrested; they were further suspended by the charge of "mental illness," and were not restored until his release after thirteen years of imprisonment. When he was brought before a jury of his "peers", the jury unhesitatingly accepted the testimony of the government psychiatrists that he was insane. Pound was never examined by a psychiatrist of his own choosing, and has not been to this day.

On October 19, 1954, Dag Hammarskjold, Secretary General of the United Nations, reviewed the contemporary scene at the Museum of Modern Art. In his speech, he said, "Modern art teaches us to see by forcing us to use our senses, our intellect, and our sensibility, to follow it on its road of exploration. It makes us seers —seers like Ezra Pound when, in the first of his *Pisan Cantos,* he senses 'the enormous tragedy of the dream in the peasant's bent shoulders.' Seers—and explorers—these we must be if we are to prevail."

In December, 1954, Ernest Hemingway was awarded the Nobel Prize for literature. He was not the first of Pound's disciples to receive this award, which was to have been given him in 1953; political considerations dictated the choice in favor of Winston Churchill. Awarding the Nobel Prize to Churchill for his pompous, overblown and heavily-clichéd prose ("The din was incessant"), and singling out for praise a style that was as plump, red-faced, arrogant and false as its creator, really destroyed whatever literary value the prize might have had. It was like giving Truman the Nobel Peace Prize for starting the Korean War—a choice that was seriously advanced! However, Pearl Buck, the creator of Chinese soap opera for our time, had received the Nobel Prize for literature in 1938, so things couldn't get much worse.

Hemingway accepted the prize money in 1954, saying, "I believe this would be a good year to release poets." He went on to denounce the continued imprisonment of Ezra Pound in a statement that was quoted all over the world, and even in the American press. His stand was the first streak of light to pierce Pound's long night. He was quoted in *Look* Magazine, September 4, 1956: "Some erudite midshipmen had been by in the early afternoon to ask my views on Ezra Pound. These views are succinct, although the subject is complicated. Ezra, I told them, should be released from St. Elizabeths hospital and allowed to practice poetry without let or hindrance."

It was odd that Hemingway never came to see Pound at the hospital, for he frequently visited the States to collect his movie royalties. He had advanced some money when Pound was brought, penniless and in chains, to his nation's capital. Cummings also put up one thousand dollars. It was a rather risky thing to do, for, although it was *de rigeur* for State Department officials to contribute to an Alger Hiss Defense Fund, it was quite another matter to contribute to Pound's assistance. Ezra has explained Hemingway to me as follows: "Hem tried to do all he could and still work *within* the system."

Hemingway was quoted by Harvey Breit, in the New York

Times, September 17, 1950, as saying, "All the contact I have had with it [politics] has left me feeling as though I had been drinking out of a spittoon."

The Papini Committee in Italy had become the focus of an impressive movement to free Pound. In 1955, Papini sent a note to the American Embassy in Rome, asking that Clare Boothe Luce, the American Ambassadress, intercede on behalf of Pound. He said, in part, "In the very moment when the chiefs of the Kremlin are sending back pardoned German war criminals, we can not believe that the descendants of Penn and of Lincoln, of Emerson and Walt Whitman, wish to be less generous than the successors of Lenin and Stalin."

Mrs. Luce apparently claimed no kinship with Penn or Lincoln, for she ignored the note, if indeed she ever saw it. Some weeks later, I was with the Pounds when they received a communication from Papini, expressing his regret that Pound no longer wished to regain his freedom and was willing to remain in custody. Pound notified him at once that he had made no such statement. We later learned that a minor official on Mrs. Luce's staff had finally replied to Papini's request by saying that Mr. Pound had been contacted and that he had no desire to leave St. Elizabeths! Neither Ezra nor his wife had ever discussed this matter with anyone in the State Department, and certainly not with anyone in the Rome Embassy.

Our officials in Italy continued to be plagued by the Pound question for several years. Our government was then deporting to Italy a number of gangsters who had done very well in America. The Italian press set up a great clamor about this. The editors wrote bitterly to the effect that these lads would never have become gangsters if they had grown up in the civilized atmosphere of their native Italy, but since they had come to maturity in the jungle cities of America, of course they had had to become gangsters in order to survive. Now that they had been overcome by their evil environment, the United States government wished to send them back to plague their native land. "If you must send people back to Italy," wrote one editor, in a statement that delighted Pound, "send us back Ezra Pound, whom you despise, but do not send back any more Italian boys whom you have trained to be vicious gangsters."

Disregarding the element of chauvinism in the Italian press, there was some basis to these complaints. It is a fact that there are more Italian gangsters in the city of Chicago than in all of Italy, and Italy does have the lowest "juvenile delinquency" rate in the world. Perhaps there is something in the atmosphere of America that creates a more volatile population, and exuberant mass that must be ruled by the machine guns of the mob, in the absence of a more effective government.

In September, 1955, I published the strange story of Mrs. Luce and the Papini Committee, including the answer that had never been made to a question that had never been asked. In February 6, 1956, Mrs. Luce's husband published an editorial in *Life* Magazine that pulled out all the stops in demanding the release of Ezra Pound and commented, "He is one of the best translators of verse who ever lived." Despite the fact that the Luce publications were supposedly quite influential with the Eisenhower administration, and had been more than generous in their appraisal of his leadership, Pound spent more than two years in prison after this demand for his release.

Meanwhile, another voice was heard among the half-dozen people in the United States who were asking freedom for Ezra Pound. This was Westbrook Pegler, who had long been interested in the Pound case, but had done nothing about it. He was moved to write a few columns in his defense by an odd chain of events. Pegler was trying to find a novel by Colonel Edward M. House, called *Philip Dru: Administrator* (New York, B. W. Huebsch, 1912), a strange work that outlined the entire New Deal program two decades before Roosevelt came to power. All copies of the book mysteriously had disappeared, but Pegler remembered that George Sylvester Viereck had ghostwritten a series of articles for Colonel House, which appeared in *Liberty* Magazine. Viereck had a copy of the book, which he lent to Pegler.

Viereck then suggested that I meet Pegler, since he enjoyed a good connection with him. I replied that Pegler couldn't do anything for me, but I did wish he would write something in defense of Ezra Pound. He responded with several sizzling columns about

Pound's long imprisonment without trial, which was an important step toward his eventual liberation. In one of these columns, Pegler said:

"There is afoot among us a movement which may amount to a conspiracy to permit the commitment as lunatics of individuals who express political views which are offensive to the left.

"The case of Ezra Pound, the poet, is a dramatic instance. Pound lived in Italy during Mussolini's reign and heartily endorsed Fascism. For that matter, so did many prominent Americans, including politicians who later affected to loathe Fascism as the enemy of an undefined ism called *democracy*.

"Winston Churchill thought well of Fascism for Italians and admired Mussolini as the genius of this stimulating and efficient experiment.

"It is alleged that during the war Ezra Pound broadcast opinions hostile to *democracy* which has no legal or constitutional sanctity in our country. It is alleged that he also criticized F. D. Roosevelt as many of us did here on the home front.

"After our Army had mopped up Italy, Pound was brought back to Washington under charges. However, he was never brought to trial but, by consent of counsel appointed by the court, was examined and adjudged to be more or less crazy.

". . . Pound was committed to St. Elizabeths hospital, a typical, old-style bughouse on the outskirts of the Capital. He has been there all these years so if he was not nuts when he went in, he easily could be now."[2]

"Tyler Kent is another case in the same category", Mr. Pegler wrote in the New York *Journal American* on October 19, 1960, "except that he was not adjudged insane. I will tell you about that one later in developing a theme. The theme is this: That the cult of the left is restoring to the occult phony science of psychiatry to either put its opponents under glass or discredit them as poor, overwrought fools."

After the Pegler onslaught, feelers were sent out from the White House, and we wondered if Eisenhower would "do something for Pound." Ezra, willing to grasp at any straw after more than ten years of imprisonment, told me that he had been informed that Milton Eisenhower was urging his brother to release Pound.

I took the story of "Brother Miltie" with a grain of salt, for Eisenhower could have brought about Pound's release at any time since 1952, merely by requesting that the Department of Justice drop the indictment. I hardly thought that he was ready to do it in 1956, and despite Pound's optimism, he spent two more years in prison.

During these dreary years, Pound's visitors maintained a heavy correspondence while seeking aid for him. The brilliant sociologist, Dr. Pitirim A. Sorokin, director of the Harvard University Research Center in Creative Altruism, wrote to me on March 4, 1957, "I enjoyed your literary note on Ezra Pound and share your criticism of a stupid imprisonment and undeserved punishment meted out to him."

Public interest in his plight was encouraged. Rex Lampman had begun to buttonhole people on Capitol Hill who owed him favors. His father had published a newspaper in Fargo, North Dakota, and Rex and his brother, Ben Hur Lampman, had been fulltime newspapermen before they were six years old, setting type and operating the press, as well as writing stories and poems. Ben Hur Lampman settled down in Portland as the editor of the Portland *Oregonian,* and many of his pieces appeared in *The Atlantic Monthly,* but Rex became a newspaperman in the old journeyman tradition. Some of the North Dakota politicians, including the pair known as "B'Langer" and "B'Lemke" because of their longstanding friendship, had gotten their start through support from Rex's father. Rex's astute advice had been responsible for some of their successful campaigns, and he went to ask a favor, the first time he had ever done so, for Rex was an independent man.

Senator William Langer was not inclined to do much for Pound, despite the fact that he was obligated to Rex. I had expected this, because I had gotten George Sylvester Viereck to go after Langer several years earlier, hoping that he would help Pound, but nothing had come of it.

Finally, Rex found his maverick. In this monolithic age, the only effective counterpart to the state is another monolithic organization, a powerful religious or racial group that is set up on totalitarian lines. As an artist and an individual, Pound had always refused to serve such an organization, and when he got into trouble with the state, no organization offered him assistance. But all mono-liths are really inverted pyramids, a massive superstructure of myth built upon a minuscule bit of truth or reality, and this tiny base is susceptible to attack by mavericks, or those who refuse to fall into line. Such are few indeed, because almost everyone is persuaded to attack the massive superstructure, rather than the base, and their attacks fail. Rather than answer Pound's attack on its base, the monolithic liberal state imprisoned him. Now he needed another maverick to maneuver from the outside, and Rex found him in Congressman Usher L. Burdick of North Dakota.

Burdick caught fire when Rex explained Pound's dilemma. It is interesting to note that most admirers of Pound's poetry were content to see him remain in prison, about ninety per cent of the purchasers of his works being liberals who admired his genius and slept more soundly because he was in jail. Many of his partisans, on the other hand, had little interest in his poetry. Burdick, who caused his release, was among this number.

On August 21, 1957, Burdick introduced House Resolution 403, demanding a full-scale investigation of the Pound case. His fellow-Congressmen could not ignore the resolution, although none of them spoke in favor of it. As was customary with a "maverick resolution", they put it in limbo, as the various committees and other means of pigeonholing legislation are known. In this case, the resolution was turned over to the Legislative Reference Service of the Library of Congress, the only department of that institution that has any direct connection with Congressional work. The LRS was asked to prepare a report on the background of the case, it being tacitly understood that the report could be completed in 1958 or 1968, or whenever the LRS got around to it, as no date of completion was set.

As luck would have it, the research assistant who was assigned to the report, H. A. Sieber, became greatly interested in the sub-ject. He made an intensive study of the considerable Pound material at the Library of Congress, and on March 31, 1958, only seven months later, the report was submitted. *The Medical, Legal, Literary and Political Status of Ezra Pound* contained much of interest, including a photograph of the death cage in which Pound had been kept at Pisa.

The report was a damning revelation of the inadequacy of the government's case against Pound. With this information available in a paper that had legal status as a Congressional document, it was obvious that he could not be kept in jail much longer.

Meanwhile, H. R. Meacham, of Richmond, president of the Poetry Society of Virginia, had been waging an effective letter campaign on behalf of Pound. He had first visited Pound early in 1957, and had resolved to end his imprisonment. He enlisted other Virginians in this cause, and he persuaded James J. Kilpatrick, editor of the Richmond *News Leader,* to print several fiery editorials demanding that Pound be released. On February 7, 1958, a *News Leader* editorial stated, "to all intents and purposes, he (Pound) remains a political prisoner—in a nation that prides itself upon political freedom."

The Richmond *News Leader* was the only important metropolitan daily in the United States to publicly advocate Pound's release, although many leading European newspapers had been doing so for years. It is true that European editors saw in the Pound case a welcome opportunity to reiterate the usual remarks about "the only nation which has gone from barbarism to decadence without an intervening period of civilization," but generally their attitude was conditioned by the fact that a writer or an artist in Europe enjoys a certain status that he is denied in America.

It may be true that America has no need of poets, which would explain why there is no need to pay them for their work, but the isolation of the Coventry into which she drives her intellectuals may in the long run be preferable to the role of government propagandists that the Soviets assign to their writers. Some bitter satisfaction may be derived from the fact that only third-rate poets and writers have ever found favor with the liberal regime in Washington, or been given government subsidies or assignments.

On January 27, 1958, after an advance look at the Sieber report, Congressman Burdick was amazed to find that the Pound case was an even more flagrant case of injustice than Rex had led him to believe. He demanded that the treason indictment against Pound be dropped, so that he could be released from St. Elizabeths.

He said that this remedy "would relieve the American government of an embarrassment that has persisted for over a decade."[3]

On April 1, 1958, the Justice Department announced that the treason charge against Pound might be dropped, this being the only condition of surrender which Pound would accept. Indirectly, Ezra had informed the authorities that if the charges were quashed, he would be willing to leave the country and return to Italy. He offered no alternative, and would accept none.

It may seem odd that a lone individual, without funds, without organized political support, and without an effective group behind him, should be able to dictate his terms to the most powerful government in the world. By the simple method of tenaciously outlasting them, he forced them to accept his terms.

This David and Goliath story has considerable historical overtones. The regime that imprisoned Ezra in 1945 was dying in 1958. Eisenhower had been called in as the last Pro-Consul of a government that had no future, nowhere to go. It had not been repudiated at the polls, because it was such a strange animal that, like the Loch Ness monster, the inhabitants preferred to stare at it rather than to attack it. Its *raison d'être,* the preservation of Soviet Russia from the military menace of Germany, had been fulfilled in 1945. During the years that Ezra was in jail, the men who had imprisoned him were desperately seeking some reason to go on living. There was none. If they defected to Russia, as some of them did, they would be even more out of place there than they were in America. An American traitor would still be regarded as a traitor, and rightly so, even if he chose to live in Moscow.

The Justice Department officials agreed with Pound's contention that it would be impossible to give him a fair trial fifteen years after the committing of the "offense", nor would it be possible to overcome the public conviction that he was guilty, an impression that had been built up by a steady barrage of such terms as "the mad traitor" and other epithets that the free press had used to describe Pound during his imprisonment. Therefore, Pound's terms were not so unreasonable as they might sound to someone who was unfamiliar with the case. He was willing to sail away and leave the liberals in control of the American people, who perhaps deserved them. What more could be asked? His powerful voice would not be raised again in his native land on behalf of freedom and justice. The liberals would be safe.

The April 1 announcement mentioned that T. S. Eliot and Ernest Hemingway had intervened on the poet's behalf. In passing, Frost's name was also included. This was the first time that Frost had been mentioned in connection with Pound's imprisonment.

In the issue of April 19, 1958, *The Nation* noted that a motion to free Pound had been filed in the Federal District Court in Washington, but did not mention Frost. The motion had been entered on April 14, 1958, "United States of America vs. Ezra Pound, Defendant, Criminal No. 76028". Statements by thirteen well-known writers, including Frost, gave reasons why Pound should be released. The signers who had been influenced in their careers by Pound included T. S. Eliot, Ernest Hemingway, Marianne Moore, Archibald MacLeish and Allen Tate.

On April 18, 1958, Pound appeared in court with his wife and his son Omar. In a brief and perfunctory proceeding, Judge Bolitha Laws, who had presided at Pound's commitment to St. Elizabeths twelve years before, dismissed the treason indictment, the government attorneys having stated that they offered no objection to the motion. Pound was represented by Thurman Arnold, of the law firm of Arnold, Fortas and Porter, a Washington law firm with important political connections. A few minutes in court disposed of this historic case, one which had done the United States great damage abroad, a political error, which, spawned by the malice of liberals, would never be lived down.

The nation's press suddenly discovered that Pound was "good copy". The *Wall Street Journal,* in an editorial on April 17, 1958, had suggested that he could be released. On April 28, 1958, *Life* printed a fine photograph of him wearing a long scarf with Chinese characters embroidered on it. The New York *Times* commented on his release on April 19, 1958:

"Yesterday wartime treason charges against him were dropped, opening the way for his return to Italy. In winter months at St. Elizabeths he has somehow managed to make himself oblivious to the disturbed patients who share his ward and to the continuously blaring television set. He has worked with the utmost concentration on composing new poetry, making new translations, and revising and editing previous writing."

Surprisingly enough, newspaper accounts of Pound's release began to give Robert Frost complete credit for the event. Since Frost had never visited Pound, and was not in court when the charges were dismissed, this was an odd conclusion, even for reporters who were accustomed to treat the facts with drunken abandon. The patient work of many others, such as T. S. Eliot, who had begun to protest the brutality of Pound's treatment as long ago as September, 1945, when he was still confined in Pisa, was ignored by the press.

When Mary McGrory of the Washington *Star* interviewed Pound on April 29, 1958, she noted, "He (Pound) was asked about an old friend, the completely non-political and much venerated poet, Robert Frost, whose intervention in the case last summer is largely credited with bringing about his release. . . . 'he ain't been in much of a harry,' Mr. Pound said dryly."

To those who know nothing of Frost's relationship with Pound, this may seem like ingratitude. Frost was one of the many poets whom Pound launched on their careers, and who forever afterward shuddered with fear that their names might be linked with his. The fact is that Frost had consistently refused to visit Pound or to have anything to do with him during the twelve years of his imprisonment at St. Elizabeths. Frost was not concerned about Pound's plight, even though Pound had been his first booster.

Frost was in his late thirties when, unable to get his poems published in the United States, he went to England. His resources were nearly gone when he met Pound, who, with his characteristic enthusiasm, at once went to work to make a reputation for him. After Pound played a key role in Frost's acceptance in England, Frost returned to the United States, an established poet. He never referred to the help that Pound had given him.

In his autobiography, John Gould Fletcher says, "One day he [Pound] spoke to me very highly of Robert Frost, an obscure New England farmer who, at the age of forty, had come to live in England . . . At my very next visit to Pound's lodging, as I recall it, he picked up a typewritten manuscript lying on the table and proceeded to read it aloud. The title was *The Death of a*

Hired Man; the author was Frost. Pound read it to the last syllable with every mark of admiration."[4]

In August of 1915, Pound wrote to the editor of the Boston *Transcript,* "I don't know that it is worth my while to call any one of your reviewers a liar, but the case has its technical aspects and the twistings of malice are, to me at least, entertaining. I note in 'Current Opinion' for June a quote from your paper to the effect that my friend Robert Frost has done what no other poet has done in this generation, 'and that is, unheralded, unintroduced, untrumpeted, he won the acceptance of an English publisher on his terms etc.' Now seriously, what about me? Your (negro?) reviewer might acquaint himself with that touching little scene in Elkin Mathews' shop some years since.

'MATHEWS: Ah, eh, ah, would you, now, be prepared to assist in the publication?

'POUND: I've a shilling in my clothes, if that's any use to you.

'MATHEWS: Oh well, I want to publish 'em. Anyhow.'

"And he did. No sir, Frost was a bloated capitalist when he struck the islands, in comparison to yours truly, and you can put that in your editorial pipe though I don't give a damn whether you print the fact.

"You might note en passant that I've done as much to boom Frost as the next man. He came to my room before his first book *A Boy's Will* was published. I reviewed that book in two places and drew it (to) other reviewers' attention by personal letters. I hammered his stuff into *Poetry,* where I have recently reviewed his second book, with perhaps a discretion that will do him more good than pretending that he is greater than Whitman. . . . Of course, from the beginning, I have known that he would ultimately be boomed in America by fifty energetic young men who would use any club to beat me; that was well in my calculation when I prophesied his success with the American public, and especially with the American reviewers, and I rejoice to see that it has caught on. But your critic's statement is caddish."[5]

This is one of the few references that Pound has ever made to the fact that he helped other writers. He was goaded to it by the unpardonable ignorance of the Boston *Transcript* reviewer regarding his own career, or perhaps to the malice that led the reviewer to ignore Pound's achievements in England. Frost could easily have corrected the error by a letter to the Boston *Transcript,* but he did not, and he remained silent when *Current Opinion* gave the story wider circulation.

The scene now changes to Washington, in 1950. I had stopped in at the Library of Congress to visit with Elizabeth Bishop, only to find that usually demure lady out of sorts.

"Don't tell me that Washington is getting you down," I joshed.

"It isn't Washington so much as it is poets," said Elizabeth. "The awfullest thing has happened. You know, Robert Frost has been down here to make some records of his poetry for the Library, and I merely said to him yesterday, 'Well, I suppose you'll be going out to the hospital to see Ezra.' He went into a furious tirade, and kept saying what a terrible person Ezra is, and that he doesn't want anything to do with him, and so on. I never saw him in such a temper."

"Oh well, that's typical of Frost, isn't it?" I said. "I don't know him, but I've heard he has quite a temper."

"It certainly left a bad taste with me," replied Elizabeth. "You know about him and Ezra, don't you?"

"No, I never heard Ezra mention him," I answered.

"Why, Ezra was the one who got him started, years ago in England," said Elizabeth. "That's why I got so upset about it."

At that time, I knew nothing of Pound's efforts in launching Eliot, Joyce and many others. Neither he nor his wife ever mentioned that they had gotten them started. I could understand why Elizabeth, with her strict moral code, was horrified by Frost's rudeness. She must have been very surprised when the news reached her in South America that Frost had been given credit for effecting Pound's release.

The most generous pronouncement on Frost's talent that has any relation to reality was made by Edmund Wilson in *The New Republic,* June 30, 1926. He said, "Robert Frost has a thin but authentic vein of poetic sensibility, but I find him excessively dull, and he certainly writes very poor verse. He is, in my opinion, the most generally over-rated of all this group of poets."[6]

Since 1926, the "authentic vein of poetic sensibility" has gotten noticeably thinner, and the verse is duller than ever. Perhaps this is why newspapermen admire him so much. American journalists still bemoan the passing of George Sterling.

One thing is certain—he writes simple poetry for simple people. One of his admirers is Dwight D. Eisenhower, which may account for Frost's involvement in the Pound situation, and for Frost's subsequent appointment to the quasi-official post of Consultant in Poetry at the Library of Congress. When the Eisenhower administration finally decided to squirm out of the Pound imbroglio, Frost was chosen as a go-between. He also was a friend of Sherman Adams, who may have dictated his choice as emissary between the White House and the bughouse.

It is difficult to believe that government officials could ignore pleas from writers like Eliot and Hemingway for thirteen years, but that Robert Frost had merely to make a telephone call for Pound to be released. Yet this is Frost's own version, as recorded in an interview with Carter Barber in the Los Angeles *Times,* May 22, 1958. Frost said,

"I don't particularly like Pound. Ezra was a self-boomer. He's not so good a poet as Santayana. No, I don't mean that. No comparisons. I leave that to my friend T. S. Eliot. He's the critic. Magnanimity was the thing about getting Ezra out of jail. So many well-meaning people worked at it for so many years. They wrote all sorts of people. Lawyers, government officials. They formed groups. Archibald MacLeish was trying for a long time. No luck. Well, I happened to be in Washington and said I would try. Archie had just about given it up. He was going away for awhile.

"Well, I got this letter from Hemingway. He felt well toward Ezra too. And Eliot was Ezra's great friend as well. They all said, 'You can speak for us.' Well, I called up a man named Rogers at the Department of Justice. He's the head of it. I told him I was representing Hemingway, Eliot and Archie and we wanted to know about getting Ezra out of the hoosegow. Rogers said there were no particular reasons for keeping Ezra any more. 'Go get Ezra a lawyer, and we'll see what happens,' he said. 'But it will have to be in court.' That part about going to court scared me. I knew I had to hire a lawyer. I was out of my field. Well, Rogers is a young man. Very nice. He's a plain Republican.

Very likable. For Ezra, I got hold of Thurman Arnold, also likable and a far-left Democrat.

"I just got the two of them together on the phone. In fact, there were only three people of any importance in the case: Rogers, Arnold, and Dr. Overholser. They freed Pound. I haven't seen Ezra since 1915. I was off speaking someplace the day he got out. But he was his old self, and got up a costume for his court appearance. They tell me he wore a flapping old black hat on his head and a yellow scarf on his neck . . . But we are all glad Ezra is out. It was just a thing of magnanimity."

As Frost luxuriates in the sensation of great magnanimity, we can only marvel at his gall in terming Pound, the critic who first drew attention to his work, a "self-boomer". His frequent references to "Ezra", a man he has not spoken to for forty-three years, suggest a familiarity that exists only in his own mind. If it is true that Attorney General Rogers informed Frost that "there were no particular reasons for keeping Ezra any more," one can hardly believe that it was "magnanimity" to keep him in prison. Why was he being held, and why was the name Frost the "Open Sesame" that unlocked the grim doors of St. Elizabeths?

Frost began his request for Pound's release with the amazing statement, "I am here to register my admiration for a government that can rouse in conscience to a case like this."[7] His statement was not very complimentary to Pound, but he was full of admiration for the government that had kept the poet in prison for thirteen years without a trial.

Notwithstanding Frost's jokes about "magnanimity", the administration was forced to bow to the great pressure for Pound's release that was being generated here and abroad. It was a surrender, and there was nothing magnanimous about it, just as there had been nothing magnanimous about the death cage in Pisa, the violence of Howard Hall, and the quieter hell of Chestnut Ward. Frost was a government poet, who was called in by the government as a face-saving gesture. Congressman Burdick's demand that Pound be freed was the first move by an American politician to help him, but the government knew that more politicians might speak up, now that Burdick had done it and survived.

The Library of Congress report on Pound showed that the government had no case that would stand up in court, as Pound and his friends had been reiterating for more than twelve years. T. David Horton, who had just been admitted to the bar in Washington, was prepared to make a motion to quash the indictment when Frost and the New Deal law firm stepped in.

Horton had been conducting an effective radio campaign for Pound's release, supported by his sponsors, "The Defenders of the American Constitution." "The Defenders" was composed of authentic military heroes, men who had led American troops in combat. Prominent members included Brigadier General Merritt Curtis of the United States Marines; Colonel Eugene C. Pomeroy; and Lieutenant General Pedro A. del Valle, who commanded the First Marine Division during the battle of Okinawa. With the support of these rugged defenders of America, Horton waged a campaign against the "armchair generals" who insisted on keeping Pound in prison.

Meanwhile, M. Koehl and I had publicized Pound's plight in lectures at the University of Illinois, Northwestern University, and other schools. Most of the students were amazed to learn that he was a political prisoner. Their professors had always told them that the only countries that had ever imprisoned men for their political beliefs were Nazi Germany and Fascist Italy. I felt like a missionary bringing light to a retarded group, for no one is so completely shut off from the benefits of learning as a student in an American university.

When I jubilantly wrote to Rex Lampman, who was then in Hollywood, that his contact with Congressman Burdick had been the breakthrough in obtaining Ezra's release, he modestly urged me not to mention it, because so many other people had worked to that end. His attitude is in marked contrast to Frost's strutting about in the white glare of "magnanimity".

H. R. Meacham of Richmond, who also is very modest about his efforts to aid Pound, wrote to me on May 6, 1959: "I wish I could lay claim to having known Mr. Pound for many years, for my life would—I'm sure—have been richer. Actually, while I've been reading him most of my life, I first visited him at St. Elizabeth's early in 1957. I made up my mind then that I would do what I could to get him out. I knew that Hemingway, Williams, MacLeish and other international figures had spoken out in Mr. Pound's behalf; I also knew that there had been no organized or sustained effort. Someone would make a statement, and there would be a little flurry of activity and sporadic and ineffectual efforts to free him. But the strength and influence of these people seemed wasted because it had not been co-ordinated . . . I asked Mr. Pound to give me a list of men and women throughout the world who were sympathetic and whom he thought would be helpful. Over a period of months, I communicated with all on EP's list. Frankly, I felt that some of the people might further prejudice his case—since prejudice played so large a part anyway —and a few were dropped. Then all of us wrote letters to the Attorney General. In fact we wrote two—because Rogers came in smack in the middle of the campaign.

"I asked the editors of several newspapers to write an editorial urging Pound's release, but so far as I know, the only one who responded was J. J. Kilpatrick, Editor of the Richmond *News Leader,* and he wrote two!

"Late in 1957 Mr. Pound wrote me: 'I don't think you shd/ have too narrow a program or bore people with my personal sorrows. BUT with yr/ admirable aim to eliminate captivity of yrs. truly, you might mix a few germane ideas into yr/ conversation.'

"The timing was perfect; actually, we tapped a reservoir of good will—or guilt—and things began to happen. You know all about this, and more, and I don't know why I repeat it unless I do so in the hope that I may throw a little light into some dark corners. I should like to know the entire story of his release, for I think it would be of great interest to future generations. For instance, I found (or thought I found) Archibald MacLeish at the core of this thing. The attached reprint from the Washington *Merry Go Round* is, I think, a lot of guess work. I don't know how active Hammarskjold was, but I had several letters from him, and I know he did what he could. I know he was sympathetic. This article refers to the influence of Frost, Eliot, and Hemingway. I know Hemingway was active, for I heard from him, also.

"As to Frost, while I have no proof of this, I'm convinced that he did what he did at the urging of MacLeish. I don't think he likes Pound—never did—and I think he was most reluctant to acknowledge—even in his own mind—that he was under obligation to Mr. Pound. All of us know about that.

"When Frost did go to Washington, I believe Mr. MacLeish was with him, and there is little doubt that as the Great White Father, he carried a good deal of weight. I believe he saw both the Attorney General and the President. Unless I am much mistaken, Mr. Pound mentioned casually that his release was decided at a Cabinet meeting.

"A couple of days after Mr. Pound's release, I went out to lunch with him at a nearby chop suey joint. He'd just seen some editorial in which it was pointed out that, in urging Pound's release, Frost had repaid a debt of some 40-odd years' standing. Mr. Pound smiled and said that Frost repaid that debt when he published the North of Boston series.

"I thought that magnificent, and I thought, also, that it was perhaps a clue to his character and his genius. He felt no one should be obligated to him for anything he had done, and he, in turn, has never been beholden to anyone. The only acknowledgement he ever made of my efforts (I wanted none and would have been embarrassed had he mentioned them) was indirect. He spent a weekend at my home in Richmond shortly after his release and autographed one of my books (I found this later) inscribed, 'With thanks for his subterranean activities.' "

The "Washington Merry-Go-Round" column, which Mr. Meacham refers to, was written by Drew Pearson's assistant, Jack Anderson. In faithful imitation of the great smear artist's style, Anderson began, "The backstage wire-pulling that freed the mad poet Ezra Pound has now been uncovered, ending a seven-month-old mystery. The hidden wires were manipulated by no less than former assistant president Sherman Adams, Under Secretary of State Christian Herter and United Nations Secretary General Dag Hammarskjold."

Just who had been mystified, outside of Pearson's office, has not yet been revealed. The story which appeared in many newspapers on December 28, 1958, was part of the campaign against Sherman Adams. No doubt the strategists felt that to link him with the "mad poet" would be even more damning than his famous Oriental rug.

Anderson also mentioned that John Kasper had supported Pound for President in 1956. New York subways were plastered with "Pound for President" stickers, which greatly upset Walter Winchell, but despite his obvious vote-getting propensities, both major parties ignored this popular figure.

Anderson commented in this column, "When Pound added the Chinese classics to his intellectual activities, Assistant Attorney General William Tompkins raised an official eyebrow." Apparently Tompkins had "official eyebrows" at the age of four, when Pound began translating the Chinese classics.

No study of magnanimity would be complete without quoting an editorial from *The Nation,* April 19, 1958: "It will be a triumph of democracy if we set Pound free, not because he is a martyr, but because a sick and vicious old man—even if he were not the brilliant poet he is, with a luminous side that all but transcends his faults—has his rights too. In Italy, he may yet write a few more beautiful pieces, and in that cracked but crystal mirror of his hold up to us once more the image of a civilization that too often drives its best creators into self-exile and political horror."

In this touching demonstration of liberal magnanimity, *The Nation* makes a stirring plea for "a sick and vicious old man."

XV

AS SOON AS the treason indictment had been dropped, government officials stated that there was no longer any objection to Pound's release from St. Elizabeths Hospital. This substantiated what both his friends and enemies had said all along—that he was not insane, and that he should either be tried or released.

Even a vindictive critic might have agreed that he could be freed by 1950. Alger Hiss had served but three years and eight months for lying about his activities as an espionage agent for Soviet Russia, and five years would have been sufficient punishment for Pound's patriotic broadcasts, that is, for airing political views in wartime. A predecessor of Pound in the continuing fight for the Bill of Rights, Chief Justice Roger Taney, had resigned from the Supreme Court in disgust after President Abraham Lincoln suspended the right of *habeas corpus* during the Civil War.

Pound's case recalls another *cause célèbre* of the Civil War, the strange story of Doctor Mudd. Like Pound, Doctor Mudd had been confined in a grim fortress, shut away from his countrymen, because of his involvement in a political matter. He was sent to Fort Jefferson, Florida, a medieval type of fortress, which could only be reached by boat from the mainland. In obedience to his Hippocratic oath, he had tended the wounds of John Wilkes Booth, although there is a strong likelihood that he was imprisoned because he had learned too much about the strange circumstances of Lincoln's death.

When it was announced that Pound was to be released, the manager of Radio Station KART in Jerome, Idaho, offered him a job as commentator. Had he accepted, this would have been his first visit to his home state since he departed in the Blizzard of '88.

Pound was no less controversial because of his release. Frederick Kuh, chief of the Washington bureau of the Chicago *Sun Times,* wrote a feature for the April 11, 1958 issue of that paper about Pound's planned trip to Italy. Kuh said that the Italian government did not wish to let him land before the May 25 general elections, as his appearance might upset the political structure of the entire nation! No doubt a coup such as Napoleon's return from Elba was feared.

Kuh noted that Pound had "toed the Axis propaganda line, denounced his native land and glorified fascism." This upheld the conventional liberal line that Brooks Adams is fascist propaganda and that to criticize F. D. Roosevelt is to denounce all that America stands for. Kuh displayed his usual journalistic accuracy by commenting that "Pound spent twenty years in Italy before American troops arrested him in 1943 (*sic*)."

On learning that Ezra had been freed, I went on safari from the jungle city of Chicago to the jungle city of Washington, in order to visit with him again before he departed these inhospitable shores, where so many had fallen. Meanwhile, he had invaded Virginia, as the guest of H. R. Meacham. It is an understatement to say that Pound took Richmond. The Richmond *News Leader* published an interview with him on May 1, 1958:

"Shortly after that [his college career] he [Pound] began 40 years as an expatriate in Europe. Why the long exile?

" 'To keep down the overhead,' Pound snapped.

"In Europe he taught a cluster of brilliant young writers. Why?

" 'I suppose it was that I wasn't afraid of them,' he said. 'I didn't think they could do it better than I could.'

"Pound carried two pairs of glasses in a little canvas bag around his neck, and as questions came from near or far, he shifted the glasses to bring the speakers into focus. All this switching lent considerable motion to the conversation.

"What one thing did he want most when released from St. Elizabeths?

"Pound jumped to his feet, bristling.

" 'Why, what about having a little constitutional government in this country?'

"But then he sank back into his chair, saying that 'having spent 13 years in the bughouse I ought to be excused from active service.' He owed it to his wife and daughter to 'keep quiet a little,' he said.

" 'I want to see my grandchildren in Italy,' he added.

"Much of his talk ran to the nation's 'magnificent Constitution' and the dangers he sees in modern college curriculums 'where they offer programs for the future instead of having the students study the past where they might learn something.'

"Nowhere in his own education did anybody introduce him to Sir Edward Coke, the British jurist, Pound complained.

" 'It's outrageous for a man to have to wait until he's 72 to get his hands on Coke and the Magna Carta,' Pound said. 'I'm in my second kindergarten.'

"Mostly he spoke with his head leaned back, his eyes closed, and there was no chance to feel pity for him when his gray eyes flew open in a hawk-like glare. His complexion was pink and fresh, more like a young man's made up for an old man's part.

"When Mrs. James Branch Cabell reported that her ill husband sent the 'thanks he owes you for many happy hours,' Pound was ready to ditch the party. 'Can't we go hold his hand?' he wanted to know, eagerly.

"A question put to Pound tends to disappear into a maze of reminiscences from which the answer pops gopher-like 15 minutes later.

" 'I don't have a one-track mind,' he said.

"To those who find his talk disjointed, Pound replied, 'It's disconnected only because I have an orderly mind and want to be sure my interlocutors get the start of it . . . There is so much to say.'

"After all, he said, when the whole of Europe explodes over a man's head, it's like a museum falling around him.

" 'You have to hunt the pieces,' he said.

"When Pound was taken during war in Italy, he was put in a cage, under guard, and had to cover himself with papers.

" 'Few men of letters have those opportunities,' he said yesterday.

"Arriving at St. Elizabeth's—jaunty Pound refers to it as 'St. Liz'—he was placed in the hospital's violent ward, 'the hell hole.'

" 'I needed a five-year rest cure, and they gave me a fifteen months' endurance test.'

"He continued to write and publish, but as to reading, he declared, 'I hate it . . . the only excuse to read is to find out something . . . it's abominable.'

"But he ranged nimbly over modern day writers yesterday from Yeats, under whom he had studied ('a much better writer than I am but a gargoyle') to Hemingway whom he taught ('one of the best').

" 'Hem,' the tough old man said, had sent him 'The Grave of the Unknown Sailor,' a set of shark's jaws.

"Pound's defense for his wartime broadcasts has been that he did them as an individual American, on his own, to help the world, and not for the few lira, about $15, he received.

"As the party broke up yesterday, a reporter leaned over Pound and asked him if he felt he had been a traitor to his country in any degree.

"The old man looked up calmly, steadily. 'I certainly do not,' he said."

The interviewer was impressed by Pound's amazing vitality. His youthful complexion and vibrant manner often startled newcomers at the hospital. One visitor described him as creating the impression of "an old-time seaman, aged but still spry from climbing the rigging every day, sitting at his ease in a coffee house or tavern between voyages of exploration or privateering on the Spanish Main."

This is a remarkably exact description, for Ezra was always a Captain Morgan, who preyed on the Spanish Main of the intellect. At the first sight of his sail, the landlubbers would dive for their cellars, chattering like hens in the shadow of the hawk's wing.

One by one, the slow, heavy galleons of the world's literature fell beneath his guns, and were plundered to outfit that new vessel, the *Cantos*.

Another visitor to St. Elizabeths complained that Ezra had a "cruel shark's mouth". To me, Ezra was always a Viking, "aged but still spry", who had many raids ahead of him. Elizabeth Bishop thought that he looked diabolical; other visitors were surprised to find that he looked like a genial, retired professor.

When I arrived in Washington in May, 1958, I found Ezra at Professor J. C. LaDriere's apartment. LaDriere, one of the faithful visitors to Chestnut Ward, is a scholar, devoted and uncompromising, a type who has been shunted aside in our universities to be replaced by flamboyant entrepreneurs from business and political and military groups—men who invade our institutions of higher learning in search of temporary status.

I took some more photographs of Pound, and we adjourned to the Aldo Café for lunch. An acquaintance at the Italian Embassy had misinformed Ezra that the garden was open, and we took our *pasta* in the crowded dining room. We were joined by Marcella Jackson of Texas, T. D. Horton, and General Curtis. Ezra was in high spirits, enjoying his first springtime of freedom in thirteen years.

The next morning, I accompanied Ezra to the National Gallery of Art, where we visited with Huntingdon Cairns. I left Ezra to browse through the Mellon collection, the first time he had seen it, and joined Dorothy Pound for lunch at the Athens Restaurant. She was obviously relieved that the long years of waiting were over, and now she was impatient to get back to Italy. The two governments were still arguing as to when it would be safe for Ezra to take to the high seas. She found these extra weeks of waiting in the humid swamp an unforeseen and exasperating "additional punishment".

We lingered in the pleasant atmosphere long after the other diners had gone. It seemed hard to believe that it had actually happened, that Ezra was free. I had given up hope after five years of effort, in 1954, because I could not find the slightest relaxation of the government officials' relentless attitude toward him. Now the happy event seemed to have taken us both unaware. Perhaps we regretted somewhat that there would be no more afternoons on the lawn at St. Elizabeths, but certainly we were thankful that we would never have to look up and see him standing behind the narrow, barred window of Chestnut Ward again.

During the weeks that Ezra waited in Washington for his government clearance, there was no effort of any kind by any civic group, college or foundation to persuade him to remain in the United States. In retrospect, this seems unbelievable. Here was a man described by the outstanding authorities in the literary world as America's most important poet, but his fellow Americans thought nothing of the fact that he was leaving these shores, never to return. One could only ask, "Why this fear and distrust, this intense dislike of Pound's ideas, this resolve to pretend that he does not exist?"

First of all, America fears ideas. Dr. Overholser, testified that Pound "speaks in bunches of ideas." America has not had an idea since 1800, but the ideas produced between 1750 and 1800 were sufficient to make her the greatest nation in the world.

These riches, these inherited ideas, are our legacy, and one always fears losing a legacy. Also, one tends to live off of them, and splendid though they are, we cannot live off of them forever. Perhaps that is why they have degenerated into materialism. There is a growing feeling in America that ideas will destroy our tinsel world, cause our Cinderella coach to turn back into a pumpkin, our steeds into rats. Ideas might even have a depressing effect on the sale of mechanical appliances. And well they might, but our forefathers would not have spurned ideas on that ground.

Spoiled by this rich inheritance of ideas, we have forgotten how to think. This was the gist of Pound's broadcasts to America —"Think, dammit!" Cummings wrote to Pound, "You damned sadist! You want people to think!" In strong contrast to the liberals, who insist that you can think what you like as long as you attribute your sources to Marx or Freud, Ezra never tried to dictate to his pupils. He referred to the personal mission of the artist in *The Little Review* of May, 1917: "The shell fish grows its own shell, the genius creates its own milieu."

At one time, the United States afforded the artist great freedom because of the guarantees which had been written into the Constitution. But the United States and Soviet Russia have proven that a Constitution offers no barrier to the development of a monolithic state. The only barrier to such a monstrosity is individual virtue. Pound discovered the basis for this in two Confucian principles: *ching ming,* or precise definition, verbal precision; and *humanitas,* or *jen.*

It was obvious that a mind like Ezra's must be banished, for who could stand up to it? The intellectually mature person does not merely receive ideas—he has mental reproductive powers as well as physical ones. The sperm ideas do not merely lie down and go to sleep; they get busy and have other ideas. This quality gave Ezra an unfair advantage over those sterile minds who make up the intellectual world in America, a world that is prostrate in shameful obeisance before the state, so off with him!

Nietzsche explains this situation in "Homer's Contest":

"If one wants to observe this conviction—wholly undisguised in its most naïve expression—that the contest is necessary to preserve the health of the state, then one should reflect on the original meaning of ostracism, for example, as it is pronounced by the Ephesians when they banish Hermodorus: 'Among us, no one shall be the best; but if someone is, then let him be elsewhere and among others.' Why should no one be the best? Because then the contest would come to an end and the eternal source of life for the Hellenic state would be endangered . . . Originally this curious institution is not a safety valve but a means of stimulation: the individual who towers above the rest is eliminated so that the contest of forces may reawaken—an idea that is hostile to the 'exclusiveness' of genius in the modern sense and presupposes that in the natural order of things there are always *several* geniuses who spur each other to action, even as they hold each other within the limits of measure. That is the core of the Hellenic notion of the contest: it abominates the rule of one and fears its dangers; it desires, as a protection against the genius, another genius."[1]

America has twisted this idea of protecting oneself against genius by setting up another genius, another champion, another hero, to offset him; modern democracy claims that the best protection against a genius is to do away with all genius! "Genius is harmful, undemocratic, psychotic!" cries the American chorus of professors, psychiatrists, and millionaires. This idea is also touched upon by Nietzsche, when he says, "Whereas modern man fears nothing in an artist more than the emotion of any personal fight, the Greek knows the artist *only as engaged in a personal fight.*"[2]

Because Ezra engaged in a personal fight, he found every group up in arms against him. He too found another genius, Confucius, as a sparring partner and comrade-in-arms. One day he showed me a battered book whose binding was in shreds and heavily patched with Band-aids and pieces of Scotch tape. This was James Legge's version of Confucius' *The Four Books.* Ezra said that this book had carried him through the Pisa experience. "Without it," he wryly remarked, "I really would have gone nuts."

As Ezra had warned his people in one of his broadcasts, "Some day you will need to know, need to know more than you do at present." This statement, made against the background of a war, was ignored, because the only thing one needs to know in wartime is how to survive.

But now the moment has arrived when Americans "need to know," need to know more than the pap that is fed them by the professors and the journalists. This need can be filled by the work of Ezra Pound, even though he has returned to Italy. The only thing that prevents the American people from reading Pound is the fear that knowledge may be more challenging than slavery.

When the governments of the United States and Italy finally agreed that it was safe to let Pound go abroad, T. D. Horton and his wife accompanied the "exiles" to New York. They stopped on the way to visit the old home in Wyncote, Pennsylvania, and on the following day drove to Rutherford, New Jersey, where they spent several days with William Carlos Williams before sailing.

In Italy, Pound has continued to work on his *Cantos.* Since his return, he has published *Impact,* a volume of essays, and *Thrones,* a new section of the *Cantos.* Giacomo Oreglia interviewed him for one of Europe's most important newspapers, Stockholm's *Dagens Nyheter,* November 5, 1958, and I quote, in part:

". . . Showing old-fashioned chivalry Ezra Pound, together with his wife Dorothy Shakespear, a finely-built, reserved lady, and his amiable, well-educated daughter Mary de Rachewiltz met me at some distance from Castel de Fontana.

"In the 13th century Castel Fontana was built on old Roman ground. Shortly after the second world war Boris de Rachewiltz bought it. Of all the old castles in Sud-tyrol none is more wrapped in old tales. People are whispering of great riches buried in the ground and known only to the devil. I was also told, by the local inhabitants, that one, at night, can see burning fires on the battlements and a gigantic, golden calf close to the castle. Those legends don't frighten Ezra Pound. He is a sporty and agile man of medium height. His hair is silver white, his eyes steel grey, sometimes flashing with a piercing fire. When walking he sometimes favours a wooden cane, but in spite of his seventy-three years and the hardships he has met with, he seems far from tired or finished, and it's difficult not to be excited by his nervous vivacity and rapid changes of moods . . . Pound speaks an Italian impressive by the amount of words he knows and the outstanding linguistic imagination. Sometimes he pauses, for a short while, and one who is not used to his way of talking may easily think he's lost the thread. But then, fast as an arrow, comes the absolutely perfect and precise word."

In the spring of 1959, Ezra wrote to me that the altitude at the castle bothered him, and that he was returning to Rapallo. There he has remained, annoyed by the osteo-arthritic condition of his neck vertebrae, but even more annoyed by the steadfast refusal of his countrymen to "Think, dammit!"

Some years ago, Rex Lampman contributed to *Nine* magazine an epitaph for Ezra, which delighted him. It read,

> Here lies the Idaho Kid,
> the only time he ever did.

Rex later sent me a longer version,

> E.P.
>
> Here lies noisy Ezra Pound,
> Mute as Adam's eldest hound.
> Here he lies, the Idaho Kid,
> The second* time he ever did.
>
> *First was when E.P. told T.S.
> Eliot he thought Eliot could
> become a great poet.

Rex claims that this is the only known epitaph with a footnote. But Rex's genial posthumous view of Pound seems unlikely to be echoed by the little minds of the Academy and the State, who can only regard him with boiling emotions compounded equally of rage and envy. To them, he will always be known as "this difficult individual".

APPENDIX

CHAPTER FOOTNOTES

I

1. *Letters of John B. Flannagan,* edited by W. R. Valentiner, New York, C. Valentin, 1942, p. 37.

2. Olga Lengyel, *Hitler's Ovens,* New York, Ziff-Davis Publishing Co., 1947, p. 179.

3. Flannagan, *op. cit.,* p. 37.

4. Robert H. Sherard, *Bernard Shaw, Frank Harris and Oscar Wilde,* London, T. Werner Laurie, Ltd., 1937, p. 43.

5. Richard Reese, a Washington commodity broker.

6. Ezra Pound, "Canto LXXIX," *The Pisan Cantos,* New York, New Directions, 1948, p. 66.

7. Pound, "Canto XI," *The Cantos of Ezra Pound,* New York, New Directions, 1948, p. 51.

II

1. Phyllis Bottome, *From the Life,* London, Faber & Faber, Ltd., 1946, p. 76.

2. *The Autobiography of William Carlos Williams,* New York, Random House, 1951, p. 53.

3. *Ibid.,* p. 58.

4. *Ibid.,* p. 64.

5. *Ibid.,* p. 57.

6. *The Selected Letters of William Carlos Williams,* edited by John C. Thirlwall, New York, McDowell, Obolensky, Inc., 1957, p. 6.

7. Malcolm Cowley, *Exile's Return,* New York, The Viking Press, 1959, pp. 123–24.

8. "Talk of the Town," *The New Yorker,* August 14, 1943, p. 16.

9. *Ibid.,* p. 17.

10. *Ibid.,* p. 17.

11. *The Autobiography of William Carlos Williams,* p. 57.

12. H. Glenn Hughes, *Imagism and the Imagists,* Palo Alto, Stanford University Press, 1931, p. 224.

13. It was said that *The Yellow Book* turned grey in a single night.

14. Percy Muir, *Minding My Own Business,* London, Chatto & Windus, Ltd., 1956, pp. 2–3.

15. *Ibid.,* p. 7.

16. *The Letters of Ezra Pound: 1907–1941,* edited by D. D. Paige, New York, Harcourt, Brace & World, Inc., 1950, p. 62.

17. T. S. Eliot, *Ezra Pound: His Metric and Poetry,* New York, Alfred A. Knopf, 1917, pp. 18–19.

18. Cowley, *op. cit.,* p. 121.

19. Pound, "Canto 104," *Thrones: 96–109 de los cantares,* New York, New Directions, 1959, p. 96.

20. Violet Hunt, *I Have This to Say,* New York, Boni & Liveright, 1926, p. 11.

21. Douglas Goldring, *South Lodge,* London, Constable & Co., Ltd., 1943, p. 16.

22. Hunt, *op. cit.,* p. 11.

23. Ford Madox Ford, *Thus to Revisit,* London, Chapman & Hall, Ltd., 1921, p. 169.

24. *Ibid.,* p. 167.

25. *Ibid.,* p. 172.

26. Ford, *Return to Yesterday,* New York, Horace Liveright, Inc., 1932, pp. 373–75.

27. *The Letters of Ezra Pound,* p. 72.

28. Ford, *Return to Yesterday,* p. 374.

29. *Ibid.,* p. 375.

30. Ford, *Thus to Revisit,* p. 167.

31. *Ibid.,* p. 167.

32. Ford, *New York Essays,* New York, William Edwin Rudge, Inc., 1927, p. 37.

33. *Ibid.,* p. 35.

34. *Ibid.,* pp. 35–37.

35. *Ibid.,* p. 45.

36. Douglas Goldring says that Violet Hunt's mother, Margaret Hunt, was a best-selling novelist of the day, and a fairly competent one as well. Her father was Alfred Hunt, landscape painter. Violet was once proposed to by Oscar Wilde, and she became a best-selling novelist in her own right.

37. Ford, in his impractical way, imagined that he could go to Germany for a short time and renew his German citizenship, a formality that would enable him to get a German divorce from his wife. He took Violet to the university town of Giessen, and applied for the divorce. The authorities were unsympathetic to the proceeding, and perhaps Ford had not filled out the papers properly. Months went by, and he heard nothing from the German government. At last, he and Violet returned to England, intimating to their friends, that a divorce had been granted to Ford. "The Governess," a gossip writer in an illustrated paper, referred to Violet Hunt as "the new Mrs.

Ford Madox Hueffer." The original Mrs. Hueffer sued the paper for libel and won a substantial sum in damages.

Although Ford and Violet were not party to the suit, and did not have to testify, some of their friends pointedly asked to see the divorce papers. None were forthcoming, and many of Violet's friends dropped her. The situation between her and Ford became more and more acrimonious, and in the summer of 1915, he enlisted in the army, as the best method of breaking off with Violet. When he was "demobbed," he married one of Pound's circle in London, an Australian girl named Stella Bowen.

Violet continued to live alone in South Lodge, hoping that Ford would return. During the 1920s, she was one of the literary luminaries of London, giving parties that were attended by the socialites of the time. By the 1930s, she was becoming aged and, as Douglas Goldring says, "tiresome." She had published her last novel in 1921, but in 1932, she published one of her best books, *The Wife of Rossetti*. Most of her friends drifted away, and she died during a bombardment of London in 1942.

38. *The Letters of Ezra Pound*, p. 28.

39. Ford, *It Was the Nightingale*, Philadelphia, J. B. Lippincott Co., 1933, p. 156.

40. Pound, "Hugh Selwyn Mauberly," *Personae*, New York, Liveright Publishing Corporation, 1926, p. 195.

41. Eliot, *Ezra Pound: His Metric and Poetry*, p. 5.

III

1. Pound, *Polite Essays*, London, Faber & Faber, Ltd., 1937, p. 8.

2. Robert Graves, *The Crowning Privilege*, London, Cassell & Co., Ltd., 1955, p. 115.

3. Louis MacNeice, *The Poetry of W. B. Yeats*, New York, Oxford University Press, 1941, p. 106.

4. *The Letters of W. B. Yeats*, edited by Allan Wade, London, Rupert Hart-Davis, Ltd., 1954, p. 543.

5. *The Selected Letters of William Carlos Williams*, pp. 210–11.

6. *Ibid.*, p. 320.

7. *John Butler Yeats' Letters to His Son, W. B. Yeats, and Others*, edited by Joseph Hone, New York, E. P. Dutton & Co., Inc., 1946, p. 133.

8. John Masefield, *Some Memories of W. B. Yeats*, New York, The Macmillan Company, 1940, pp. 6–9.

9. Goldring, *South Lodge*, p. 49.

10. Alexander Norman Jeffares, *W. B. Yeats: Man and Poet*, London, Routledge & Kegan Paul, Ltd., 1949, p. 167.

11. *Ibid.*, pp. 176–77.

12. *Ibid.*, p. 165.

13. Edmund Wilson, in "The Permanence of Yeats," *Selected Criticism*, New York, The Macmillan Company, 1950, pp. 22–23, cites this passage as evidence of a "new austerity," but attributes this development to "the frustration of early love, apparently."

14. Richard Ellman, *Yeats: The Man and the Mask*, New York, The Macmillan Company, 1948, pp. 211–15.

15. Joseph Hone, *W. B. Yeats, 1865–1939*, New York, The Macmillan Company, 1943, pp. 308–9.

16. *The Letters of Ezra Pound*, p. 25.

17. Ellman, *The Identity of Yeats*, New York, Oxford University Press, 1954, pp. 131–32.

18. *The Letters of W. B. Yeats*, p. 585.

19. *John Butler Yeats' Letters to His Son*, p. 175.

20. *The Letters of W. B. Yeats*, pp. 589–90.

21. Pound, "Canto LXXXI," *The Pisan Cantos*, pp. 99–100.

22. Edith Finch, *Wilfrid Scawen Blunt, 1840–1922*, London, Jonathan Cape, Ltd., 1938, p. 337.

23. *The Letters of Hart Crane*, edited by Brom Weber, New York, Hermitage House, 1952, p. 88.

24. Goldring, *op. cit.*, pp. 48–49.

25. T. R. Henn, *The Lonely Tower, Studies in the Poetry of W. B. Yeats*, London, Methuen & Co., Ltd., 1950, p. 97.

IV

1. John Gould Fletcher, *Life Is My Song*, New York, Farrar & Rinehart, Inc., 1937, p. 59.

2. *Ibid.*, p. 60.

3. Eliot, *Selected Essays, 1917–32*, New York, Harcourt, Brace and Company, 1932, p. 49.

4. Pound, *Make It New*, London, Faber & Faber, Ltd., 1934, p. 335.

5. Richard Aldington, *Life For Life's Sake*, New York, The Viking Press, Inc., 1941, pp. 134–35.

6. Michael Roberts, *T. E. Hulme*, London, Faber & Faber, Ltd., 1938, pp. 21–22.

7. *The Letters of D. H. Lawrence*, edited by Aldous Huxley, New York, The Viking Press, Inc., 1932, p. 128.

8. *Ibid.*, p. 145.

9. *Ibid.*, p. 174.

10. *Ibid.*, p. 183.

11. Norman Douglas, *Looking Back, An Autobiographical*

Excursion, New York, Harcourt, Brace and Company, 1933, p. 287.

12. Harold Munro, *Some Contemporary Poets,* London, Leonard Parsons, Ltd., 1920, p. 93.

13. Oliver St. John Gogarty, *As I Was Walking Down Sackville Street,* New York, Reynal & Hitchcock, Inc., 1937, p. 59.

14. Fletcher, *op. cit.,* p. 103.

15. *Ibid.,* p. 239.

16. S. Foster Damon, *Amy Lowell,* Boston, Houghton Mifflin Company, 1935, p. 237.

17. *Ibid.,* p. 238.

18. *Ibid.,* p. 239.

19. Fletcher, *op. cit.,* p. 151.

20. *The Letters of Ezra Pound,* p. 44.

21. Damon, *op. cit.,* p. 238.

22. Amy Lowell, *A Critical Fable,* Boston, Houghton Mifflin Company, 1922, pp. 90–1.

23. *Ibid.,* p. 91.

24. *Ibid.,* p. 94.

25. Damon, *op. cit.,* pp. 635–8.

26. *Ezra Pound, A Collection of Essays,* edited by Peter Russell, Peter Nevill, Ltd., 1950, p. 29.

27. Pound, *Personae,* p. 112.

28. Graves, *The Common Asphodel,* London, Hamish Hamilton, Ltd., 1949, p. 148.

V

1. Wyndham Lewis, *Blasting and Bombardiering,* London, Eyre & Spottiswoode, Ltd., 1937, pp. 254–55.

2. *Ibid.,* p. 255.

3. *Ibid.,* pp. 280–81.

4. Pound, *Instigations,* New York, Boni & Liveright, 1920, p. 215.

5. Pound, *Gaudier-Brzeska, A Memoir,* London, The Bodley Head, 1916, pp. 45–46.

6. Aldington, *Life for Life's Sake,* pp. 165–66.

7. *Ibid.,* pp. 165–66.

8. Jacob Epstein, *Let There Be Sculpture,* New York, G. P. Putnam's Sons, 1940, p. 37.

9. Hunt, *I Have This To Say,* p. 114.

10. Ford, *No Enemy,* New York, The Macaulay Company, 1929, pp. 206–12.

11. Ford, *New York Essays,* p. 59.

12. Gaudier explained to Frank Harris how he had financed a period of art studies in Munich. He had turned out fake Rembrandt drawings, which were yellowed with tea extract, and sold them to

dealers who specialized in the American trade. Perhaps some of our finest "Rembrandt" drawings are worth as much as "Gaudiers."

13. *The Letters of Ezra Pound,* p. 26.
14. Pound, *Personae,* p. 148.
15. Pound, *Gaudier-Brzeska,* p. 116.
16. *The Letters of Ezra Pound,* p. 25.
17. Hughes, *Imagism and the Imagists,* p. 229.
18. Sophie Brzeska later died in an insane asylum.
19. Pound, *Gaudier-Brzeska,* p. 141.

VI

1. Iris Barry, *The Bookman,* October, 1931.
2. *The Letters of Ezra Pound,* p. 26.
3. *Ibid.,* p. 29.
4. *Ibid.,* p. 60.
5. *The Selected Letters of William Carlos Williams,* p. 29.
6. *Ibid.,* p. 42.
7. Cited by Frank Harris, *Contemporary Portraits,* New York, Brentano's Publishers, 1923, p. 149.
8. Barry, *op. cit.*
9. *The Letters of W. B. Yeats,* pp. 606–7.
10. *Passages from the Letters of John Butler Yeats, Selected by Ezra Pound,* Dublin, The Cuala Press, 1917, p. 2.
11. *Ibid.,* pp. 9–10.
12. *Ibid.,* pp. 24–25.
13. *Ibid.,* p. 25.
14. *John Butler Yeats' Letters to His Son,* p. 279.
15. *The Letters of W. B. Yeats,* p. 672.
16. Almost four decades later, during one of his broadcasts, Ezra said, "Those that missed the Little Review did not catch up with the bandwagon, I'll say they did not."
17. Pound, "Advice to a Young Poet," *The Little Review,* December, 1917, pp. 58–59.
18. Pound, *Imaginary Letters,* Paris, The Black Sun Press, 1930, pp. 1–5.
19. *Ibid.,* pp. 10–11.
20. *Ibid.,* pp. 23–31.
21. *Ibid.,* pp. 37–40.
22. *Ibid.,* p. 49.
23. *The Little Review,* November, 1918.
24. *Ibid.*
25. *The Little Review,* January, 1919.
26. Conversation with Eustace Mullins, 1950.

VII

1. *The Letters of Ezra Pound*, p. 34.

2. *The Letters of James Joyce*, edited by Stuart Gilbert, New York, The Viking Press, Ltd., 1957, pp. 23–24.

3. *The Letters of W. B. Yeats*, p. 598.

4. *The Little Review*, January, 1918.

5. *The Letters of W. B. Yeats*, p. 698.

6. Herbert Gorman says that a portion of Gosse's letter was exhibited during the Centenary Exposition of the *Revue des Deux Mondes* (*James Joyce*, New York, Farrar & Rinehart, Inc., 1939, p. 340).

7. Lewis, *Blasting and Bombardiering*, pp. 270–77.

8. *The Letters of James Joyce*, p. 95.

9. *Ibid.*, p. 183.

10. *Ibid.*, p. 219.

11. *Ibid.*, p. 255.

12. *Ibid.*, p. 277.

13. *The Letters of Ezra Pound*, p. 202.

14. *The Letters of James Joyce*, p. 249.

15. *Ibid.*, p. 277.

16. Pound's eager interest in those whom he sponsored is shown by his concern for their health as well as by his promotion of their work. Herbert Gorman writes, "Ezra Pound had insisted more than once that a major cause of Joyce's eye troubles was the condition of his teeth. He advised that they be extracted. Therefore, in 1923, the writer willing to follow any advice that sounded sensible, went to a Parisian dentist and suffered the agony of having most of his teeth drawn out. A number of them turned out to be abscessed. One good result of this multiple operation was the cessation of the attacks of iritis that had annually tortured Joyce for eighteen years." (*James Joyce*, p. 328.)

17. Gogarty, *Intimations*, New York, Abelard Press, Inc., 1950, p. 67.

VIII

1. Pound, *Indiscretions, Une Revue De Deux Mondes*, Paris, Three Mountains Press, 1923.

2. Fletcher, *Life Is My Song*, p. 284.

3. *Ibid.*, p. 57.

4. *Ibid.*, p. 28.

5. *The Letters of Ezra Pound,* p. 41.

6. *Ibid.,* pp. 169–70.

7. *Ibid.,* pp. 171–72.

8. Eliot, *On Poetry and Poets,* New York, Farrar, Strauss & Cudahy, 1957, p. 164.

9. Eliot, *Milton,* London, G. Cumberlage, 1948, p. 13.

10. *The Collected Essays of John Peale Bishop,* New York, Charles Scribner's Sons, 1947, p. 38.

11. Cowley verifies this statement in a letter to the publisher dated April 1, 1960. He cites his authority as John Peale Bishop.

12. Bishop, "Homage to Hemingway," *The New Republic,* November 11, 1936.

13. Charles Fenton, *The Apprenticeship of Ernest Hemingway,* New York, Farrar, Straus & Young, 1954, p. 227.

14. John Hyde Preston, "A Conversation," *The Atlantic Monthly,* August, 1935, pp. 187–94.

15. Gertrude Stein, *The Autobiography of Alice B. Toklas,* New York, The Literary Guild, 1933, p. 246.

16. *The Letters of James Joyce,* p. 141.

17. Robert McAlmon, *Being Geniuses Together,* London, Secker & Warburg, 1938, p. 19.

18. *Ibid.,* pp. 334–35.

19. Ford, *It Was the Nightingale,* p. 156.

20. *Ibid.,* pp. 283–84.

21. Pound, "Canto 95," *Section: Rock-Drill, 85–95 de los cantares,* New York, New Directions, 1956, p. 106.

22. Ford, *It Was the Nightingale,* p. 313.

23. *Ibid.,* p. 333.

24. Goldring, *The Last Pre-Raphaelite,* London, Macdonald & Co., Ltd., 1948, pp. 255–56.

25. Van Wyck Brooks, *The Opinions of Oliver Allston,* New York, E. P. Dutton & Co., Inc., 1941, p. 240.

26. George Antheil, *Bad Boy of Music, passim.*

27. Cowley, *Exile's Return,* pp. 121–24.

28. *Ibid.,* p. 176.

29. Margaret Anderson, *My Thirty Years' War,* New York, Covici, Friede, 1930, pp. 243–44.

30. *Ibid.,* p. 244.

31. McAlmon, *op. cit.*

32. In a memorial note for Dunning in *This Quarter,* 1930, Samuel Putnam says that when Dunning was taken to the American Hospital at Neuilly, "I learned that he had refused to eat for weeks, that he had wanted to die. But he had been very tranquil. He had conceived a fancy for his nurse, who, he insisted, looked like an Egyptian. He was an Oriental to the last."

33. McAlmon, *op. cit.*, pp. 300–1.

34. Cowley, *op. cit.*, p. 123.

35. John Espey, *Ezra Pound's Mauberly*, Berkeley and Los Angeles, University of California Press, 1955, p. 103.

36. Peggy Guggenheim, *Out of This Century*, New York, The Dial Press, Inc., 1946, p. 59.

IX

1. Alfred Alvarez, *Stewards of Excellence*, New York, Charles Scribner's Sons, 1958, p. 48.

2. *The Letters of Ezra Pound*, p. 189.

3. Louise Cann, *The Pound Newsletter*, October, 1955, p. 25.

4. *The Letters of Ezra Pound*, p. 190.

5. Guggenheim, *op. cit.*, pp. 69–70.

6. Elizabeth Delehanty, *The New Yorker*, April 13, 1940.

7. Aldington, *Life For Life's Sake*, pp. 104–5.

8. Yeats, *A Packet for Ezra Pound*, Dublin, The Cuala Press, 1929, p. 1.

9. *The Letters of W. B. Yeats*, p. 758.

10. *Ibid.*, p. 771.

11. Lewis, *Blasting and Bombardiering*, p. 285.

12. *The Letters of W. B. Yeats*, p. 733.

13. *Ibid.*, pp. 733–34.

14. *Ibid.*, p. 739.

15. In this respect, God is the highest creation of the gentleman.

16. Pound, *The Unwobbling Pivot and the Great Digest of Confucius*, New York, New Directions, 1951.

17. Russell Kirk, *Beyond the Dreams of Avarice*, Chicago, Henry Regnery Company, 1956.

18. *The Letters of W. B. Yeats*, p. 718.

19. *Ibid.*, pp. 772–73.

20. *Ibid.*, p. 774.

21. *Ibid.*, p. 807.

22. Yeats, *The King of the Great Clock Tower*, New York, The Macmillan Company, 1935, pp. v–vii.

23. *The Letters of W. B. Yeats*, p. 827.

24. *W. B. Yeats and T. Sturge Moore, Their Correspondence, 1901–1937*, London, Routledge & Kegan Paul, Ltd., 1953, pp. 153–54.

25. Yeats, *Essays, 1931–1936*, Dublin, Cuala Press, 1937, p. 41.

26. *Letters on Poetry from W. B. Yeats to Dorothy Wellesley*, edited by Dorothy Wellesley, New York, Oxford University Press, 1940, p. 25.

27. Pound, "Canto LXXXIII," *The Pisan Cantos*, p. 106.

28. Yeats, *A Packet for Ezra Pound*, p. 2.

29. Pound has variously termed the *Cantos* "the tale of the tribe" and "an epic poem containing history."

30. Allen Tate, "Ezra Pound's Golden Ass," *An Examination of Ezra Pound*, New York, New Directions, 1950, pp. 66–72.

31. Eliot, *Ezra Pound: His Metric and Poetry*, p. 28.

32. Aldington, *Ezra Pound and T. S. Eliot*, Hurst Berkshire, Redcocks Press, 1954, p. 18.

33. *The Selected Letters of William Carlos Williams*, p. 132.

34. *The Letters of Ezra Pound*, pp. 196–97.

35. Caresse Crosby, *The Passionate Years*, New York, The Dial Press, Inc., 1953, p. 256.

36. Alfred Perles, *My Friend Henry Miller*, London, Neville Spearman, Ltd., 1955, p. 20.

37. This interview was reprinted in a collection of Pound miscellany, *Pavannes and Divigations*, New York, New Directions, 1958, pp. 153–55.

38. Pound, *ABC of Reading*, Norfolk, New Directions, 1951, p. 50.

39. *The Letters of Ezra Pound*, pp. 255–56.

40. Desmond Chute, *The Pound Newsletter*, October, 1955, p. 12.

41. Stella Bowen, *Drawn from Life*, London, Collins Publishers, 1941, pp. 142–3.

42. Goldring, *People and Places*, Boston, Houghton Mifflin Company, 1929, p. 264.

43. Chute, *op. cit.*, pp. 13–14.

44. Pound, "Canto 92," *Section: Rock-Drill*, p. 81.

45. Chute, *op. cit.*, p. 14.

46. Pound, *Impact*, Chicago, Henry Regnery Company, 1960, p. 222.

47. Pound, *Polite Essays*, p. 193.

48. Conversation with Eustace Mullins.

49. Conversation with Eustace Mullins, September, 1950.

50. Washington *Daily News*, April 30, 1958.

51. *The Selected Letters of William Carlos Williams*, pp. 177–78.

52. Pound, *The Pisan Cantos:* "Canto LXXIV," p. 11; "Canto LXXVI," p. 39; "Canto LXXVIII," p. 59; "Canto LXXX," p. 87.

x

1. Bottome, *From the Life*, pp. 70–73.

2. In *Culture* (Norfolk, New Directions, 1959), Pound says that "Sovereignty rests in money. The United States Constitution is the greatest document yet written, because it alone of them all, clearly recognizes this power and places it in the hand of Congress."—p. 270.

As Professor Giovanni Giovannini, Professor of English at Catholic

University, Washington, D.C., comments on this passage, "For Pound, the Constitution implies an economic wisdom ancient and modern, found in Bacon whom he quotes, 'Money is like muck, no good except it be spread,' and in a Confucian maxim which he translates: 'Rake in wealth and you scatter the people. Divide the wealth and the people will father to you.' "—"The Strange Case of Ezra Pound," *The New Times*, Melbourne, August 26, 1955.

3. Stanley S. Kunitz and Howard Haycraft, *Twentieth Century Authors*, New York, H. W. Wilson Co., 1942, p. 1122.

4. In 1879, Nietzsche wrote that "The mother of dissipation is not joy but joylessness"—*Mixed Opinions and Maxims*, No. 77.

5. New York *Times*, August 19, 1949.

6. Pound, *America, Roosevelt and the Causes of the Present War*, London, Peter Russell, Ltd., 1955.

7. Quoted in *The Medical, Legal, Literary and Political Status of Ezra Pound*, by H. A. Sieber for the Legal Research Division of The Library of Congress, 1958.

8. "The Strange Case of Ezra Pound," *The New Times, op. cit.*

9. Pound, "Coke on Misprision," *The European*, London, August, 1958.

10. George Morgenstern, *Pearl Harbor, The Story of the Secret War*, New York, Devin-Adair Company, 1947.

11. *The Letters of Ezra Pound*, p. 322.

12. *Ibid.*

13. Luigi Villari, *The Liberation of Italy*, Appleton, Wisconsin, C. E. Nelson Publishing Company, 1959, pp. 196–97.

14. Sisley Huddleston, *Terreur 1944*, Paris, Editions de la Couronne, 1947; *France: The Tragic Years, 1939–1947*, New York, The Devin-Adair Co., 1955.

15. Pound, "Canto LXXIV," *The Pisan Cantos*, p. 8.

16. *Ibid.*, "Canto LXXXVI," p. 36.

17. *Ibid.*, "Canto LXXI," p. 97.

18. Kirk, *The Conservative Mind*, Chicago, Henry Regnery Company, 1954, p. 76.

19. Pound, "Canto 86," *Section: Rock-Drill*, p. 25.

XI

1. Pound, "Canto LXXVIII," *The Pisan Cantos*, p. 60.

2. *An Anthology of Famous English and American Poetry*, edited, with an introduction, by William Rose Benét and Conrad Aiken, New York, Modern Library, 1945.

3. Pound, *Personae*, p. 116.

4. *A Casebook on Ezra Pound*, edited by William Van O'Connor and Edward Stone, New York, Thomas Y. Crowell Company, 1959.

5. Edmund Wilson, *The Triple Thinkers,* New York, Harcourt, Brace & Company, 1938, p. 206.

6. *The Case Against the Saturday Review of Literature,* p. 9.

7. *Ibid.,* p. 9.

8. *Ibid.,* p. 9 (and other citations).

9. *Ibid.,* pp. 19–20.

10. *The Partisan Review,* May, 1949, p. 518.

11. *The Letters of Sherwood Anderson,* selected and edited with an introduction by Howard Mumford Jones, Boston, Little, Brown and Company, 1953, p. 119.

12. *Ibid.,* p. 365.

13. John Cournos, *Autobiography,* p. 235.

14. *Ibid.,* p. 236.

15. Charles Norman, *The Case of Ezra Pound,* New York, The Bodley Press, 1948, p. 56.

16. *The Letters of Ezra Pound,* p. 240.

17. *Ibid.,* p. 225.

18. Pound, "Canto LXXX," *The Pisan Cantos,* p. 72.

19. William Barrett, "A Prize for Ezra Pound," *Partisan Review,* April, 1949, pp. 334–47.

20. Pound, "Canto 85," *Section: Rock-Drill,* p. 11.

21. Pound, "Salutation the Third," *Personae,* p. 145.

XII

1. Harold Loeb, *The Way It Was,* New York, Criterion Books, Inc., 1959, p. 61.

2. *The Correspondence of Nicholas Biddle, 1807–44,* edited by Reginald C. McGrane, Boston, Houghton Mifflin Company, 1919, p. 278.

3. Pound, "Canto 97," *Thrones,* p. 22.

XIII

1. Pound, "Introduction," *Money Pamphlets,* edited by Barbara Villars, Washington, D.C., Square Dollar Series.

2. Kunitz and Haycraft, *op. cit.,* p. 1122.

3. This is not an uncommon lack of knowledge concerning Pound's influence. No less a critic than Edmund Wilson, reviewing Pound's *Poems, 1918–1921* for *The New Republic,* April 19, 1922, chided him for imitating Yeats and Eliot. He adds the note, in a collection of these reviews, *The Shores of Light,* that "I did not know at that

time that both Eliot and Yeats had been influenced by Pound." (New York, Farrar, Straus and Young, Inc., 1952, p. 44.)

4. Eliot, "Isolated Superiority," *The Dial*, January, 1928, p. 5.

5. Letter to Eustace Mullins.

6. Letter to Eustace Mullins.

XIV

1. Robert Hillyer, *The Saturday Review of Literature*, June 18, 1949.

2. Westbrook Pegler, "As Pegler Sees It," New York *Journal-American*, April 15, 1955. Mr. Pegler's subsequent stories on Pound appeared in the *Journal-American* of June 15 and September 16 and 21.

3. *The Congressional Record*, January 27, 1958.

4. Fletcher, *Life Is My Song*, p. 74.

5. *The Letters of Ezra Pound*, pp. 62–63.

6. Wilson, *The Shores of Light*, p. 240.

7. *A Casebook on Ezra Pound*, p. 135.

XV

1. Frederic Nietzsche, *The Portable Nietzsche*, New York, The Viking Press, pp. 36–37.

2. *Ibid.*, p. 37.

INDEX OF PROPER NAMES